CULTURE AGAINST MAN

CULTURE
AGAINST
MAN

JULES HENRY

VINTAGE BOOKS

A Division of Random House

NEW YORK

VINTAGE BOOKS

are published by A<small>LFRED</small> A. K<small>NOPF</small>, I<small>NC.</small>

and R<small>ANDOM</small> H<small>OUSE</small>, I<small>NC.</small>

© *Copyright, 1963, by Random House, Inc.*

Manufactured in the United States of America

To my daughter PHYLLIS

PREFACE
AND ACKNOWLEDGMENTS

I HAVE FINISHED THIS BOOK IN APRIL 1962, IN THE TENTH month of my sabbatical year. The earth looks good from my window: the last protective brown leaves are falling from the oak and little yellow-green ones start from the twigs and branches of the willow; the Japanese quince is full of tiny leaves, and the tinier buds of the quince blossoms are already pink among them. The peach tree that my wife planted from a pit is ten feet high this spring, and the dogwood is gray with a foam of new buds. It seems scarcely possible that the world should be in the state I describe in this book.

I started to write, or, rather, to rewrite *Culture Against Man* in 1956, and there is practically nothing of the original manuscript left. By 1958 *Culture Against Man* was basically recomposed, and it has lain around while I learned more and became involved in the variety of research the reader will find here. There was an enormous advantage in waiting six years to finish the book, for the world changed a great deal in that time. Probably one must write a book about his society in order to really understand what change is, in society and in one's self. Something else happens when one writes a book about which he feels deeply: he becomes a creature of his book, for as he pours ideas and emotion into it the process shapes him, so that he can never be the same again. Writing clarifies positions and commits one's soul—often far beyond what one ever imagined possible. In order to remain placid and uncommitted, I would say, never write a book that has deep meaning for you.

In writing this book I have been helped much by my wife

whose unfettered originality is a constant inspiration, and by my daughter who in her growing and thinking made me sensitive to the problems of children. Random House has been important to me; not so much because they are my publishers, but because they have been daring enough to take a gamble on a book of violent prejudices. This is the nature of the publishing business in a democracy. Weston LaBarre, who read the original draft, was able to see through its weaknesses and encourage me to go on, even as he advised me to throw it away. I am grateful to him. I am grateful also to Carl Withers for having read the sections on Rome High School, and to the anonymous readers for Random House, who made so many helpful suggestions.

Since a great deal of foundation and Government money has gone into the research discussed in this book, I want to express my appreciation here. I am grateful to the University of Chicago's Sonia Shankman Orthogenic School and particularly to its director, Dr. Bruno Bettelheim, for the opportunity to participate in the School's research program. I want to express my gratitude also to the Research Institute for the Study of Man, the Rockefeller Foundation, the National Institute of Health (Grant GN 5535), the Ford Foundation, the World Health Organization, and the United States Children's Bureau and, particularly its Youth Project Director, Carl Withers, for the opportunity to work on projects financed by them.

Finally, I want to thank Washington University for a number of things: First, for its bracing climate of academic freedom, where one can teach what ideas one pleases, and find students alert and intelligent enough to listen and "fight back." Second, for its composure in the presence of the waves of political and social prejudice that have swept over the country. In its acceptance of academic freedom as the very breath of the University, and in its composure in the presence of random social and political lunacy, Washington University is a perfect expression of the intellectual life in a democracy. Third, I am grateful for the grants made to me by the University for research, and last, but far from least, I appreciate the sabbatical year during which *Culture Against Man* was completed.

It seems to me that, in the interest of encouraging younger people who may be dismayed by foundation "turn downs," I should acknowledge the foundations that have rejected my petitions. I believe the Wenner-Gren Foundation for Anthropological Research turned me down at least four times; and I have lost count over the years of the number of times I was rejected by Guggenheim.

I would like to acknowledge by name the many students who have participated in the research that has gone into this book. Yet, since the research areas are highly sensitive it seems to me best to withhold their names in order to protect the anonymity of the persons and institutions studied. Finally, I am indebted beyond my capacity to repay to all the institutions and persons that have opened their doors to our inquiring research eyes.

J. H.

St. Louis, Missouri

CONTENTS

PART ONE

No event can be beyond expectations,
fear contradiction, or compel surprise, for Zeus,
father of Olympians, has made night at full noon,
darkness mid the brilliance of the sun—
and pale fear has seized men.
Henceforth nothing for them is certain:
one may expect everything,
and none among you should be astonished to see,
one day, the deer, preferring the sonorous tides
of the sea to the land,
borrow from the dolphins their sea pasture,
while the latter plunge into the mountains.

ARCHILOCHUS, 700 B.C.

1: Introduction

THIS BOOK IS ABOUT CONTEMPORARY AMERICAN CULTURE —its economic structure and values, and the relation of these to national character, parent–child relations, teenage problems and concerns, the schools, and to emotional breakdown, old age, and war. *This is not an objective description of America,* but rather a passionate ethnography; the emphasis is on description and interpretation rather than on program for change. Though in parts of this book I suggest ways of changing conditions I deplore, in much of it I do not, because over the six years spent in writing I have not been able to perceive immediate possibilities for change. For example, though I deplore the fact that the elementary school pitches motivation at an intensely competitive level, I see no sense in altering that approach, because children have to live in a competitive world. Thus though I often describe rather grim situations, I try also to be aware of the complex interrelationships in culture and of the fact that even though one may regret what one describes, usually he cannot make practicable suggestions for change.

Most of this book is based on studies in which I have participated either as director or researcher or both, and much of the research has been by direct observation. However I do not *use research as proof* in any rigorous sense; rather I write about the research from an interpretive, value-laden point of view. Since I have an attitude toward culture, *I discuss data as illustrative of a viewpoint and as a take-off for expressing a conviction.* So I do not consider statistical frequency or regional differences, but have, rather, settled for the attitude that the materials reflect feelings, ideas, and conditions that seem to occur often enough in the United States to merit deepest consideration.

I doubt that there is any country in the world more suitable for anthropological study as a whole than the United States, for not only do towns and institutions open their doors to research, but the United States Government Printing Office is an inexhaustible source of information on everything from how to repair a home freezer to analysis of the military budget,[1] and Government officials are tireless in giving answers to all questions. Millions of pages of *The Congressional Record* provide a running ethnography on some of our most crucial concerns; and over and over again these millions of pages are condensed into brilliant reports by nameless anthropological geniuses employed by the Government. In addition to all this are our newspapers, particularly great journals like the *New York Times* and the *New York Herald Tribune,* for not only do they carry a continuous report of our daily goings-on, but even their biases, their omissions, and their trivia provide deep insights into our culture. Whereas in primitive culture the anthropologist often has to work to ferret out information, in our great democracy the printing presses inundate him with it, and his greatest task is to sort it out and interpret it. So, although much of the material of which I speak comes from "research projects," much is derived from contemporary printing presses.

THE AMERICAN CHARACTER AS IT PERSISTS AND AS IT CHANGES

In this book I am much concerned with our national character in a culture increasingly feeling the effects of almost 150 years

[1] Department of Defense Appropriation Bill, 1962. House of Representatives 87th Congress, *1st Session.*

of lopsided preoccupation with amassing wealth and raising its standard of living. This may be somewhat less than it was when Tocqueville visited us in 1831,[1] but it still constitutes a focus of such enormous interest that it raises the question, "What has our great concern with raising our standard of living done to us?" When we realize that the rest of the world has the same orientation, a study of what has happened to the American national character may give some insight into what to expect in other parts of the world from Paris to Moscow, to Peiping, Rangoon, Calcutta, and Rhodesia.

In Tocqueville's day we were 24 states and 13 million people. A thoughtful and meditative visitor, Tocqueville admired our independence, our peacefulness, our justice (though not our jurists!), and our enterprise, though there was much about us that saddened him too. He thought us "the most prosaic of all peoples on earth," and we clearly bored him to death. He considered Americans empty-headed, in mortal dread of being different from their neighbors, and lopsidedly occupied with making money and obtaining material enjoyments. Tocqueville found us sunk in personal pleasures and so frightened of having a deviant opinion that he wrote:

> When I survey this countless multitude of beings, shaped in each other's likenesses, among whom nothing rises and nothing falls, the sight of such universal uniformity saddens and chills me, and I am tempted to regret that form of [aristocratic] society which has ceased to be. . . . (Vol. 2, p. 825.)

Enmeshed as he was in the political turbulence of France, he looked upon our own politicians as political cowards, and the population as no better. On the other hand he saw us as courageous to the point of recklessness when in search of personal fortune, whether on the open seas or in the loneliness and danger of our forests. He admired the "manly independence" of Ameri-

---

[1] Alexis de Tocqueville, a Frenchman of noble descent, visited the United States for somewhat less than a year in 1831–1832 and wrote his classic *Democracy in America* on the basis of that trip. All citations from his work derive from the Henry Reeve translation, published by D. Appleton and Company, New York, 1901. My book was practically completed before I read Tocqueville's book.

cans, but he felt also that, standing lonely on his own two feet, the American cared little for anyone outside his family and narrow coterie of friends:

> As in ages of equality no man is compelled to lend assistance to his fellow-men, and none has any right to expect much support from them, every one is at once independent and powerless. . . . His independence fills him with self-reliance and pride among his equals; his debility makes him feel from time to time his want of some outward assistance, which he cannot expect from any of them, because they are all impotent and unsympathizing. (Vol. 2, p. 786.)

There are many similarities between what Tocqueville perceived in the American character and what I, and many others, see today. Yet such resemblances cannot be understood simply in terms of some vague tendency of personality to persist. Rather, so it seems to me, one must search for those cultural factors in each period of history that sustain traits present in previous epochs, and for those cultural factors which cause other character traits to drop out. Of course, to argue that anything as insubstantial as a trait of personality "persists" unchanged is to be absurd, for everything changes. What looks the same most surely has altered in subtle ways. The problem is to discover the nature of the alteration. For example, the insatiability Tocqueville found in 1831 arose from the hungers and strivings brought from the Old World by immigrants to a social order of unlimited equality of opportunity, to a continent apparently limitless in its wealth, and to a community beset by great shortages of workers of all kinds. Insatiability gripped the entire population, as Tocqueville saw it, and was expressed in private exploitation of land, in commerce, and in activity in the nascent professional life. Nowadays insatiability takes different forms depending on social class, and the "feverish" drive for self-improvement is no longer related to boundless frontiers. The same holds for the restlessness, the impulse to change, and the "evanescence" of American life that Tocqueville discerned: though these traits are present in America today, they are sustained by different social conditions. And so, finally, are the sadness Tocqueville perceived in us in the midst of our enjoyments and successes, and the grimness with which Americans in his day seemed to go about acquiring the good things of life.

Some of what Tocqueville saw in the American national character has been tamed or transferred to a separate class. For example, "feverishness"—which I call "drivenness"—is the property of the executive, the business, and the professional groups nowadays; the others—those millions who man the production lines, handle the billions of telephone calls, file the letters, type the letters and reports, etc., and who are rapidly being replaced by automated machinery—have abandoned drivenness for an anxious hope for security. The only desire for security of which Tocqueville was conscious in Americans was security from public criticism, for in America in 1831 acceptance of mere economic security was contemptible.

Thus apparent persistences are marked by subtle alterations and have become subject to changing social factors which have distributed them in special ways in the population. Other traits, such as religiosity and "puritanical" morality, have almost disappeared.

One trait of contemporary America—obsessive fear of annihilation by a foreign power—Tocqueville could not imagine; it was not only absent when he visited us, but our army was so tiny (6000 men), our navy so ridiculously small, our absorption at home so complete, our peacefulness so evident, that he was impelled to speak of us as the most "unmilitary people in the world" (Vol. 1, p. 310). Nor could Tocqueville, though he saw many of the human consequences of the emerging new technology and science, imagine the phantasm of death they would create; or that it would become commonplace for scientists and statesmen to imagine hundreds of millions of corpses.

> . . . . I still exceedingly regret the necessity of balancing these hazards [from the fallout consequent on aerial bomb-testing] against the hazards to hundreds of millions of lives which would be created by any relative decline in our nuclear strength.[1]

Tocqueville, for all his genius and insight into the future, could not foresee the creation of a *new kind of imagination* that would

[1] President Kennedy in his address on plans for resuming nuclear testing, March 2, 1962.

become preoccupied with thoughts of *imminent annihilation* and so commit enormous national wealth to the elaboration of instruments to accomplish and defend against it. In this he "failed"— but who in his right mind would not have?

Every culture has its own imaginative quality and each historic period, like each culture, is dominated by certain images. Who would deny that the Doric imagination was different from the Hellenistic; that the imagination of the Murngin of Australia is different from that of the Dakota Indians of the United States —or that the American imagination of Tocqueville's day was different from our own? And every culture and every period of history has its phantasms, is ruled by its Great Nightmares. The nightmares of the ancient Hebrews were the Philistines and their own God, constantly threatening them with annihilation if they disobeyed his law. The Athenian nightmare was Sparta and that of the Pilagá Indians was sorcery. In Tocqueville's day the American nightmare was what he called the despotism of the majority, the absolute power of the majority to control thought. Nowadays the same tyranny broods over us, but we have in addition the great, the encompassing Fear Incarnate, Russia, which clamps a vise on our intellectual powers so strong that men who are brilliant in other walks of life are so stupified with terror of the Soviet Union that though they may long for peace they cannot think of how to get it, and find it easier to brood on war and death.

SOME COMPARISONS BETWEEN THE MODERN AND PRIMITIVE WORLDS

When we compare our own with primitive culture we perceive differences and similarities, and in the body of the book I refer to many of them. It is necessary to give a somewhat extended explanation of certain points at the outset, however, since they occupy an important place in my theoretical orientation.

Outstanding among the differences between simpler societies and our own is the absence in the latter of what I call *production-needs complementarity* and *coincidence*. In primitive culture, as a rule, one does not produce what is not needed; and objects are made in the quantity and at the time required. Thus there is a congruence or complementarity between what is produced and what is desired, and there is a coincidence with respect to timing. This helps to give primitive culture remarkable stability. The primitive workman produces for a known market, and he does not try to expand it or to create new wants by advertising or other forms of salesmanship. On the whole he has a relatively firm demand, and he is content to be underemployed at his craft if it does not keep him busy. There is thus a traditional and relatively stable relationship not only between production and material needs, but also between production and psychological ones: the craftsman does not try to invent new products to sell or to exchange, nor to convince his customers that they require more or better than they are accustomed to. On the other hand, neither are they moved to come to him with unmet yearnings they must satisfy with new products. In primitive culture there is an implicit understanding that wants and production shall remain unchanged; and where tradition does not provide a large demand for his product the artisan usually makes up for that by farming, fishing, and so forth.

The contrast between primitive culture's assumption of a fixed bundle of wants and our culture's assumption of infinite wants is one of the most striking—and fateful—differences between the two cultural types. It contributes to stability in the one and restlessness in the other. If one imagines the capacity to want infinitely as anchored at one end to food and clothing but spiralling outward and upward toward the moon and the infinitude of outer space, one can then understand that the difference between our own and primitive culture is vast indeed. There is a contemporary cultural dynamics that contrasts qualitatively with primitive cultural dynamics.

Related to our contemporary dynamics is the lack of a *property ceiling*. Most, though by no means all, primitive societies are provided with intuitive limits on how much property may be accumulated by one person, and the variety of ways in which primitive society compels people to rid themselves of accumulated property is almost beyond belief. Distributing it to relatives, burning it at funerals, using it to finance ceremonies, making it impossible to collect debts in any systematic way—these and many other devices have been used by primitive culture, in veritable terror of property accumulation, to get rid of it. Rarely does primitive society permit the permanent accumulation of vast quantities of wealth. The fact that our society places no ceiling on wealth while making it accessible to all helps account for the "feverish" quality Tocqueville sensed in American civilization. Meanwhile, the concept of no ceiling on wealth has ripped the sky away, so that the idea of limitless space has come to play an enormous role in the twentieth-century imagination. It is no accident, therefore, that Russia, The Great Nightmare of our time, should be imagined as vaulting in upon us from outer space to rob us.

The absence of production-needs complementarity and coincidence and a property ceiling represent two critical differences between our own and primitive culture, and are therefore important in my thinking about the genesis of American character. It is obvious that since most of the world called "modern" shares these contrasts with the primitive world it must have in common with the United States many character traits. Throughout the book I suggest this.

There is one fundamental similarity between our own and primitive culture which it is well to take up in this Introduction. It derives, like all such similarities, from the fact that *Homo sapiens,* regardless of race, language, or culture, is a single species. The similarity is found in the tendency of human culture to provide remedies for the conflict and suffering it creates. The strong inherent tendency of *Homo sapiens* to search for solutions to problems he himself creates ranges from a therapy like psychoanalysis, which is an effort to heal the emotional ills generated by society, to social revolution. *Homo sapiens* has thus made of misery itself an evolutionary force; it is the misery man himself creates that urges him up the evolutionary tree. We perceive that *Homo sapiens* has the capacity to extort new adaptations from his suffering, and that if he does not destroy himself too soon, he may eventually come upon a destiny of great beauty. I say "may" rather than "will" because of *Homo sapiens'* well-known capacity—from bow and arrow to atomic nucleus—to use his discoveries against himself. Even an outright healing art like psychoanalysis has been used against man to exploit him for "motivational research," "public relations," and similar pecuniary purposes. This capacity to use his culture against himself may yet overtake man and destroy him while he works on his ultimate problem—learning to live with himself.

Since man, unlike lower animals, has no genetically determined, inborn mechanisms for governing interpersonal relations, he has to learn in each generation how to manage with other men; and since he has been on earth only half a million years or so, he is, naturally, still in elementary school so far as learning how to get along with his fellows is concerned. Of course he is more intelligent than other animals; still, when we consider that it took about two billion years to produce the human brain and when we see how men fumble in their relationships with one another, it becomes clear that Nature takes a long time to get anything done and that a million years is but a moment in evolution. Learning how to live with his species, then, is among man's tasks in evolution; the process has been largely trial-and-error and mostly disappointing.

If this book can be said to have a message it is that man *wrings* from culture what emotional satisfactions he obtains from it. But this is part of the evolutionary process. Man shall not wait 200 million years, like the giant tortoise within his carapace, until some organic mutation determines his course; rather shall he hunt, in anguish and perplexity, for a pattern of decent relations with his fellows. For man is deprived of inborn ways to interpersonal satisfaction and thus is compelled to search for them, evolving along the resulting pathways of dissatisfaction and intrapsychic conflict.

In this strain toward decency man is heir to a primitive condition which continues to confuse his social and personal life. Throughout history, in jungle and desert and on the coral atolls and stone pavements inhabited by men, society has been established primarily for the purpose of guaranteeing food and protection. And from this primitive necessity has emerged the central problem of the human species: the fact that inner needs have scarcely been considered. Man has been so anxiously busy finding ways to feed himself and to protect himself against wild animals, and against the elements, and against other men, that in constructing society he has focused on these problems and has let even sex (not marriage) take care of itself. Within its formal legal institutions, no organized society has stipulated the procedures and guarantees for *emotional* gratification between husband and wife and between parents and children, but all societies stipulate the relationships of protection and support. The very efficiency of human beings in ordering relationships for the satisfaction of these external needs has resulted in the slighting of plans for the satisfaction of complex psychic needs; everywhere man has literally had to force from an otherwise efficient society the gratification of many of his inner needs. The one-sided emphasis on survival, however, has provided man with an evolutionary impulse, for in the effort to gratify himself emotionally and to rid himself of emotional conflict with himself and his fellows, man constantly works on his institutions and on himself and thus becomes self-changing. Meanwhile, the orientation of man toward survival, to the exclusion of other considerations, has made society a grim place to live in, and for the most part human society has been a place where, though man has survived physically he has died emotionally.

This is another reason why, although culture is "for" man, it is also "against" him. And that is why I do not say much about the "good" things in American culture, for I am concerned and deeply worried that unthinking subjection to the primordial impulse to survive is simply producing new varieties of destruction.

2: Contemporary America

SINCE A CENTRAL PURPOSE OF THE BOOK IS TO SHOW THE relation of our institutional structure and values to the rest of our culture, this chapter outlines some of our basic institutions and values. Through them I interpret everything in contemporary American life.

VALUES AND DRIVES

Ours is a driven culture. It is driven on by its achievement, competitive, profit, and mobility drives, and by the drives for security and a higher standard of living. Above all, it is driven by expansiveness. Drives like hunger, thirst, sex, and rest arise directly out of the chemistry of the body, whereas expansiveness, competitiveness, achievement, and so on are generated by the culture; still we yield to the latter as we do to hunger and sex. Side by side with these drives is another group of urges, such as gentleness, kindliness, and generosity, which I shall call values, and in our culture a central issue for the emotional life of everyone is the interplay between these two. Values and drives—other than physiological drives—are both creations of the culture, but in the lives of Americans, and, indeed, of all "Western" men and women, they play very different roles. A value is something we consider good; something we always want our wives, husbands, parents, and children to express to us, to shower on us when we are gay, to tender to us when we are miserable. Love, kindness, quietness, contentment, fun, frankness, honesty, decency, relaxation, simplicity belong here.

Fundamentally, values are different from what I call drives, and it is only a semantic characteristic of our language that keeps the two sets of feelings together. To call both competitiveness and gentleness "values" is as confusing as to call them both "drives." Drives are what urge us blindly into getting bigger, into going further into outer space and into destructive competition; values are the sentiments that work in the opposite direction. Drives belong to the occupational world; values to the world of the family and friendly intimacy. Drives animate the hurly-burly of business, the armed forces, and all those parts of our culture where getting ahead, rising in the social scale, outstripping others, and merely surviving in the struggle are the absorbing functions of life. When values appear in those areas, they act largely as brakes on drivenness. Though the occupational world is, on the whole, antagonistic to values in this sense, it would nevertheless be unable to function without them, and it may use them as veils to conceal its underlying motivations.

In our own culture the outstanding characteristic of promotable executives is drive.[1] It is no problem at all to locate jobs requiring an orientation toward achievement, competition, profit, and mobility, or even toward a higher standard of living. But it is difficult to find one requiring outstanding capacity for love, kindness, quietness, contentment, fun, frankness, and simplicity. If you are propelled by drives, the culture offers innumerable opportunities for you; but if you are moved mostly by values, you really have to search, and if you do find a job in which you can live by values, the pay and prestige are usually low. Thus, the institutional supports—the organizations that help the expression of drives—are everywhere around us, while we must search hard to find institutions other than the family which are dedicated to values.

[1] C. Wilson Randle, "How to Identify Promotable Executives." *Harvard Business Review,* May-June, 1956, pp. 123–134.

Americans conceive of drive as a consuming thing, and in some people a drive may grow so strong that it engulfs the person who has it and those who come in contact with him. In the American conception, drives can become almost like cannibals hidden in a man's head or viscera, devouring him from inside. Urged on by drive, the American then may consume others by compelling them to yield to his drivenness. Values are merely ideas about good human relations, and though they do give people direction, they lack the compelling power of drives because they do not have institutional support. Americans get heart attacks, ulcers, and asthma from the effects of their drives, and it seems that as exotic cultures enter the industrial era and acquire drive, their members become more and more subject to these diseases.[1]

A phenomenon that is important to an understanding of our culture and, indeed, of the contemporary world is the underlying assumption of the modern world that one does not really know what one thinks one knows; that it is likely, on close investigation, to turn out to be wrong. This assumption of probable error inherent in all decisions helps create a condition of uncertainty, so that the torment of always being possibly wrong, or at least of not having the "best" answer to any of life's problems, becomes a dominating characteristic of modern life. Uncertainty in contemporary culture feeds upon itself, for each new "truth" becomes a new error, and each new discovery merely opens the door to new uncertainties. If you put together in one culture uncertainty and the scientific method, competitiveness and technical ingenuity, you get a strong new explosive compound which I shall call *technological drivenness*.

TECHNOLOGICAL DRIVENNESS

Among the first to describe the driven quality of industrial society was David Ricardo, whose central discovery was that it is driven by its productive forces to a constantly spiraling expansion and change. Unless the reality of this process and its capacity to drive the culture inexorably is understood, the fate

[1] Dr. John R. Rees, Director of the World Federation for Mental Health, personal communication.

and the dilemma of the American people are not comprehensible.

The vast natural resources of the United States made possible, though they did not determine, the coupling of great industrial development with technical creativity. Put to use in the laboratories of basic science, creativity results in new discoveries and inventions, which produce industries offering new products. Since they are new, demand for them must be stimulated, and the creation of new wants results in further industrial expansion; but since constant industrial expansion depletes and exhausts natural resources, scientists are paid to find new ones so that America itself will not become exhausted. The effort to increase productive efficiency is an expression of industrial growth, and that effort has pushed scientists, engineers, and inventors still further into research and discovery, with the result that still more industries have been born.

In view of all this, it is not surprising that the ideal American is an inexhaustible reservoir of drive and personality resources; one who, while not using up what he has, yet exploits his personality to the best advantage. To function inefficiently, to permit one's accomplishments to fall short of one's potentialities, is the same as using one's industrial capital inefficiently and is considered a symptom of neurosis.

The increase in the population of the United States and a rising living standard during nearly a century of rapid growth of productive facilities have helped solve the problem of the spiraling relationship between production and the need for an expanding market. Often primitive people cannot permit too many children to survive, for, given their technology, there simply is not enough to feed a large population in a harsh and niggardly environment. In America, until recently, the situation was the reverse: the productive machine seemed so efficient and nature so generous that a growing population appeared necessary to buy all that could be produced. Whereas in the Far East government officials might worry about overpopulation, in America even as late as 1961 the Government welcomed every infant as a potential customer. Early in 1957:

A huge electric chart in the lobby of the Commerce Department building [in Washington, D.C.] registered the 170

millionth inhabitant of the United States. . . . Sinclair Weeks,
Secretary of Commerce, was present to see the 170 millionth American chalked up. . . . "I am happy to welcome
this vast throng of new customers for America's goods and
services," he said. "They help insure a rising standard of
living and reflect our prosperous times."[1]

And again in December 1961:

The population of the United States, as measured on the
"census clock" in the Commerce Department lobby, reached
185,000,000 at 3:01 P.M. today.

Commerce Secretary Luther H. Hodges led a round of
cheers as the numbers on the clock moved to that figure.

The growth of 5,000,000 since last year "gives some idea
of the future needs of the country from the economic standpoint," he said.[2]

In 1962, however, the impending danger from automation,
which had been hidden by Government and industry in the
economic closet for seven years,[3] could no longer be denied,
for it was eliminating jobs so fast, while the population was still
growing, that chronic unemployment had become a persisting
source of anxiety.

In America there is an asymmetry and imbalance among products, machines, wants, consumers, workers, and resources. It
is never certain in our culture that a new product will be wanted
or that an old one will continue in demand; on the other hand,
there are always some economic wants that are unfulfilled. There
is a continuous race between consumers and products: consumers must buy or the economy will suffer, and there must
always be enough products to satisfy consumer demand. There
must always be enough workers to man the machines, and there
must always be just enough machines turning to absorb enough
workers. Finally, there must always be enough raw materials to

---

[1] *New York Times,* February 16, 1957.

[2] *New York Times,* December , 1961.

[3] The ritual of denial is embalmed in the classic *Automation and Technological Change,* Hearings before the Subcommittee on Economic Stabiliza-
tion of the Joint Committee on the Economic Report. 84th Congress. First
Session. United States Government Printing Office, 1955.

manufacture the needed goods, and the proper instruments must be produced in order to provide the raw materials necessary for manufacture. Unlike the ancient Greeks, the Americans have no gods to hold their world in equilibrium, and for this reason (and many others) America gives a visitor—and even a sensitive resident—the feeling of being constantly off balance, though many of our social scientists maintain that society is in equilibrium.

Imbalance and asymmetry, however, are necessary to America, for were the main factors in the economy ever to come into balance, the culture would fall apart. For example, if consumer wants did not outstrip what is produced, there would be no further stimulus to the economic system and it would grind to a halt and disintegrate. If there were ever a perfect balance between machines and workers to man them, then new industry would be impossible, for there would be no workers for the new machines, and so on. True equilibrium—balance, symmetry, whatever one wishes to call it—is poison to a system like ours.

In the United States, facilities for producing increasing quantities of products in constantly growing variety increase faster than the population, and since the lag must be taken up by the creation of needs, advertising became the messiah of this Era of Consumption, so well described by Riesman and Eric Fromm.

The fact that in stable cultures whatever is produced has a complementary need suggests the existence of a vast potential of human needs. For after all, if in stable cultures all over the world almost every object, however bizarre it may seem to us, is found to have a complementary need, it is only common sense to suppose that human beings have the potential for developing an enormous variety of needs. If the Ashanti of West Africa, for example, need golden stools, the natives of the South American jungles need curare, intoxicating drugs, dyed parrots, feather cloaks, shrunken heads, and flutes several feet long; if the Incas of Peru needed fields of flowers made of silver and gold and the Kwakiutl Indians needed totem poles, slat armor, engraved copper plates six feet square, and painted cedar boxes inlaid with mother of pearl, one can realize without even looking at Greece, Rome, Babylon, Egypt, and modern America that human beings have the capacity to learn to want almost any conceivable material object. Given, then, the emergence of a modern industrial culture capable of producing almost anything, the time is ripe for opening the storehouse of infinite need! But bear in mind that since our equation states that a necessary condition for cultural stability is perfect economic complementarity, it follows that lack of complementarity—a modern condition in which new objects are constantly seeking new needs, and new needs are constantly chasing after new objects—involves cultural instability. Meanwhile, we know that the storehouse of infinite need is now being opened in America. It is the modern Pandora's box, and its plagues are loose upon the world.

The following, from a full page ad in the *New York Times,* illustrates the American preoccupation with creating new wants. Under the picture of a large, outstretched, suppliant hand at the top of the page appears, in capitals almost an inch high, the *first commandment* of the new era:

CREATE

MORE

DESIRE!

Now, as always, profit and growth stem directly from the ability of salesmanship to create more desire.

To create *more* desire . . . will take more dissatisfaction with time-worn methods and a restless quest of better methods! *It might even take a penchant for breaking precedents.*[1]

This formulation stands on its head the anthropological cliché that the function of culture is to satisfy a relatively fixed bundle of known needs, for in America, as elsewhere in industrialized cultures, it is only *the deliberate creation of needs* that permits the culture to continue. *This is the first phase of the psychic revolution* of contemporary life.

There is probably nothing to which industrialists are more sensitive in America than consumer desires, and in that respect there is a striking resemblance between the businessman watching consumers' wants and an anxious American mother watching her child eat. The slightest sign of a decline in consumer demand makes the business world anxious, but this very petulance in the

[1] *New York Times,* July 12, 1949.

consumer stimulates the manufacturer to throw new products
on the market. The following gives the tone:

> Merchants and manufacturers faced even with a slight
> increase in reluctance to buy must take steps to *restimulate
> consumer appetite* for their goods. The tradition of Ameri-
> can ingenuity will come to their aid. New fashions, new
> models of mechanical goods and new designs are all in
> the order of the day. . . .
> Even slight lags in consumer interest have brought new
> products to the market quicker than they might otherwise
> have been introduced. . . . In the automobile field the lag
> in sales appears to have stimulated development of the gas
> turbine cars that give promise of more economical trans-
> portation and lower car prices.[1] (Italics supplied)

So if the reluctant consumer stops to count the change in his
pocket, the businessman is there, eager to count it for him and to
put it into his own pocket. If buying lags, the manufacturer
lures the consumer with a new car style, color TV, or a pocket-
size transistor radio. But this very reluctance to buy, though it
troubles the manufacturer, propels him into new productive
ventures, which in their turn give jobs to new hands, but also
foster new troubles.

The second modern commandment, "Thou shalt consume!"
is the natural complement of the first—"Create more desire!"
Together they lead the attack on the key bastion of the Indo-
European, Islamic, and Hebrew traditions—the impulse control
system—for the desire for a million things cannot be created without stimulating a craving for everything. This is the second phase
of the psychic revolution of our time—*unhinging the old impulse
controls*. The final phase will be the restoration of balance at a
new level of integration.

The attack on the impulse control system, that is, on our
resistance to inner cravings, is related then to technological
drivenness. In its onward rush, technological drivenness eats up
natural resources at such a rate that international combines must
be formed to find and exploit new ones. It helps, through
constantly increased advertising pressure, to lower the defenses

[1] *New York Times,* June 24, 1956.

against inner compulsions to express insatiable needs, while it harnesses human effort to the very machines that nourish the consuming appetites.

Born into a world where uncertainty was already a living principle, technological drivenness has intensified uncertainty by magnifying the economic imbalances on which it pivots, and the tension of uncertainty stimulates some to buy almost as a nervous man eats to calm himself. Industry, pressed by the drive for greater profits, by competition, and by the uncertainty of the market, commits ever larger sums to sales promotion. In the jargon of advertising in America, "education" means educating the public to buy, and "inspiration" means "inspired to buy."

As technological drivenness mines the earth of wealth, so it mines the desires of men; as the strip-shovel rips coal from the earth, as the pump sucks oil from the bed, so advertising dredges man's hidden needs and consumes them in the "hard sell." But without constant discovery and exploitation of hidden cravings, all of us would starve under the present system, for how would we be fed and clothed otherwise? Where would we be employed?

Were human wants to regress to a primitive level, there would be universal misery in America. No government could cope with the unemployment that would ensue, and at present there is no visible middle ground between the needs of the caveman and the cravings of space-man.

Meanwhile, advertising does not deserve all the (dubious) credit for destroying our impulse controls. After all, if they still served a social purpose we would keep them. If holding ourselves in check led to satisfaction in work, to a position of community respect, or to immortality, we would not let ourselves go so easily for fun and for the ever higher standard of living. But for most Americans, self-denial seems to lead nowhere any longer, for heaven has become detached from society, and for most people work is merely a dreary interlude between nourishing hours with one's family. Man in our culture has always bargained his impulses against higher goods—he has always sought to trade one day of abstinence against economic gain or against an eternity of supernatural blessings. But when the sacrifice of impulse release no longer assures rewards either on earth or in heaven, he will no longer keep his cravings under control unless he is punished, so that nowadays advertising merely opens the door to impulses clamoring to come out anyway.

TECHNOLOGICAL DRIVENNESS AND DYNAMIC OBSOLESCENCE

The idea of obsolescence—or, better, "dynamic obsolescence"—has become such a necessary part of contemporary American thinking and life that it deserves a place, along with achievement, competition, profit, and expansiveness, among the drives. "Dynamic obsolescence" is the drive to make what is useful today unacceptable tomorrow; to make what fitted the standard of living of 1957 inappropriate even for 1960. It is the "new-car-every-year" drive. Technological drivenness is admirably served by dynamic obsolescence, for it compels us to throw away what we have and buy a newer form of the same thing or something entirely different. It is the technological complement to impulse release.

"Dynamic obsolescence" was formally installed as a cultural drive in a speech given by Mr. Harlow Curtice, President of General Motors, at the dedication of General Motors' wonderful new Research Center. No occasion could have been more appropriate for this historically unique phenomenon: the recognition and crowning of a new cultural drive. The only thing that was missing from the ceremony was a Miss Dynamic Obsolescence of 1956. Some excerpts from Mr. Curtice's speech on the occasion will give the tone:

Continuing emphasis on change, on a better method and a better product, in other words, on progress in technology, has been the major force responsible for the growth and development of our country. Some call this typical American progress "dynamic obsolescence" because it calls for replacing the old with something new and better. From this process of accelerating obsolescence by technological progress flow the benefits we all share—more and better job opportunities, and advancing standard of living—the entire forward march of civilization on the material side. . . .

The promotion of the progress of science and the useful arts is of crucial importance . . . [but] there is a *far more*

vital consideration. I refer to the importance of technological progress in assuring the continuance not only of
American leadership in the free world, but of the democratic processes themselves.[1]

Dynamic obsolescence has thus become the American Fortuna,
warm, fruity, and maternal, in whom all benefits abound.

In attempting to understand Mr. Curtice, I encounter two difficulties: I cannot decide who really is the leader in the world
today; and I become lost in some of the implications of Mr.
Curtice's words. For example, the emergence of India as a
modern state seems to be the result of obsolescence not in the
material, but rather in the social sense, for what became obsolete
in India was British rule; and what is obsolescent is the caste
system. On the other hand, the rise of India as a political power
has become possible in large part also because the two grand
power configurations (the Soviet Union and the United States)
that are dynamic above all others in their (material) dynamic
obsolescence confront each other in fear and trembling, and this
gives India a chance. Thus, India's road to leadership-through-
dynamic-obsolescence is indirect—but it is there, and the Oracle
of Detroit is correct again.

Whatever role we wish to assign it in world affairs, however,
there is no doubt that in American life dynamic obsolescence is
fundamental and necessary. From the point of view of personality
this means that one's human capacities are in danger of becoming obsolete, and every man and woman therefore stands in peril
of waking up one morning to discover that he is, too. When the
entire pattern of transportation changes and a thousand railroad
stations are abolished overnight by one major road, then all the
station masters, baggage clerks, and others who manned them become obsolete;[2] when several large corporations merge into one,

[1] Printed in "'The Greatest Frontier'—Remarks at the dedication program, General Motors Technical Center," Detroit, Michigan, May 16, 1956.
Public Relations Staff, General Motors, Detroit. I am grateful to Mrs. Sydney
Slotkin for calling my attention to this speech and the remarks on obsolescence.

[2] Front page article, *New York Times*, August 21, 1956. I want to thank
Mr. Richard Meier for calling my attention to the implications for obsolescence of this article.

then many of the executives become unnecessary and obsolete;[1] and people's fear of becoming obsolete stirs hostility against Science, the paramount creator of obsolescence.

A few quotations from *Automation and Technological Change* will give the tone:

> . . . a radio poll in Detroit showed that listeners feared automation next to Russia. . . . (p. 247)
> . . . automation . . . produces various sorts of fears in various sorts of individuals—fear of change, fear of technology itself, fear of displacement, fear of unemployment, fear of machines, *fear of science in general.* (pp. 262-3) (Italics supplied)

> We know of cases where some workers have gotten sick on the steps of the new [telephone company automated] toll center; others developed various illnesses which could be traced to fear of new work operations. We have been told of mature women crying in restrooms, improperly prepared for new methods and fearful of losing their jobs. . . . The tragedy of the mature worker whose skill area suddenly disintegrates and is incorrectly retrained is profound. (pp. 341-2)

As professors encounter their colleagues in the corridors of "progressive" American universities, they silently evaluate them as "obsolete" or "alive"; in order for a professor to stay "alive" in an American university that is not obsolescent, he must indeed change from year to year like an automobile, refrigerator, or washing machine.

The fear of becoming obsolete is so powerful that the sense of being useless is a common element in emotional crisis in America. However this fear is rooted not only in the fear of obsolescence, but also in an industrial system that obliges too many people to do what they have so little interest in doing. In this respect

---

[1] "National Job-Hunting Group Established To Aid Unemployed Executives Over 40." *New York Times,* August 30, 1956. Between 1910 and 1950 the number of proprietors, managers and officials declined by nearly 7 per cent (*Economic Forces in the U.S.A. in Facts and Figures.* U.S. Gov't Printing Office, p. 29) even though productive facilities and the gross national product have increased many times that.

America's industrial progress has made many people spiritually useless to themselves.

THE JOB AND THE SELF

Most people do the job they have to do regardless of what they want to do; technological driveness has inexorable requirements, and the average man or woman either meets them or does not work. With a backward glance at the job-dreams of his pre-"labor force" days the young worker enters the occupational system not where he would, but where he can;[1] and his job-dream, so often an expression of his dearest self, is pushed down with all his other unmet needs to churn among them for the rest of his life. The worker's giving up an essential part of himself to take a job, to survive, and to enjoy himself as he may is the new renunciation, the new austerity: it is the technological weed that grows where the Vedic flower bloomed. What makes the renunciation particularly poignant is that it comes after an education that emphasizes exploitation of all the resources of the individual, and which has declared that the promise of democracy is freedom of choice.

This renunciation of the needs of the self—this latter-day selflessness—is, paradoxically, a product of the most successful effort in human history to meet on a mass basis an infinite variety of material needs. The man who accepts such a renunciation does indeed approach fulfillment of the wants the engines of desire-production have stirred within him, and whoever refuses to renounce his very self will get few of the material things for which he has been taught to hunger. The average American has learned to put in place of his inner self a high and rising standard of living, because technological drivenness can survive as a cultural configuration only if the drive toward a higher standard of living becomes internalized; only if it becomes a moral law, a kind of conscience. The operator, truck driver, salesclerk, or bookkeeper may never expect to rise much in "the firm," but he can direct his achievement drive into a house of his own, a car, and new furniture.

[1] Gladys L. Palmer, "Attitudes toward work in an industrial community," *American Journal of Sociology*, 43 (1957), 17–26.

The massing of so much drive behind the living standard in our culture has brought it about that the very survival of our culture depends on a unique and fantastic material configuration created for us by technological drivenness, and to which the standard of living has been fastened psychologically by pressures from within and without.

As numberless selves have been ground up by the technological system, the popularity and usefulness of psychoanalysis have grown so that America is one of the most psychoanalytically-minded countries on earth; and clinical psychology and learning theory have covered the country with practitioners—bad as well as good, of course. Though this flowering of psychology has much to do with the technological system, and though much of it has grown up either in order to speed the technology or to ameliorate its lethal effects, nevertheless, to the degree that psychology has expanded our understanding and deepened our sensitivity, it is a medicine wrung from the very system that inflicts wounds upon us.

Meanwhile, one should remember that the great rise in real income suggests that we have gotten what we paid for; but how far we have yet to go is suggested by an estimate that by 1965 half the babies born in New York City hospitals will be the off-spring of "indigent parents."[1]

Along with the emotional problems they create, all cultures provide socially acceptable outlets or anodynes. In America some compensation for personality impoverishment is provided by the high-rising standard of living, but another available outlet is job change. More than half the American workers had from two to four jobs between 1940 and 1949, and in those ten years every worker shifted around an average of three times.[2] Beneath this continuous tidal movement in and out of jobs[3] lie deep narcissistic wounds whose pain the worker tries to ease by moving around, searching restlessly for the "perfect" job, as a sick man painfully

[1] *New York Times,* October 30, 1957.

[2] Gladys L. Palmer, *Labor Mobility in Six Cities.* N. Y., Social Science Research Council, 1954. It is to be regretted that later figures of equal comprehensiveness are not available.

[3] Professor Irvin Sobel reminds me that many semiskilled workers shift around from activity to activity within the same company at approximately the same level of skill. He tells me also that automation has now made even younger workers so apprehensive about job security that they move around less.

shifts his body about in bed to find a more comfortable position. Of course, he never does. I have called this movement in and out of jobs tidal because it is a slow, never-ceasing trickle from many sources, from many industries and many occupations, and in the long run it has reached such proportions that millions are spent to analyze it, and some of the best brains in the land devote their lives to fascinated study of it. What keeps a worker on his job? Why does he move? Why does he *not* move if he doesn't? Are workers satisfied? If not, why not? What does "satisfied" mean? Can we measure the boundary line between satisfaction and dissatisfaction? So far, the mass study of "job attachment" shows that the American worker's involvement in his job is so insubstantial that it is next to impossible to define the term "attachment."

Meanwhile, industry is hostile to workers who move too often because it is costly to train new hands, and because a missing employee disturbs production. That is why American psychology considers frequent job change as a symptom of emotional disturbance. It ought to be pointed out, however, in view of the fact that frequent job change is used routinely to diagnose emotional instability, that there are vast differences in the cultural pattern of job stability, for while over half the laborers had three or more jobs between 1940 and 1949, only two-fifths of the service workers had that many, and only a third of the professional workers.[1] At any rate, the man who changes jobs "too frequently" is simply manifesting in extreme the characteristic American tendency to job-flux.

Paradoxically, while it detests worker instability, industry must at the same time love it, for it is this very lack of involvement in, lack of loyalty to, the job that makes the rapid growth of industry possible. If a new factory making a new product is built, all that is necessary to get workers is to advertise, for the workers' lack of attachment to the jobs they have and their obstinate hope for better working conditions, a few cents more an hour, or a pleasanter boss, make it easy to attract them away from what they have to something new.[2] Were there firm and devoted attachment to the job, industrial growth would be much more

---

[1] Palmer, *op. cit.*
[2] This applies especially to younger workers. As a unionized worker acquires seniority, he is less likely to change employers.

difficult, for new enterprises would not be able to find trained workers if they loved it where they were. Since we require of most people that they be uninvolved in the institution for which they work, it follows that the ability to be *un*involved is a desirable quality in the American character. Meanwhile, since loyal workers are valued because every replacement cuts into profits, we have a paradoxical situation in which, since *un*involvement— "What do *you* give a damn, bub?"—is valued also, loyalty is obtained through higher wages, fringe benefits, and seniority. This emotionless connection that finally pins a worker to his job is called "attachment" in the ambiguous language of labor economics.

The recent social invention—the "coffee break"—fits this situation perfectly, for during the "break" the worker escapes from a task in which he has little or no interest, takes up his preferred and necessary role as consumer, and relaxes his impulse controls. In the uninvolved flirtations and sociability of the coffee break the worker can renew his self-esteem, badly battered through performance of the meaningless task, and assuage some of the anxiety and hostility stirred up by it. The coffee break is on-the-job therapy.

The fact that the majority have little or no involvement in the institutions for which they work means that work, which in most *non*industrial cultures of the world is a strong and continuous socializing agency, is, in America, also *de*socializing. In the first place, for the overwhelming majority of Americans, the job itself—not the union or the associates on the job, but the institution in which they work—is precisely the mechanism that cuts them off from their most significant emotional involvements —family, friends, and Self; and in the second place, since the great majority of the tasks at which Americans work are routine, requiring little or no initiative and imagination,[1] most persons in the labor force never have the opportunity to develop, through work, characteristics that might contribute to the enrichment of society. Furthermore, the rising labor turnover since World War II[2] suggests that the pleasures of the "work group" have little binding force on the worker who wants to change.

To almost any American his working companions, however

[1] *Economic Forces in the U.S.A. in Facts and Figures,* pp. 28–29.
[2] *New York Times Magazine,* May 19, 1957.

enjoyable, are *inherently replaceable*.[1] The comradely group a man has on one job can be replaced by a similar one on the next. The feeling of being replaceable, that others can get along without one, that somebody else will be just as good, is an active depressant in the American character.

By the Ice Age man had discovered that he could bind his fellows to him by sharing work and its fruits. This discovery was so valuable that establishing solidarity through work and sharing became a stable human tradition, so that whether on an atoll in the South Pacific, in the jungles of South America, or in Arctic wastes, this aspect of early life has persisted. Since one of the many revolutions of industrial society has been the sweeping away of the unifying functions of work, work has lost its human meaning. Although it is true that on the job some pleasure is obtained nowadays in socializing, the hold of the worker's fellows on him is slight. This lack of deep positive involvement in the people with whom one spends most of his waking life derives in part from the fact that he does not work *for* the person he works *with*, for the fruits of activity are not shared among workers but belong to the enterprise that hires them.

Except for professionals and executives most Americans are emotionally involved neither in their occupation (what they do) nor in their job (the place where they do it).[2] What finally relates the average person to life, space, and people is his own personal, intimate economy: his family, house, and car. He has labelled his occupational world "not involved," and turned inward upon his own little world of family, hobbies, and living standard.

WORKER DRIVES AND THE DRIVES OF THE ELITE

The majority of workers—the factory hands, mechanics, laborers, truck drivers, minor clerical and sales workers, all those

[1] Nancy C. Morse and Robert S. Weiss, "The function and meaning of work." *American Sociological Review*, 20:191–198, 1955; also, Palmer, "Attitudes toward work," *loc. cit.*, and personal communication from Mr. Robert Weiss.

[2] *Fortune*'s study of executives reports a rapidly mounting turnover among them. See *The Executive Life* by the Editors of *Fortune*. New York: Doubleday, 1956. Professionals and executives care much about *what* they do, but have the characteristic American lack of loyalty to the organization *for* whom they do it.

millions (61 per cent of the labor force)[1] engaged in routine
work requiring little education or initiative—is concerned largely
with raising their living standard and grasping for security[2] (the
worker drives). Competitiveness, profit, achievement, and expansion (the élite drives) belong more to scientists and other
professionals, to corporation executives and managers—that is, to
the élite and to their satellites and imitators. Few Americans,
of course, are innocent of any one of these drives, and it is this
broad dissemination of drive potential in all classes in a modern
democracy that makes possible recruitment of workers into the
élite. It is in the latter group, however, that profit, achievement,
expansion—the drives that maximize the culture—appear with
greatest strength, are given the freest expression, and play over
the most numerous areas of life.

All cultures offer, through prescribed channels, some outlet
for the emotional problems they create; they stipulate, in addition, what emotions may be expressed, by whom, in what quantity,
and the circumstances of their expression. For example, in American culture erotic interest must be expressed differently by men
and women, and hostility is more acceptable in a male than in a
female. Furthermore, except in war or under other very special
circumstances, hostility must be contained in public, and its expression veiled. In contrast, the profit, achievement, living standard, and expansion drives can be expressed almost without
limit and in public; there are no laws against maximizing profits
or the standard of living in public, and newspapers devote many
pages to their discussion.

All of this is obviously accomplished through an act of ap-
portionment—of distributing the cultural baggage among the
culture carriers, according to the circumstances. In modern industrial societies the routine workers learn to make the drives toward
security and a higher living standard most completely expressive
of their selves; and what they harbor of other drives is channeled
into those two consuming working-class hungers. To an industrial
worker, for example, to be a "success" is to have job security. In
the jobs and occupations that are the lot of the routine worker,

[1] *Economic Forces in the U.S.A. in Facts and Figures*, pp. 28–29.
[2] Palmer, *op. cit.* As the Editors of *Fortune* point out, security is important
to executives too, but it is not their life's goal as it is for workers.

the élite drives really play a secondary role. This is primarily because since there is a very definite limit on how far the routine worker can rise in his work, expansion, achievement, and the rest have little emotional meaning for him. The aspirations of the élite, as we shall see, have no limit; for them expansion is a passion yearning in the flesh.

What the American industrial system does not offer the routine worker can be appreciated best by contrast with what it does offer one of its élite groups, scientists and engineers. By the same token, the personality *deprivations* of the average worker can be appreciated by a view of the personality *expectations* of this élite.

THE CULTURAL MAXIMIZERS

All great cultures, and those moving in the direction of greatness, have an élite which might be called the *cultural maximizers* whose function is to maintain or push further the culture's greatness and integration. In ancient Israel, where the pivot of greatness was religion, these were the Prophets. In Rome, as among the Dakota Indians also, the cultural maximizers united within themselves qualities of violence and statesmanship, for they had to be warriors as well as wise men. The functions of a cultural maximizer include organization (i.e., maintaining the level of integration of the culture as it is) and contributing certain qualitative features necessary to the continuance of the cultural life. His function is never to alter the culture radically. He may help to give more intense expression to features that already exist, but he never wants to bring about a fundamental change. Thus, those who have the capacity to maximize culture in this sense are among the élite in all highly developed civilizations.

In our own culture there is no group that deserves more recognition, and hence a position among the élite, than the scientists and engineers. They are the central power from which emanate the new technical ideas and industrial products so necessary to the continuation of our culture. Insofar as they are able to expand the array of lethal weapons so necessary to a warlike people, they are in the truest sense cultural maximizers.

In America the scientifically trained élite is one of the most mobile segments of the population.[1] Because of their scarcity relative to the demand for them, and because, as with other American workers, their institutional loyalties are weak, large sums are spent by industry to attract them, and they are offered many psychic rewards. In the advertisements for scientists and engineers is the essence of the American dream—the dream that every American is supposed to realize in his lifetime work, but which is approximated only by the élite. A few examples will give the flavor:

The following is a third-of-a-page advertisement, addressed to "electronic and mechanical engineers and physicists":

> An invitation to a better
> way of life . . . from MELPAR

The Washington D.C. Area provides a stimulating environment for professional and intellectual growth under conditions of minimum stress. Melpar laboratories are located in Northern Virginia, suburban to the Nation's Capitol. The area enjoys the country's highest per capita income, is free of heavy industry, and virtually depression proof. Cultural, recreational, and educational facilities abound. Housing is fine and plentiful.

Should you join Melpar you would tie your own professional growth to that of a Company which has doubled in size every 18 months for the past decade.[2] Melpar maintains a policy of *individual recognition* which enables our engineers to progress according to their own time tables, not prearranged ones. Performance primarily determines advancement. Age, tenure, length of experience are only secondary considerations. . . .[3]

The chance to grow, to achieve recognition for performance as an individual—precisely what is denied most workers—is offered the élite as a special lure; such inducements are not found in advertisements for most other jobs. The phenomenal growth of this company is interesting, because one of the commonest words in advertisements directed to cultural maximizers is "expand."

[1] *Occupational Mobility of Scientists*. Bulletin 1121, United States Department of Labor Statistics, 1953.

[2] This would mean that the company had increased in size about 64 times.

[3] From the *New York Times*, June 7, 1956. Although these advertisements are some years old, a glance at the ads for scientists on the last few pages of the financial section of the contemporary *Times* will show that if anything the advertising for scientists has become even more hyperbolic.

It is a rare advertisement that emphasizes permanence or stability as such, since in the circles in which the élite move, expansion *is* stability. That is to say, cultural maximizers in America abhor stability; what interests them, or better, what drives them, is expansion, and the permanence of their world is seen in terms of its limitless growth. But in actuality, "growth" does not quite cover the case for cultural maximizers, for growth does not of itself imply the outward-in-all-directions-at-once kind of increase that fires their imagination. Rather, their phantasy is the expanding universe of the astronomers, and that is also their concept of stability.

International Business Machines placed this advertisement in the *New York Times;* it was arranged as if spelled out on a Scrabble board:

```
          D
     ELECTRONIC
          V    E
     ENGINEERS
          L    E
          O    A
          P    R
          M    C
          E    H
          N
          T
```

How to spell out a winning future

. . . .

The IBM engineer is confident of his future because he knows that digital computer development, design, and manufacture is perhaps the one "unlimited" field in electronics today . . . and that IBM is an acknowledged world leader in this permanently significant field.

Ideas . . . ideas . . . and more ideas are the raw materials of successful engineering. And at IBM you expand your ideas in a small team, where they are immediately recognized and rewarded. IBM's awareness of each engineer's individual performance is expressed in the great number of challenging positions awaiting men who prove their abilities at IBM.

Right now there are career openings at IBM that offer *you* every opportunity to grow in professional stature to the fullest extent of *your* abilities.[1]

Here the feeling of expansiveness is communicated through an emphasis on having ideas—an experience largely irrelevant to the work-life of men on the assembly line. Shrewdly, IBM's advertisement (which reads as if it had been composed after running a thousand answers to a questionnaire on "What do you most desire in a job?" through an electronic sorter to find out what words appeared most often) emphasizes immediate recognition and reward of ideas by the company, an experience reserved almost exclusively for cultural maximizers.

Another of the world's giant corporations placed the following advertisement:

ENGINEERS
What are the attractions at General Electric? To men who think ahead, this expanding department offers the opportunity to pioneer in the creation and development of important, new projects, plus the advantages of living in Utica, at the gateway to the Adirondacks.

Within easy reach of your home you'll find 5 golf courses . . . over 8,000 acres of parks . . . an unspoiled countryside of lakes noted for fishing and swimming.

Openings for Experienced
Mechanical engineers—for creating new airborne equipment to operate under prodigious conditions of shock, (etc.) . . . The "Specs" will be written *after* your job is done. We want mechanical engineers with vision, horse sense and the courage of their convictions.

Electrical engineers—These projects from science fiction require rational dreamers who possess a high starting and operating torque.[2]

Through the advertisements, many of them a quarter of a page or more in size, run the themes of challenge, creativity, initiative, personal growth, expansion, novelty, individuality, the taking of responsibility, stimulation through professional on-the-job contacts, and achievement. The majority of American jobs, however,

[1] *New York Times,* June 24, 1956.
[2] *New York Times,* May 29, 1955.

are remote from these. What is most striking is that realization of these things should be offered as *inducements:* the very form of the advertisements is an acknowledgment that in America most jobs are not challenges, that no creativity or initiative is desired.

But what of these "dreamers" with "high starting and operating torque"? Do their dreams come true? For a very large number of the Ph.D.'s entering the American industrial system they do not. With its characteristic detachment the Bureau of Labor Statistics states the case:

> The figures . . . indicate that more than two-thirds of the scientists who left the government, private industry, or a foundation for another type of employment entered educational institutions. *The largest numbers entering education from other types of employment came from private industry.*

> The fact that the universities were able to compete successfully with other types of employers in attracting and retaining scientists is noteworthy in view of the low salary levels prevailing in educational institutions. Apparently, the advantages of university employment, such as *freedom of research,* are sufficiently strong to countervail, in the minds of many scientists, the economic handicaps such employment imposes. [Italics supplied.]

Their figures show also that while two-fifths of the scientists whose first position is in private industry take one in a university for their second, only 16 per cent of the Ph.D.'s whose first job is on a campus take their second in industry. As a matter of fact, "the [scientist] recruits into . . . industry have come in large numbers from the ranks of *newly created* doctors of philosophy rather than from among scientists already established as educators."[1] [Italics supplied.]

Thus, it is hard experience that teaches the young, and usually deeply committed, scientist that industry is not the place for him. Attracted at first by the startling pay and the lure of pleasant

[1] *Occupation Mobility of Scientists.* Bulletin 1121. United States Department of Labor, 1953, p. 42.

living, he finds these are no compensation for personality loss. *Executive Life* tells the same story:

> "A help-wanted ad we ran recently," one executive ex-
> plains, "asked for engineers who would 'conform to our
> work patterns.' Somebody slipped on that one. He actually
> came out and said what's really wanted around here."

In view of the relative hysteria that has arisen in connection with our shortage of scientists and engineers it might be well to stop for a moment and review some stimulating observations on scientists and engineers gleaned from the *New York Times* over the years. I start with Devon Francis' *Some Dreams F.O.B. Detroit:*

> . . . much of the time they sit at their desks performing such
> grubby tasks as redesigning an engine camshaft or doing
> surgery on a rear axle because the company sales depart-
> ment has decreed a change to meet competition. (*N. Y.
> Times* Magazine, Oct. 25, 1959.)

Vance Packard in *The Waste Makers* has also pointed to the subjection of scientific and engineering brains to the whims of the market. An advertising executive commenting on the recruitment practices of companies looking for scientists and engineers, observed:

> . . . many recruitment ads failed to give a valid picture of
> the employer—a factor that tends to increase engineering
> turnover. The average engineer changes jobs about once
> every two and one half years, according to the study [car-
> ried out by his agency]. (*N. Y. Times,* Jan. 27, 1961.)

As a matter of fact the companies themselves are aware of the deceptions, for in attempting to pirate researchers from one another they use appeals like the following:

> "If those glamorous projects you were promised you'd
> work on haven't materialized. . . ."
> [These appeals] are typical of a barrage of newspaper
> help-wanted advertisements that appeared today [in Los
> Angeles] before 3,000 participants in a joint national meet-

ing of the American Rocket Society and the Institute of Aeronautical Sciences. . . .

The advertising barrage was part of the most intensive talent-raiding episodes in recent industrial history. Large corporations constantly engage in the process colloquially called "body-snatching." (*N. Y. Times,* June 16, 1961.)

All of this enables us to make a discovery in connection with the present panic in America over the lack of scientific brains in industry; for we see now that when industry does get scientists it cannot hold them, because it interferes with their autonomy and growth. This élite shows the same tidal movement as the plebe, and for the same reasons. The difference is that this élite can get out of the industrial system, but the plebe cannot. The university, with its unpainted walls, its preposterous architecture, poor lighting, petty politics, status hunger, and trailing clouds of pipe smoke is still a refuge of the human spirit. Of course, as consulting fees mount and professors rush around garnering them, even this function of the university becomes problematic—as does the existence of the "human spirit." Professors have no immunity against the effects of the high-rising standard of living.

FEAR IN AMERICA

Most American workers have learned to put the constantly rising standard of living in place of progressive self-realization. Only the élites—the professionals, the corporation executives, and the successful businessmen—have a real chance to express the most highly rewarded cultural drives or to try in their occupational lives for some kind of self realization not comprehended within the retail price index.[1] On the outer fringes of this group are millions of "little men" who struggle along in their own businesses and whose failures are numbered in the ever-increasing tens of thousands. They are the men who yearn to "go in business for myself," and who, though animated by the drives of the élite, also have other, more intimate, possibly more determining motives.

[1] A composite statement, with approximate values, of the things Americans buy, published regularly by the Bureau of Labor Statistics and formerly known as the "cost of living index."

When a man goes into business for himself he is moved not only by the élite drives but also by the wish to have self-respect, to not have somebody else tell him what to do, to be able to work when he pleases and stop when he pleases. Being his own boss means keeping for himself what he makes and using his own ideas rather than somebody else's. In short, "my own boss" means that the little man controls himself rather than being controlled by someone who has no interest in him other than a pecuniary one. To be used up for somebody else's drive realization goes against his grain; he wants to survive in his own interest and not be consumed in somebody else's; he wants to be protected.

It is because going into business for one's self expresses such deeply rooted yearnings that the traditional American drama of big and little business has its perennial appeal. In it something big (Big Business) is always pushing somebody small and helpless around and depriving him of his right to life and self, and Americans respond to the drama with vigor and passion because most of them feel pushed around. While it is true that the restraints exercised on the economy by the great concentrations of industrial capital are real, the repeated congressional investigations of big business and the plight of little business reflect widespread folk anxieties. The following from "Teen-Agers Views of Big Business" gives the tone:

> "Big Businesses run everything in America—they have all the money." This reaction of a 16-year-old high school girl in Tucson, Arizona, sums up the attitude of many of our young people toward big business. . . .
>
> Nearly 31 per cent of those interviewed thought of big business in a negative sense, as sort of a giant monopoly spread across all America. They feared the future will see all free enterprise swallowed up in one or two gigantic trusts. The consensus was that in the next decade and a half there will be one or two large companies representing each individual industry.[1]

The opinions of this cross-section of American youth reflect fear of the enormously ramifying network of controls exercised

[1] *St. Louis Post-Dispatch,* October 5, 1956. Article based on interviews with 1923 teen-agers in 42 American cities.

over the American economy by big business. While the giant American enterprises help raise the standard of living, contribute brilliantly to the élan of American capitalism and are necessary for its survival, and represent in some ways the approaching climax of a creative type of economic organization, they nevertheless fill many Americans with a feeling of mingled anxiety, hostility, and dependence. Thus, although the teenagers previously quoted are angry at and fearful of big business, the majority of the boys are yet eager to become dependent on it:

> Only one out of eight young men in high school expects or has any desire to go into business for himself. The majority hopes to find security and success in positions with important national companies. The "reach for the sky" dream of American youth seems to have suffered a setback in the period since the end of World War II. Young men would rather put their trust in management of large concerns than set out on their own.[1]

This is self-renunciation again—only this time the American does it because he is intelligently afraid to try his hand alone.

Anyone can readily understand why youth should feel as it does about starting out on its own, for even without their intuitive sense of the limited chances of survival, there is the obvious reality that new and little businesses die off rapidly.[2] The new man and the little one are forced to go into businesses which are the easiest to enter and where, therefore, competition is keen, profits low, and business mortality high. Even in boom times, it is difficult to gain a foothold, for then big business borrows the

[1] *Ibid.*

[2] Dun and Bradstreet report that there were more business failures in 1961 than in any other year since 1933. The 1961 failures represent the present peak of a mounting trend. Of the 2,647,671 businesses listed by Dun and Bradstreet in 1956, half are worth less than $10,000 and only 5 per cent are worth more than $125,000. (*New York Times*, January 8, 1962.) It is of this 95 per cent of American business that I speak. Dun and Bradstreet's figures on failures do not, obviously, take account of the number of businesses that quietly disappear without going bankrupt.

For general statements on the plight of little business, see *The Congressional Record*, 1956, p. 8359; Kurt Mayer, "Small business as an institution," *Social Research*, 14: 332-349, 1947; the following articles in the *New York Times*, August 26, 1956, Section 3: "Credit Shortage Overhangs Boom" and "The Merchant's Point of View."

loose money available in order to finance expansion, thus making money hard for others to come by and compelling them to pay higher interest than big business. For these and other reasons, nearly half of new business never reaches its second birthday.

A further factor that gives big business increasing advantage over the new and the little man is the capacity of big business, aided by social psychology and psychoanalysis, to channel unconscious cravings into consumption. Since the new man and the little one often lack the financial resources necessary to do this, they cannot move with as much assurance as the big enterprise into areas as yet unexploited, and where the chances of success may be greater. In this way, big business, with its new capacity for diversification—the ability of one enormous enterprise to expand in a variety of directions with a variety of new goods and services—and with the money to finance advance market research, is reducing the possible areas of success for the little man. To all of this must be added the natural reluctance of banks to lend money to new ventures by little people.

Thus, the man who seeks to be "independent" by starting his own business cannot make a free choice of what he shall do, and having made his enforced choice, he has about a 50 per cent chance of surviving. If he survives, he will remain small and earn a modest income.[1]

Thus, the little businessman stands out in the open, fearful of other little men and of the large enterprises.[2] But his fear is not of economic destruction only; what he fears also is loss of the remnants of his self-hood embodied in his business. In this he is little different from the worker, for the protection a worker wants from his union is not only against low pay, insecurity, and poor

---

[1] Kurt Mayer, *loc. cit.* Much of what is in Professor Mayer's restrained and scholarly paper is stated vigorously on the basis of broad personal experience by Frederick W. Copeland, retired successful corporation president, in his article "The Illusion of Owning a Business" in the *Atlantic,* September 1956, pp. 66–68. Mr. Copeland is now a management consultant and has had experience with hundreds of small businesses.

[2] The almost total disappearance of independent butchers and grocers in some towns is, of course, related to the development of supermarket chains. At present they threaten the variety stores because of the increase in their nonfood lines—drugs, cosmetics, phonograph records, kitchen accessories. The newest development is the expansion of supermarket chains into sale of TV and other electrical home appliances.

working conditions: what he wants also is a safeguard against humiliation, for that is spiritual murder.

Out of the fears inherent in technological drivenness have arisen unique economic institutions. The giant corporations' drive to diversification is an expression not only of the will to profit but of the fear of loss of markets. The trade unions arose out of the fear of the arbitrary, humiliating power of employers. The vast quantity and quite unbelievable quality of American advertising expresses not only the will to riches but also the fear of competition and consumer indifference. Thus, technological drivenness derives much of its motive power from fear. But we can go even further than this and say that the economy *relies* on fear. Take away fear of competition, of failure, of loss of markets, of humiliation, of becoming obsolete, and the culture would stop; take away the fear the union man has of the boss and the union would blow away.

But it is not merely fear of one another that keeps us driving hard; there is also the Great External Fear—fear of the Soviet Union. Without it the automobile industry would drop to almost half its size, the aircraft industry would dwindle to a shadow,[1] and numberless businesses that supply them or live on the paychecks of their workers would shrink or vanish. Without the Great External Fear, indeed, Latin America, India, Southeast Asia, and the Near East would starve at our gates while we continued to digest our billions. Thus fear impels us to maximize production at home and abroad and casts us in the role of reluctant Samaritan.

It is now possible to understand better why some scientific talent leaves American industry. Industries that hire most of the engineers and scientists depend heavily on military contracts, and since they must produce the instruments of attack and defense against the Great Fear, they are often compelled to concentrate on fear-created technical problems. Most of the advertisements

[1] The Subcommittee on Antitrust and Monopoly staff report, "Bigness and Concentration of Economic Power—A Case Study of General Motors Corp." Offprint from *The Congressional Record* of the 84th Congress, 2nd Session, 1956, p. 24. The Subcommittee on Defense and Procurement to the Joint Economic Committee report, "Economic Aspects of Military Procurement and Supply." Offprint from *The Congressional Record* of the 85th Congress, 2nd Session, 1960. For a popular summary see *Life*, June 18, 1956

for scientists specify the particular mechanism or problem on which the scientist is expected to work and sometimes a company actually specifies in detail, as on an examination, precisely what the Ph.D. is expected to do. For example:

1. How does the AGC bandwidth affect the accuracy of the angle-tracking radars?
2. What are the statistical factors to be considered in calculating the detection probability of a search radar?
3. What is the effect of atmosphere turbulence on high gain antenna performance?
4. How is the sidelobe level of radar antenna affected by random perturbations of phase and amplitude over the aperture?

If you have answers to any of these four related questions, then we would like to talk to you.

We are looking for engineers and physicists with inquisitive and imaginative minds. . . .

To a scientist it must seem that such meticulous statement of the problem implies a lack of interest in "inquisitive and imaginative minds," as the editors of *Fortune* point out.[1]

In the course of evolution it has appeared that the greatest asset of an organism is its potentiality for "adaptive radiation," the capacity to develop new forms to suit new conditions of life. What we see in a fear-ridden human being is loss of adaptability, a tendency to become frozen in unchanging patterns of behavior and thought. As far as scientists are concerned, the record of their departure from industry for the campus speaks for itself: quite a few are unwilling to suffer the loss of adaptation potential required by the fear-dependent milieu in which they must work. Of course, fear-*dependent* does not mean fear-*ridden*, but the consequences are the same. Though it is not implied that the drafting and thinking rooms of industry are atremble with the Great Fear, what is clear is that the Great Fear dictates the problems and accounts for the uniformity of scientific offerings in the advertisements for scientists. A further paradox inheres in a drive for a knowledge that is dictated by fear; for in the

[1] *The Executive Life*, pp. 75–6.

long run, the product of fear is a certain vital ignorance—an
ignorance of all that does not help allay the fear, that does not
contribute to attack or defense against an enemy.

Fear has served the animal kingdom well; without it, oysters,
apes, and man would perish. Yet when fear penetrates all aspects
of culture and becomes a dominant driving force, the culture
freezes in fixed attitudes of attack and defense, all cultural life
suffers, and the Self nearly dies in the cold.

FUN IN AMERICA

But really the Self does not die, given half a chance. Even
poor, sick, aged, depersonalized, bedridden patients in a bare
public hospital preserve (as we shall see in Chapter 10) a
spark of Self that can be blown into a flame, for Nature has
endowed all life with a capacity to seize any opportunity to stay
alive. This capacity for "adaptive radiation" is a primal endow-
ment of the cell and dies with it. The Self is the spiritual mani-
festation of this capacity in man.

Fun in America is an adaptive radiation, for it is the expression
of the American's determination to stay alive. It is an under-
ground escape from the spiritual Andersonville in which technological drivenness has imprisoned us. In fun the American saves
part of his Self from the system that consumes him. Fun, in its
rather unique American form, is grim resolve. When the for-
eigner observes how grimly we seem to go about our fun, he is
right; we are as determined about the pursuit of fun as a
desert-wandering traveler is about the search for water, and for
the same reason.

But though fun revives people so that they can carry on with
work in which they have no interest and out of which they get
little psychic reward, fun in America is also a clowning saboteur
undermining the very system fun was meant to sustain. For
having fun is the precise opposite of what is necessary to keep
the system driving hard. The system needs students who will
work at "tough subjects," and it needs executives who will take
work home and find their principal pleasure in driving hard on
the job. But since fun is opposed to all this, it undermines the
system; it is impossible to educate children to want fun ("Learn-

ing can be fun!") and not expect the fun ideal to eventually blow the ideal of hard work to pieces, and with it the system hard work supports.

In this way, by its curious dialectic, the Self still manages to save itself. To wring "heaps of fun" from a culture that is harsh in so many ways is an American adaptive radiation. Europeans think we work too hard at having fun, but we know better.

Fun is a creature out of the Id, the repository of all untamed instinctual cravings that surge within us. Within every man and woman, says Freud, is an Id, a volcano of seething impulse, held in check only by society, whose controls become our conscience, our Super Ego. In contrast to the Id, which urges us to seek only pleasure, the Super Ego commands that we work hard, save, and control our impulse life. But nowadays, as the Super Ego values of hard work, thrift, and abstemiousness no longer pay off, and technological drivenness presses the Self so hard; nowadays, when the high-rising standard of living has become a moral ideal, the Id values of fun, relaxation, and impulse release are ascendant. Only a people who have learned to decontrol their impulses can consume as we do. So the consequence of technological driven-ness is the creation of a people who, though reared to support it —by being trained to heroic feats of consumption—are quietly undermining it by doing the least they can rather than the most, not only because it is hard to get anything out of the system but also because they have stayed up so late the night before having fun!

3: Advertising as a Philosophical System

ADVERTISING IS AN EXPRESSION OF AN IRRATIONAL economy that has depended for survival on a fantastically high standard of living incorporated into the American mind as a moral imperative. Yet a moral imperative cannot of itself give direction; there must be some institution or agency to constantly direct and redirect the mind and emotions to it. This function is served for the high-rising living standard by advertising which, day and night, with increasing pressure reminds us of what there is to buy; and if money accumulates for one instant in our bank accounts, advertising reminds us that it must be spent and tells us how to do it. As a quasi-moral institution advertising, like any other basic cultural institution anywhere, must have a philosophy and a method of thinking. The purpose of this chapter is to demonstrate the character of advertising thought, and to show how it relates to other aspects of our culture. In order to make this relationship manifest at the outset I have dubbed this method of thought *pecuniary philosophy*.

THE PROBLEM

Since the problem of truth is central to all philosophy, the reader is asked to ask himself, while perusing the following advertising, "Is it literally true that . . ."

. . . everybody's talking about the new *Starfire* [automobile]?

. . . *Alpine* cigarettes "put the men in menthol smoking"?

. . . a woman in *Distinction* foundations is so beautiful that all other women want to kill her?

. . . *Hudson's Bay Scotch* "is scotch for the men among men"?

. . . if one buys clothes at Whitehouse and Hardy his wardrobe will have "the confident look of a totally well-dressed man"?

. . . *Old Spice* accessories are "the finest grooming aides a man can use"?

. . . *7 Crown* whiskey "holds within its icy depths a world of summertime"?

. . . "A man needs *Jockey* support" because *Jockey* briefs "give a man the feeling of security and protection he needs"?

. . . one will "get the smoothest, safest ride of your life on tires of *Butyl*"?

. . . the new *Pal Premium Injector* blade "takes the friction out of shaving" because it "rides on liquid ball bearings"?

. . . *Pango Peach* color by Revlon comes "from east of the sun . . . west of the moon where each tomorrow dawns" . . . is "succulent on your lips" and "sizzling on your finger tips (And on your toes, goodness knows)" and so will be one's "adventure in paradise"?

. . . if a woman gives in to her "divine restlessness" and paints up her eyelids with *The Look* her eyes will become "jungle green . . . glittery gold . . . flirty eyes, tiger eyes"?

. . . a "new ingredient" in *Max Factor Toiletries* "separates the men from the boys"?

. . . when the Confederate General Basil Duke arrived in New York at the end of the Civil War "*Old Crow* [whiskey] quite naturally would be served"?

. . . *Bayer* aspirin provides "the fastest, most gentle to the stomach relief you can get from pain"?

Are these statements, bits of advertising copy, true or false? Are they merely "harmless exaggeration or puffing"[1] as the Federal Trade Commission calls it? Are they simply para-poetic hyperboles—exotic fruits of Madison Avenue creativity? Perhaps they are fragments of a new language, expressing a revolutionary pecuniary truth that derives authority from a phantasmic advertising universe. In the following pages I try to get some clarity on this difficult and murky matter by teasing out of the language of advertising some of the components of pecuniary philosophy I perceive there.

Pecuniary Pseudo-Truth. No sane American would think that literally everybody is "talking about the new *Starfire,*" that Alpine cigarettes literally "put the men in menthol smoking" or that a woman wearing a *Distinction* foundation garment becomes so beautiful that her sisters literally want to kill her. Since he will not take these burblings literally, he will not call them lies, even though they are all manifestly untrue. Ergo, a new kind of truth has emerged—*pecuniary pseudo-truth*—which may be defined as a false statement made as if it were true, but not intended to be believed. No proof is offered for a pecuniary pseudo-truth, and no one looks for it. Its proof is that it sells merchandise; if it does not, it is false.

Para-Poetic Hyperbole. *7 Crown* whiskey's fantasies of icy depths, Revlon's rhapsodies on *Pango Peach, The Look's* word pictures of alluring eyes, and similar poesies are called para-poetic hyperbole because they are something like poetry, with high-flown figures of speech, though they are not poetry. Note, however, that they are also pecuniary pseudo-truths because nobody is expected to believe them.

Pecuniary Logic. When we read the advertisements for *Butyl* and *Old Crow* it begins to look as if *Butyl* and *Old Crow* really *want* us to believe, for they try to prove that what they say is true. *Butyl*, for example, asserts that "major tire marketers . . . are now bringing you tires made of this remarkable material"; and *Old Crow* says that the reason it "would quite naturally be served" to General Duke in New York was because he "esteemed it 'the most famous [whiskey] ever made in Ken-

---

[1] An expression used by the Federal Trade Commission in dismissing a complaint against a company for using extreme methods in its advertising.

tucky.'" When one is asked to accept the literal message of a product on the basis of shadowy evidence, I dub it *pecuniary logic*. In other words, pecuniary logic is a proof that is not a proof but is intended to be so for commercial purposes.

There is nothing basically novel in pecuniary logic, for most people use it at times in their everyday life. What business has done is adopt one of the commoner elements of folk thought and use it for selling products to people who think this way all the time. This kind of thinking—which accepts proof that is not proof —is an *essential* intellectual factor in our economy, for if people were careful thinkers it would be difficult to sell anything. From this it follows that in order for our economy to continue in its present form people must learn to be fuzzy-minded and impulsive, for if they were clear-headed and deliberate they would rarely put their hands in their pockets; or if they did, they would leave them there. If we were all logicians the economy could not survive, and herein lies a terrifying paradox, for *in order to exist economically as we are we must try by might and main to remain stupid.*

The problem has now been stated and briefly illustrated: pecuniary thinking can be analyzed into component parts each one of which serves a specific purpose in marketing in our own peculiarly constructed economy. In the next section, I shall present some of the tribulations of the pecuniary system of thought and then go on to a more extensive analysis of its complexities.

PITFALLS TO PECUNIARY PHILOSOPHY

Like all philosophies pecuniary philosophy has its limitations. The central issue in the viability of philosophies is the truth they assume and what they try to explain. Every philosophy must work in its own backyard, so to speak; that is why Buddhism, for example, has no place in a physics laboratory or logical empiricism in a Buddhist temple. When one philosophy "encroaches" on the "territory" of another's universe it runs into difficulties. Now pecuniary philosophy may be satisfactory for selling cosmetics or whiskey but when it tries to "sell" health or any other form of human welfare it becomes vulnerable to attack by the more traditional logical methods. At such a point the question, "Does aspirin *really* provide the fastest relief for pain, and is its effect on the digestive tract literally gentler than that of any other pain-killer?" cannot be answered by a logic whose only test is whether the product sells, but must be answered by the more traditional truth-logic. Pecuniary philosophy has two problems here. In the first place, human suffering is at issue; in the second place, terms like "relief," "fast," and "gentle" have specific, identifiable physiological referents, and physiology is the province of true scientific research and discovery. Each has its own sphere, and traditional logic and science are as inappropriate for selling nail polish in American culture as pecuniary reasoning is for selling medicine. When medicine is to be sold the canons of traditional reasoning must be respected; when one is selling whiskey or electric razors "folk-think" and pecuniary logic will, perhaps, serve. Put another way, government, with the connivance of the people, permits the exploitation of wooly-mindedness up to a certain point, in the interests of maintaining an irrational economy; but this cannot be allowed if it results in obvious physical suffering, since the right to seek, without trammel or deceit, relief from physical anguish, has become an inviolable value of the American people.

I will have more to say about the use of pecuniary logic in the sale of medicine.

PECUNIARY TRUTH

Most people are not obsessive truth-seekers; they do not yearn to get to the bottom of things; they are willing to let absurd or merely ambiguous statements pass. And this undemandingness that does not insist that the world stand up and prove that it is real, this air of relaxed wooly-mindedness, is a necessary condition for the development of the revolutionary mode of thought herein called *pecuniary philosophy*. The relaxed attitude toward veracity (or mendacity, depending on the point of view) and its complement, pecuniary philosophy, are important to the American economy, for they make possible an enormous amount of selling that could not otherwise take place.

Every culture creates philosophy out of its own needs, and ours has produced traditional philosophies based on truths verifiable by some primordial objective or supernatural criteria, and another, pecuniary philosophy, derived from an irrational need to sell. The heart of truth in our traditional philosophies was God or His equivalent, such as an identifiable empirical reality. The heart of truth in pecuniary philosophy is contained in the following three postulates:

> Truth is what sells.
> Truth is what you want people to believe.
> Truth is that which is not legally false.

The first two postulates are clear, but the third probably requires a little explaining and a good example. A report in *Science* on the marketing practices of the *Encyclopaedia Britannica* is just what we need at this point.

> One of the tasks of the Federal Trade Commission, according to the Encyclopaedia Britannica, is to order business organizations to stop using deceptive advertising when such organizations are found to be so engaged. A few weeks ago Encyclopaedia Britannica, Inc., was ordered by the Federal Trade Commission to stop using advertising that misrepresents its regular prices as reduced prices available for a limited time only. . . .
> Some of the company's sales practices are ingenious. The FTC shows, for example, how the prospective customer, once he has gained the impression that he is being offered the Encyclopaedia and accessories at reduced prices, is led to believe that the purported reduced prices are good only for a limited time. This is done by two kinds of statements, each one being true enough if regarded separately.
> The first kind of statement, which appears in written material, says such things as "This offer is necessarily subject to withdrawal without notice."[1]

Science explains that the second kind of statement is made by the salesman when he applies pressure to the prospective customer by telling him he will not return. The Federal Trade Commission, in enjoining the *Encyclopaedia Britannica* from using this kind of sales technique, argued that the first statement plus

[1] *Science,* July 14, 1961. Reprinted from *Science* by permission.

the second created the impression in the customer's mind that if he does not buy now he will lose the opportunity to buy at what he has been given to think is a reduced price. Actually, *Science* points out, it is not a reduced price, for the price has not changed since 1949. Since it is literally true that a business has the right to raise prices without advance notice, the *Britannica* advertisement is not legally false, even though it reads like a warning that prices will go up soon. I have coined the term *legally innocent prevarication* to cover all statements which, though not legally untrue, misrepresent by implication.

Having given some preliminary illustrations of the character of pecuniary philosophy, I am now ready to review the structure of method and idea in one of its great modern classics, Rosser Reeves' *Reality in Advertising*.[1]

A brief biography of the author

At 51, the author of *Reality in Advertising* still has a solid frame and a full head of black hair. He speaks in a loud resonant voice, booming words at his visitors in a deep Virginia drawl. Mr. Reeves, a hard-driving, aggressive man, says he often puts in a 90-hour week at his office, retreating to his nearby apartment late in the evening. He maintains a small apartment in the east Fifties [New York City] as well as large homes in Larchmont, New York and Montego Bay, Jamaica [British West Indies].

When not conducting the affairs of the Bates agency Mr. Reeves is an omnivorous reader (his library contains some 8,000 volumes) and a dedicated sailor. He owns a 33-foot sloop. . . .

. . . . Mr. Reeves insisted that the book has turned out to be the most successful single advertising presentation[2] in the history of the profession.[3] He said that companies repre-

---

[1] Alfred A. Knopf, New York, 1961. Some of the American tributes paid to this work are to be found on the back of the book's jacket. Characteristic expressions of praise are: "A great polemic . . . intelligent forceful, refreshing . . . the master of the hard sell . . . the definitive book on advertising. . . ."

[2] A "presentation" is a statement or proposal of how an agency would attempt to sell a client's product.

[3] Note the use of the term "profession" for advertising. The professionalization of advertising is a very important status-yearning of Mr. Reeves in

senting some $70,000,000 in billings have approached his
agency as a direct result of reading *Reality in Advertising.*
. . . . After its top officials had read the book, Pakistan
International Airlines recently dispatched two executives
to New York to confer with Mr. Reeves. As a result the
$1,500,000 account was assigned to Bates' London Office.[1]

Possibly the most important implication of this account is that
pecuniary philosophy is a world movement, not a unique miasma
boiling up from the asphalt swamps of Madison Avenue. If it
were not, why the world-wide influence of the book? And why
would the Pakistanis, people of an apparently different culture,
come to see Mr. Reeves from the other side of the world?
But let us get on to the book!
Morality and the Veneration of Truth. Reeves' commitment
to the fundamental postulates of pecuniary truth can be inferred
from the advertising campaigns and slogans he admires. Some
examples are:

1. Do you have tired blood?[2]
2. Pink toothbrush.[3]
3. Wonder Bread helps build strong bodies twelve ways.[4]
4. A TV ad for a hair tonic in which a pair of gloved
    feminine hands strokes first the head of a man wearing the
    advertised tonic and then the head of a man using a com-
    petitor's product. The picture shows that the gloves come
    away greasy in the latter but not in the former.[5]
5. A magazine ad for *Dodge* automobiles in which two
    pictures of the car were shown, one of the car plunging
    through a sandpit at high speed, and the other of the beauti-

---

spite of his numerous dwellings, his sloop, and the fact that his book is enjoying an astonishing sale abroad and has been translated into eleven languages,
including Japanese and Hebrew.

[1] From the *New York Times,* October 12, 1961. Copyright by *The New
York Times.* Reprinted by permission.

[2] A slogan for a "vitalizing" nostrum, quoted in *Reality in Advertising,*
p. 81.

[3] A slogan for a toothpaste that claimed to help prevent pyhorrea and
bleeding gums, quoted in *ibid.,* p. 53.

[4] Quoted in *ibid.,* p. 68. Any ordinary bread provides adequate nutritional
materials.

[5] *Ibid.,* pp. 110-11.

fully polished car standing on a showroom floor over the
legend *"Powders her nose in a sandpit, wins honors at a
beauty show."* Another advertisement showed the car being
rolled off a cliff and then driven away on its own power; still
a third had elephants standing on top of the car to show how
strong it is.[1]

Reeves' attitude toward such advertising is one of veneration. As
a matter of fact there is a rhapsodic sublimity in his writing
about advertising in general. Consider, for example, the following quote:

> No longer can the [advertising] copywriter, like Tenny-
> son's Lady of Shalott, view life through his own magic
> mirror. No longer can he live in that state the saints call
> *Innigkeit*, or "inwardness." For him, no longer, can private
> planets shine in some solipsist universe where his delusions
> can be treated as reality. He must make his imagination
> function under the strict discipline of attaining a com-
> mercial goal. . . .[2]
>
> So let your tree reach for the sun! In fact, clear away the
> advertising underbrush and give it a chance to grow and
> breathe. You can own a towering giant, with its roots deep
> in the earth, safe against even the most raging advertising
> storms.[3]

Sometimes his feeling is so strong that it leads him to trespass
on areas venerated in the more traditional philosophy, where
other matters are sublime. For example, carried away by his
thoughts of the power of advertising words, he compares them to
the power of

> Our Father Which art in Heaven
> Hallowed be Thy name.[4]

But then, when has not inspiration carried some of us away?
Of course, Reeves has a strong moral sense. To his way of
thinking, immorality in advertising consists in basing a claim on

[1] *Ibid.*, pp. 135-6.
[2] *Reality in Advertising*, pp. 121-2.
[3] *Ibid.*, p. 33.
[4] *Ibid.*, p. 80.

a trivial ("minuscule") difference between products. Of this he says, scornfully:

> This is idea bankruptcy, leading to the distortion, ex- aggeration, fake claims, and hucksterism that has given all advertising a bad name. . . . It is bad not only in *moral* principle, but bad in commercial results.[1]

An inevitable consequence of violation of this moral principle is "destruction of the product" by a kind of pecuniary lightning. Thus while traditional morality relates to human beings (is "per- son-centered"), pecuniary morality relates to products (is "prod- uct-centered"). It is very consistent: in the traditional philosophy the divinity is God; in pecuniary philosophy it is the Market. Divine lightning strikes people dead; pecuniary lightning strikes products dead! Orthodox morality prevents the destruction of human beings; pecuniary morality preserves products.

> A campaign that stresses a minuscule difference . . . also accelerates the destruction of the product.[2]

We turn now to a more central theme of the pecuniary system, *pecuniary psychology*.

PECUNIARY PSYCHOLOGY

The fundamental concepts of pecuniary psychology are the "brain box" or, more simply, "the head," and "penetration." The head is a repository for advertising "claims" or "messages," and these enter the head by virtue of their penetrating power. Quotes from Reeves' book will make the matter clear:

> There is a finite limit to what a consumer can remember about 30,000 advertised brands. . . .
> It is as though he carries a small box in his head for a given product category. . . .
> Do you doubt this?
> Then, take one man and subject him to an exhausting depth interview. Measure his total memory of advertising in any one field—be it cereals, razor blades or beer. . . .

[1] *Ibid.*, p. 60.
[2] *Ibid.*, p. 61.

You will be able to chart the size of the theoretical box in his head. Now, do this with tens of thousands of people. . . .

You will begin to see the tremendous difficulty of owning a bit of space in the box.[1]

Our competitor's penetration is moving down as we seize a larger and larger share of the consumer's brain box.[2]

Thus pecuniary psychology pivots, like any system of thought, on a conception of mind.

Other important concepts are: the advertiser's "claim," "finiteness" of head content, "measurability" of head content, transitoriness. Transitoriness is really an implicit underlying idea or parameter extracted from Reeves' thinking by me. Fundamentally it implies impermanence, instability, evanescence—disloyalty, so to speak, of consumers, for consumers are viewed (rather ungratefully, I think) as being constantly on the verge of deserting one product for another. It seems to me that Reeves is a little confused in his attitudes here, for not "product loyalty" but product *dis*loyalty is the foundation of our economy. After all, if everyone stuck with a product once he had tried it, how would dozens of other manufacturers enter the field with identical ones? And where would Reeves be? His inability to grasp the importance to our entire way of life of this *socially necessary evanescence* seems a curious weakness in one so brilliant.

The conception of the head or "box" involves the hidden assumption of mental passivity, for the brain box is conceived of as an inert receptacle which the advertiser enters by penetration, i.e., his "campaign" gets a claim inside the box. Reeves must be right, for if the box were not relatively inert advertising would be a failure.

Since many products are very similar to one another and hence must compete intensely for the same brain boxes, struggles develop between claims. I shall call these struggles *The Wars of Pecuniary Claims.*

In the battles of The Wars of Pecuniary Claims the consumer is passive, while the wars are fought by claims competing for his brain box. It is something like a fort which, though inanimate, is

[1] *Ibid.*, p. 39.
[2] *Ibid.*, p. 42.

a provocation to the adversaries because of its strategic importance. Triumph means that the victor plants his flag—symboliz-
ing beer, electric razors, soap, toothpaste, etc.—on the consumer's
head. The brain box has been penetrated! My simile is not quite
perfect because whereas generals in traditional wars understand
that fortresses may be destroyed in the struggle for them, Reeves
does not discuss the possibility of the destruction of the consumer.

But the consumer can be destroyed, especially by drugs prescribed by wooly-minded doctors and bought by wooly-minded
people. "Many more people will be killed by some drugs," said
Dr. Haskell Weinstein, former medical director of Charles Pfizer,
at Senate hearings on the drug industry, "than by all the contaminated cranberries and stilbesterol chickens[1] combined." Perhaps the most terrifying revelation before the Senate Committee
came in connection with the examination of the advertising
policies of the *Journal of the American Medical Association,*
where it was brought out that an advertisement for a drug called
Norlutin bore no warning that thirty-six pregnant women had
given birth to sexually abnormal daughters after being given the
drug. Meanwhile, according to the testimony, the very issue of
the *Journal* carrying the article that made these disclosures had
an advertisement for *Norlutin* also. The ads continued for three
months thereafter.[2]

There is a breathless excitement in Reeves' writing as he discusses the Wars of Pecuniary Claims; one might say that the
smoke of pecuniary battle is always in his nostrils. It is perhaps
this that gives him an intense sense of *pecuniary history.*

PECUNIARY HISTORY

Pecuniary history evolves naturally from the Wars of
Pecuniary Claims, and just as orthodox history has its famous
men and battles, so pecuniary history has its own type of emi-
nence. Thus there are a "great laxative," "a great mouthwash,"
"a great headache remedy," "a great advertising campaign."
There are "a famous dental cream" and "a famous toothpaste."

[1] A chicken that has been fed the hormone stilbesterol to promote growth.
[2] Reported in the *New York Times,* July 22, 1961.

The battles of pecuniary history in which armies of claims, bearing the ensigns of embattled mouthwash, headache remedies, and laxatives, have surged around the consumer's wooly head have brought forth on this continent new Gettysburgs, new Bull Runs, and a ragamuffin pecuniary hall of fame to which advertising pays rhapsodic reverence.

PECUNIARY BIOLOGY

Pecuniary biology deals with "product evolution," and Reeves, modestly deferring to a great predecessor, says that "The whole concept, in a way, is straight out of Darwin." Reeves, however, is not concerned with the theory of natural selection alone. He has thought much about lethal mutation, also, and has adapted recent genetic theory (a bit carelessly, perhaps) to the more fundamental Darwinian system. The following will give the flavor.

> There do appear, for a short while on the economic scene, wild mutations in products; they are senseless, and they are stupid; but such products are sooner or later doomed—like the pterodactyl, the brontosaurus, the archeopteryx—to vanish into some economic Mesozoic shale.[1]

Reeves is not talking in metaphors; he thinks in strict biological terms; for to him, the changes and improvements in products, as well as their decline and extinction, are simply manifestations in products of the same evolutionary process that operates in the plant and animal world. We must bear in mind meanwhile that transformations in products are true cultural changes, and some of my anthropological colleagues hold to the same theory of cultural evolution.

PECUNIARY PHILOSOPHY AS A TOTAL SYSTEM

Every culture produces, in an unbelievably appropriate and rigid way, a philosophy that fits its needs like a glove. Pecuniary philosophy is a total system, embracing, like some great classical

[1] *Ibid.*, p. 143.

school, not only a metaphysics and morality, but also a psychology, a biology, a history, a poetics, and so on. It has also a theory of birth and death—the birth and death of products. Fundamentally what pecuniary philosophy does is place the product in its proper perspective in our culture, for the product and its attached claim are considered central, while the inert consumer, or rather his head (box) is placed where it belongs—in secondary or, perhaps, merely adventitious position. Consumers are necessary to the existence and evolution of products; consumers (like air and water) are the environment in which products (in a way similar to plants and animals) evolve and have their being; and just as deprivation of air and water causes plants and animals to die, so loss of consumers causes the death of products.

Thus advertising rests on a total system of thought and pursues ends that are fundamentally at odds with the traditional academic philosophies of our culture. And because it is at odds with these philosophies and their old-fashioned morality, it is vulnerable to attack from them. On the other hand, however, the contribution pecuniary philosophy makes to our economy is so great that in spite of the fact that it flies in the face of orthodoxy, it needs to be defended. This is accomplished, in great part, through starving the agencies of Government that have been specifically established to supervise it. In 1960, for example, Congress appropriated only $33 million for the Federal Trade Commission, the Federal Communications Commission, and the Food and Drug Administration—about three-tenths, of 1 per cent of what was spent for advertising that year.

Having sketched the general character of pecuniary philosophy I will now go on to an examination of details. I begin by returning to para-poetic hyperbole and the brain box.

PARA-POETIC HYPERBOLE AND THE BRAIN BOX

Revlon, manufacturer extraordinary of cosmetics, often picks for the central figure in its advertisements in *Life* magazine a woman with the good looks of a lower-middle-class working girl dressed up for a place she will never get to; a destination *sans merci,* an empty port on the technicolor Sea of Lower-Middle-Class Dreams. Sales clerks, routine office workers, lower-middle-

class housewives can identify with these average looking females
in fancy costumes floating on a Saturday night cloud. Para-poetic
hyperbole thus begins with the hyperbolic picture, as the advertisement zeroes in on a deprived target (the lower-middle-class
working girl or housewife) who started life with a Self but lost
it somewhere along the way. Revlon will fix all that, for Revlon
is medicine man and magician to the soul. Consider the advertisement for *Pango Peach*, a new color introduced by Revlon in 1960.
A young woman leans against the upper rungs of a ladder leading
to a palm-thatched bamboo tree-house. *Pango Peach* are her *sari*,
her blouse, her toe and finger nails, and the cape she holds. A sky
of South Pacific blue is behind her, and the cape, as it flutters in
the wind, stains the heavens *Pango Peach*. "From east of the sun
—west of the moon where each tomorrow dawns . . ." beckons the
ad, in corny pecuniary lingo. But when you are trying to sell nail
polish to a filing clerk with two years of high school you don't
quote Dylan Thomas! The idea of the ad is to make a woman
think she is reading real poetry when she is not, and at the same
time to evoke in her the specific fantasy that will sell the product.
Millions will respond to poetry as a value and feel good when
they think they are responding to it, and this process of getting
people to respond to pseudo-values as if they were responding to
real ones is called here *pecuniary distortion of values*.

In the ad *Pango Peach* is called "A many splendoured coral . . .
pink with pleasure . . . a volcano of color!" It goes on to say that
"It's a full ripe peach with a world of difference . . . born to be
worn in big juicy slices. Succulent on your lips. Sizzling on your
fingertips. . . . Go Pango Peach . . . your adventure in paradise."
Each word in the advertisement is carefully chosen to tap a particular yearning and hunger in the American woman. "Many-
splendoured," for example, is a reference to the novel and movie
Love Is a Many Splendored Thing, a tale of passion in an Oriental
setting. "Volcano" is meant to arouse the latent wish to be a vol-
canic lover and to be loved by one. The mouthful of oral stimuli—
"ripe," "succulent," "juicy"—puts sales resistance in double
jeopardy because mouths are even more for kissing than for
eating. "Sizzling" can refer only to *l'amour à la folie;* and, finally,
"Your adventure in paradise," is an invitation to love everlasting
with a dark-skinned man in a tree-house on the island of Pango.

Whether anybody reads such advertisements is really not my

concern, although the fact that Revlon repeats them year after year suggests that women do read them[1] What is most interesting is Madison Avenue's opinion of the females to whom these ads are addressed, for what this and other Revlon advertisements project is a female who does not believe in herself, has yearnings toward a sexuality which she holds back within her like a rumbling volcano, and who has fantastic dreams. Is this indeed the mask that looks at us from the Revlon ads? Is this girl of fragile poise, tricked out in pecuniary scenery, the one that leans on the boy friend's arm on Saturday night on all the subways, on all the Main Streets across the land? Are these in their millions mothers of Americans? Could it be true?

Advertising helps while it profits by this female, for some new cosmetic may make her imagine for a moment that she *is* something. But such "help," such *product therapy,* is merely palliative at best and lethal at worst; for products in fancy dress sustain and support underlying flaws, while assuring these girls that they have nothing to offer a man but allure. So again a culturally patterned defect, as Fromm would call it, becomes the maid of all work for the economy, for this girl will buy almost anything that will make her feel good.

> Fill her wanting eye
> with wishes, her will-
> ing ear with answers.
> She will never be more
> open-to-buy.

> *The same thing that*
> *makes her buy . . . pure*
> *emotion.*
>   *They feel be-*
> *fore they think,* they
> perceive before they
> see, *they buy more on*
> *impulse than on purpose,*
> *they do more on inspiration than*
> *by plan.*

[1]Revlon sales increased from $33,604,000 in 1954 to $110,363,000 in 1958 (*New York Times,* November 5, 1959, p. 28). Some of this increase is due, of course, to Revlon's rigged TV quiz shows.

says *Glamour*[1] talking intimately to its Madison Avenue brethren and other businessmen.

When you dress up a girl, surround her with tropical scenery, and put her in a bamboo tree-house on the island of Pango, it makes sense to talk about volcanoes, sizzling finger tips, and adventures in paradise, for you have manufactured a dream for a sex that is *scenery-prone.* Industry spends billions exploiting the capacity of American women to lend themselves to unreality. Since our culture gives women no firm role except an erotic one, but rather surrounds them with ambiguities, they fit readily into tree-houses or any other kind of commercial fantasy. Men are more intractible in this regard; it is more difficult to metamorphose them into make-believe creatures because their roles are more real. Hence there is a poverty of hyperbole in the advertisements addressed to men. Hence also the monotony of the appeal, playing constantly on the tired themes of virility and status. Only occasionally does hyperbole appear, like a fresh rosy neon light. The following advertisement for *Excello* shirts is one of the rare examples of para-poetic hyperbole in the masculine vein: A picture of the upper body of a broad-shouldered, ruggedly handsome, deeply troubled and rather driven-looking man occupies almost all of the frame. He is between thirty-five and forty years old and wears a somewhat rumpled but clean shirt and a tie. His brows are knit, his arms and shoulders are disposed in dynamic tension, and the veins on his right hand bulge. In a sense, he is what every man who can afford "quality" shirts would like to be and fears he may not be: drive-packed, masculine, achieving. The copy burbles in purest para-poetic hyperbole:

> A shirt is the day's beginning, a special semaphore signaling the forward thrust of endeavor. A shirt is the morning mood of man, his ebbing effort at evening. A shirt is Excello.

The *New York Times,* May 17, 1961, says of the ad

> The Meyers [advertising] agency believes that the contrast of emotion and realism will produce psychological undertones that "should gain increased attention for the product."

Well, what are the emotions and what are the "psychological undertones" (sometimes referred to by others as "unconscious

[1] In the *New York Times,* October 3 and 5, 1961.

motivations") that Meyers is reaching for here? I think that in the first place they are trying to transmute commonplace and even somewhat unpleasant things, like going to work in the morning and going out in the evening when you are tired and would rather stay home, into something vibrant; they are attempting to convert industrial time and its inexorable demands into a poetic thing. This conversion I call *hyperbolic transformation*. In the second place I think they want men to identify with the executive-appearing male wearing the rumpled shirt, while they say to us, "You are just like this man of high drive, for whom morning is a forward thrust of endeavor and evening a time when, exhausted from his driving labor, he, with his last ebbing effort, dons a fresh shirt to go out and relax." This is *pecuniary identification*.

The *Excello* advertisement adeptly exploits the mood-meanings of time—morning mood and evening mood—and the desire for status. What emotions American men experience on starting out in the morning and what yearnings toward or satisfactions they may have in the executive position, are spun by the advertising copy into a para-poetic statement tying them to shirts. This is what I would like to call the *monetization* of time and status, and I shall use the term *monetization* where cultural factors not usually thought of as entering the processes of production and sale are used to make money. Another example of monetization would be the exploitation of women's feeling that they have nothing to offer but allure, for this transmutes feelings of inadequacy into cash.

MONETIZATION

Since values like love, truth, the sacredness of high office, God, the Bible, motherhood, generosity, solicitude for others, and so on are the foundation of Western culture, anything that weakens or distorts them shakes traditional life. The traditional values are part of traditional philosophy, but pecuniary philosophy, far from being at odds with them appears to embrace them with fervor. This is the embrace of a grizzly bear, for as it embraces the traditional values pecuniary philosophy chokes them to death. The specific choking mechanism is *monetization*.

Let us consider the following advertisement for a popular

women's magazine: Against a black sky covering almost an entire page in the *New York Times* of June 2, 1960 is chalked the following from the New Testament: "Children, love ye one another." Below, the advertising copy tells us that *McCall's* magazine will carry in its next issue parables from five faiths, and that

> Such spiritual splendor, such profound mystical insight, seem perfectly at home in the pages of *McCall's*, where the editorial approach is all-inclusive, universal, matching the infinite variety of today's existence.

Guilt by association is familiar enough to the American people through the work of various sedulous agencies of Government. *McCall's*, however, has discovered its opposite—*glory* by association, or, in the language of this work, pecuniary transfiguration. Since "spiritual splendor" and "mystical insight" are traits of holy books, and since examples of these are printed in *McCall's*, it is by that fact a kind of holy book. This is what I mean by the use of values for pecuniary purposes; this is value distortion through monetization.

Consider now the following report from the *New York Times*, July 27, 1961:

> It is understood that President Kennedy for the first time has authorized the use of his name and photograph in an advertisement.
>
> The ad will be one of a series of institutional advertisements run in behalf of the magazine industry. The President's picture will appear together with a statement discussing the role of magazines in American life.
>
> An element of controversy has surrounded the use of President Kennedy's name and photograph in advertising. Last week the National Better Business Bureau criticized the unauthorized use of the President's name and likeness and warned that White House policy forbade such practices. The bureau noted such items as a "Kennedy Special" fish stew, J.F.K. rocking chairs and so forth.

The reason certain forms of logic are abandoned is not because they are wrong, but rather because they have proved inadequate to new problems and new knowledge. The old logics cannot make distinctions that must now be made, or they make distinctions that are no longer necessary. In the *Times* article we perceive such a situation, for obviously practitioners of pecuniary logic have somehow used the President's name inappropriately in naming a fish stew after him. Consider the following imaginary slogans:

John F. Kennedy, President of the United States, endorses the American way of life.
John F. Kennedy, President of the United States, endorses our fish stew.
John F. Kennedy, President of the United States, endorses American magazines.

One can see instantly that endorsement of the American way of life by the President would make one feel comfortable, whereas presidential endorsement of fish stew would cause one to feel vaguely unhappy and perhaps a little sick. The third statement might merely stimulate a little wonder that the President could do anything so brash. However, if magazines can be linked by pecuniary transfiguration to a basic value like "the American way of life," then it becomes reasonable to bring in the President. Herein lies the genius of the Madison Avenue logicians—the wave of the future—for though in the present case they have avoided the worst pitfalls of pecuniary logic, they have remained true to its spirit. The failure of pecuniary logic in the fish stew case lies in its inability to make a distinction between something of high cultural value ("the American way of life") and something of little or no cultural value (fish stew). This failure can be referred to the inadequacy of the basic premise, "anything that sells a product is right." In the present instance the premise was not right because it brought pecuniary thinking into collision with tradition as embodied in the Better Business Bureau. The magazine men were smarter.

Consider now the following imaginary brands:

"George Washington" Corn Chowder.
"Abe Lincoln" Blackstrap Molasses.

The reader will not very likely take offense at either of these because (a) Washington and Lincoln are dead; (b) corn chowder and blackstrap molasses have a primordial, earthy, American atmosphere about them. The fish, however, is a deprecated, rather low-caste animal in American culture, in spite of the enamoured pursuit of it by millions of week-end fishermen. Furthermore, though *fried* fish has higher status, fish *stew* sounds plebian and even hateful to many people. One can now begin to understand the instinctive revulsion of the BBB to attachment of the President's name to fish stew. Fundamentally it has nothing to do with the monetization of a national symbol. Basically BBB recoiled at the degradation of the symbol through association with fish, and at the connection of a *living* president with a commercial product. (It would not be so bad if he were dead.)

Though Americans have traditionally shown little respect for public office, some men, like the Founding Fathers and Abraham Lincoln, have become almost sacred, and their memories are still rallying points for the forces of traditional ethics in American life. Hence their names and likenesses, *downgraded,* perhaps, are yet useful for advertising many things, from banks to whiskey. This being the case, we can surmise that the reason we do not protest the use, for pecuniary purposes, of passages from the New Testament, or the widespread monetization of values is because *traditional values are losing the respect and the allegiance of the people,* even though Madison Avenue can still transmute into cash what residues of veneration they yet evoke. An important social function of the Franklin, Lincoln, and Washington sagas is to make Americans ready to patronize any institution or buy any product bearing their names. One might say, "Sell a kid on the cherry tree and you can sell him cherries the rest of his life."

In their wars of survival pecuniary adversaries will use anything for ammunition—space, time, the President, the Holy Bible, and all the traditional values. Monetization waters down values, wears them out by slow attrition, makes them banal and, in the long run, helps Americans to become indifferent to them and even cynical. Thus the competitive struggle forces the corruption of values. The best example of this comes from the frantic competitive struggle among the mass women's magazines.

Bamboo Values. Television advertising has such enormous powers of penetration that it has been growing many times faster than magazine advertising. Since, in 1960, TV advertising increased 7 per cent while magazine advertising increased only 1 per cent, competition among the magazines for readers and advertisers has intensified. It is particularly feverish in the women's field, where the magazines have not only been increasing their efforts to expand circulation—for this is what attracts advertisers —but have also been attacking one another. It is therefore reasonable to expect that advertising should become frenzied and absurd, for it is under conditions of extreme anxiety that frenzy and absurdity are most likely to occur. We have seen how the President himself has been called in to save the magazine industry and how one magazine now poses as a holy book. The following are examples of frenzied monetization of values by different women's magazines:

> "M is for *motherhood*. . . . M is also for *McCall's*. This week, when everybody, including the sophisticated, is out shopping for Mother's Day, we urge you to do the following for the mother of your choice. Kiss her. Tell her you *love* her. Either get her a subscription to *McCall's* or give her enough money to buy it at the newstand for a year."[1]

A large picture of a woman of about eighteen to twenty-two years of age shows her looking tenderly at a cake she has just baked. Above her in large type it says, "½ Pillsbury [flour]—½ *Mother Love*." Below, the copy reads, ". . . the making and serving of food is not a chore, but an act of *love* that daily restates the *devotion* of *Mother* to *family*. . . . It is understanding this attitude, and editing our food pages 'with *love*,' that makes them so much more meaningful. . . ."[2]

The copy reads: "In women's language, *love* of a *child*, of an *ideal*, of a *purpose*, is often expressed in the negative; as a refusal of permissiveness that would seem easy and relaxed—but would be in fact an act of unloving. So it is with *Good Housekeeping*. Because this magazine is womanlike in its *caring*, it must often reject what might be glitter-

[1] *New York Times,* May 5, 1960.
[2] *Ibid.,* October 30, 1959.

ingly attractive on the surface, but dangerous or *impure* in its nature or its ultimate effects."[1]

A pair of enormous, clinking glasses of champagne dominates the page, and above them the copy reads "To the most wonderful woman in the world!" Below and in between the glasses it says, "(and 6,000,000 more just like her). At the beginning of the new year, we would like to lift our glass to the millions of women who read *Ladies' Home Journal*. We would like to salute, first off, their *wisdom*. They know that a magazine's mission is more than to be 'a physical and neutral carrier of advertising messages.' Much more. Our readers prove it by their special *loyalty* to the *Journal*. In November when readers of the three leading women's magazines were asked which magazines they liked best, 50% more of them chose the *Journal* than either of the other two. We *thank* them for this *affection*. We also cheer our readers' *zest* for living. A *Journal* reader, we have discovered, is a very *special sort of person*. For one thing she's *younger*—a whole year younger—than readers of other women's magazines. She has a higher income. She's better *educated*. She *cares* more about her life and the world around her, and spends more in time and money on her *home* and *family*. And we toast our readers' *loyalty*—which gives *Ladies' Home Journal* the largest average circulation of any woman's magazine on earth. A Happy New Year to you all."[2] [Italics supplied.]

In these passages, bubbling with monetization, the monetized values have been italicized by me. The advertisements suggest a law: *the more intense competition between claims becomes, the greater the extent of monetization.* This is probably valid regardless of what the product is. The *law of competition and monetization* makes clear the fact that unbridled competition among products increases monetization, saps values, and imperils the foundations of our society.

Now, the reader may urge, nobody reads these ads and no one is gulled by this nonsense. I would urge, on the contrary,

[1] *Ibid.*, January 21, 1961.
[2] *Ibid.*, January 4, 1960.

that since the three magazines quoted above have a combined
circulation of about 20 million there must be some attractive
power in their approach, and that this consists in a shrewd capacity to exploit woman's unmet need to be loved and to feel
she is a loving, wise, caring, pure, forever young, motherly,
idealistic, loyal being. What is monetized and exploited is the
American woman's idealization of herself—a further example of
her ability to lend herself to unreality. On the island of Pango
we saw her in a house of bamboo *scenery;* here she is in a house
of bamboo *values.*

Consequences of Monetization. Well, perhaps one takes all
this too seriously and perhaps my embarrassment at the magazines' utilization of emotional hunger to push sales is just a
quaint personality distortion of my own, quite unbecoming in an
objective scientist. Perhaps, who knows, the number of women
who read the copy—instead of merely responding to the name of
the magazine—is very, very small, and perhaps many of those
who read do not grasp what is said. So in the end the advertisements have really not *hurt* anybody. Who could prove they have?
But this is really not my central concern. What I argue is that
advertising will exploit sacred values for pecuniary ends, that
the transition from relatively *harmless* distortion to relatively
harmful is gradual, and that most pecuniary philosophers cannot
tell the difference. Consider the following:

> There are rumblings from across the border to the north.
> A Canadian publisher has succeeded, by dealing with indi-
> vidual principals and teachers, in getting a thirty-two page
> exercise book called "The Educational ABC's of Industry"
> into Ontario schools. The glossy, multicolored work book
> provides a rundown of the alphabet. For $7,800 a page, an
> advertiser was permitted to buy a letter.
>
> Thus, in the book, C is for Orange Crush, G is for General
> Motors, M is for Milko and O is for Oxo. Or with a little
> different approach: H is for Health, So Keep Face-Elle on
> hand, It's Canada's finest, the Softerized brand.
>
> All went well until the children came home singing the
> jingles. Then the parents began to complain.
>
> Officials of the Ontario Department of Education said that

they did not know anything about the publication or how the booklets had found their way into the classrooms. They said that advertising material was, in fact, banned from classrooms by law.

As a result of the controversy caused by the booklet, Mr. and Mrs. John Kiernan of Toronto withdrew their daughter from the third grade at St. Basil's Separate School "because she was spending her time copying the slogans." Mrs. Kiernan commented: "We were surprised and annoyed. It smacks of brainwashing."[1]

When the report appeared in the *Times* the booklets were already being withdrawn.[2]

Since in pecuniary philosophy "educate" means to educate to buy, "inspiration" means to inspire to buy, "dream" means to dream about products, et cetera, we have, in the Ontario case merely an instance—quite understandable—of a man who took the vocabulary of pecuniary aims to mean something in the orthodox tradition: he believed literally that "educate" meant to teach to buy products, and he saw nothing wrong therefore in helping the process along by putting advertising materials in the hands of children. Neither did Oxo, Orange Crush, General Motors, etc. The borderline between delinquent and nondelinquent behavior and perception is a hair, for given the pecuniary definition of the world in terms of products and claims, there is nothing reprehensible, in the pecuniary view, in teaching children to buy all kinds of products from soups to shaving lotions. Such education takes place not only, as in the Ontario case, through matters introduced directly into the schoolroom, but also through toys which present materials to the children in miniature—as in toy kitchens stocked with miniatures of "famous" brand groceries, or in miniature bathrooms with models of shaving lotions, soaps, etc. The idea is to condition children early, to "burn" into their minds the brand names so they will be loyal customers as adults.

But why should one recoil from the exploits of the man from

[1] Reported in the *New York Times*, May 12, 1960.
[2] Paul Goodman saw these booklets in use in a New York City school. See *Growing Up Absurd,* p. 118.

Ontario or, indeed, from the widespread campaign to "burn" product messages into the brains of children? It is partly because children are unable to defend themselves, and we still resent any attack on a defenseless human being. A more powerful reason, however, is because since we have embodied in "the child" the last of our squandered human decency, we want to hold him dear. Let us remember, meanwhile, that though some may consider the exploitation of children immoral, in the world view of pecuniary philosophy the sin would consist in letting the market go untapped.

PECUNIARY PHILOSOPHY AS CRADLE SNATCHER

The Flower-eyed Wonderment of Babes;
The Phantasy of Their Play;
The Joy of Christmas

The brand-image created on
television and embedded in
the minds of children assures
good volume for these items. . . .[1]

Homo sapiens trains his children for the roles they will fill as adults. This is as true of the Eskimo three-year-old who is encouraged to stick his little spear into a dead polar bear as it is of an American child of the same age who turns on TV to absorb commercials; the one will be a skilled hunter, the other a virtuoso consumer.

In contemporary America children must be trained to *insatiable* consumption of *impulsive* choice and *infinite variety*. These attributes, once instilled, are converted into cash by advertising directed at children. It works on the assumption that the claim that gets into the child's brain box first is most likely to stay there, and that since in contemporary America children manage parents, the former's brain box is the antechamber to the brain box of the latter.

In their relations with children manufacturers and advertising agencies are dedicated cultural surrogates, like any other teacher,

[1] *New York Times,* November 11, 1960.

for since the central aims of our culture are to sell goods and create consumers, they educate children to buy. What should businessmen do, sit in their offices and dream, while millions of product-ignorant children go uninstructed? This would be an abdication of responsibility. Besides, the businessmen might go bankrupt. The argument that advertising campaigns beamed at young children are somehow sickening because such campaigns take advantage of the impulsiveness and the unformed judgment of the child is old-fashioned squeamishness, somehow reminiscent of the fight against vivisection. Time and again we have had to fight off crackpots who do not understand that animals must be sacrificed to human welfare, and that because of anesthetics vivesection is now painless. So it is with the child versus the gross national product: what individual child is more important than the gross national product? And is it not true that TV is an anesthetic?

Let us now look at a few reports on advertising directed to children.

In the span of time few things have greater memorability than a brand name learned in childhood.

As a result, many large advertisers are using toys to get their products into the hands of children. Many of the companies are providing the merchandise free or below production cost to a Pennsylvania toy manufacturer, who then sells miniature sets of products for children. . . .

John White, Jr., sales promotion manager of Chesebrough Ponds, Inc., explains:

"This is just about the only medium that affords us direct contact with future users of our products. We're very much aware of the importance of preselling the youngsters. . . . I think there's no doubt that the company whose product has been used as a play item during the impressionable years of childhood, has just that much edge on a competitor who does not engage in this type of promotion. . . ."

There was another favorable comment from Winton May, vice president of the Chicopee Manufacturing Company, whose Miracloth dishcloths are included in one of the toy sets. He said:

"This is an especially good medium for establishing brand images."[1]

[The H. J. Heinz Company has just floated a campaign aimed at the back to school trade], which they say will put "the whole world" in the hands of school children while putting Heinz tomato soup in their mouths.

The "whole world" turns out to be a plastic globe, 12-inches in diameter. The student may get the globe by sending $2 in cash to Heinz along with three Heinz tomato soup labels.[2]

A SHARE FOR JOHNNY

Like a stone cast in water that makes wider and wider concentric ripples, stock market enthusiasm is reaching a wider and wider public. But recently Cadre Industries Corporation of Endicott, N.Y., decided that children had not yet been reached effectively.

To mark its tenth anniversary, the company has published a booklet called A Share for Johnny.[3]

Educating a child to buy stocks is not, of course, the same as inspiring him to buy soup or pie, but the general principle is the same: training the young mind in spending money.

A PIE FOR BILLY

Youngsters like pie. Pies usually are made in grown-up sizes. If they are made in children's sizes, more will be sold to children.

The Wagner Baking Corporation of Newark, N.J., has been following this reasoning, and the result is the introduction of a snack-size Billy Wagner Pie, which will be promoted to children as a confection for meals, between meals and for school lunch boxes (to be eaten on the way to school).[4]

[1] New York Times, August 3, 1960.
[2] Ibid., July 18, 1960.
[3] Ibid., October 6, 1961. I would not wish to give the impression that Americans are the only ones with progressive ideas. The New York Times of November 4, 1961 reports that Lord Ritchie of Dundee, chairman of the London Stock Exchange recommended that children be instructed in school on "how the stock market operates" so that "when they were older it would seem natural for them to invest in the future prosperity of their country. . . ."
[4] Ibid., August 17, 1960.

It would be narrow, fanatical, eggheaded legalism to urge that business is merely *legally* innocent of coercion in such advertising. After all, what is the tender-eyed innocence of children for? Is it not for gazing spellbound and uncritical on the doubtful wonders of the culture?

Is it not better that American children engage in productive play such as manipulating standard brands in miniature cans, than waste their time and energy in mindless games of jacks? The outstanding characteristic of children's play in all societies has been preparation for adult life. We were deviant in this respect until advertising put us back on the right path. The charge that pitching advertisements to youngsters, *conditioning* them before they have a chance to *think,* is an arrogant and brutal *invasion of the function of judgment,* is hysterical. It reminds one of *1984.* The idea that Campbell's, Heinz, Chicopee, Texaco, et cetera, could become like "big brothers" to our children is laughable. Absurd to imagine that my grandchild, as he swings his jet-propelled road-scooter into the nearest Shell station should feel as if a speaker went off in his head saying gently, "Texaco! Remember?" And that he should then wheel away, heading guiltily for the next Texaco service station! Preposterous!

At no time is the invasion of children's judgment by advertising fiercer than at Christmas time, when the merchants of toyland, goaded by competition and by the awareness that 60 per cent of their money is made in the short Christmas season, crash through the thin Christmas ice of legal innocence. The struggle among the toy merchants for the brain boxes of the children and the dollars of their parents is indeed so keen that one could hardly blame them for a little chicanery. In order to get a feeling for the almost unendurable anxiety under which these poor men labor and in order to gain some awareness of the television Christmas spirit, let us look at a couple of reports from the *New York Times;* they will enable us to empathize also with the parents and children.

> . . . advertising toys on television is creating a demand for heavily promoted items. Many of these will be in tight supply toward the end of the holiday shopping season. . . .

The brand image created on television and embedded in the minds of children assures good volume for these items. . . .[1]

Here is a story for Christmas. It did not originate with a press agent. It was told by a mother.

Of late the television channels have been alive with advertising directed at children—a saturation campaign whose purpose was to whet the children's appetite for certain toys.

The campaign has been successful. The children are telling their parents that nothing else but these toys will do for Christmas.

The desperate parents have been combing the stores. Some have been to nine, ten, eleven, twelve stores and the answer has been pretty much the same—"sold out."[2]

If under conditions of "heavy promotion" and competitive "embedding," the channels of air "alive with advertising directed at children," their parents "desperate" to buy exactly the toy their darlings want; if under such circumstances some businessmen should "lose their north star" (*perder el norte*) as the Spaniards put it, and the merchants of toyland should blunder into the abyss of dishonesty, well, we can still not forgive them.

The disorientation of the toy business brought some afterthoughts on the heels of the Christmas advertising campaigns.

The toy industry is in trouble. A survey just completed in three major markets shows a growing, if not full-grown resentment leveled by the public at the toy industry. . . .

. . . the resentment is aimed at one specific type of toy— the heavily advertised television toy. . . . It seems that it is almost impossible for some of our leading manufacturers to put a toy on television without misrepresenting it.

We see non-floating battleships move through fog and haze, tanks crash through barbed wire blowing up enemy outposts. Toy rockets launch into space between actual film clips. Toy submarines surface and sink in front of incredible marine backdrops.

[1] *Ibid.*, November 20, 1960.
[2] *Ibid.*, December 23, 1960.

> . . . a commercial . . . shows an airplane flying through
> most of a sixty-second commercial. At the end of the com-
> mercial there is printed the words, "not a flying toy," but
> without voice accompaniment. [A father is quoted as say-
> ing:] "My youngster is only 5. He cannot read. It's a
> helluva thing to spend $15 on a toy and then see my kid sit
> down and cry because it doesn't fly like the one he saw on
> television."[1]

By Christmas 1962, however, these guilt twinges had passed,
and the toy merchants were again engaged in decent pecuniary
misrepresentation. Had they not, their ability to sell high-priced
toys—those promoted most actively on TV—would have been
impaired, and the gross national product diminished. This would
have been a pity. Even more of a pity would it be if overnight
our society should change from child- to parent-centered, so
that through television the toy industry was no longer able to
appeal *over the heads of the parents* to the children; so that
parents, in terror of the petulance of their children no more,
would not be driven into the streets searching for something to
satisfy an electronically generated whim. In a child-centered
society childish whims, abetted by irresponsible advertising,
can transform the anticipated joy of Christmas into a psychosis.
But the crazier the Christmas, the more money spent, and if toys
were simple, few, and cheap, and not promoted by TV, the
gross national product would suffer. It is obvious also that in a
parent-centered society, where parents were so firmly in the
saddle that they were not afraid of their children, such rudderless *impulse-drift*, such toyland mania, would be impossible,
for children would be happy with the parents' decision and
parents would not feel coerced. Child-centeredness, however, is
necessary to our toy economy. Any middle-class four-year-old
boy having less than 30 toys is unusual; boys tend to have about
three times as many toys as girls.[2] Take away child-centeredness
from the toy business and it would be back in the nineteenth
century. Deprive business of its capacity to appeal to children
over the heads of their parents and what would happen to

[1] From the *New York Times,* December 27, 1960, quoting from an article
in the December issue of *Toys and Novelties.*
[2] Based on my actual inventories of toys in small samples of families.

most of the cereals, some of the drugs, and many toys? If advertising has invaded the judgment of children, it has also forced its way into the family, an insolent usurper of parental function, degrading parents to mere intermediaries between their children and the market. This indeed is a social revolution in our time!

Meanwhile this arrogance is terrifyingly reminiscent of another appeal to children over the heads of their parents: that of the Nazi Youth movement, for it too usurped parental function. The way the Nazis did it was by making society state-centered. What we have done is to combine product-centeredness with child-centeredness to produce a unique American amalgam, consumption-centeredness: a cemetery of brain boxes filled with the bones of pecuniary claims.

The insatiableness of children is matched by business' hunger for profit; and many businesses, whipped on by a hurricane of competition-engendered anxiety, will use almost any device to sell: traditional values, human weaknesses, the intimacies of women, and the immaturities of children—all are transmuted, by the Midas touch of advertising, into cash. But, lest we place too much blame on the merchants of toyland, let us remind ourselves once more that they could not do as they do were ours not a child-centered society, committed to permissiveness, afloat in the tides of impulse release and fun.

THE PECUNIARY CONCEPTION OF MAN

I have, perhaps, burdened this chapter with too many new expressions; yet it seemed necessary to do this in order to make clear the fact that pecuniary philosophy is a more or less systematic method of thinking, as well as a way to make money. So I have spoken of pecuniary pseudo-truth, a statement nobody is expected to believe but which is set down as if it were to be believed. Pecuniary logic was defined as a statement made to be believed but backed up by shadowy proof, and para-poetic hyperbole was described as being poetry but not quite poetry, its function being to make a product appear rather dreamlike and fey, to transmute it. Pecuniary psychology is the "scientific" base of pecuniary philosophy, and its central concepts are the

head or "brain box," penetration, and the claim. Surprisingly
enough, pecuniary history emerges as a phase of pecuniary
psychology, for the Wars of Pecuniary Claims and the rise and
fall of products are indissolubly linked to the concepts of the
brain box and of penetration. Being a complete philosophy,
pecuniary thought has not only a truth, a logic, a history, and a
poetics, but also a biology—the evolution and extinction of
products.

This brings us to pecuniary philosophy's conception of man.
Man—or, rather, his brain box—is finite, but at the same time,
infinite. The brain box is finite with respect to the number of
claims it can contain at the same time, but it is infinite in the
things it may desire. Claims and perceptions (of products)
surge in and out of the brain box like the tides of an ocean
moving up and down a passive beach. Put another way, man is
inert while the external culture in the form of products and
claims molds him to desire. Thus if the culture (i.e., advertising)
requires that man stay at home consuming electric organs and
barbecue pits, he can readily be gotten to do so if advertising
paints mellow pictures of home and family. If, on the other
hand, it is desired that he drive around and use up gasoline,
man, in the pecuniary conception, will readily be brought to
that too, simply through "promoting" the beauties of automobile travel. If he takes his coffee weak, he will drink it strong
if advertising admonishes him to do so. If, smoking mentholated
cigarettes, he fears for his masculinity, he will lose his fears if
he is told that Alpine "put the men in menthol smoking!"[1]

How to Sell Hats

Before Christmas, Bloomingdale's tried a series of five
seven-column newspaper advertisements—one a week—
built around the idea that the store catered to the "orig-
inalist," the person "who loves to shop for or receive the
unusual, who appreciates the individual, who looks for the
exciting."

The purpose of the advertisement was to get across the
idea that Bloomingdale's was loaded with a variety of mer-

[1] See, for example the Alpine cigarette advertisements in the *New York
Times,* August 2, 1961 and in *Life* magazine, May 26, 1961.

chandise that would please the most discriminating taste
and be fun to ferret out, in the bargain.

One advertisement had for its art work a cluster of hats
on a hat tree. They were not accompanied by any price or
description. But from a single such institutional advertisement in a single newspaper, Bloomingdale's, as an immediate reaction, sold $1,000 worth of the hats on the tree
—many by mail or telephone.[1]

How to Sell Strawberries
. . . last winter, Rottelle, Inc., Bucks County, Pa., dis-
tributor for Seabrook Farms frozen foods, found itself with
a lot of frozen strawberries on hand. . . .

The problem was taken to James H. Williams Jr., national advertising manager of *The Levittown Times* and
The Bristol Daily Courier. Mr. Williams suggested an advertisement using strawberry-scented ink. In Mr. Williams'
words:

"We designed the ad to be appetite appealing, using very
little copy and featuring as a focal point a big, juicy red
strawberry. When this advertisement arrived in the homes
on Jan. 20, the rush was on. . . .

"Rottelle's records show that at the end of the first week,
10,000 packages of Seabrook Farm strawberries were
sold."[2]

How to Sell an Island
[Trans Caribbean Airlines, wanting to increase traffic
to Aruba, approached Warwick & Legler, a small advertising agency. Mr. Heller of the agency describes his approach to the problem.]

"It is the same sort of approach," Mr. Heller said, "that
is used in cosmetics advertising. An effective advertisement
for a lipstick does not simply tell a woman that there is a
new blushing pink shade available. It tells her that the
blushing pink lipstick will make her more beautiful and
more appealing to men."

[1] From the *New York Times*, December 30, 1960.
[2] From the *New York Times*, November 6, 1960.

The airline ads for Aruba, Mr. Heller said, attempt to involve the reader in the same way by asking him questions and making specific emotional appeals. . . .

Trans Caribbean is happy with the results of the campaign. The airline's passenger traffic . . . has had a dramatic increase since the campaign. Before the campaign started, flights to Aruba averaged four to five passengers. Four weeks after the campaign was under way . . . traffic to the island jumped to an average of seventy-five passengers each flight.[1]

People who like to hope that advertising is wasting its money point to the failure of big-car automobile advertising to destroy the American consumer's desire for a smaller car and the consequent encroachment on the market of small foreign cars. But one swallow does not make a summer. It is also important not to forget that the foreign manufacturers were advertising too! Insatiably desiring, infinitely plastic, totally passive, and always a little bit sleepy; unpredictably labile and disloyal (to products); basically wooly-minded and non-obsessive about traditional truth; relaxed and undemanding with respect to the canons of traditional philosophy, indifferent to its values, and easily moved to buy whatever at the moment seems to help his underlying personal inadequacies—this is pecuniary philosophy's conception of man and woman in our culture. Since it is a very contemptuous one, it appears that Madison Avenue is not so much the "street of dreams," as *McCall's* has called it, but rather the Alley of Contempt, housing thousands who, through the manufacture of advertising, pour their scorn upon the population. The following expresses this with precision: A full page advertisement by a company trying to sell to advertising agencies movies of championship bowling matches, is dominated by a lamp post carrying the sign "54th Street and Madison Avenue." The copy says, in part:

The name of this TV sports series is CHAMPIONSHIP BOWLING. It is an hour show, features the country's top bowlers in head-to-head matches. It is simple to understand, exciting and suspenseful to watch. And once you've got this

[1] From the *New York Times,* August 30, 1961.

narcotic TV viewing habit, you're hooked—as witness the fact that every year our ratings climb.

. . . we deliver almost as many people as does Football, week in, week out.[1]

When you are able to talk in a full page ad in the *New York Times* about *delivering* narcotized people, you and the newspaper have almost ceased to think of people as human. On the other hand if advertising, spending almost 12 billion dollars a year, has this conception of the public, there must be some basis for it. After all, this advertisement is from one advertising man talking to the rest, in the comfortable, intimate language of a fraternity brother. How could the ad be wrong? Where is the flaw in its assumption that the attitude of "54th Street and Madison Avenue" toward the human race is one of disdain and ridicule?[2]

The only obvious flaw in pecuniary philosophy is its perception of man as expendable, for without man there could be no products—a matter of elementary pecuniary biology.

I have pointed out that pecuniary philosophy passes by imperceptible degrees from matters it can handle to materials (drugs, for example) which are beyond its competence because,

---

[1] *New York Times*, August 7, 1961.

[2] The following correspondence about this ad took place between Mr. V. Redding of the *New York Times* Advertising Acceptability Department and me. (Mr. Redding's letter is reprinted by permission.)

Dear Sir:

I was deeply shocked by the ad on page 11 of Monday, August 7. How can you permit an advertiser to use language like:

"And once you've got this narcotic TV viewing habit, you're hooked. . . ."

Very truly yours,
Jules Henry

Dear Professor Henry:

This will acknowledge your letter of August 9.

We are most regretful that the statement in the Walter Schwimmer advertisement about which you wrote was offensive to you. It did not seem objectionable to us in the degree that would have prompted us to question it.

There are bound to be differences of opinion from time to time as to our judgment. We are not infallible but we can assure you that an earnest effort is made to protect the interests of our readers and we appreciate your taking the time to write.

Sincerely yours,
V. Redding

since it considers human beings expendable, it is unsuited to deal with matters of life and death. Because of this weakness— and all philosophies have some—pecuniary philosophy often leads its followers into errors, such as making improper claims for drugs or trying to put advertisements in the hands of babies. The last is a consequence of pecuniary philosophy's being itself misled through borrowing value words from traditional philosophy. For example, whereas in traditional philosophy "educate" means "to acquaint with ideas and skills," in pecuniary philosophy it has come to mean "to teach to buy a product." In this connection advertising's use of the traditional value words was said to accelerate loss of respect for them and decomposition of their traditional meanings.

In analyzing monetization I said that "in their wars of survival pecuniary adversaries will use anything for ammunition—space, time, the President, the Holy Bible and all the traditional values" —a discovery that lead to the conclusion that the erosion of traditional values was due in no small part to fear of competition.

The modes of thought and the view of man entertained by pecuniary philosophy have been shown to derive in great part from fear and contempt. Thus we have discovered that an industry now contributing nearly 12 billion dollars to the gross national product derives much of its dynamism from contempt and fear. It has also the most radical conception of *Homo sapiens* that has ever been proposed.

SHAME AND DEGRADATION

The pretty girl is probably the marketing man's best friend. At least he depends on her more than anything else to catch the eye of the public. . . .

The college co-ed is quite an effective marketing tool. . . .

The suburban socialite type of model . . . is a good saleswoman for products involving self-indulgence. . . .[1]

There ought to be a section of this report dealing with *parts* of the female that are the best "marketing tools." For example,

[1] Report on a study done by Social Research, Inc., a commercial outfit of high-power University of Chicago social scientists. From the *New York Times*, April 11, 1961.

I have an advertisement for a popular automobile showing a blonde, bottom up, on the roof of it. The lower part of her is clad in scarlet tights and glows arrestingly against the warm browns and yellows of the autumn background.[1] Another ad is a closeup color photo of a lovely young woman on ice skates coming to a spectacular, braking, "swoosh" of a stop. Since the camera is shooting from below upward and the girl is wearing tautly stretched tights and a tiny skirt that conceals practically nothing, the view of the buttocks, flung sideways at the lens by the sizzling half-turn is unparalleled.[2] How many points the GNP has risen on the feminine buttock is an interesting question.

I once showed several advertisements to a class of advanced graduate students in business administration, in order to illustrate how women are used by advertising in our culture. When I came to a Japanese student he glanced at the red-tights ad but quickly averted his eyes. This is *shame*. Shame seems still to live in Japan, hence the averted eyes; for the Japanese could never confront his inner self if he permitted himself to look brazenly on the publicly flaunting buttocks of a woman, even in a photograph.

The female has lost her *shame functions* in our culture; impulse has broken through the wall of shame and advertising has been quick to see the pecuniary value. I am not saying that advertising has caused a breakdown in the shame functions of women. Rather I am urging that since women have already lost their shame functions, advertising merely exploits the consequences.

By *shame function*, I mean the following: In some cultures the culturally central emotions tend to be embodied in one sex or the other, and that sex becomes the symbol of the emotion. From Lorca and Pitt-Rivers[3] we know the importance of *sangre y verguenza* in Spain: man the embodiment of courage and violence (*sangre*), woman the repository of shame (*verguenza*). Together they are the emotional underpinning of Spanish peasant culture and social life. The blood and brooding

---

[1] *Esquire,* July 1960.
[2] *Life,* January 20, 1961.
[3] See Pitt-Rivers, *People of the Sierra.*

night of Lorca's plays flow from the peril to these in the Spanish villages of which he wrote. It was not so different in our own culture not too long ago, except that the ferocity of the defense and the darkly oppressive quality of these feeelings found in Spain were not present in America. With the transformation of American culture into a consuming one, all inhibitory emotions, all feelings that contribute in any way to an austere view of life and to the constriction of impulse, had to go. Female shame, and masculine respect for female shame, are casualties of the era of impulse release and fun in the United States. As usual, advertising merely converts the casualty into cash. In doing so, however, it drives the message home: *shame has lost its force in American life,* and women, having turned their backs, lead the retreat.

Let us consider other dimensions of this problem, in the light of what might be called advertising's ingenuously prophetic gifts: its capacity to slyly tell us the truth about ourselves while not being interested in traditional truth. Consider a full-page advertisement for a famous perfume.[1] It is a picture of two expensive TV and Hollywood "personalities" trying to look as idiotic as possible. He is holding a bottle of the perfume as he looks at her, and the advertisement says, "The Facts of Life: Promise her anything but give her————"(that perfume). The truth in the advertisement is that men in our culture, often looking down on women as "nervous," somewhat feeble-minded, and vapidly whimsical, tend to soothe them with false promises; but this is acceptable because it is a "fact of life." "Quiet her down; tell her anything; you don't have to make good," is the silent communication in this message.

Here is a two-page advertisement for a famous electric shaver. Against a background of deep red reclines at full length a woman in white. One bony leg extends pastily from under her dress. The expression on her lips and in her eyes communicates a honeyed atmosphere of enticement and exploitation. The ad has her saying, "Gimme, gimme, gimme." What she wants, of course, is that shaver![2] The truth in the image is that many men retain a lurking fear of woman as seductive and material-

---

[1] *New York Times,* December 5, 1960.
[2] *Life,* December 19, 1960.

istic. The issue, meanwhile, is not that this is the way women are, but rather that this is the way an advertiser dares portray her.

Advertising's use of female ecstasy is, perhaps, the most imaginative monetization of woman. Campaigns for undergarments, soaps, sanitary tissues and napkins, perfumes, and cigarettes have pictured women swooning orgastically under the spell cast by the product. The prophetic, though unarticulated, message in the advertisements is that men and women have become so estranged from one another and from themselves that for many the love-climax has become *socially* meaningless. When orgasm is self-centered, a narcissistic experience only, and does not unite one overwhelmingly to another human being, there is no particular reason why it should not be pinched off, mimicked, monetized, and used to sell anything.

"Are we wasting women?" queries *Life* editorially.[1] The answer is, Of course not! No nation on earth has ever used them to greater advantage! Without the pecuniary uses of women—their hair, their faces, their legs and all the wondrous variety of their personality and anatomy—the economy would perish. Even the armaments race would not save it, nor could we eat enough nostrums to make up for the loss of the monetized female! But along with monetization, along with this power to hurl the economy to unimagined heights,[2] woman has been degraded. How can she permit advertising to portray her as it does? Why does she not rise up in rage? Perhaps her idealization of herself prevents the American woman from perceiving what is actually happening to her.

Of course, I do not argue that such degradation was *alone* responsible for the tremendous and unexpected rise in gross national product. What I do urge, however, is that women, by permitting themselves to be degraded, by allowing their most intimate privacies to be exploited, have made a formidable self-sacrificing contribution to national well-being. The recesses

[1] July 28, 1961.

[2] In 1947 projected gross national product for 1960 was $202 billion at 1944 prices. See *America's Needs and Resources* by J. Frederic Dewhurst and Associates. New York: The Twentieth Century Fund, 1947, p. 24. Correcting for about a 70 per cent price rise since 1947, this would give around $350 billion for 1960-61. Thus the projection erred by almost 40 per cent!

of the feminine soul have become ransom for the gross national product.

But it is never possible to say of Madison Avenue that it is all one way. The reader will remember that in the advertisements for magazines woman is portrayed as representing the following spiritual values:

> motherhood
> love
> devotion
> idealism
> purposefulness
> caring for another person
> purity
> wisdom
> mission in life
> loyalty

Perhaps everything good and spiritual Madison Avenue has to say about women is summed up in the following full page advertisement for *Cosmopolitan*.[1] Most of it is occupied by the figures of a man and a woman. Of refined loveliness, the woman's long lashes sweep against her cheeks as she pours wine from a cut glass decanter. Very close, half turned toward her, smiling in shy, empathic adoration is a handsome, refined, masculine young man. You cannot quite see, but you sense that he is wearing a dinner jacket in harmony with her expensively simple gown. They stand by a table for two whose décor breathes costly refinement. The copy:

SHE KNOWS THERE'S MORE THAN ONE WAY TO QUENCH A THIRST

She's COSMOPOLITAN! This is a woman who endows every aspect of living with her own particular grace. She lights a candle, plucks a flower, pours the wine—and a dinner à deux becomes a festive occasion. Her conversation is as piquant as her sauces, her smile as intoxicating as the wine's bouquet. Multiply her by a million, and you have a portrait of the COSMOPOLITAN reader. . . . Reach a creative, discerning woman like this, and you're reaching a market for the best of everything. [Off to one

[1] *New York Times*, June 13, 1960.

side the copy says] the best of everything in this case is wine
and liquor. She is a connoisseur of each. . . .

IS SOME ADVERTISING GOOD?

By this time the reader must be wondering whether I see
anything "good" in advertising, and in order to answer the question I shall discuss the first few ads in an issue of *Time,* a magazine read mostly by men, and the first few in an issue of
Woman's Day, read mostly by women.

The first advertisement from *Time*[1] shows, against a luminous
background of blue summer sky suffused with white clouds, a
triangle of fifteen pastel billiard balls standing on its apex.
Below, the copy reads

> Group insurance that makes men work together and *stay*
> together.
>
> Without proper maintenance, the best machines run down
> and stop. Have you ever considered that a work force is
> very much the same?
>
> Without "people" maintenance, poor workers get poorer and
> the good ones . . . leave.
>
> Today hundreds of employers are using group insurance and
> pension plans to help maintain the enthusiasm and loyalty
> of their employees. . . .
>
> Results prove when this is done, people approach their jobs
> with more enthusiasm and loyalty and think less about
> greener pastures elsewhere.

It is impossible to find any of the techniques of pecuniary philosophy in this advertisement except, perhaps, a faint monetization of the values of enthusiasm and loyalty. The symbolism of
the triangle seems a bit fuzzy and impersonal, but straight-
forward: it seems to say that just as these balls are together so
men will stay together if group insurance is used. Thus the
appeal is without frills and states, if not an absolute truth, at
least a reasonable possibility, viz., that group insurance does

---

[1] All *Time* quotes from the July 16, 1961 issue.

sometimes make some contribution to the stability of one's working force.

The next ad is for Rose's lime juice. Emerging from a background of deep, velvety black, is a classic head of a young woman crowned with a bathing cap and sprinkled with drops of water. Her eyes, shadowed by furry black lashes, look slanting at a cocktail glass, just below her left eye. A flirtatious conversation is taking place between the girl and the contents of the glass. The girl says:

> I didn't catch the name. Gimlet? Of course. That vodka, Rose's Lime Juice and ice thing. They tell me you have taste, charm, and perfect form.

Then, it seems, the glass is supposed to have said, "So do you," because the girl says, "So do I? Why Gimlet, how gallant! I just know we'll get along swimmingly." Because this ad is pure whimsy I think it is aimed at women, though my wife is convinced that men are the target. This is, then, a pecuniary hyperbole directed to men. Since we are not expected to believe that this girl would actually flirt with and talk to an alcoholic beverage, the advertisement fits the categories of pecuniary pseudo-truth as well as—with some strain, to be sure—the category of pecuniary poetry. (Better, perhaps, pecuniary drama!) The most interesting aspect of this ad, however, is its efforts to accomplish identification of the man with the gimlet. Since the girl is flirting with the gimlet in the glass, a man reading the ad is supposed to imagine that if he serves a gimlet to a girl she will flirt with *him*. The idea is to get a man to fantasy himself a gimlet. Thus girl, gimlet, and guy are woven together by this ad into an alcoholic fantasy of flirtation; and the relatively commonplace act of putting lime juice in a drink is transmuted into something exciting. A purely "female" type of appeal.

We have looked now at two advertisements taken in succession from the same magazine. The first uses the methods of pecuniary philosophy relatively little; the second is deep in the tradition. Let us look at the third.

Goodyear controls the next two pages. The picture, occupying the left-hand page, shows the front fender of an expensive pitch-black car curving above a Goodyear tire. Fender, tire, and part of the cowl dominate the page, but above them we discern, in higher tones, the imposing front of a prestige golf club; standing on the broad lawn before it are two golfers and a caddy. The advertising copy, which is long, and can only be summarized, promotes Goodyear's "Double Eagle" tire, calling it "the world's safest." The most telling guarantee of this is that

> If it *ever* goes flat from *any* cause Goodyear will (1) pay for your road service, (2) replace the inner shield free, and (3) give you full allowance for all unused tread wear if the outer tire is damaged.

What makes the tire remarkable is a "captive-air inner spare"— a built-in second inner tube that carries the weight of the car in case the first layer is punctured. Goodyear claims that this tire is "70% *stronger* than an ordinary tire."

Most of this sounds relatively orthodox, because the argument about the "inner-spare," and the guarantee seem to offer something genuine in the old tradition. One might raise questions about the tire being "the world's safest" and about the 70 per cent claim, but otherwise the ad seems relatively forthright. There is in it just one ingredient from the kitchen of pecuniary cookery—the picture, which attempts to establish a link between the tire and high status, the implication being that men who buy this tire are in a class with members of exclusive golf clubs. Obviously Goodyear does not think it enough just to cook up an orthodox ad that states simply the merits of a remarkable tire; the ad must have some pecuniary pepper too.

Thus, two out of the three first ads in *Time*, a magazine read mostly by men, contain little pecuniary philosophy. The one ad that does involves lime juice and man's relation to women. It is hard to say anything orthodox about such a combination because one is dealing at one and the same time with the un-reality of man's relation to woman in our culture and with lime juice. So, as my wife says, "I take my hat off to the agency that did the ad," for they have managed to eroticize lime juice— transforming it, through pecuniary whimsy, into vibrant un-reality!

We turn now to *Woman's Day*.[1]

[1] Advertisements quoted are from the March 1961 issue.

The first ad to be discussed is one for Angel Skin lotion and cream. The copy speaks for itself:

YOUNG HANDS are happy hands. Lovely to look at. Tempting to touch. How *sad* to let your hands look old before you do! "Old Hands" can happen to anyone because housework, hot water, wind and weather all do daily damage, *aging your hands before their time.* Pond's won't *let* this happen to you! Pond's makes this promise: *all new* Angel Skin, used faithfully and frequently every day, will work positive wonders in warding off that hated "old hands" look. *Penetressence* is the reason. *Penetressence* is Pond's own lovely secret . . . an exclusive concentrate of age-defying moisturizers, softeners, and secret essences that go *deep down where aging begins!* Your hands respond *instantly. Penetressence* is the reason young hands *begin* with
All-new ANGEL SKIN
ANGEL SKIN the *young hand* lotion by Pond's

Penetressence, lovely secret, age-defying moisturizers, et cetera, express pecuniary logic—fuzzy "proof," ambiguous claims, mysterious words, all for wooly-minded people. "Young hands are happy hands. . . . Tempting to touch. How *sad* to let your hands look old . . . lovely secret . . . secret essences . . . ," all classic pecuniary hyperbole. The psychological stimuli reach deeply into female anxiety about aging, and, having *stirred up fear* the ad offers absolute relief—a promise that if one uses Angel Skin her hands will not grow old. The pledge illustrates a new dimension of pecuniary morality, which I shall call the *pecuniary commitment*—a promise on which nobody can collect. For suppose, in spite of "faithful" application of Angel Skin a woman's hands grow old, what can she do to Pond's? Thus the pecuniary commitment is one on which nobody can collect except the manufacturer.

The next ad is for Bissell wax remover, rug shampoo, and upholstery shampoo. After reminding the housewife–reader of her endless fight against dirt, the ad says:

. . . you can get near-miracles from Bissell. Such as new Scuff 'n Wax Remover, that takes the hard work out of getting rid of stubborn old wax deposits. And the wonderful Bissell Rug Shampoos . . . the best ways there are to clean rugs at home—they leave your rugs amazingly clean and new looking. . . . Let these Bissell wonder workers make life easier. . . .

Once you are socialized to hyperbolic transmogrification all advertisements sound plausible—provided you believe the advertiser's claims—so "miracle" does not mean "a supernatural event," nor do "amazing" and "wonder worker" mean anything more than "very, very good." Actually the Bissell advertisement is making very modest claims: it is simply saying that its products are the best on the market and will make work easier and furnishings cleaner. If one accepts the linguistic reality of our culture—that the meanings of words, like the significance of values, have become soft and shapeless—many ads that look like lies in terms of traditional thinking become reasonable. This flabbiness, this *pecuniary plasticity* of words is, of course, the direct product of *fear* of competition: if Bissell used an orthodox vocabulary it wouldn't sell against similar products that use a pecuniary one.

The last advertisement to be considered is for Lawry's Italian-style Spaghetti Sauce Mix with imported mushrooms.

Occupying the upper half of the page is a picture of all the ingredients used in making spaghetti sauce: tomato paste, anchovies, spices, cheese, wine, olive oil, mushrooms, and so on. Above this picture it says, "The old way to make a *great* spaghetti sauce. . . ." Below it says, "and the new!" And just beneath these words is a picture of a package of the mix. The copy goes on:

> Face it, the quickest spaghetti sauce is in cans. But not the best. The best is the sauce *you* make when you go all-out. Now you can get the same *bravissimo* flavor from one little foil package.

The copy continues in the same vein, extolling Lawry's sauce, and there is really nothing in the advertisement but the claim —relatively unvarnished, relatively free from the methods of pecuniary philosophy.

Thus, as one surveys the creations of advertising, he finds they range from a direct presentation of the product, like an ad for beans that simply tells a woman they go well with pineapple, to wandering fantasy, and ultimately to outright false claims. Much of advertising assumes that people are wooly-minded and frightened; some of it assumes that people think straight. Everywhere the ads are permeated by a puffed-up vocabulary which by now amounts to a linguistic convention, and which reflects the fact that the cybernetic—i.e., the steering or guiding—function of our language is giving way to a *mis*-guiding function. "The Only Thing We Have to Fear is the Truth," said a sign hanging over the desk of a Hollywood press agent.[1]

Ancients of our culture sought clarity: Plato portrays Socrates tirelessly splitting hairs to extract essential truth from the ambiguities of language and thought. Two thousand years later we are reversing that, for now we pay intellectual talent a high price to amplify ambiguities, distort thought, and bury reality. All languages are deductive systems with a vast truth-telling potential imbedded in vocabulary, syntax, and morphology, yet no language is so perfect that men may not use it for the opposite purpose. One of the discoveries of the twentieth century is *the enormous variety of ways of compelling language to lie.*

Advertising in the *Slough of Dispond*

However unworthy our advertising man may be for comparison with Bunyan's Christian, he is at least an honest man with an honest set of standards, who is trying to progress from charlatanism to the status of a professional over a course set with more pitfalls than even a Bunyan could imagine.

Edwin Cox, chairman of Kenyon & Eckhardt, Inc.[2]

. . . this is a By-way to Hell, a way that Hypocrites go in at; namely, such as sell their Birthright, with *Esau:* such as sell their Master, with *Judas:* such as blaspheme the Gospel, with *Alexander:* and that lie and dissemble, with *Ananias* and *Sapphira* his wife.

John Bunyan, *The Pilgrim's Progress.*

[1] *Esquire*, January 1961.
[2] *New York Times*, December 2, 1960.

By late 1959 the advertising industry was more worried about its public image than about Federal prosecution. It is true that even as an executive was publicly declaring that much advertising was dishonest, his own agency was under scrutiny by the Federal Trade Commission for deceptive advertising; but it was not such random *contretemps* that were disturbing the advertising business, but rather awareness of public disgust. The result was an eruption of intra-fraternal scrutiny, and many emotional speeches by advertising executives at meetings in Boca Raton, Bermuda, Washington, and New York in which they accused the business of dishonesty, bad taste, not understanding "the true relationships between advertising and people," dullness, repetitiveness—even of "insulting the people's intelligence"!

In the very act of self-blame, however, advertising men committed the sins of which they were accused. This is natural, for a true protest of innocence and veritable rites of confession and purification can be carried out only according to the orthodox requirements of truth-language and not in double talk. For example, Mr. Cox, as he compares advertising men to Christian in *Pilgrim's Progress,* yet says that advertising men are unworthy of the comparison; and if, as he protests, advertising men are honest, why is he making a speech apologizing for them? And in the same vein, how can a person be honest and a charlatan at the same time? Obviously, only an advertising man is capable of this feat. In a flight of para-poetic hyperbole Mr. Cox next lists the pitfalls that lie before these honest charlatans: The Sins of the Few, Dreadful Dullness, The Stairway of Mediocrity, and the Cult of Creativity. He thus uses the language of the fraternity in addressing his brothers, while telling them what they must know is untrue—that they are all suffering for the sins of the few. Finally, Mr. Cox condemns advertising for mediocrity and dullness while calling creativity a cult. But if creativity is condemned as a cult, how can mediocrity and dullness be avoided?

We should guard against the idea that advertising men are dull-witted and slow; a group that spends $12 billion a year cannot be stupid. They do not contradict themselves or lie to one another *in terms of their own culture.* The central issue is that they have lived so long where double talk is the *only* talk, and where *contradiction is affirmation* that they do not perceive in what they say what we of the more traditional culture perceive.

Let us now turn to one of advertising's gestures in the direction of a public reconciliation. On August 15, 1960 the advertising business bought a third of a page in the *New York Times* for an advertisement explaining its role to the public. I quote some of it below.

WHAT WOULD HAPPEN IF ALL ADVERTISING STOPPED?

Within a week most radio and television stations would close up shop for lack of revenue. . . . Without advertising our national economy, our national *life,* would be bleak indeed. In many ways, advertising is the *power plant* of our society. . . .

Advertising not only gives people news about new products, but provides the *urge* for people to own and enjoy these products. The wider and deeper the penetration of our products into the life of America, the greater the need for more production. This means more jobs. More jobs mean more people able to enjoy what we make.

THE CULTURAL EFFECTS OF ADVERTISING

It's because of *advertising* that our mass media of communication can afford to command the finest talent for bringing to the American people information, stimulation, entertainment and education which in other countries are available to just a very few people. . . .

Here the very techniques for which advertising has been condemned are used in order to gain public favor. First we are terrorized by being told that if advertising were to go away we would all starve. This is the familiar technique of "frighten 'em and snow 'em," so well known from ads for hand creams, insurance, automobile tires, etc., that terrorize us with spectres of old age, insecurity, and disaster, and then tell us how we can save ourselves with a few dollars spent the right way. Next we are informed that advertising is merely there to help us enjoy ourselves—to stimulate the dormant "urge" to enjoyment. Thus fear and enjoyment are counterpointed against each other in an effort to weaken the psychological defenses of the enemy— the public. Finally we are asked to believe that advertising brings us CULTURE.

Being a separate society islanded in the winds of Madison Avenue, advertising cannot perceive how bizarre it is. Advertising is out of contact with us and so is unable to see that you do not address yourself in double talk, in "pecuniary-think," to adversaries who are criticizing you for it. Furthermore, to try to fob off on their *critics* the notion that the radio and TV catastrophes are CULTURE is beyond belief in people not harbored safely behind the protective screens of a psychiatric hospital. Let me put it this way: a fundamental index of schizophrenia is disconnectedness, so that one is unaware of how other people think and feel. When a person is crazy or merely pathogenic and functions in a schizoid way we say he is out of contact or disconnected. When a large group of people acts this way toward us we say that they constitute a separate culture.

I would urge that advertising is unable to see its ethical position relative to traditional orientations. I suggest, for example, that since the agency attacked by the Federal Trade Commission saw nothing illegal in what it was doing, its executive could talk about dishonesty, for advertising's conception of dishonesty applies to unlawfulness only, and hence *its* only concern is to be legally innocent. I would further urge that in advertising "shameful" could mean only improper display of bodily functions and parts according to public legal ordinance and has nothing to do with inappropriate use of value signs, symbols, and personalities according to the inner ordinances of the traditional conscience. Nevertheless it is in the distorted use of values, through monetization or improper comparisons, that one finds something shameful according to the traditional system. Advertising men have no sense of the inner ordinance.

Advertising considers itself the powerhouse of our society, generating the "urges" that will drive people to buy what is produced by our machines. It is by this token The Great Generator, a kind of deity, so to speak, and it is commitment to this deity that makes advertising men a "group of *dedicated* (a word they love so well) men and women." Since this dedication is combined with disconnectedness from important parts of our culture, we may call this *pecuniary otherworldliness*. Joined to a method of thought and a form of confession this transforms advertising into a vocation. Meanwhile it must be remembered that the development of this vocation is related to a very special kind of economy; that just as the monks of Cluny emerged in sackcloth and crucifix in the Middle Ages as a stabilizing force in the church, so the vocation of advertising, with all *its* trappings, stabilizes our irrationality. This problem is reviewed briefly in the next section.

ADVERTISING, CONSUMPTION AUTARCHY, AND THE SELF

Consumption autarchy is the term I have coined for the condition in which a country consumes all it produces. In 1960 the United States exported 4 per cent of its gross national product.[1] This closeness to consumption autarchy is made necessary by the low purchasing power of much of the rest of the world and by reduction to a mere trickle of exports to the communist countries. Thus advertising's extreme behavior is inseparably connected with the *world* consumption pattern and fear-ridden international relations.

Advertising methods are related also, however, to a first tenet of American business: profits must increase without limit. Given consumption autarchy and the tenet of limitless increase, only the wooly-minded consumer, trained to insatiability, can put the tenet into effect; and advertising alone can excite him to the heroic deeds of consumption necessary to make of the tenet a concrete reality.

In the background of all of this is the collective Self of the American people which has been educated to put the high-rising living standard in the place of true Self-realization. Consumption autarchy, the drive toward higher profits, and alienation from Self are the factors that account for advertising. To ignore these while considering America's problems of production, con-

[1] United States Department of Commerce, World Trade Information Service. *Statistical Reports.* Part 3, No. 60–30. September 1960. 4.1 per cent, the actual figure given by the Department of Commerce, includes military supplies and equipment and other forms of foreign aid.

sumption, and advertising is to ignore the ocean while studying the tides.

Configuration and Subculture.   Unique to the so-called high cultures of the world is their capacity to constantly generate within their vast bellies subcultures which, while having some connection with the archetypal, the so-called great or traditional culture, are somehow remote from it and encapsulated. Members of these subcultures talk mostly to one another, receiving in this way constant reassurance that their perceptions of the world are the only correct ones and coming to take for granted that the whole culture is as they see it. What has frustrated the efforts of social scientists to analyze the United States as a configuration, as a unitary system of ideas and activities, is the fact that it has so many apparently separate subcultures. Yet they are all connected with and depend on one another and on the fundamental orientations of the American configuration—toward private property, the high-rising standard of living, competition, achievement, and security. Thus the *stupefied* TV audience is the natural and necessary complement to the *alert* advertiser; and the merchants of *confusion* on Madison Avenue are a necessary complement to hard-pressed industry, pursuing economically *rational* ends. The *dubious modes of thought* of pecuniary philosophy integrate with the *undemandingness toward truth* characteristic of American folk, and their desire for a higher living standard makes them susceptible to the advertising that assails them with increasing pressure to raise it. And so it goes. The *survival anxiety* among products and claims is matched by the worker's *worry* about his job. He *passively awaits* the turn of the system—whether it will support him or let him drift—while industry and advertising collaborate in a fierce survival *fight* for markets. The worker measures his fluctuating *security* in terms of the steadiness of his job, advertising in terms of the *steadiness* of its billings: worker employment seems no more fickle and *uncertain* than advertising accounts, as they *shift around* from one agency to another.

WHAT'S TO BE DONE?

What shall we do? The ideal might seem to be to resocialize all these men, but this is obviously impossible. Ideally we should send them all to a "truth school" where, under the direction of wise and benevolent philosophers of the old tradition, they would have classes in (1) the difference between pecuniary and traditional truth; (2) the nature of values and their social function; (3) the nature of human dignity: problems of human feelings and why they should not be exploited; the importance of shame, female and other; problems in human degradation (self and other). It is unlikely, however, that such retraining would accomplish much. Furthermore, advertising is self-selective, so that youngsters with a traditional ethical sense avoid it; as late as September 20, 1961 Thomas B. Adams, president of the Campbell-Ewald Company, a big Detroit agency, was " 'shocked' at the degree to which promising young men were shunning the advertising profession because they believed it 'dishonorable.' "[1] Those that do not believe it dishonorable can only be young people perfectly socialized to the corrupt system, who will enthusiastically practice the pecuniary ethic of legal innocence. Thus the dishonesties and distortions of advertising are bound to be self-renewing. The most we can expect in the long run, therefore, is some diminution of unlawfulness, some sparking up of the campaigns in order to eliminate dullness and repetition, and more elaborate and whimsical art work—for example, a larger, cuter and more intensely *green* green giant advertising Green Giant vegetables; better looking, more tastefully dressed women occupying more space in advertisements for cosmetics; more realistic and more carefully color-photographed children poring over encyclopedias, et cetera.

Spontaneous moral regeneration is thus impossible for advertising because it does not know what the problem is and is self-selective in recruitment of personnel. Furthermore, since business competition will grow more intense (projected expenditures for advertising are about $25 billion by 1970), the chances of self-regulation are illusory. In view of the increasing competition and the expanding operations of advertising, greatly increased budgets of the FDA, FTC, and FCC should be countermoves against advertising's strong inherent tendency to misrepresent. Federal regulatory agencies, however, find it difficult to deal effectively with anything but legal dishonesty. It seems possible, however, to set up, within the FCC a division, the function of which would be perusal of the *non-legal* aspects of the commercial uses of the

[1] *New York Times*, September 20, 1961.

mass media. If such a unit were to take a project a year or a subject matter a year—toys, women's magazines, cosmetics—and publish its findings, it would have a tremendous effect on advertising through exercising a moral force, bringing the attention of the public to the nature of the corrosive influence. Such publication would be a kind of textbook of clean advertising practice which, over the years, might gradually re-educate the older generation of advertising men while providing fundamental principles to younger personnel. It would have the further effect, through naming agencies and products, of keeping the young job-seeking generation out of companies responsible for copy that is nauseating, insulting, or merely legally innocent.

The fact that advertising expenditures are running currently at 12 billion dollars yearly and will soon double bears repetition, for such enormous expenditures in the mass media exercise great pressure on the morals of the country. It is common knowledge that advertising firms and their clients, in bending the mass media almost exclusively to pecuniary ends, have come to play an important *regulatory* role and have, therefore, usurped the functions of Federal regulatory agencies. The least the Government can do is treat advertising itself as a public utility, and regulate it accordingly.

POSTSCRIPT: A LATE RECOVERY

By 1962, with unregenerate bumptiousness, advertising had decided that the best defense was to admit everything and declare that everything was good. Mr. William D. Tyler, executive vice-president of Benton & Bowles and co-chairman of the Joint Committee for the Improvement of Advertising Content, challenged all critics in a voice of brass. Advertising, he declared,[1] reflects our society more accurately than anything else does.

Esthetes and apologists can rail at its vulgarity, its brashness, its aggressiveness, its insistence, its lack of cultural values, its crass commercialism, its loudness, and its single-mindedness— but let them rail, he contended.

These are the qualities "that have built the nation," Mr. Tyler said. "They are qualities of virility."

[1] As reported in the *New York Times,* December 27, 1961.

The agency executive went on: "This is not to say that advertising should glory in vulgarity. But let's face up to the fact that frank and honest materialism is not a weakness. It is a symptom of strength. So if advertising reflects us as vulgarly virile, let's not blame advertising. Let's change it, but not blame it. Because the mirror does not lie. And let's accept it as a lusty fact of life, not necessarily admirable, but nothing to wring your hands about either."

4: The United States and the Soviet Union: Some Economic and Social Consequences of a Twentieth-Century Nightmare

The nation which indulges toward another an habitual hatred or an habitual fondness is in some degree a slave. It is a slave to its animosity or to its affection, either of which is sufficient to lead it astray from its duty and interest.

GEORGE WASHINGTON

THE MOST IMPORTANT SINGLE FACT IN AMERICAN HISTORY since the Revolution and the Civil War is the pathogenic fear of the Soviet Union. Over a period of nearly twenty years it has distorted our economy and our traditional attitude toward freedom, cut us off from trade with half the world, and undermined our gold reserves. For sheer dynamic power this dread has no parallel in our past.

Let us consider these problems first in the context of the armaments race.

ARMAMENTS[1]

> *. . . a large number of giant corporations*
> *obtain up to 100 per cent of their business*
> *solely from defense procurement.*
>
> EA. p. 7[2]

Most obvious among the fear-engendered phases of our current life is the armaments race, for this has brought it about that nearly two-thirds of the expenditures of Government are for arms procurement and for maintenance of the military establishment. When one realizes that in 1947 a group of experts projecting our military budget for 1960 could not imagine expenditures beyond $6 billion[3] at 1940 prices (about $10.2 billion at 1960 prices), whereas today they are estimated at about $55 billion,[4] one surmises what happened: the projection was based on the assumption that *"some form of international arrangement for peace will be operating on a fairly stable basis,"*[5] because the experts could not believe that mankind would ever drive itself to war again. Wishful thinking and national unwillingness to tolerate the idea of a new war put a delusive end to the traditional bellicosity of Western man.

When Alexis de Tocqueville wrote *Democracy in America*, he was able to say the following about us:

> The same interests, the same fears, the same passions
> which deter democratic nations from revolutions, deter
> them also from war; the spirit of military glory and the spirit

[1] Much of what is said in this section is derived from the following U. S. Government sources: "Economic Aspects of Military Procurement and Supply." Report of the Subcommittee on Defense Procurement.1960(EA); Department of Defense Appropriation Bill 1962(DA 1962); Report of the House Subcommittee for Special Investigations.1960(SI); Availability of Information from Federal Departments and Agencies. 27th Report by the Committee on Government Operations.1958(AI); *Export Control.* 54th Quarterly Report by the Secretary of Commerce.1960(EC)

[2] EA, DA, SI, etc., are code letters for the reports mentioned in the previous note.

[3] In *America's Needs and Resources.* J. Frederic Dewhurst and Associates. New York: The Twentieth Century Fund, 1947, p. 500.

[4] Text of President Kennedy's Message and Budget Analysis. *New York Times,* January 19, 1962.

[5] *America's Needs and Resources,* p. 480.

of revolution are weakened at the same time and by the same causes. The ever-increasing numbers of men of property— lovers of peace, the growth of personal wealth *which war so rapidly consumes*, the mildness of manners, the gentleness of heart, those tendencies to pity which are engendered by the equality of conditions, that coolness of understanding which renders men comparatively insensible to the violent and poetical excitement of arms—all these causes concur to quench the military spirit. [Italics supplied.]

Tocqueville could not imagine a nation where property is *revived* and *increased* by war; this has been another American revolution. It is so well known that today our economy responds euphorically to war or threat of it that the Russians attribute to our statesmen a deliberate policy of war in order to avoid economic collapse. But *this* is not our problem; rather that since American industry expands and unemployment declines in the presence of a war atmosphere, the usual economic and emotional deterrents to war do not exist for us. Thus since *fear of war is anesthetized by heightened economic well-being, we become accustomed to living comfortably under conditions of impending annihilation.* That is why a decision to go to war, or to the "brink," can be accepted much more readily than if the economy were placed in jeopardy by war. The fact that the Soviets are in the opposite situation has helped to save us, for since their way of life is threatened by war, they lack the temptations we have. The reader need only imagine what his own attitude toward war would be if mere *preparation* for it meant that his clothes would become tattered, he would taste meat only once a week, he would have no butter or coffee, gasoline would be available only once a week and in two-gallon allotments and he would have to wait in line for it; that if his car needed repairs he would have to make them himself or wait weeks to get the job done, etc. In such a case even the most warlike statesmen would think a thousand times before announcing the possibility of war. The fact that war-*fear* is partly narcotized by consumption-*euphoria* habituates us to living with The Great Fear.

Basic expenditures for the military establishment are not, of course, a complete measure of the dependence of the economy on

fear. Every dollar spent directly on military requirements stimulates the metals, ceramics, electronics, chemicals, and other industries that supply them, and their payrolls keep the consumer
industries booming. Meanwhile, since diversion of productive capacity to production-for-fear removes much industrial potential
from other possible fields, we have to rely on other countries for
things we might be making ourselves. If billions spent by Government on armaments research were spent on nonwar research,
it would be possible, though not convenient, to deluge the world
with goods instead of being reduced, as we are now, to an export
level currently running at a laughable 4.1 per cent of gross national product.[1] If industrial firms, instead of shifting to production-for-fear when in economic difficulties, were encouraged to go
into other—exportable—lines our balance of payments would not
be so chronically bad as to induce in us a kind of gold hemophilia.
Young and adventurous men gravitate nowadays to war industry,
for that is where money is made most rapidly.[2] Thus their talents
for planning and organization are not directed outward, but inward, musing on death and the profit in it.

Dr. Walter H. Heller, chairman of the President's Council of
Economic Advisers, put the matter as follows:

> Other countries have benefited . . . from systematically
> investing a bigger share of their gross national product in
> plant expansion and modernization. With less of their total
> income going to military and foreign-aid expenditures, they
> have been able to spend more on automation and other
> forms of industrial improvement without squeezing their
> output of consumer goods.[3]

It is not only a laughable export level from which we suffer,
but a growing vulnerability to imports also, for as diversion to
production-for-fear expands and income rises, production of some

[1] "Exports in relation to U. S. product, 1959. . . ." World Trade Information Service, Statistical Reports, Part 3, No. 60–30. U. S. Department of
Commerce.

[2] In a short and incomplete list of corporations occupied in defense industry the EA report gives some examples of "per cent of profit on capital."
Some examples are: North American Aviation, 802 (1954); Lockheed Aircraft, 238 (1953); Boeing Airplane, 110 (1954); Glenn Martin Co., 81
(1954).

[3] *New York Times*, May 8, 1961.

consumer goods can remain at high domestic price levels. We then become more fearful than ever of imports of "cheap" foreign goods—cars, steel, cameras, radios, textiles, clothes, typewriters, and so on. Thus while some manufacturers press upon the American consumer because of need to unload the fruits of their high-priced expanding production, others fly fearfully from him to engage in production-for-fear.

Meanwhile, as we import more than we should and export less than we might, we are compelled to enter deals with any institution or nation that will help correct our loss of exports and gold reserves,[1] and we, consequently, run the risk of appearing before the world either as bullies, suppliants, or weasels. As pride retreats before anxiety, we become fearful of the decline of our foreign "image." You cannot have one obsessive fear without having a thousand!

Finally, the growth in economic power of firms dealing in production-for-fear[2] makes it difficult for others to obtain financing; and since they could play an important role in export, such difficulty is disastrous to them and to the economy. Furthermore, since fear (i.e., defense) contracts are sound investments, banks lend more eagerly to companies having them than to others. The situation is made even more trying by the fact that domestic loans are more readily collectable than foreign ones; banks more easily lend to companies working for defense than to exporters shipping to troubled Latin America, Asia, and the Near East. Domestic fear is a better investment than foreign uncertainty. If anyone should ask me how to invest his money, I would say, "Invest in domestic fear. Fear and dollars grow together like root and branch."

The armaments race has placed the development of such a large segment of American industry so firmly in the hands of the military establishment that even the ecological pattern of industrial development is subject to its decisions. For example:

---

[1] In this connection see "Germany: Chronology of Monetary Developments 1960–1961," dittoed report, U. S. Treasury, Office of International Finance; and especially also *Monthly Report of the Deutsche Bundesbank.* June 1960. Frankfort (Main), Germany, p. 9 *et seq.* In these reports there is set forth a detailed analysis of the steps taken by Bonn to correct our loss of gold reserves.

[2] In 1958 the 10 largest American companies received 37 per cent of the total contracts for fear-products. (EA, p. 26)

For the fiscal year 1959, the allocation to California was
. . . 24.3 per cent of the total [military procurement]. By
comparison, the next four largest recipients were [New
York, 11.1; Texas 6.0; Massachusetts 5:3; Ohio 4.] So the
highest five States had 51.4 per cent of the total and the
lowest 37 as much as the single highest.

By contrast also, some of the States with heavy areas of
unemployment had these percentages of the total: Pennsylvania, 3.1 per cent; West Virginia, 0.1 per cent; Tennessee,
0.5 per cent; Kentucky, 0.2 per cent. (EA, p. 37)

Moreover companies having the heaviest armaments contracts
also employ the largest number of retired admirals and generals.[1]
The Great Fear has welded industry and the armed forces. This
union, however, is not destined to be stable or easy, for since the
games theory-computor-and-symbolic logic boys with Ph.D's in
mathematics, physics, chemistry, and economics are increasingly
planning weapons and strategies that the military cannot, guidance of warfare itself is slipping away from the military under
the impact of The Great Fear.[2]

Since the consequences of this are revolutionary, a little time
ought to be spent on Sir Solly Zuckerman's ideas. He says:

. . . the amount of military input into modern weapons
systems, and particularly complex strategic systems, is declining rapidly, with a complementary increase in the technical input provided by the non-military man. This change
is associated with increasing specialization of single-purpose
weapons systems. By "military input" one means, of course,
the fruits of actual military experience. The simplest illustration of this proposition is that no military genius or ex-

[1] In July 1960, for example, General Dynamics, the corporation having the
largest per cent of armaments contracts (by dollars), had 27 retired generals
and admirals on its payrolls. The *total* number of retired officers of all ranks
employed by General Dynamics, however, was about 200. Its closest competitor was United Aircraft, with 171. The actual figure for General Dynamics in the SI report is 186, but not all questionnaires were returned. (EA,
p. 26; EI, pp. 167–170 and attached Appendix 4: "Statistical breakdown of
retired officers in defense industries.")

[2] (EA, pp. 32–37) But see also Sir Solly Zuckerman's fundamental paper,
"Judgment and Control in Modern Warfare" in *Foreign Affairs,* January
1962.

perience has gone into the conception or design of I.C.B.M.s.
If one wishes to push it that far, there is no logical need for
such a weapon to be deployed by the military, as opposed to
some other agent of government. If the name Moscow, or
New York, or London, or Paris were written on each
I.C.B.M., the missiles might be deployed and operated by
the firms which produced them. The complex operations of
the U. S. National Aereonautics and Space Administration
(NASA) are not military operations, even though the men
who go into space may all be military men.[1]

What this means is not so much that the military are being pushed
out of war, but that civilians are being sucked into it; that the
best civilian minds, once drawn into the military *Walpurgisnacht*
are so influenced by the environment that they cannot think of
peace. In former epochs one always drew a line between military
and civilian populations; but no more. Under the rain of bombs,
civilians gained the privilege of dying like soldiers; now we have
obtained the right to think like them. Is it possible? Is it possible
that in the late Twentieth Century *the outcome of the liberation
of the mind by science is merely its imprisonment by fear?*
Imagine a moving mass of sheep discoursing on science and ap-
praising the stars, while bleatlessly falling into an abyss they
do not see!

Attracted by salaries paid by companies working on war contracts, and by the much higher than government or university pay
offered by 350 nonprofit corporations[2] engaged in military research, the sharpest (though not the deepest) minds are drawn
into the war net, the net of fear. This means that what conscience
remains to scientists is put to sleep by high pay and "fun in
games"—the war game. And I *mean* fun, for if ever there was
scientific writing that breathed the high joy of fun-in-games it is
writing of the weapons-systems ilk.[3] There is no reason, of course,

[1] *Ibid.* Sir Solly Zuckerman is Scientific Advisor to the Minister of Defense and Chairman of the Defense Research Policy Committee, London.

[2] *New York Times,* August 6, 1961. Article: "Kennedy Orders Research
Review."

[3] A good example is Herman Kahn's *On Thermonuclear War* (Princeton:
Princeton University Press, 1960). Dr. Kahn, the jacket says, "has been a
member of the RAND Corporation [a nonprofit organization specializing in
weapons systems and military strategy] since 1948. During the past twelve

why the Russians should not be playing the same kind of games with their computors. The destruction of Hiroshima and Nagasaki has made the contemplation of greater holocausts easy.

The following is an account of the RAND[1] Corporation, most famous casino of fun-in-death games in the country. It is by the sea in Santa Monica, California, the state with the highest percentage of war contracts.

RAND Corporation Furnishes Brain Power for the Air Force[2]

The RAND Corporation is a non-profit institution, which has been called "the Air Force's think factory" . . . and 90 per cent of its work is still done for and supported by the Air Force. . . .

Here 500 scientists and 400 aides pursue their studies in a thought-provoking atmosphere overlooking the Pacific. Protected by security measures as strict as the Pentagon's, sport-shirted scientists informally develop theories and recommendations that tomorrow may become the nation's basic defense policies.

"Get the best brains and turn them loose on the problems of the future." [That is to say, war.]

That, in essence, was the instruction given by the late General H. H. Arnold and his aides to F. R. Collbohm [the first chairman].

The RAND Corporation was established in 1948 with the financial support of the Ford Foundation . . . [Military philanthropy, so to speak.]

There is no such thing as a casual visitor at RAND. Visits are by specific appointment and all visitors are tagged by plant security officers in the reception lobby. . . .

Wastebaskets are carefully checked and contents burned nightly. . . . Classified papers must be locked up in safes overnight, and security officers continually remind overly absorbed scientists of the fact. . . .

The flexibility and initiative that RAND encourages makes recruiting relatively simple. RAND attracts the cream of scien-

---

years, which he spent in studying the intricate and critical relationships between weapons and strategy, he has served as a consultant to the Gaither Committee, the Atomic Energy Commission, and the Office of Civil and Defense Mobilization."

[1] RAND = Research and Development.

[2] From the *New York Times*, May 22, 1960. Copyright by *The New York Times*. Reprinted by permission.

tific graduate schools despite offering new Ph.D's less than $10,000 a year, considerably below the going scale in industry.

To some extent, RAND gets the visionary type who, in the words of one close observer, "wouldn't be caught dead in a factory or aircraft plant. . . ."

Typical of the younger leaders at RAND is Robert W. Buchheim, 35-year-old head of the aeroastronautics department. The program he directs seeks, among other things, new metals for missiles and improved defense systems against constantly improving intercontinental weapons. . . . Mr. Buchheim was project engineer for the Snark missile guidance system at North American Aviation before joining RAND in 1954. . . .

Richard Bellman, a wide-ranging mathematician, is the Renaissance man type. He is the founder of dynamic programming, a mathematical theory of decision-making with the aid of highly sophisticated computors. . . .

War *games* play an important part in RAND formulations. *Game* theories frequently evolve into doctrines of military strategy. *Playing games* simulating attack conditions provides answers to such problems as how to supply threatened fighter bases around the globe, and how to defend cities against bomber or missile strikes or even satellite bombings. . . .

RAND specialists, particularly engineers and economists, are constantly on the move, consulting with Air Force heads in the Pentagon and at bases everywhere. RAND also maintains a staff of thirty in Washington and has a reserve of 300 consultants. . . .

Their . . . reflection and discussion with colleagues occasionally results in some sharp updating of theory and policy by Washington politicians, not just the Air Force. [Italics supplied.]

Cultural maximizers and élites impel a culture toward its goals, and in our culture the chemists, physicists, mathematicians, and engineers are cultural maximizers. Inasmuch as they are engaged extensively in the manufacture, deployment, and fantasy of death, it follows that they are the élite of death, and that what is maximized in our culture is the goal of death. The seerlike insight of Freud has therefore been proved correct, for in *Beyond the Pleasure Principle* he assumed a "death instinct" that drove all men ineluctably toward death. My only difference with him would be that while he thought the impulse to death was instinctive, I believe it culturally determined.

THE SPECTRE OF DISARMAMENT

It is generally agreed that the greatly en-
larged public sector [in the economy]
since World War II, resulting from heavy
defense expenditures, has provided ad-
ditional protection against depressions,
since this sector is not responsive to con-
traction in the private sector and provides
a sort of buffer or balance wheel in the
economy.[1] *[Emphasis supplied.]*

Though a politician may think once before he allocates money to the military establishment, he appoints panels and committees and establishes agencies to inquire anxiously into the economic consequences of disarmament. The latest, the panel that produced the above quotation, having provided a properly sponsored theory of the *absolute economic necessity* of armaments, ought to be made known by their names, for they constitute a kind of inner priesthood of arcane economic lore.

Members of the Panel

Emile Benoit, Chairman; Associate Professor of International Business, Columbia University, and Director, Research Program on Economic Adjustments to Disarmament, New York, N.Y.

Blanche Bernstein, Bureau of International Organization Affairs, Department of State, Washington, D.C.

Prentice N. Dean, Chief, Foreign Economic Policy Division, Office of the Assistant Secretary of Defense, Department of Defense, Washington, D.C.

Marvin Hoffenberg, Military Economics and Costing Division, Research Analysis Corporation,[2] Bethesda, Md.

Richard R. Nelson, Council of Economic Advisers, Washington, D.C.

[1] In *Economic Impacts of Disarmament*, United States Arms Control and Disarmament Agency, Publication 2. Economic Series 1. United States Government Printing Office, 1962, p. 13.

[2] Must be one of those 350 nonprofit corporations set up by the Department of Defense in order to get better brains than exist in Government. See *supra*.

Robert M. Solow, Council of Economic Advisers, Washington, D.C.

Robert F. Steadman, Economic Adjustment Adviser, Office of the Assistant Secretary of Defense, Department of Defense, Washington, D.C.

Nat Weinberg, Director of Special Projects and Economic Analysis, United Automobile, Aircraft, and Agricultural Implement Workers of America, Detroit, Michigan.

When a panel of economic cardinals announces that expenditures for death are "a sort of . . . balance wheel in the economy," we must believe. When they affirm that death stands at the balance wheel I am prepared to believe the unbelievable. Now, finally, in the face of all previous denials, truth has been received, and Death has won pecuniary sanctification. It is long overdue. Saint Death, I salute you! Here in the United States *death sustains life.*

The findings of the panel project economic, political, and psychological uncertainties that must make a statesman hesitate before undertaking disarmament.[1] Thus the democratic process, when entangled in a web of fear, becomes its own enemy; for who, wishing to retain the affections of the people would take the economic risks? The path to increased armaments and industrial stability is clear; the road to peace unclear and improbable. The improbability of disarmament resides essentially in the "balance wheel" theory, the "deadly adversary" theory, and in the "blueprint" characteristics of modern warfare.

I have already pointed out that the "balance wheel" theory makes disarmament impossible. The view of the Soviet Union as a deadly adversary that at any moment may destroy us also makes real disarmament unlikely; and suggests that instead of getting rid of our arms we will merely rest on them. This attitude of suspicion, of peace-with-anxiety, of watching the adversary constantly out of the corner of the eye, produces ambiguities even

---

[1] Professor Benoit, however, in a letter (February 27, 1962) to me, says the following: "I believe it would be possible to avoid economic disorder even at a much faster rate [than 12 years] of disarmament if appropriate measures were taken." The reader is urged to consult Gerard Piel's thoughtful paper "On the Feasibility of Peace" in *Science,* February 23, 1962.

in those most optimistic about the possibility of disarmament. Consider first the following from *Economic Impacts of Disarmament:*

> . . . in a period of disarmament the United States would be *glad* to adopt any measures of a defense character [i.e., civil defense] which would *increase* its physical security and not be incompatible with the disarmament agreement. They might be viewed as a desirable form of insurance against possible breakdowns in the disarmament program, especially during a period before all nations were participating. Nor would such a program reduce the *deterrent power* of the Peace Force; on the contrary, *it alone* could render the exercise of such power credible.[1] [Italics supplied.]

This matter is explained a little more fully in Professor Benoit's letter. Speaking of his belief that disarmament could go faster than actually proposed in *Economic Impacts of Disarmament,* he says:

> The reason for the slower pace of disarmament is exclusively to make it possible that each stage be adequately inspected and that the required international police and deterrent forces be established.

I would urge that an attitude of "peace-with-deterrence," of "peace-with-defense" is unregenerate dread, a twentieth-century version of an ancient condition of man in which adversaries never gave themselves up to peace but merely accepted a truce of exhaustion and suspicion. An armed armistice is not disarmament; nor, as a matter of fact, does *Economic Impacts* envision American expenditures on armaments at less than 10 billion dollars by 1977.

While *Economic Impacts* projects a drop in expenditures for research and development from 21 billion dollars in 1965 to 1.5 billion by 1977, a billion and a half dollars is still a great deal of money. Taken together with the 9 billion dollars contemplated in 1977 for building up the NASA (National Aeronautics and Space Administration) program, it would permit the Govern-

[1] *Op. cit.,* p. 28, fn. 3.

ment to maintain the brains of the military establishment—for example, some of the nonprofit corporations—on a stand-by basis, working on blueprints for new weapons and strategy. The seed of the fear would, in such a case, merely remain in a state of tillering—the beginnings.

To a people already accustomed to a military budget of 55 billion dollars, reduction of expenditures to 10 billion dollars must look like an enormous cut; but when we realize that in 1932 total expenditures for the military establishment were only about a billion and a half dollars[1] one can see that the culture of war and death has brought such vast and unconscious changes in our imagination and world view that 10 billion dollars seems a small sum. It must also seem "natural" to people who have lived a nightmare to project their lives into the future as a nightmare, so that a budget for "civil defense" in 1977 when, presumably, peace is maximal, is identical with the budget for 1965!

It thus is unlikely that those who have learned to fear would learn to disarm or, put another way, it is hard for a people that has thrived on fear to live without it. In a second letter (March 10, 1962) Professor Benoit writes:

> The balance wheel has been created not by defense expenditures as such but by a larger program of public expenditures than would otherwise have occurred. The balance wheel in effect would be equally useful if it came from non-defense public expenditures. The danger is solely that with a reduction in defense expenditures *it will be hard to induce the Congress to provide non-defense public expenditures of anywhere near comparable magnitude.* [Italics supplied.]

Fundamentally, my reasoning should be correct regardless of whether we ever solve our "Russian problem" or not; for the theoretical point is that the institutions, values, and emotions of a culture are so amalgamated that fundamental changes become almost unthinkable. The amalgam becomes so much a part of

[1] This sum is obtained by taking the 1932 figure for "Military forces," which includes all expenditures outside of veterans' pensions, and multiplying it by two in order to account for price increases. The source of the data is *America's Needs and Resources, op. cit.*, pp. 468 and 480.

every person that it determines his slightest and his greatest sensitivities. The fact that Congress is reluctant to spend great sums on anything but death simply means that the habit of responding to fear is easy, whereas a response to other stimuli is difficult.

"Don't Convince 'em; Scare 'em" writes James Reston in describing Congress' propensity to respond readily only to fear:

> . . . the Administration has done what it always does when it goes to Capitol Hill. It has appealed to fear; fear of Soviet competition, fear of a savage "trade war" with the European Common Market countries, fear of a loss of export markets and of jobs if the trade bill is not passed, and of chaos and communism in the underdeveloped nations if the foreign aid bill is not passed.
>
> *Maybe this was inevitable.* It has got so you can't get money for a school or a road from Congress without arguing that failure to build them will mean the triumph of communism for a hundred years. . . .
>
> . . . The question now is whether the Administration is going to concentrate on scaring the Congress or convincing it.[1] [Italics supplied.]

A nation that will respond only to fear cannot govern itself wisely, for it has no destiny but fear, while its overshadowing goal is to defend itself.

INTERNATIONAL RELATIONS

We can count as fortunate consequences of The Great Fear the fact that we devote much of our wealth to raising the miserable peoples of the world from the dirt and hunger into which they were born, and the fact that the populations of Latin America, Asia, and Africa whom we formerly treated with contempt, are now assuming human shape in our eyes. Under the stimulus of The Great Fear *nigger, chink, jap,* and *greaser* are slowly disappearing from our language (although, as we know, *nigger* will probably be the last to join the junk heap of obsolete American slander).

[1] *New York Times*, March 14, 1962.

Throughout history *Homo sapiens* has tended to reward his friends and punish his enemies. As a nation we follow this course as truly today as mankind in the dawn of culture. Today, using the definitions "red" and "non-red" we reward and punish the underprivileged of the earth in their diseased and famished millions. What will become of us on the day those we punish become our equals? The "starve the reds" amendment to the 1961 agriculture act cannot but grind forever into the minds of the Chinese, begging to be allowed to exist on 1500 calories a day, the conviction that the United States wants them to die. If China follows the "hard Stalinist line" toward us, it is certainly nourished by famine.

In the long run an obsessive fear irrationally divides the world into what can be touched and what is taboo. It is difficult to believe that such a syndrome could grip a modern, enlightened nation. It is hard to believe—but it is also true—that our foreign policy is scarcely more enlightened than that of the redskins!

CONSUMPTION AUTARCHY AND THE RESTRICTION OF TRADE

High tariffs, economic isolation from the Communist countries, and the fact that much of the non-Communist world is too poor to buy from us, have made it necessary to consume at home most of what we produce. This is *relative consumption autarchy*. The growth of advertising is the institutional response to this, and the era of self-indulgence and fun is the emotional one.

But consumption autarchy is not a viable form in an industrial nation, and billions of dollars have gone abroad looking for quicker and higher profits in countries where markets are expanding more rapidly than ours. The resulting loss of gold has become a constant headache because of the threat to the value of the dollar. When we cut ourselves off from Communist trade we open our own veins.

Thus we come to one more delusion created by The Great Fear—the delusion of the effectiveness of economic warfare. It is delusive on two counts: first, it is not hurting the Russians; second, we are the only ones who think it important. Let us consider this problem further through examination of some newspaper reports. I begin with a dispatch from the *New York Times*:

United States sales to the [Communist] bloc countries last year came to $193,000,000—and three quarters of it to Poland[1]—compared with Western European sales to the Communists of $2,400,000,000. The great majority of the European sales are manufactured goods such as metals, machinery and chemicals. Europe's more generous export policy toward the Communists is well established, and has long been a frustration to this country's efforts at restriction.

When the Kennedy Administration took office, its makers of trade policy were thinking in the direction of easing restrictions, because *the restrictions were having no important economic effect,*[2] *and because the easing might improve relations with the Soviet Union.* Those thoughts came to abrupt halt at midsummer in the heat of the Berlin crisis and mounting pressure from Capitol Hill.[3] [Italics supplied.]

Considering the fact that "the restrictions were having no important economic effect" this angry hitting back could only be a phantom blow, more harmful to ourselves than to the Russians. I continue with some more dispatches from the *Times.*

. . . West European countries . . . had refused United States requests to curtail the granting of credits to the Soviet Union. Italy . . . avoided giving credits and, instead . . . put up a five-year $100,000,000 guarantee against losses by Italian exporters to the Soviet bloc.

Italy was . . . furnishing material for a Soviet pipeline to Europe from Black Sea oil ports in exchange for Soviet oil priced at about half the Persian Gulf price posted by Western oil companies.[4]

Meanwhile, even in the presence of an oil glut, American oil companies were raising their prices and were being sued successfully by the Attorney General for price-fixing.

The British Vickers-Armstrong organization has received a contract amounting in value to more than £14,000,000 to

---

[1] Mostly food and one plant for making galvanized steel.
[2] See also, *Soviet Economic Power* by Robert W. Campbell. Boston: Houghton-Mifflin, 1960, pp. 47 *et. seq.*
[3] *New York Times,* Sept. 25, 1961.
[4] *New York Times,* Feb. 10, 1961.

supply the Soviet Union with a complete factory for producing Nylon-66, a form of nylon used primarily for technical purposes. With this and other Vickers-Armstrong
equipment, the Soviet Union will soon be able to have an
integrated process for nylon production, from output of raw
materials to the final product.

The contracts signed with major Italian factories provide
for delivery to the Soviet Union of equipment for plants to
produce menthanol, acetylene, ethylene, titanium dioxide,
cellulose and other products.[1]

Validated export licenses are required for shipments of the last
five chemicals to the Soviet Union.[2]

Of late . . . the $500,000,000-a-year ferro alloy industry
has run into some stiff problems. Imports have been increasing. Recent expansions by domestic manufacturers have
given rise to problems of overcapacity.[3]

The Positive List of commodities—those for which a license is
required for exports to certain countries, including the Soviet
Union—contains seven ferro alloys (Schedule B, Nos. 62230-
62290). There are also additional ferro alloys which require a
validated license for shipment to the Soviet Union.

Italian shipbuilders were gratified today to learn of the
agreement signed in Moscow yesterday whereby Italian
yards will build six 48,000-ton tankers for the Soviet
Union. . . .[4]

The chairman of the . . . Federal Maritime Commission
said that the Soviet Union was having 200 merchant ships
built in nine countries.[5]

[1] Ibid., June 4, 1961.
[2] Letter to me, March 6, 1962 from Geraldine S. DePuy, Director, Operations Division, U.S. Department of Commerce, Bureau of International Programs, Office of Export Control. Export Control Office File 7340-HLF. A
fairly complete statement of American trade policy toward the Communist-
bloc countries is contained in Export Control, 62nd quarterly report by the
Secretary of Commerce. This report contains the "Positive List" of commodities for which export licenses are required to Communist-bloc countries.
[3] New York Times, August 14, 1960.
[4] Ibid., Sept. 23, 1961.
[5] Ibid., Oct. 14, 1961.

Japan has signed an agreement to export some 30,000 tons of steel sheets valued at $4,720,000 to the Soviet Union. . . . In turn, the Russians are to sell Japan some 60,000 tons of pig iron valued at about $3,000,000.

Japan's trade with the Soviet bloc countries last year was more than double the average of the previous three years, the Japanese, Soviet and East European Trade Association reported today.[1]

On February 23, 1962 the *New York Times* reported the completion of a pipeline from the Soviet Union to Czechoslovakia. The United States had embargoed steel pipe to the Soviet Union; much had been obtained from Italy, and the sections of pipe were welded together over the 260 miles by automatic spiral pipe-welding machines bought from West Germany. "The export of any pipe-welding machinery for use in the construction of a pipeline in an Eastern European Soviet bloc country, would have to have the specific approval of" the Department of Commerce.[2]

There is little reason to believe that we are impeding Soviet industrial growth; on the other hand, there is no doubt that we are impeding our own and furthering that of Western Europe and Japan as they pick up the business we turn down. In this way we render our allies "hidden" economic aid. The Soviet Union has repeatedly pressed us to renew trade with her, but we have refused. It is time to abandon our delusions as *the first step toward peace*.

The Great Fear resembles a true obsession: like all obsessions its perceptions and anxiety-reducing measures transgress the bounds of reality; fly in the face of the facts; have widely ramifying, unanticipated consequences; and, most important, are self-destructive over the long run. A person with an obsession takes steps that give him *immediate* relief from his anxiety, seizing upon what seems at the moment to be the element that immediately threatens his survival, only to discover later that he has chosen wrongly. A person in such a state is driven also to bizarre ways of protecting himself. For example, his under-

[1] *Ibid.*, Feb. 9, 1962.
[2] Personal communication to me from the Department.

lying anxiety may find partial expression in a fear of red. He then not only avoids all red objects—finding himself, for example, in acute terror of stoplights—but he also avoids all people whose names begin with *R, E,* or *D,* or contain the syllable *-red,* for example, *Red*mond, Alf*red,* Wilf*red.* He seeks to protect himself further by removing all red objects from his room, even, perhaps, extending his activities to mixtures of red such as orange or purple. Ultimately, if he does not find his way to a psychiatrist, he becomes afraid of going out for fear of being driven home, wild with terror, by the sight of any object that even suggests red. This is madness.

The American public has been so thoroughly educated to fear that statesmen think they would risk their political future by coming to an accommodation with the Russians on the only firm basis possible—the resumption of trade. But without it disarmament is only a dream, for we cannot continue economic *warfare* and expect that disarmament will bring military *peace.*

INFORMATION

In all cultures the part to which people commit most of their resources is the part where the main components of that culture meet. At such core units in a culture conflicts are most acute, and the intellectual gifts and drives of the cultural maximizers are most exercised. The search for such a core unit in our political structure suggests the Department of Defense, for that is the organ of Government that spends most, that utilizes national resources most, and that occupies most scientific and technical talent. Charged as it is with protection against The Great Fear, the Department of Defense, in all its ramifying activities, is the agency of Government most under the sway of the national dread, and hence most controlling of information and most permeated by the drives, the conflicts, and the irritations inherent in the culture as a whole.

In 1955 interference by the Department of Defense in the dissemination of information about its activities had reached such proportions that the House of Representatives established a Special Committee on Government Information in order to study the problem. Hearings, beginning in 1956, extended into 1959, and produced almost 3000 pages of data and a report.[1]

Considering the number of services contained in the Department, one would expect competition to be acute among them, and that the Department would resemble business in the competitiveness and secrecy between these subdivision. Since each service was animated by its own loyalties and by its own convictions about how to defend us against The Great Fear, competition was exacerbated by a sense of mission. As the anxiety generated in this way drove the different services to seek public support for their views and to make derogatory statements about one another, it became a question of whether, for example, the Navy was more interested in defeating Russia or the Army. This intra-Departmental competition became an important source of information leaks, for in order to present the claims of one branch of the armed services to a national audience, its members would inform the press of their superior rights to develop a particular weapon. Journalists, of course, were eager to listen to the leaks because they made money for the paper and enhanced the status of the lucky reporter. By 1955, therefore, leaks had become such a source of embarrassment to the Department that it had developed a veritable "leak-anxiety" which expressed itself in the belief—unsubstantiated by careful investigation—that important documents had been "purloined."

In this way The Great Fear, competitiveness, self-advertising, and the achievement drive flowed together, piling little fears on top of big ones.

To the fear of leakage was now added the underlings' fear of releasing any information at all that might conceivably be interpreted as "embarrassing" to the Department or as giving aid and comfort to the enemy. In these circumstances every employee ran the risk of a surprise reprimand for releasing even the most innocuous information, and it therefore became a regular practice for Department workers in all echelons to stamp as "secret" or "confidential" documents that could have no imaginable value to the enemy. It was repeatedly brought out in the hearings that any employee who had his head screwed on right would sooner withhold a document than release it to the public,

[1] AI, *op. cit.*

for however harmless it might seem to him, there was no telling
when one side of the Pentagon might fall capriciously on him.
To the "aid and comfort to the enemy" deterrent was added,
meanwhile, the sensitivity of superiors to criticism by the press,
by Congress, by members of rival services, et cetera, so that it
soon began to appear as if, could the specks of dust on the
Pentagon desks sustain a stamp, they would have been stamped
"Top secret!" Thus anxiety begets anxiety in a self-reinforcing
cycle, until warehouses and libraries throughout the country were
bursting with "classified" documents and the country was becoming sealed off from its own history!

> The stipulation in Executive Order 10501 ordering that
> whenever practicable classified documents bear a date or
> event for subsequent declassification is being almost totally
> ignored. *Unless some operative system of declassification
> is developed in the near future, we may find ourselves com-
> pletely walled off from our past historical achievements as
> well as from future progress in basic science.* (AI, p. 117)
> [Italics in the original.]

> Mr. Coolidge [of the Coolidge Committee][1] testified that
> 6 billion documents were classified during World War II
> alone, and that the rate of classification had increased since
> then. (AI, p. 117)

> *Harvard* [the Widener Library] *finds itself . . . bur-
> dened with the cost of storing and protecting secret mate-
> rial which no one at Harvard can look at and which
> Harvard can't get declassified* [who'd take the chance? JH],
> *can't return to the Government, can't give away, and can't
> burn. At the same time, material which would be of value
> to scientists and scholars is padlocked beyond their reach.*
> (AI, p. 118). [Italics in the original.]

Contributing to the fearsome orientation of the Department
were features introduced directly from business. Since the Department handles millions of procurement contracts each year
(38 million between 1950 and 1959. See EA, p. vii), it must
employ businessmen who know about contracts. Furthermore,

---

[1] A special committee appointed to aid Congress in its investigation.

Government has taken the position that the best Secretaries—of Defense or otherwise—are businessmen. In addition, it is natural and proper that, in the presence of such extensive cooperation with business, and with businessmen swarming in Pentagon corridors, the Department should acquire the climate of a businessman's club. From the standpoint of this section, however, what is most interesting is the effects of the business *Weltanschauung* on information policy; for it is normal, in view of business's natural proclivity to withhold information from competitors and also from its own underlings, that the leakage-anxiety natural to business should find piquant expression in the Department of Defense. The matter was stated incisively in the AI report (p. 153):

> Men appointed to public office after a background in private business sometimes have failed to realize their new *responsibility* for maintaining a free flow of public information, especially *adverse* information. Self-serving secrecy, considered proper in personal affairs, has no place in Government. The public's *right to know* must be paramount, within the bounds of security, in the attitude of the public official. [Italics supplied.]

While it is obvious that if the public were informed of all the adversities of Government people would fall into irreversible anxiety and depression, we may pass over this to note that responsibility to the public and recognition of its "right to know" must appear bizarre to many businessmen, for a businessman has responsibility to his *business;* the customer—the public—has a right to know only what promotes business. In the Department of Defense the inherent tendencies of businessmen to keep information to themselves are intensified and readily legitimized by The Great Fear. An illustration from the world of business will make the matter clearer.

> Some [business] clients are suspicious of their [advertising] agencies. They want all sorts of marketing help from their agencies but they refuse to give them any information about sales or profits. They are fearful that this information will be leaked to competitors.[1]

[1] From statements by Barton A. Cummings, president of Compton Advertising, Inc. Quoted in the *New York Times,* February 28, 1962.

Thus business introduces into the heartbeat of a fearful nation the same self-destructive forces that threaten business. How could it be otherwise?

I have often wondered how well Franklin Roosevelt's statement that "The only thing we have to fear is fear itself" is understood. The case of the Department of Defense illustrates his meaning well, for there we see that fear is to be feared because it tends to paralyze action, thought, and Government. Yet more important, perhaps, than the institutionalization of fear in the Department, is the influence it exerts on *all* channels of information and on freedom of discussion. Consider, for example, the eighty-year-old woman lying with her sick heart at death's door in a nursing home, and her anxiety that her remark, "The country is going to the dogs," might be reported to "the authorities"; or my student who was afraid to write to the Department of Commerce for information on trade with the Soviet Union, although this information is published in the Department's bulletin, *Export Control.*

In order to be accepted in a culture one must accept or adopt an uncritical attitude toward its customs and its fears. In contemporary America whoever does not obsessively hate and fear the Soviet Union isolates himself, for public opinion (or, rather, the public dread) tolerates only a rigid, negative attitude. A consequence of this is unthinking acquiescence and extinction of all possibility of solving the underlying problem. When such fear is joined to the "tyranny of the majority" (as Tocqueville called it) and to the fortunes of political parties, extinction of fear becomes problematic. Since the fate of the political parties is tied to the will of the majority, and since the majority, drilled in fear, responds so readily and blindly to it, the easiest way to retain power is by maintaining the fear. When, in addition, fear leads directly to economic euphoria through expenditures for armaments, there is little hope for the emergence of new ideas.

Leaders who inspire their followers with fear of an external enemy become the prisoners of their followers, for once the life of the people becomes adapted to terror, the leaders can no longer change, even if they would. Immersed in a sea of terrified people, the leader becomes a captive of the general dread. He is dragged along by the current of his own actions as reflected to him by a terrified public.

Since fear, obsession, and isolation are directed by Government, and abetted by business, the press, the schools, the armed forces, and the lunatic right, it is clear that the existence of the Nightmare sustains a certain national character, a certain conception of man, and a certain view of the world. Central to our national character today must be fearfulness and a tendency to acquiesce. The anxiety latent in our insecure and competitive life has been rationalized—made real and specific—by the emergence of the Soviet Union as the contemporary Incarnation of fear. If ever an incarnate nightmare stalked our American earth it is Russia, and use of the Nightmare to call our survival in question makes the American soul flexible as wax, depriving a proud people of its power to think. Since in the mid-twentieth century obsessive fear of the Soviet Union is part of our survival neurosis, reliance on a fearful and acquiescent American public is at the base of many important Federal decisions. This fits our world view, primordial in its simplicity, as uncomplicated as the outlook of the forest nomad sitting, alert with fear, beside his midnight fire, listening for the stealthy footfall of the enemy. Having reduced the entire world to two essential categories, friend or foe, we have largely forgotten its great variety of human riches.

But the Soviet Union fears us as much as we fear them and therefore its internal and external policies are subject to comparable influences. Hungary, East Germany, and the Berlin wall are the direct outcome of Russia's American Nightmare. As long as we stand in obsessive dread of each other there can exist between us little more than self-fulfilling evil prophecies.

PART TWO

INTRODUCTION

In Part One, I outlined our institutional structure
in order to prepare the ground for a study and interpretation
of the more intimate aspects of American life and
character. Unless one first examines basic institutions
any interpretation of national character seems to hang in
mid-air no matter how psychologically perceptive one is.
On the other hand, once the institutional underpinning is
understood the lives of people and their character
seem to fall easily into place and become comprehensible.

In Part Two the relations between parents and children
and among children are seen as consequences of the
dynamics of American society. The configuration of
satisfactions, tensions, aspirations, disappointments, and
possibilities that is shown in Part One to be inherent in the
institutional dynamics becomes, in Part Two, the matrix
of analysis of the more intimate aspects of American life
and character. Thus Part Two traces the influence of the
general American configuration on the relationships
of people to one another.

5: Parents and Children

IN CHAPTER 2 I ARGUED THAT TECHNOLOGICAL DRIVENNESS created a work environment with few gratifications and much tension. I said that the industrial system generates hostility, insatiability, and fear of being obsolete and unprotected, and that for most people their job was what they had to do rather than what they wanted to do; that taking a job, therefore, meant giving up part of their selves. I urged, also, that on the job people cared precious little about one another, all working companions being inherently replaceable. I said further that under the urgencies of consumption, and the feeling that hard work was not worth the effort, the ancient impulse controls were breaking down, and that we were therefore shifting from a society in which Super Ego values (the values of self-restraint) were ascendant, to one in which more and more recognition was being given to the values of the Id (the values of self-indulgence). The loss of self and the rise of the values of the Id have combined to create a glittering modern pseudo-self, the high-rising standard of living, waxing like the moon in a *Midsummer Night's Dream* of impulse release and fun.

It is against this background that we can understand the

American family, for it is in his family life that the American
tries to make up for the anxieties and personality deprivations
suffered in the outer world. Most of the pleasure he gets out of
being alive is obtained within and through his family; for most
people, friends are extensions of the family circle and are enjoyed
within it. As a matter of fact, it is only when he has a family
that a man can fully come into his pseudo-self, the high-rising
standard of living, for on whom but his family does a man shower
the house, car, clothes, refrigerator, TV, etc., which are the material components of the high-rising living standard? But in addition to this, autonomy, peace, contentment, security, relaxation,
co-operation, freedom, self-respect, recognition, even challenge
and creativity as well as sense of worth and usefulness must be
sought in the family. Since the emotional satisfactions denied by
our occupational culture are sought hungrily in the family, it
must serve therapeutic and personality-stabilizing needs which,
in many cases, are overwhelming.

American family life is shaped in large part by the industrial
system. The economic system prevents involvement; it is within
the family that people struggle to become involved in one another. The economic system generates competition; it is within
the family that parents and children must try—and often fail—to
live a life without competition. The occupational world creates
feelings of inadequacy; it is within the family that the members
attempt to prove themselves adequate. The economic system
causes hostility, fear, and suspicion; it is within the family that
these feelings must be worked through and subordinated to love.
The emphasis on love in the American family seems almost in
direct proportion to the orientation toward profit, competition,
destructiveness, and de-personalization of the outer world. "Out
there" a man is a boss, a member of the "labor force," or a mass-
produced customer. Only in his family does he have a chance to
be a human being.

As the American struggles to make home and family a haven
from the outer world, business cheers him on with billions in
advertising. As he turns from the world inward on his own intimate economy, the American seeks, in an attractive home, an
environment that will island him warmly with his wife, children,
and chosen friends. Business loves family "togetherness" because

it means sales. See what Macy's, the largest store in the world, says about it: "Togetherness," says Macy's, is "the priceless ornament" for your Christmas tree.[1]

> What is Christmas made of? A family around a bountiful table, a beautiful tree, a pyramid of gifts . . . for nothing is more precious at Christmas than the joy of being together. The togetherness of Christmas starts with you. But its glitter and gaiety start at Macy's . . . where the Trim-a-Tree Shop is dazzling with decorations for inside and outside the house . . . So many families enjoy shopping our Trim-a-Tree Shop together. Yours will, too.

A list of forty-five tree and home decorations follows. Macy's pushes togetherness not only in winter, but in the springtime and in the summer, too. Here is one[2] for springtime. A full-page ad features a photo of a pony cart with two expensively dressed kids in it and a youthful mother and father standing beside it, obviously taking great pleasure in the children. Beneath the picture the copy burbles:

> In spring even the birds and the bees yearn towards togetherness. For this is the season when being alone is lonely. That's why you see families walking side-by-side, enjoying their togetherness. They're proud of how they look as a family. And they're proud of their new clothes. Families with a strong sense of togetherness shop at Macy's . . . together.

Above is a lonely-looking pony (so different from the pert one in the other picture) attached to an empty cart, *surrounded* by the words, "It's so lonely without TOGETHERNESS."

Because family purchases mount steeply with the standard of living, the family is the darling of American business; witness the anxious concentration with which business studies family psychology, growth, development, consumption, and reproduction. More sermons on the joys of family life are preached by advertising in one day than from pulpits in a month of Sundays.

[1] *New York Times,* November 19, 1956.
[2] *New York Times,* March 14, 1956.

FATHER, MOTHER, AND KIDS

In the history of the culture in which America has most ancient roots, the male has been the symbol (though often not the reality) of law, restraint, industry, severity, and aloofness—the Super Ego values—and woman has stood for closeness, warmth, softness, yielding, and guile—the values of the Id. In America the "emotional" wife has been the complement of the unshakable husband of iron dignity.

But it is not clear that fathers *enjoyed* the position of dominance-without-warmth to which the requirements of war and the turmoil of the socioeconomic organization assigned them. In the high cultures of recorded history, strength and tenderness have always been opposed, so that, although tenderness was not entirely excluded from his life, the ideal male avoided it for fear of emasculation. Behind outward harshness and containment of self, nevertheless, fathers have reached toward their children.

Though Proust was French, his description of his father fits the view that I urge here. In *Swann's Way* Proust relates how, as a child, he one evening plotted to steal a kiss from his mother by waylaying her on the staircase when his father was in another room. The kiss had to be stolen because, according to theory in the Proust family, too much tenderness would weaken the boy's will. The child's plan failed:

. . . my father was upon us. Instinctively I murmured, though no one heard me, "I am done for!"

I was not, however. My father used constantly to refuse to let me do things which were quite clearly allowed by the more liberal charters granted me by my mother and grandmother, because he paid no heed to "Principles," and because in his sight there were no such things as "Rights of Man." For some quite irrelevant reason, or for no reason at all, he would at the last moment prevent me from taking some particular walk, one so regular and so consecrated to my use that to deprive me of it was a clear breach of faith; or again, as he had done this evening, long before the appointed hour he would snap out: "Run along up to bed now; no excuses!" But then again . . . he could not, properly speaking, be called inexorable. [This time] he looked at me for a moment with an air of annoyance and surprise, and then when Mama had told him . . . what had happened, said to her: "Go along with him then . . . stay in his room for a little."

"But, dear," my mother answered timidly, "whether or not I feel like sleep is not the point; we must not make the child accustomed. . . ."

"There's no question of making him accustomed," said my father, . . . "you can see quite well that the child is unhappy. After all, we aren't gaolers. You'll end by making him ill, and a lot of good that will do. . . . I'm off to bed, anyhow; I'm not nervous like you. Good night."

It is quite clear that this traditional maleness of Proust's father was not uncontaminated by tender impulses, against which he fought by declaring to his wife, "I'm not nervous like you," and by stalking off to bed, "an immense figure in his white nightshirt, crowned with the pink and violet scarf of Indian cashmere. . . ."

Proust's father was arbitrary and unpredictable, like any man caught between impulses without clearcut values to direct him; as Proust says, his father "paid no heed to 'Principles'" because there were no obvious ones.

Even at the moment when it manifested itself in this crowning mercy, my father's conduct toward me was still somewhat arbitrary, and regardless of my deserts . . . and due to the fact that his actions were generally dictated by chance expediencies rather than based on any formal plan . . . for his nature . . . prevented him from guessing, until then, how wretched I was every evening . . . but . . . as soon as he had grasped the fact that I was unhappy he had said to my mother: "Go and comfort him."

My argument is simply that there is much of Proust's father in American fathers, but their emotional qualities and yearnings are no longer so concealed, and they have moved closer to their children. Feelings that were latent and contained in the elder Proust are more manifest now in American fathers, because they do not have to be as restrained as formerly. Unlike Father

Proust, beneath whose outward strictness there was a certain
warmth that could be touched, in the contemporary American
father we now perceive his emotional needs which, surging outward, are still, however, repeatedly frustrated by the requirement that he appear before his family in the old-fashioned
imperial nightshirt of authority.

Deprived in his work life of personality aspirations, the American father reaches deeply into the emotional resources of his
family for gratifications formerly considered womanly—the tenderness and closeness of his children; and his children reach
thirstily toward him. Confused by the mass and contradictory
character of available values, however, the American father can
no longer stand for a Law or for a Social Order he often can
neither explain nor defend sensibly against the challenges of his
wife and children. So, too, for a man the struggle "in the world"
is hard, and often, he thinks, not worth the restraint, the hard
work, and the imagination he may have put into it. It seems to
him better to relax and have fun. Meanwhile, since fathers cannot abandon their efforts to control children (and even wives),
because the consequences of yielding entirely seem too grave,
the man is caught between his need for gratifying his tender
impulses and the requirement that he be an old-fashioned
authority figure, too.

In the past, woman took revenge for her subordination to man
and for the condescension with which she was treated by quietly
stealing the children. Let her husband have his power and pride;
she would have the children's warmth, by gratifying their emotional needs, while their father sat aloof on his ice-cold Super
Ego. Now this is changing, and while the not-always-silent tussle
for the children goes on day and night, father, too, is learning
to fight with the values of the Id. But it is difficult, for it is a new
weapon, and he struggles within himself because he knows—
or half-knows—that it is wrong to capitulate to impulse and to
give the children all the candy they want.

Because nowadays both parents are concerned more and more
with the gratification of their own impulses and with a variety
of emotional yearnings, father and mother are thrown into collision. This occurs because the old Super Ego values are losing
caste; because since father desperately craves gratification he is

eager to give it, and because there is pressure to reduce the areas of restraint and the unbearable tension generated by a driven culture, and so to relax and have a good time. It is in this context that we can understand the new role of the American father as feeder, diaperer, and bather of the baby. It is true, of course, that the increased activity of women in economic life tends to reduce the differences between male and female roles, but the cause of the alteration in these roles lies also in the decline of the ancient values and the unshackling and unmasking of a masculine hunger for emotional gratifications.

In the following section, the children themselves tell what their attitudes are toward their fathers and mothers and in this way throw light on the changes I have been discussing and on the relation between family life and the rest of our culture. About 200 ordinary school children have written out for me[1] answers to the question, What do you like most and what do you like least about your father (and mother)? Freshly and frankly, their answers point up the issues raised here and in the preceding chapter.

THE CHILDREN SPEAK

The first answer is from a lower-class twelve-year-old girl:

FATHER	MOTHER
I like my father because he is kind, good and funny, when he is with my brothers and sisters and I. When I bring my friends home with me, he is very nice to them, and shows us a good time. He also lets me go to Plankville[2] to see my grandparents, aunt and uncle, and my two cousins every summer. This summer he	I like my mother because she lets me go to visit my friends often. She lets me invite them over whenever I please. If it was up to her, I would get a lot more allowance than I do. She lets me help her fix supper when I want to, and is very nice about it, when I make a mess (even though I have to clean it up). She also lets

[1] I am grateful to the teachers who have collaborated with me in this research by asking their children the questions.
[2] Fictitious name.

talked Mother into letting me go to Bigtown,[1] with my aunt, uncle, and cousins.

me do almost anything I want.

I don't like my father because he doesn't believe in letting me go to the show at night, and he won't let me wear lipstick. Even if he knows that he is wrong, he won't admit it to anybody. He insists on wearing his hair in a crewcut, even though he is losing most of it.

I dislike my mother because she gets mad so easily. On Saturday morning she makes me clean the house, while she goes shopping. She won't let me wear lipstick, or go to the show at night. She makes me take care of my brothers and sisters (ugh).

"Let" is the pivotal word in most of these compositions, for it reveals the triangular tension—mother-child-father—in most households: the child tugs at each parent as his impulses hammer at him, and his parents yield or resist as they are swayed by their own impulses toward their children. What one can learn from children's answers to the question is that they expect mothers *and* fathers to be yielding ("permissive") and giving, and that it is impossible to tell which parent actually does give most and from which one the children expect most. For example, though this girl's father "talked mother into letting me go to Bigtown," in other compositions it is the mother who prevails upon the father to yield to something the child wants, and in the present case the mother favors a larger allowance than does the father.

The closeness of mother and father roles shows again in the child's feeling of closeness to both of them, and also in the child's "dislikes," for she blames both parents for not letting her go to the show at night and for not letting her wear lipstick. In this composition, the girl blames her mother for forcing her into the feminine role—cleaning house and taking care of the children—but in some cases the father is blamed for the same thing. When mother–father roles are so close, when the child

[1] Fictitious name.

can expect the same thing from both of them, the ancient competition for the children between mother and father gains renewed vigor, and the competitiveness in our culture from which the family is supposed to give shelter enters through the back door. Under these circumstances, the temptation of one parent to try to steal the child from the other by overpermissiveness can become irresistible, and is in fact a plague in some American households.

When this child says that even when her father "knows that he is wrong, he won't admit it to anybody," she reminds one of Proust's observation that his father had no "principles." This child cannot see that her father's most important principle is his personal autonomy, which is so vulnerable in the outer world that it has to be defended vigorously within the family. When mere maleness is no longer an overriding law, when it is no longer an armor, giving men a pseudo-invulnerability against the emotional and intellectual demands of their families, then a father with an archaic self-image has to be irrational in its defense. Such a self-image is learned from previous fathers and grandfathers, and from the little-boy peer group, where strength is still the law; for it is there that the most conservative traditions of American culture flourish.

The final note in this child's criticism of her father is her annoyance with his crewcut. This "young lad" aspect of her father may frighten her, for she wonders, perhaps, how a boy with a crewcut can take care of a family, and she is embarrassed by the incongruity of a balding man wearing his hair like a youth; she is upset by a man with a wife and three children who is himself not grown up. Perhaps this is an American father-epitome— a balding man with a crewcut! The crewcut, however, is a last defiance in the face of impending obsolescence.

We listen next to an upper-middle-class girl of eleven talk about her parents:

FATHER	MOTHER
My father is a wonderful man. He has likes and dislikes which I like, and ones I dislike.	

I Like

1. He usually does what we want him to do.
2. I like him because he is usually very sweet.
3. I like him because he is very giving and when he happens to have a little change in his pocket, he reaches in and gives each one of us kids some money.
4. I like him because he gives me a large allowance.
5. He usually lets me do what I want.

I Dislike

1. He sometimes is very stubborn, and just to be mean he won't do a little chore around the house.
2. I dislike him because he sometimes teases me and my sisters.
3. I dislike him because he sometimes gets out his camera and has to have everyone in the pictures.
4. I dislike him because he sometimes makes me do things such as wash dishes and he won't even touch them.

Likes

I like her because
1. When Dad is mad, she protects me.
2. She doesn't get mad easily.
3. She does what I want her to.
4. She believes me when I get in a fight, usually.
5. She usually lets me do what I want to.
6. She wants to move to a nice farm when we find one.

Dislikes

I dislike her because
1. She gives up too easily.
2. She gets mad when I start the subject HORSES.
3. I like horses she doesn't care for them for she is afraid of most of them.
4. She gets your hopes up so high then drops them.

The subtle differences between this mother and father become clear if the sexes are reversed, as follows:

My mother is a wonderful woman. She has likes and dislikes which I like, and ones I dislike. She usually does what we want her to do. I like her because she is usually very sweet. I like her because she is very giving and when she happens to have a little change in her purse she reaches in and gives each one of us kids some money. I like her because she gives me a large allowance. She usually lets me do what I want.

She sometimes is very stubborn, and just to be mean *she won't do a little chore around the house.* I dislike her because she *sometimes teases me and my sisters.* I dislike her because she sometimes *gets out her camera and has to have everyone in the pictures.* I dislike her because she sometimes makes me do things such as wash dishes and *she won't even touch them.*

I like him because when Mother is mad he protects me. He doesn't get mad easily. He does what I want him to. He believes me when I get in a fight, usually. He wants to move to a nice farm when we find one. I dislike him because *he gives up too easily.* He gets mad when I start the subject HORSES. I like horses, he doesn't care for them for *he is afraid of most of them.* He gets your hopes up so high then drops them.

I have italicized what seems least likely to be associated with the parent when the sex is reversed in the text. For example, it seems most unlike an American child to accuse her mother of not doing a chore around the house; it seems unlikely that an American mother would tease her children, that she would get out her camera and make everybody get in the picture, and so on. This brings out the striking fact that what this child likes least about her father are some of his efforts to maintain a masculine role, and what she likes least about her mother are certain of her expressions of the traditional feminine role. After all, isn't it womanly to "give up" to the dominant male in the family, and isn't it truly feminine to fear horses? But many expressions of traditional masculinity and femininity are now felt by children to be intolerable.

Such attitudes on the part of children set up an emotional undertow in the American family against which parental Super

Egos are almost powerless, for the parent, in his need for love
—a need that is greater than his need to train the child to dignity
and citizenship—tends more and more to become almost drift-
wood in the tides of his child's demands. What we see so much
in America, then, is that the psychoanalytic metaphor according
to which the child introjects the parent (copies the parent, tries to
come up to parental expectations) is stood on its head, and the
parent copies the child. In America today it is not alone that
the child wants to live up to parental expectations, but that the
parent wants also—often desperately—to live up to the child's
expectations. And just as the traditional child was torn between
what he wanted and what his parents wanted, so the contemporary American parent is buffeted between what he thinks
he believes to be good for his *child* and what he thinks he
knows would gratify him in relation to his child. In these circumstances, the children themselves tend to become more disoriented. The need to follow the child contributes to the impulses
that produce the crewcut on the balding father, and, lest we
forget, the "accent on youth" in the mother.

In these compositions the children's values come out, too—
as much in what they do not say as in what they do say. For
example, parents are rarely liked or disliked for their scholarship,
religious fervor, or dedication to persons or causes outside the
family. Rarely is a parent liked because he does not exploit
people or does not care about money, or because he is earnest,
tough, tender, orderly, simple, gentle, and so on. What the children talk about most is whether the parent "lets me" or "doesn't let
me." What permits impulse release is "good" and anything that
blocks it is "bad."

Anger is also "bad"; a common complaint about parents, especially about fathers, is that they "get mad" and yell. Anger is not
experienced by these children as a natural expression of a clash
of wills but as an intolerable poison. Since anger is a universal
human characteristic and since without it mankind could not
endure, it is hard to understand why this is so. A lack of tolerance
for anger is probably related to the fact that since modern American parents often attempt to create a home atmosphere of permissiveness and yielding, the appearance of anger finds the child

relatively unprepared. It may also be that the parent himself is uncertain about his own anger; anger is almost immoral in the contemporary American family, and mothers show great anxiety over their impulses to scream at their children.

The following is written by an eleven-year-old lower-class boy:

FATHER	MOTHER
Things I like about my father.	1. She's the Best! ! ! person in the world.
My father is interested in sports. He manages a baseball team in the Local League. He also teaches me other sports. He gives me as much as he can. But he never gives me a spanking when I've done wrong. Mother does that.	2. She always understands me.
	3. She helps me on my homework.
	4. She spanks me when I need it.
Dislikes	*Dislikes*
He doesn't like the opera and Mother does.	NONE! ! !

Spanking is rare among the children studied; to have punishment, and especially such punishment, coupled with pleasure, is twice rare; but to have it consciously associated with giving is strange indeed. What this child seems to be saying is that the father, who gives "as much as he *can*," cannot give what the child feels he needs in order to make him a person: just punishment for his wrongdoing. It is startling for people in a permissive culture to learn that *not* to be given pain can be felt as a deprivation. Yet it is more painful for some children to bear guilt unpunished than to get a spanking. Though it would appear that this boy values spanking excessively, his general problem—the feeling of a need to be punished in order to become a person—points the direction in which permissiveness may lead.

In this family, the father is valued because he gives companion-ship (togetherness) but mother is valued because she gives un-derstanding and help in homework. Among these children both togetherness and helping with homework are often valued as fatherly characteristics, too, as we shall presently see.

A twelve-year-old boy has the following to say about his lower-middle-class father:

> I like my dad because he usually takes interest in activities of mine. He usually lets me stay up late to watch a late movie on school nights. I dislike my dad because he will say I can do something and then turn around and say I can't.

Of his mother, he says:

> I like my mother because she will give me extra spending money when I need it. I don't like my mother because she will crab at me every time I do something wrong.

The second child discussed in this chapter was annoyed with her mother for getting "your hopes up so high and then dropping them." Here the father bears a similar charge. In the case of the previous boy, he liked his mother because she punished him; now we have a boy who dislikes his mother for the same act. We see also that sometimes it is the mother, sometimes the father, who gives extra money.

In the present case the father is liked because he is his son's companion in the son's activities. Rarely does a child like his father because he is allowed to participate in the father's activi-ties. This is extraordinary when viewed in the perspective of the cultures of the world and even in the perspective of the not-too-distant rural past in America. There the son—and the daughter, too—took pleasure in being permitted to take part in the parent's activities. In American culture the demand is more often that the parent, especially the father, enter the child's world; not the other way round. In America the realm of adult action that the child really wishes to enter is the world of impulse release.

The emergence of the father as an imp of fun is a revolution in our time, and the following, from an upper-middle-class twelve-year-old girl, illustrates the point.

FATHER	MOTHER
Likes	*Likes*
1. He "fights" with me all the time.	1. She is considerate of us.
2. He always brings little things home with him, and is always doing things for my sisters and myself.	2. She is always willing to have a good time.
	3. She isn't the goody-goody type that spoils you.
3. He isn't "stingy."	4. When your sick she doesn't smother you with sympathy that makes you feel bad.
4. He is always ready for fun.	
5. He turns up with wonderful ideas at the oddest times.	5. She has taught us about and is willing to tell us more if we ask about sex relationship.
	6. She is a good mother in general.
Dislikes	*Dislikes*
1. He's moody.	1. She nags at times.
2. He likes football games.	2. She worries a lot about little things.
3. He won't ever go to P.T.A., etc.	
4. He is gone often on business trips.	

In a previous example, an upper-middle-class girl dislikes her father because "he sometimes teases me and my sisters"; here, however, an upper-middle-class girl likes her father for a similar thing. Playful aggressiveness, which includes mock boxing, sometimes painful "roughing," and teasing, is masculine American communication. In male–female relations in American culture, this is the male accommodation to feminine timidity and weakness; in male–male relations it is an accommodation to the need for male solidarity: it is partly a demonstration that "a guy can take it." It is also the compulsive masking of male affection in a culture that cannot tolerate tenderness between men because it would frustrate the destructive violence required in the economic system. In the American family, a father's teasing, "fighting" approach to his twelve-year-old daughter is an effort to get close without violating the unwritten emotional law of culture that when a daughter approaches adolescence, physical expressions of affection by Daddy must diminish, for the kissing, caressing, and fondling that were acceptable forms of tenderness in childhood are unacceptable at adolescence.

If there yet remains one distinction between mother and father roles that seems consistent in the American family, it is that fun and a good time are more frequently associated with father than with mother. This girl, for example, says that she likes her father because "He is always ready for fun," and children often speak of liking father because he takes them places. Thus, the father's appeal is more open. The father, since a number of factors interfere with his ability to give regular, routine gratification at the primary level, must make a more dramatic, direct, conscious appeal to the child. He does not routinely feed the children or comfort them when they are hurt, as the mother does. He does not receive them when they come home from school, guard the kitchen and refrigerator or dispense their contents as the mother does. If a father wants to please his children and if he wants the gratification they can afford him, he must find ways that are not available as part of his routine and necessary functioning. He must invent and improvise, and dramatize himself. This is why the imp of fun is male—or rather, has been male. Now women, too, are learning to play this role, as we are told in an ad for hair dye in which a ten-year-old boy looks with adoring eyes at his pretty, blond young mother and she looks back at him coquettishly. The copy reads:

Hair color so natural only her hairdresser knows for sure!

You can see it dancing in his eyes . . . the *fun* and *pride* in having a mother whose *happy spirit*, whose radiant hair keeps her looking younger, so pretty *all* the time!

And with Miss Clairol, it takes *only minutes* . . . to add clear, shining color to faded hair . . . to *hide gray* . . . [Italics supplied.][1]

But the face of the father-imp is the face of the tired and deprived father, who seeks surcease in his children. Out of his eyes

[1] *Life*, December 17, 1956.

look those of the little-boy father, who recaptures in his present family some of the warmth he himself once had known in his childhood family, but which is now missing for him in his daily life in the outer world. And so a twelve-year-old lower-middle-class boy says:

> I like my father because he takes a lot of time out for me. He usually brings 16 mm. films home on Monday nights. *He has a boyish heart.* He is always cracking jokes. He is pretty considerate. He takes part in a lot of sports. If he gets a chance he takes me to a baseball, football or basketball game or other places. [Italics supplied.]

When a man acts like a boy, he has the impulses of one; often he wants to be a boy because as a child he was protected, though as a man he is vulnerable. The hostility, competition, and strain men experience in their occupational lives make them feel exposed and fearful. When a man acts like a boy in the bosom of his family, he can feel that he is as accepted and protected by his family as he was by his father and mother when he was a child.

What this twelve-year-old says about his mother brings out the routine but important sources of emotional involvement with her:

> I like my mother because she is very kind. She often plays ping pong with me. She always prepares good meals. *She always has a snack ready for me when I come home from school.* She often takes me out places. [Italics supplied.]

Because the father cannot provide a snack, because he does not give love through good meals, he has to work harder at loving and has to invent and improvise signs of affection. Mother, because she runs the refrigerator, does not have to bring home 16 mm. movies, and because she is a good cook, she doesn't have to crack jokes. The American father has to create the conditions for "togetherness" if he wants to be loved, and the condition of choice is *The Midsummer Night's Dream,* where Daddy is Puck; where, 'mid lunar mists, "He turns up with wonderful ideas at the oddest times."

The twelve-year-old girl who "fights" with her father likes her

mother because, among other things, she doesn't make her feel
guilty. "When your sick she doesn't smother you with sympathy
that makes you feel bad." Since we have met guilt before, in
the boy who liked his mother because she spanked him, we
ought to have a closer look at it. A twelve-year-old girl, daughter
of a professional man, has the following to say about her father:

> My dad is very kind to me, he never seems to mind giving
> up a fishing trip to go somewhere with me. He goes along
> with what my mother says and he usually cooks supper.
> The only thing I dislike about my father is that when-
> ever I am bad he doesn't punish me he just tells me why I
> shouldn't do what I did. It makes me feel so sad when he
> tells me so kindly that it hurts him too when I do some-
> thing bad.

Guilt, like love, gratitude and many other emotions we cover
with a single word, is a complex phenomenon which is really
made up of a number of feelings: regret at having done or not
done something, desire to make restitution and expiation, nameless anxiety and a specific fear of punishment, self-depreciation
(the feeling of unworthiness), desire to conceal the act. Though
not all of these are present every time a person feels guilty,
one of them is constant—a feeling of unworthiness, the intolerable
pain that makes it so hard to live with one's self. What is so
interesting, therefore, in American children is their rebellion
against the tyranny of guilt, for it is the enemy of the Id as water
is the enemy of fire. Since father, who was once the source of
the Super Ego and of guilt, now wears the moon-emblem of
Puck, the victory is easy, for the militia has deserted to the
rebels. One horn of this modern American dilemma is father,
who must be Id *and* Super Ego; the other is mother who,
when she competes with permissiveness against the father for
the child, helps to sap the structure of the childish Super Ego
and its most formidable fortress, guilt.

The fact that the American father actively advertises to his
children his love for them and courts them through appeals
to their primary needs; the fact that he is not a remote but a
close and engaging figure; the fact that the mother often
punishes as much or more than the father, while the father often
diapers, feeds, bathes, and keeps the nocturnal vigils—these

must bring about some peculiarly American modulations in the
classical Oedipus Complex.

Thus, in its intimate and intricate way the American family
meshes with the larger society. In their hunger for one another, parents and children express a warmth and affection for
which the economic rough-and-tumble has little use. On the
other hand, the Id values—impulse release and fun—though
exploited in the outer world as sources of consumption energy,
are nurtured in the family also.[1] Enveloped in the atmosphere of
Id, the roles of mother and father draw close to one another.
Fathers are no longer aloof, controlling figures, and both parents
seek gratification from the children at the level of deep feeling;
meanwhile, since permissiveness has come to loom large in the
child's appreciation of either parent, they can now compete for
the child more openly and on a more equal footing than in the
past. Parental roles thus resemble each other; both parents now
draw closer to the children and also become more equal to them
in a modern version of American democracy—equality in impulse
release.

In this atmosphere the children are becoming intolerant of
guilt and of parental anger. Guilt, of course, retires before the
Id as the devil before the Cross in this contemporary reversal
of the medieval religious tales. But how account for the intoler-
ance of anger? It may be explained in part by the fact that anger
is, along with guilt, just another instrument of parental control
and hence insufferable to children. More important, though, may
be the child's awareness of the roots, the volume, and the meaning of his parent's anger. Perhaps he feels that only part of the
hostility is related to his fault and that it is really directed
against the forces that are destroying his parent's Self; that the
rage poured out on him belongs elsewhere. It is the unrealistic,
disproportionate aspects of anger that frighten and disconcert
the child.

Finally, parental anger must seem contradictory in the en-

---

[1] Note, for example, the enormous emphasis on self-demand, permissiveness, and fun in such influential works as Gesell and Ilg's *Infant and Child
in the Culture of Today* and in the most recent Children's Bureau pamphlet
on child care. Martha Wolfenstein has written a penetrating essay on this
pamphlet in *Childhood in Contemporary Cultures,* edited by Margaret Mead
and Martha Wolfenstein, University of Chicago Press, 1955.

vironment of permissiveness. Here is the parent who has been constantly "letting," finally forbidding. When the parent explodes, the impact on the child is violent because the explosion must seem unreasonable and disproportionate, and what is disproportionate is bound to be hated. Furthermore, the child has become unusually sensitive to anger, for when parents dam up their anger because it does not fit with permissiveness, because they are afraid of their own rage, because they are unsure of their ground, and because anger blocks the demonstrations of affection they desperately need, its sudden and disproportionate release finds a child who is not prepared to cope with it.

Thus, anger and guilt are being carefully weighed in the American family: they, too, are becoming casualties of "dynamic obsolescence." But when anger and guilt join the other junk in the cultural dump, thought, too, tends to obsolescence. To think deeply in our culture is to grow angry and to anger others; and if you cannot tolerate this anger, you are wasting the time you spend thinking deeply. One of the rewards of deep thought is the hot glow of anger at discovering a wrong, but if anger is taboo, thought will starve to death. It is the same with guilt, for where there is none there is no impulse to moral self-criticism, and in place of it is set self-examination merely as it relates to group conformity and getting ahead.

6: The Teens

THE PERSONAL COMMUNITY

In many primitive cultures and in the great cultures of Asia, a person is born into a personal community, a group of intimates to which he is linked for life by tradition; but in America everyone must create his own personal community. In cultures where one's group is determined before birth, even one's wife may be selected in advance by traditional arrangements. Where one is born into an inalienable personal community, social "appeal" is relatively unimportant, and it is in part because of this that so many Asiatics strike us as being "so delightfully unaffected." But in American culture, where no traditional arrangements guarantee an indissoluble personal community, every child must be a social engineer, able to use his "appeal" and his skill at social maneuvering to construct a personal community for himself. This is the child's task from the day he leaves the established security of his mother's orbit, and he works hard at it as he tries, through making himself "appealing," to bring new friends into his personal community. Meanwhile other children try to lure him into their personal communities, and still others try to win his friends away from him into their own spheres, as they attempt to build their worlds out of stones taken from his. Elsewhere it is unusual for a child to be surrounded by friends one day and deserted the next, yet this is a constant possibility in contemporary America.

Since men in industrialized America move from job to job, up and down the social ladder, from neighborhood to neighborhood, from city to suburbs and from suburbs to the country, and so on, the establishment of enduring and secure interpersonal relations is difficult for children. Since, additionally, the American child, having made and lost many friends, learns to commit himself deeply to none, he often cannot hold tightly even to what he has because he has suffered and hence withdrawn. Thus the battle of interpersonal relations sometimes cannot be won because of an unwillingness to commit personality resources, and the resources cannot be committed for fear of waste.

This is the context in which conformity and the wish to be popular can be understood, for popularity is insurance against uncertainty in interpersonal relations. It is the analogue in the adolescent world to diversification in the industrial world: both aim at the elimination of uncertainty. "Popularity" is not a nasty American disease, but the adolescent's effort to stabilize his perpetually precarious situation. It is a sort of bank—a person-bank, where one stores up friends against a rainy day, for if you have many people in your person-bank because you are popular, you can afford to take some losses, too. However, you are also subject to the vicissitudes of the market: you must watch your person-stock, not to see how *it* rates, but how it rates *you*.

When the personal community is unstable and must be constantly worked on and propped up, individual idiosyncracies become dangerous and must be ruled out in favor of tried and true skills that ring bells 100 per cent of the time in the endless American game of interpersonal pinball. American conformity therefore is an American necessity; it is the American's intuitive effort to hold American society together. Here again, as is so often the case, the adolescent is ahead of his critics among the intelligentsia at home and abroad.

Although it is true that the price of social acceptance is conformity and loss of freedom, that one builds a personal community by mortgaging his individuality, the tough-minded kids who, for one reason or another, cannot fit in with the majority and are squeezed out of the conforming groups join forces with one another, reinforcing each other's differences, gaining strength to set themselves against the majority and stimulating each other's creative élan.

In America, the absence of predetermined personal communities plus great mobility brings it about that in one of the great populations of the world people have become scarce commodities and compete with one another for one another as industry competes for natural resources, for manufactured objects, and for consumers. The fact that everyone can be chosen or rejected by others, that he never knows why he is rejected if he is, and the fact that those he numbered in his personal community one day may not be there the next, makes for enormous uncertainty in interpersonal relations; it makes for great sensitivity to looks, stares, smiles, and criticism, and originates the endless inner questioning, "Am I liked?"

It is against this background that we can, perhaps, come to understand why, when teen-agers are asked the question, "What are your main personal problems?"[1] interpersonal relations are paramount.

GOSSIP AND POPULARITY

Since 250 cases is a small number on which to base generalizations about the whole United States, I prefer merely to discuss the answers to the question "What are your main personal problems?" rather than trying to generalize. However, there are certain differences between boys and girls, which, though sometimes small, demand some attempt at explanation. The outstanding differences are the more frequent reference by girls to malicious gossip among themselves, and their greater preoccupation with courtship and popularity.

My conjectures about the differences are as follows: Beginning with school days, boys' society pivots on games requiring teams, and there are few boys' games of any prestige that can be

[1] The majority of the 250 who replied to the questionnaire discussed in this chapter are from the upper middle class.

played individually. Even sand-lot track and field meets, where boys pit themselves as individuals against one another, require relay teams. Boys' games are played according to rules, and a boy takes his place on a team in terms of his skill. In boys' society there is no nonsense about this and in the actual play every boy is judged by how good he is. It is hard for a boy to stay out of a group if he has any skill at sports, for, since he is necessary to complete the team, he is constantly being dragged cheerfully into play and hence into groups where he must play fairly and according to the rules, where he learns the morality of good sportsmanship and the tenets of masculine "decency." It is difficult for a boy to avoid group life and "teamwork."

Though girls play games, the team-game life of a boy is consuming. During the baseball season, for example, he talks practically nothing but baseball when he is alone with his peers. He not only discusses his own and his friends' play, but also the world of professional baseball. He knows the batting averages of the major league players, their errors, assists, and so on. He may even know how much each player cost, who was traded for whom, who is a rookie and who is on his way out; and this is more or less the same for each sport as its season comes up. The faithfulness of boys to sports is a striking characteristic of American life. As the season for each sport arrives, the boys are out in the field or in the street playing it with dogged loyalty, and the patter of information about the game is a counterpoint to the determined, excited play. There is a total, almost a religious, community of sport among boys, in which maleness, masculine solidarity, and the rules of the game are validated year in and year out.

Little girls play with their dolls, their sewing, their cut-outs, or their jacks, and their talk is not about rules of the game, about trying hard and winning, but about the trivia of their semi-isolated play. And as they grow toward adolescence, girls do not need groups; as a matter of fact, for many of the things they do, more than two would be an obstacle. Boys flock; girls seldom get together in groups above four whereas for boys a group of four is almost useless. Boys are dependent on masculine solidarity within a relatively large group. In boys' groups the emphasis is on masculine unity; in girls' cliques the purpose is to shut out other girls.

Since girls do not have teams but cling closely to "best girl friends," fighting to hold them against other girls who might steal them in order to make them *their* best girl friends, gossip develops as a consequence. Gossip, the interpersonal ballistic missile, emerges first in little-girl groups as the weapon with which each will defend her personal community against attacks on its frontiers by others. With gossip she attempts to blast all those who, she thinks, might invade her sphere, stealing her friends, laying her life in waste. But those who live by the sword shall die by it, and since personal communities are unstable, the girl who reinforced one's slander of others on Monday may bomb one from the rear on Tuesday. The following answer by sixteen-year-old Lila to the question, "What are your main personal problems?" shows extraordinary insight:

> It seems to me that teen-agers would have much more to do than spread gossip about their best friends. I am as much a part of this as anyone, I suppose, and realize the wrong in doing it, but we all are this way. Trying to grow up and become mature adults has its problems and I guess without thinking about it we are so conscious of getting ahead, of being liked, we step on others and push them away without realizing it.

To be able to relate destruction of others to the need to be liked takes a long head indeed, though we should be careful never to underestimate the really great capacity of children to understand their own problems.

In the next example we deal with thirteen-year-old Charline's loneliness in a predatory world.

> . . . . I don't have many friends because people who call themselves your friends are really your enemies, sweet in front of your face and gossips behind your back. If you call those kind of people your friends, then I guess I have as many as anybody else if not more. But it would be nice to have a real friend, one to tell all your problems to. All I have to tell my problems to is my diary.

And diary sales are high in this age group of girls.

Competition for boys penetrates the gossip complex, becom-

ing part of its disintegrating function. Sixteen-year-old Milly
says:

> Another problem which I have is trying to get along with
> a certain bunch or clique of girls . . . They are all cute and
> nice, but they are such terrible gossips I can't stand them.
> All girls gossip a little, but these girls carry it out to such a
> large extent, I felt I couldn't go out with someone new, and
> say anything about the date, without it going around the
> school very exaggerated.

One might say that Milly describes the destructive impact of
gossip at the "benign" level, where it is merely destructive without
planned intent. In the next observations by thirteen-year-old
Bonny, however, it is possible to see the underlying motivation
of all gossip:

> There is this one girl that all my life I have never really
> gotten along with. We are fighting almost constantly. When
> we get into a really big fight she has to tell everyone about
> it. She has to make especially sure the boys find out about
> it, too.

Bonny summarizes so eloquently and frankly what appears in a
scattered and half-articulated way in the majority of the letters
that we ought to have a look at the rest of what she says.

3) I am also worried constantly if the girls and boys like
   me.
4) I am always worried if people are whispering about me.
5) Sometimes I feel as if everybody hates me.
6) I always try to be pretty friendly but I know sometimes
   I am sort of a snob. The thing that hurts my feelings
   most are—
1) When I am walking with someone and another person
   that I know comes up to the person I am walking with
   and says Hi to them and not to me.
2) Some people try to hurt my feelings on purpose it seems
   like. Maybe they don't but they hurt me very much.

The writing in this note is excellent, the language clear, and
the self-analysis could hardly be better. Bonny speaks with

the voice of her age-group: sorrowful, lonely, and afraid. The hysteria that Elvis Presley and Jimmy Dean evoke in these children has an agony at its core.

Sixteen-year-old Karen speaks of jealousy:

> . . . . girls are too vicious to everybody and including one another. They aren't satisfied by degrading other people (girls), but when they're apart from one another they tear one another apart, and when two girls have an almost perfect friendship, they're jealous of them, so they try to spread false rumours in order to break up the friendship.

In a competitive culture one envies anything good that happens to anybody else; it is enough to know that somebody—anybody—has something good, for one to become depressed or envious or both. In a competitive culture, anybody's success at anything is one's own defeat, even though one is completely uninvolved in the success.

The boys' group is the place where every boy tests and validates or loses his masculinity. Since he needs the group to prove himself, he must work at holding it together and at showing the group that he is masculine. He does this partly by obeying the rules of masculine life. If a boy cannot be a good athlete, he can always play fair. What does a girl need a group for? How can a girl prove she is feminine, now that taking care of babies, cooking, and doing other household chores have become loathsome, degrading, and symbolic of subservience to parents? She can do it by attracting boys.

The idea that a woman does not have to *do* anything to prove herself, that she need merely *be*, and that in the fullness of motherhood, as she produces one child after the other, her femininity will be obvious for all to see, does not fit contemporary America. It does not square with Madison Avenue, where a lot of money is spent for advertising that tells a woman how to prove to the world and to herself that she is every inch a female. According to Edward Weiss of the advertising firm of Weiss and Geller, "Women . . . want, first, reassurance of their own femininity. . . ."[1] The answers by girls from twelve to seven-

---

[1] John Crosby in the *St. Louis Post-Dispatch*, April 8, 1953.

teen to the question, "What are your main personal problems?" strongly support Mr. Weiss.

By the time she is twelve, an American girl is preoccupied with proving, by becoming "popular" with boys, that she is female, and in this task she is alternately cheered and goaded by her family. But the task is difficult because she has played mostly with girls and does not know the ways of boys, and because the monolithic solidarity of the boys' groups gives boys so much support that the girl, now predatory on the boys' group as she was on the girls', has to work to detach the boy. In junior high and high school the girls can be seen hovering around the boys, while the boys lean against the walls in the school corridors looking detached and unmoved, though inwardly they are slowly yielding.

Much of the time when girls talk about "popularity" they mean "sought after by boys"; they mean that they have been able to reverse the boys' tendency to seek gratification exclusively in the boys' group and orient it toward themselves. Though being popular validates a girl's femininity and guarantees her boy-community, it is hard for a girl to stay popular because few girls have the necessary characteristics. For American boys and girls, then, the "steady" is the answer to the instability, emptiness, and anxiety inherent in other types of boy–girl relationships, and becoming "steadies" sometimes gives the boy–girl relationship solemnity, dignity, and meaning. The implications of the "steady" relationship are, however, naturally quite different in the boys' crowd and in the girls' crowd. Boys' steadies become integrated into the semi-sacred boys' society, and the rules of the game apply: no boy would steal the steady of a member of his group, though he might dream about it and hang forlornly (though chivalrously) around the edges of a steady pair, hungering for the girl, hoping that his buddy and she will break up. However, until they do, their relationship is taboo to him; he will protect the girl, watch over her, talk to her, but never declare himself. A girl must understand this, for if, while going steady, she makes eyes at another boy in her steady's group, both boys will drop her.

Within the girls' group, however, a steady is not taboo, and a girl's readiness to steal her best friend's steady fits the predatory interpersonal pattern of girls' culture. So Edna says:

It seems that every boy I start to like my best girl-friend starts liking the same boy or the boy likes her. But I'll find someone else I guess to like.

Girls begin to escape from the irritation of the female world when, at thirteen or fourteen, they start going after boys in a determined way. Boys become the grand preoccupation not only because the girl must validate herself as a female by proving she can attract boys, but also because her little-girl hostility to boys must now be replaced by niceness toward them and because boys, since they are fearful of what was once hostile remain anchored so warmly in the masculine group that they are hard to get at. If boys were easy to reach, if the girl's self-image were not so threatened by failure to attract them, and if once attracted the boys would *stick,* girls would not be so anxious. The courting age is an anxious as well as a gay age; every teenage party hides anxiety beneath its outer gaiety.

The best way to feel the impact of these problems on thirteen-to-fourteen-year-old girls is to read a series of their answers to the question, "What are your main personal problems?"[1]

Abby: My greatest problem is boys. All the boys that I like, don't even notice me. Then when it comes around to dances at school the boys I don't care for, ask me. I don't know what I'm going to do.

Beatrice: I think about popularity and hope to become very popular. One reason is because my mother worries about my popularity and nags me about it and is always saying, why aren't you like her and her. Whenever she gets mad at me she gets back at me by talking about my popularity.

Belinda: I go steady with a boy 14 years old. He goes away to Military School and I only see him once out of every three months. My mother says it is silly for me to go steady with a boy that I can't even see. We like each other very much and we don't want to break up.

[1] Names are in alphabetical order.

Belle: I would like to be more popular with boys. I'm probably not popular with boys cause I am shy. I would like to be able to talk to people with more ease.

Carlotta: My personal problems are: How can I get popular. The boy I like is shy and I'm pretty sure he likes me and how I can find out if he likes me . . . If I'll ever go steady. How can I get a certain boy to stop bothering me and trying to kiss me in class. How I can get another certain boy to stop staring at me every time he sees me. How I can get one boy to stop cussing me out.

Carol: There is also a dating problem. I don't mean I'm unpopular. I get plenty of dates, but hardly ever with the person I really want to go out with. After thinking it over I think about boys most of the time, having parties and going to affairs. I love to dance, but it's hard to find a boy who can dance as equally as well.

Charline: My personal problems are: Every time I like a boy he never likes me, maybe because they don't know I like them. They probably wouldn't like me anyway because I always like the popular ones. I sure wish one of them would like me, too.

Daisie: . . . . my mother does not like for me to go steady. If my boyfriend asks me to go steady I hate to say no to him because I really want to and then I have an argument with my mother.

Daphne: There's a boy I have liked since last year and he likes me. We have gone to parties and to the movies and we have had a lot of fun together, but now I am getting tired of him and sorta like another boy. I don't know how to *not* go around with the other boy without hurting his feelings.

Debby: When I dance with any boys I never know what to say. Maybe its that I don't dance well, but they never ask me again. My older brother is popular and everybody expects me to be. And they look at me and talk to me they lose interest.

Dorothy: My one main problem is one certain boy and whether he likes me or not. I only wish he wasn't so shy. And I wish he would go bowling or to the show because I never see him out of school.

Eleanor: My personal problems are, that I worry too much about being popular with the boys. Some people tell me that some cute boys like me as a girlfriend but I don't know if it is true or not because they never call me up on the phone. Though they always act real nice to me in school.

Elizabeth: I always have trouble because I like boys that like other girls. Because we go away for the summer, I have different boy-friends in summer that I don't see in the winter. I like 6 boys all the same time and I am going steady with another.

Emma: My main problem is boys. My mother says I'm boy crazy. When I get interested in a boy I don't eat, sleep, and sometimes my working habits fail. In one particular insident I like this boy very much and I think he likes me. But he is very shy towards me and all he does is sit and stare at me and I get self-conscious and don't know what to do with my hands or anything. He talks to all the other girls but he gives me special looks. Maybe something will become of it.

Abby, Carol, and Charline have one of the commonest problems—liking someone who doesn't like them, just as in the occupational world where one often has what other people don't want. In the occupational system, where a man has no place until he makes it for himself, a worker, in order to get a job, compromises with the system by renouncing part of his personality. It is the same in the world of girl–boy relations—the girl anxiously asks herself why she is not liked and what she can do to make herself liked, pruning and cultivating herself experimentally until she finds the personality configuration that seems to "click." "It" at the personality level is the analogue of "job appeal" at the occupational level.

Charline illustrates one of the factors that lies behind the difficulty in liking those who don't like you. Charline likes only boys approved by other girls and sought after by them. There is a kind of "Approved" label pasted on the fortunate boy, and she doesn't really have to examine the product! One might also remark that Charline's condition is characteristic of our culture in general: she shows an extreme sensitivity to light emanating from what is hard to get. This goes together with a sensation that what you have is not as good as what you haven't got, and that what is really valuable is not what you have, but what everybody wants. The reason you do not value what you have is because you are not involved in it; you are drawn toward distant hills because you cannot sink roots in those on which you stand.

When girls like Abby and Carol do go out on dates they often go with second choices—with boys that like them but whom they do not like—and both are degraded to the level of mechanisms going through an empty cultural form. Distrust is bred between them, for the boy feels the girl goes out with him just for the date and the girl senses the boy's dejection and hostility. But since the girl often cannot stand the feeling she has as a consequence of dates without feeling, and the boy is indignant at what has happened to him, both may later rush into ill-considered relationships. The girl exaggerates to herself any liking she feels for a boy, and the boy gets involved with the first girl who really shows she likes him. Since in both cases the underlying feeling is superficial, the result is often disaster.

Of course, one of the difficulties that Abby, Charline, Carlotta, Eleanor, and nearly all the girls suffer from is never knowing where they stand with the boys: why they are liked or not liked, how long it will all last, etc. Not knowing what to do, not knowing how to make people like you is a state of mind that can arise only where people are not naturally outgoing but have to be brought out by personality tricks. One then has to work with tools the exact nature of which nobody really knows, and which are imagined as assembled out of certain inborn characteristics and certain manners that can be copied from others. The simple affirmation, "I like you," is not enough to win another human being, even were it not taboo to say these words to another person without long preparation of the ground. Since in American culture it is not easy to express one's feelings about another person directly to him, regardless of what the feelings are, they can come out only indirectly.

Charline's problem is the same as that of many others: she likes people who don't like her because they don't know she likes them. It must mean that in her judgment they feel that she either dislikes them or is indifferent to them. The underlying assumption of a person in any mass society is that most people are indifferent to him or dislike him and that only a tiny minority like him. Under such circumstances it is hard to imagine what could poison social relations more than withholding signals of affection and approval. Here is a culture where children hungry for love reach invisibly toward one another yet dare not give a sign, for to do so indicates weakness and may bring contempt in a society that admires strength. There is also the danger that anyone who shows that he can be had easily will be held cheap in this culture, where what is valued most is what is "hard to get."

It is not enough that the girls should have to flounder in this jungle of interpersonal shadows, but, as with Beatrice, their families may badger them because they are not good hunters. In this way, the courting pattern becomes a ceremonial through which the family self-image is validated and an instrument which can be used against girls in the family to punish them. An interesting thing about American families is that though they like their girls to be popular—to have many superficial relationships with many boys—they often, as in the case of Daisie and Belinda, oppose the "steady" relationship, though it has greater possibilities than popularity for emotional development and for learning. The family's objection to a girl's going steady is the last island of resistance in a perimeter of sexual defenses that is rapidly crumbling. But though the parents are afraid of the girl's getting too deeply involved, one of the central problems in our culture is the American's difficulty in becoming deeply involved at all. Daphne and Elizabeth illustrate the point.

MID-TEEN SOLEMNITY

The illustrations in the preceding section were from compositions written by girls, because girls are *preoccupied* with gossip and popularity, while boys are not. It is not that boys are free of these concerns, but they are not besieged by them the way girls are. In the present section I do not limit the discussion to one sex because it seems to me that the solemnity of which I speak—a product of inner questioning and self-examination —is just as much a quality of boys as of girls in the mid-teens— from fifteen to seventeen.

Though the title of this section seems to imply a theory of stages of development, nothing could be further from my mind. On the other hand, what I do discern from careful analysis of the data, is that as one moves out of the early teens there is relatively less preoccupation with the external facts of gossip and popularity and a greater tendency to inner questioning. This does not mean that concern with externals disappears at this age or that in the earlier teens there is no self-questioning. It simply suggests that as the child grows older in our culture he becomes so absorbed in self-examination that other problems diminish relatively. At the same time, regardless of sex, worry about the personal community remains important: the children worry about where they stand, how they can attract others, how they can overcome their shyness, and how they can control their general tendency always to do the wrong thing. Interpersonal relations remains the wellspring of anxiety, and it emerges in many forms; most striking is the tendency of the children to attack themselves. Thus the fluctuating, evanescent, will-o-the-wisp character of the personal community, having created the questions, "What is wrong with me? What can I do to be liked?" ends by producing the answer, "I am no good. I must change myself so that people will like me."

> I sometimes worry what people think about me [says 15-year-old Flossie] and times I feel alone . . . I guess my main problem is that I don't feel I'm as good as everybody else sometimes. I feel very lucky because I have a good homelife and understanding parents though.

> *Frank,* age 15: As a teenage boy of the twentieth Century I have many problems. Because of my age I guess I kind of feel inferior to the rest of my class even though I have many friends. Also when I come to school with a new article of clothing on I am afraid that some person will make

some remark. I know I am not the best dressed boy at Park High but I guess I do my best with what I've got.

Freddie, age 16: I don't believe I make friends easily. In other words, I avoid going places where I will be among a group of strangers.

George, age 16: The problem of making friends and then retaining them is always confronting me. But I try not to worry about this very much.

Gertie, age 15: Let me see. I think my biggest problem is in living with people my age. It is probably overly important to me to be accepted by them, and I am sure I too often wear my feelings on my sleeve, which results in getting them hurt easily. I am young for my years in school; and do not always feel at ease with my classmates, probably because, though I wish to be accepted and thought of as one of them, I am really not ready to take part in all their activities.

Glenn, age 16: . . . . my third problem is being wanted and excepted by my friends . . . and I think I am but I wish I could be more popular with more people and not just a group of about 20 or 30 kids. This year I have been friendly more with the seniors but I would like to become more friendly with other kids my own age; and more known to kids of other surrounding high schools.

Taking one's self apart as Flossie and Frank do is the source of strong competitive impulses, for since they feel inferior to others they must try to come abreast of or surpass them. In this way the self-destructive self-analysis that springs from a personal community that is the product of a mobile, fluid, evanescent industrial society helps to provide the very competitive impulses on which it feeds. Thus the economy draws, from the very anguish it creates, energy to drive it. This then creates greater instability in the personal community, which leads to increased competitiveness,[1] which contributes to further driven-

[1] On January 7, 1957, in the article "Heart Disease Seen Peril to Young Men," the *New York Times* reported a study showing that "The alarming trend in heart disease is that the ailment is becoming increasingly frequent among men in their 20's and 30's. . . ."

ness. The ultimate brake on this process is now appearing: giving up hard work as an ideal, and increased emphasis on teamwork and getting along, rather than on individual striving.

Glenn's insatiability for friends is an expression of a people whose hunger for others cannot be satisfied because the deprivation has been too sharp and because they cannot really incorporate what sustenance they get; they have given up involvement because it is too costly, and they cannot hold what they have because they cannot become involved in it. Yet such people are often charming and even seductive. The hunger from which Glenn and many Americans suffer can be understood only if one has starved, either for food or for people.

Lack of self-confidence is a toxin in the emotional stream of most of these children. "How do you improve your personality?" asks sixteen-year-old Hannah. "I am kind of shy when it comes to talking to new acquaintances." Or, at more length, sixteen-year-old Hilda says:

> I am a girl of sixteen. Although a teenager has many problems, I think my greatest problem is learning how to overcome shyness. It seems that whenever I am with any of my friends I don't have any trouble talking with them at all. But whenever I meet a stranger or most of the boys in my classes, I can't seem to carry on a conversation and begin feeling very shy.
>
> Another problem I have is being very quite [quiet], which isn't actually unusual because a person that is shy is often a very quite person as well.

Lack of self-confidence dries up the personality by holding the sufferer back from new experience—"I'm afraid of strangers"—impoverishing life by limiting it to the tried and the true. But since it also makes a man hold himself cheap and take whatever comes along, it fits the economic system like a bargain basement.

Lack of self-confidence, endemic in the mid-teens, poisons emotional life as undernourishment would sap it physically. Occasionally some unusually articulate or suffering youngsters will write like sixteen-year-old Hal:

Probably my worst problem is that of gaining self-confidence. The lack of self-confidence marks everything I do. I have no confidence in myself in sports even though I make the teams. All the time I am asking for help in things I should do myself and I am always asking others if I should do this or wear that, etc.

The times when my confidence is completely lacking are when I am with girls or have to ask someone out on a date. It takes me the longest time to ask a girl out or even get up my nerve to ask her. Then when I have the date I am continually wondering whether or not she is having a good time. I worry so much over this point that I can't relax enough to let myself have a good time. Lately, I haven't been as bad for I met someone I like and have had a lot of fun going out with her. *But she likes someone else better and besides she's going out of town in 25 days.* I hope that I will soon achieve self-confidence or grow out of this stage or something.

Another problem I would like to overcome is that most of the time, I am too self-conscience. I worry too much over what kind of clothes to wear or whether I look good. Then if anyone stares at me or makes a remark, I draw up into a little hole as if I was a turtle. [Italics supplied.]

A person lacking in self-confidence says to himself, I cannot do what *I* want to do; I cannot do what *others* expect of me; I cannot *give* others what they want; I am not as *others* want me to be; I am not the way *I* want to be. If he is like Hal he will throw himself upon others, alternately warmed by their approval and affection and shrinking "up into a little hole as if I was a turtle." Some, like sixteen-year-old Helen, permanently withdraw:

Before the Christmas holidays and for the past year there was one problem that I thought I would never lick. I am the kind of person that is hard to get to know. The first impression that people get is that I am conceited and self-centered. That is the viewpoint of my friends that are my age. The older people I associate with take a different impression. However, they too feel that they do not really know me. Within myself I felt that there was

a stone wall which I could not break. I felt somehow
that it would keep me from marriage because my husband could never know me.

When the Christmas holidays arrived I began thinking
deeply about this problem. I came to the conclusion that
if I continued worrying about this so called problem it
would just get worse and worse. So I made a kind of deal
with myself to just forget about it and be myself. In
doing so I find that I am much easier to talk to and am
a great deal happier. I have learned to accept it as a
characteristic rather than a problem.

And Helen may go through life inaccessible: she has "solved"
her problem by denying it—by "just forgetting about it"; by
magically transforming it from a problem to a "characteristic."
In this way self-acceptance has become, paradoxically, self-
denial. But Helen should learn that though walls are a defense,
they are also a prison; if others cannot get to Helen, neither
will she come to know them.

Helen does not tell us how she came to raise this wall, but
since most children suffer from feelings of inadequacy, inferiority, incompetence, and unattractiveness, we can guess
that she attempts to cope with hers by sealing herself off
defensively from the world. Howard, who says he is sixteen
and seven-eighths years old, makes it clear:

My personal problem is my fear and consequent rejection
of people. Although I use to be forward and outgoing, I
am now rather inward and afraid to meet people.

Thus, though Americans must find in marriage and family the
warmth that is lacking in the outer world, their capacity to do
so may be impaired by social experiences that seal them off from
or make them extremely demanding of one another. Helen and
Ruthie (see p. 166) seem to be girls who, one morning, on awak-
ening beside their husbands, will ask themselves, "Who is this
man?"

The fact that there is no marked difference between the intimate needs of boys and girls in the mid-teens means that men
and women enter marriage with many similar problems, require

the same kind of help from one another and from their children, and therefore tend to assume similar roles in the family. This helps to account for the absence of sharp differences between father and mother in the answers we have earlier heard young children give to the question, "What do you like most and what do you like least about your father/mother?"

Joe is a good example of a sixteen-year-old boy who is facing, a little crazily, a variety of problems with girls:

Females, Females, Females. You can't live without them, and you can't live with them. Let us take, for example, a simple date on a Friday night. Did I say simple? Well, maybe they are simple, but they're more expensive than a formal dance. After you pick up the girl you ask her where she would like to go. She replies, "A show." Then you ask her what show she would like to see and nine out of ten of the times you end up at the most expensive show in town. After the show you ask her if she would like to have a little snack—big joke! Snack, heck! She orders a nice big steak, three double thick chocolate malts, and a triple decker banana split. That is when you begin to feel that *emptiness* inside you. You pay the bill and the required tip on a steak dinner and leave half unconscious. You take your date home. She says she had a wonderful time and would like to do it again sometime. Ha, Ha, Ha.

If you would like to spend all the money you own in a very short time, then this is probably the best way I know of. A female will *drain* every cent you own and then when she finds out that you are broke, she won't speak to you. Females, Females, Females. Let's don't kid ourselves that they're simply *wonderful*. [All italics except *wonderful* are supplied.]

If we knew Joe better we would understand why he formulates his fear of girls in this particular way. However, throughout our history men and women have feared being used by one another. Men have been afraid of not meeting the challenge to their masculinity posed by physical relationships with a woman and they have feared that the woman, having used them up, would throw them away. Joe's jocular and somewhat fantastic account

of what happens when he takes a girl out tells us how he perceives his relationship to girls: they will *drain* him. Since his
mother has always fed him, a reversal of roles in which he must
feed females stirs frightening fantasies. The fear of being
used by a "female"

> "... just like a toy children enjoy,
> Loved, and then thrown away."

as the old tin-pan alley ballad moans, is nowadays the product
of a socioeconomic system that does exploit people, that does
use them up and drop them.

One wonders how boys and girls ever come together at all
at this age. Reading what they write, one often gets the feeling
that both sexes are projected into courtship too early. Both
talk so much about their shyness, about not knowing what to
do, and about not knowing where they stand. There is one
thing, however, which girls discuss that boys never mention:
an irresistible feeling of detachment, an overwhelming sensation of estrangement that leaves them feeling guilty, unhappy,
and empty. Ruthie is a good example:

> There is one particular problem I have which has been
> troubling me for over three years. Strangely enough it has
> to do with boys. Like most girls, I like to have dates, to be
> popular and just plain "have a ball," but feelings which
> I cannot control often sneak in and ruin my little dream
> world. Here is an example of what I mean.
>
> I'll begin to date a boy. Pretty soon we aren't just
> dating, we're actually "going together." Everything's swell:
> I'm happy, carefree, all perfect. Then, one day I look at
> him and I get that horrible feeling that I've had with every
> boy I've gone with since 9th grade—I don't like them. It
> happens just all of a sudden. It sounds *fairly normal,*
> I guess, until you stop to realize that maybe a few minutes
> or a few hours or maybe the next day I like them again,
> maybe more than ever, but, yet, give me time and first
> thing I know I have that feeling again—*it's awful.* The
> strange thing is that while I've got them I usually take
> them for granted, BUT if I should lose them I'd just die.

My parents have tried to tell me it's normal, but if that's being normal—I'm not sure I want to be, because it's not fair to the boy to keep going with him, and I know I'd just suffer if we broke up. I'm afraid this sounds like a Martha Carr[1] letter, but then maybe it should be. [Italics supplied.]

It will be recalled that among the thirteen-year-olds Beatrice was being pushed into popularity by her family, and that Daphne and Elizabeth were suffering from sexual detachment. Sixteen-year-old Joanne seems to bring the whole matter together:

My one problem is the boys I date. I have gone out with many boys from a variety of homes, wealth, and family lives, but no matter how much they are interested in me I seem to never like them. I have problems in turning down dates with these boys because I would rather do something with just girls rather than go out with any boy I don't like. *My parents don't think I should feel this way,* after a boy has taken me out 2 or 3 times and I turn him down after these dates. They think I should be nice to all boys whether I I like them or not and just go out and have fun. They think I should not have to like a boy to go out with him. But I feel if a boy wants to spend money on a girl and have fun he should take a girl out who he knows likes his company and therefore I turn down these dates. I have trouble because *my parents think I don't go out enough with boys* when I keep turning down dates and they can't believe I am perfectly happy staying home or going out with some girls.

Also if a boy has taken me out two or three times, and I still don't enjoy his company, and I have a party at which I am to ask a boy, my parents feel that I should ask this boy who has just taken me out rather than someone else whose company I enjoy better. They think it is my duty to invite this certain boy who has taken me to nice places and spent money on me. [Italics supplied.]

A similar value system animates reciprocal gift-giving among the natives of Tikopia, but it is applied here to sexual relations

---

[1] A local Miss Lonelyhearts.

rather than to the exchange of yams. In this way parents attempt
to shove their cocktail party ethos down Joanne's throat. In the
writings of these children we yet see the floundering nobility
of childhood, that still focuses the problems of human relations
clearly before the corrosive forces of the adult world have
degraded people to yams. Parents like Joanne's are well-meaning;
they want their daughter to be happy too. Yet this pushing and
meddling and muddying the perceptions of their children creates
dilemmas like Ruthie's, Helen's, and Daphne's. The common explanation of the girls' troubles is likely to be that when girls discover they are too powerfully attracted sexually to a boy, they
withdraw and this is what Ruthie experiences as suddenly "not
liking them." We learn from Joanne, however, that, urged on by
powerful environmental forces, girls can go out repeatedly with
boys with whom they are not involved in the first place.

For Joanne's parents the morality of fun has taken precedence
over involvement and interpersonal decency, because for them
fun is a paramount value; it is more important even than being
human. In the *metaphysic of fun*, fun is what gives reality to
the world; no matter whom you are with, if you have fun together all will be right and the world will hold together. Mixed
up in this is the fuzzy idea that youth should be a swirl of
fun-having kids, out of which eventually will crystallize a
permanent marriage. However, it is not recorded that the
bacchantes remembered each other's names in the morning. So
we see that Joe's problem might turn out to be his girls' *parents*
rather than the girls themselves: the girls go along just for the
ride because that is the parents' point of view and when Joe
is broke (drained) and cannot give fun, then the girls leave
him alone. This is the morality of the car market: when yours is
used up, trade it in for a new one! Another factor is that since
boys are expected to be more "animal" than girls in American
culture, the middle-class boys' impulses toward girls are partly
released in masturbation.[1] But since boys get release this way, the
girls become anxious because the boys *can* hang back, and this
makes the girls try all the harder. Middle class, college-oriented
boys' masturbation gives the girls unfair competition.

Meanwhile another difference between boys and girls makes

[1] See Kinsey, Pomeroy, and Martin, *Sexual Behavior in the Human Male.*
Philadelphia: W. B. Saunders, 1948.

the middle-class girl's task even more challenging. At this age, though twice as many girls as boys worry about dates, twice as many boys as girls worry about study and career. Thus boys ruminate about their place in society and girls ruminate about boys.

ADOLESCENT MARRIAGE

Technological drivenness and its ally, impulse release, push the marriage age down in all social classes. By the time he is seventeen a working-class boy can earn at a machine nearly as much as his father. Why should he go to college and postpone his gratifications any longer, especially since his wife can work and help assemble the cash they need to set up housekeeping before the first child comes? For both of them marriage seems to solve all the problems of sex, loneliness, instability of personal community and feelings of not being wanted, just as installment buying settles all the residual economic difficulties not encompassed in their combined earnings. And why should his parents put up with him, as his impulses hammer at him, making him difficult to handle at home, especially since his mother, now that her children are growing up, can get a job and does not need the son's income in the home?

The situation is not essentially different in the middle class, where some of the boys will go on to the professions. The storming impulses, never really held in firm control by the new ethos of permissiveness with children, make the middle-class adolescent difficult to manage also. Into this situation step the large corporations bidding against each other for the students in engineering, physics, chemistry, and business, before they have their degrees. Marriage seems simple under these circumstances: Johnny will be making his seven to eight thousand a year as soon as he graduates, so why shouldn't the parents support him and Mary for a couple of years until he gets his degree? Marriage will "settle" both of them and relieve their parents' anxieties about Johnny's flunking and Mary's possible unmarried pregnancy. Besides, even if he doesn't get that Ph.D. in electrical engineering before he gets married, Missile Dynamics Corporation will educate him at its expense while he gets his Ph.D. on the job.

So a little social revolution is taking place in the middle class: parents are supporting their young married children "until they get on their feet," when they finish school. Of course the middle-class girl can work too, to help put her husband through his professional training.

All of this puts girls under unbearable pressure at ever younger and younger ages to get their man before all the young men are snatched up. As the marriage age declines the girls are forced into competition sooner and sooner. This starts them experimenting with courtship while they are still in the sixth grade of primary school, so that in some cities the local movie is noisy as the rendezvous of ten-year-olds every Friday night.

The net result of the decline in the age of marriage is a growing emphasis on quick and certain economic returns on the job a man takes, a rise in consumer spending for hard goods, and an increasing conflict in girls about their education, for if they try to give their time to study they impair their chances of getting a husband. It stands to reason that every minute one girl gives to study, some other girl is out there "playing the field." To forego a husband too long is to lack social status, be tagged as an "oddball," and to run the risk of classification as a "loose woman" in a culture that has not reconciled its ancient (and illusory) moral code with the realities of *The Midsummer Night's Dream*.

Thus technological drivenness penalizes girls possibly more than boys. Just as women seemed to be truly entering the promised land of equality with men, the competition among the girls becomes more intense, upsetting their personal communities, compelling them to give up the dreams of self-realization the approaching era seemed to hold out to them. In place of their dreams they take husbands—often still inadequate to the burdens thrust upon them—whom they subsequently push to "make good" and to justify their wives' renunciation of self.

WHY STUDY?

At sixteen the problem of distributing himself efficiently among his obligations hits the middle-class boy hard. Kenny expresses it well:

> My problem is the controversy between girls and studies. In order to make good grades I should stay in and study at nights and on week ends. These conflicts with my social affairs. I usually take one night a week and go out. But then if I have a date I cannot see my male friends as much as I want to and if I don't take my girl out she gets angry.

Since the hold of his pals on Kenny is still strong, his girl has to fight it by getting angry when he doesn't show her enough attention. At the same time Kenny has to get good grades to get into the college he wants. Thus he is torn between pals, girl friend, school and parents. He says:

> Another of my problems is the purpose of applying my time to my best advantage in study. When I get home in the afternoon there is usually work that my mother wishes me to do and it takes most of the time before dinner to complete. I finally get to study then it is broken up by dinner and then my father has me help him in the basement with his tools. By the time I get through I either have no time left to study or the things I have studied are forgotten.

Each of the four—pals, girl, school, and parents—makes demands on Kenny almost as if the others did not exist. The demands of each are often in the opposite direction from the others, and each wants all of him; few who make demands weigh carefully an individual's capacity to give, for in a competitive culture, if you yield an inch you may lose a mile. It is said that in our culture a "neurotic" cannot measure "reality"; but it is equally certain that "reality" uses primitive ways of measuring the capacity of human beings. The most primitive way of measurement of other human beings is simply by the dimensions of one's own desires, as an infant measures its mother. If it is true that the "neurotic" makes excessive demands for love, attention, and approval, it is equally certain that the American environment makes insatiable demands; the middle-class American ethos conceives of people as inexhaustible wells of personality resources and recoils from the man who says, "I am exhaustible."

Though it is true that a middle-class boy has a hard time

choosing among conflicting claims on his energies, the question is, "Why do the alternatives conflict?" Why, for example, isn't the middle-class boy's drive to learn and get on with his career powerful enough to override all his other interests? It is often argued that the presently moribund interest in study is caused by bad teachers and boring subject matter, but the truth goes far deeper than that. Since America devalues learning that does not contribute to income, schooling tends to become meaningless except in terms of some distant and uncertain economic goal. Even if he is able to perceive a goal, a child is often not sure that he wants it, or that his knowledge will, in the long run, ever get him where he wants to go. Few American children are able to say inwardly, "I will not fail"; indeed, their sense of inadequacy is so profound that one wonders whether they don't ask themselves, in addition to "Will what I am doing in City High ever do me any good?" the more searching question, "Can I be *done* any good?" Since this takes place while they are trying to become personalities—to become selves—an important issue is, Is the self the high school is training them to express the self they want to be? All this is quite apart from any inherent quality of interest the subject matter may have (whatever we mean by "inherent interest"), for obviously what qualities of interest a subject matter may have is related to the needs of the student.

Shifting from the schools to the children as scapegoats, critics attack children as softies who do not want to work hard. It is true that many do not want to work hard at school, and this is because they have been trained in impulse release, not in impulse restraint, the motor of hard work. American children are *Id*-creatures, living in the moonlight of consumption ecstasy. How could anybody expect them to work hard? Besides, since they see that their hard-working daddies are little at home and burdened with the irritations, coronaries, and ulcers of their work, why should they not conclude that hard work is for the birds?

It is against this background that I have tried to understand the mid-teen boy's school difficulties. Sixteen-year-old Kirk states some issues quite well:

My main problem right now is having enough time to do the things I am required to do. I go out for three sports during the school year and this takes care of all my after school time. At night I try to get all my homework done, but there is never enough time. I am always up later at night than I should be, working on school work.

On week-ends I have little time for pleasure because of my various obligations to school and to two other outside organizations.

It is a problem to me whether I should sacrifice my grades in school for some pleasure of my own or eliminate some after-school athletic activities.

I might be taking too many hard courses than I can handle. I have five solid subjects and there is usually an hour or more homework in each subject which I should do in order to make a good grade in these subjects. I am getting too little sleep and I am very tired in school during the day after a hard night of studying.

What is a "hard course"? Is it a course that is inherently "hard"? Or is it a course that, given all the other things that Kirk feels "required" to do, saps his energies? Kirk is required to take part in athletics and outside organizations though he gets no pleasure from them—a typical enough American school situation, and one that ought to be openly recognized. Since so many participate in athletics and other extracurricular activities not for the fun of it but because they are obliged to do so, it is absurd to continue to view it as fun. Since, basically, people like Kirk do not do things to please themselves but to please others, they try to make doing something for others fun, with the result that all the fun is taken out of fun. Meanwhile, since principals and coaches have to validate their jobs to the Father's Club, the PTA, and the Board of Education, coaches and principals team up with the peer group to dragoon students into athletics and clubs while teachers and parents hammer at them to get good grades. Since the culture knows neither measure nor pity in the demands it makes, students caught in this trap are held in it physically but remain emotionally uninvolved.

Karl at sixteen has a different kind of problem:

I have a problem with school work. I cannot get myself interested enough in my studies to put out my best work. I don't feel that I am working up to my ability. I try to get interested but I get nervous and then I usually stop working and do other things. I don't watch much television so I don't think that that is the problem. It must be an inability to concentrate.

I am worried about what I want to do in future years. I have always thought I wanted to be an engineer but when I really think about it I am not sure. Also I can't decide which college to attend. This is probably because I don't know what I am really interested in.

Another problem I think is that I worry too much about other people and how they are treated.

Karl says he's not interested in his work, he doesn't do his best in it, it doesn't express his real ability, and homework makes him so nervous he escapes into "other things." Whatever the cause, he can't "concentrate." He's worried about the future: Does he really want to be an engineer? Would that be *him* being an engineer? Could he really *be* an engineer? Maybe, he muses, he should be preparing himself for a career worrying about other people instead of about equations. Fear of failure, in the sense that the world will evaluate him not in terms of his real capacities but by narrow standards that give him no quarter, frightens Karl away from his work, making failure even more certain. Having picked engineering, a career with high cultural visibility and prestige, Karl is worried that his choice was the wrong one for *him*. But if he devotes his life to worrying "about how people are treated," he will have a job of low prestige and low income, for in America the rewards for worrying about others are small indeed and the "do-gooders" are an untouchable caste, contaminated by the intangible muck of failure picked up in the dwellings of those they have helped. For just as the shadow of an untouchable carries a contagion that, falling upon the food of a high-caste Hindu, poisons it, so in the West, devoting one's life to failures contaminates one's social personality because somehow the odor of the disease has been communicated from the failure to his samaritan.

There are those who think the world is imposed on them from without and there are others who feel that all their problems come from inside themselves. Kirk is among the first group and Karl belongs to the second. Kirk feels trapped because somebody or something requires and obliges him to do things against his will; Karl feels that his difficulties all spring from "inability to concentrate."

Leonard, who is sixteen, is more like Kirk:

I think that probably the problem that often disturbs me is the disagreement with such matters as how late should I stay out at night, allowance, how I should spend my time, and the useless things that I spend my well earned money on. My parents try to make me a boy who would impress them if they would meet me the first time, and since they are not the only people in the world who I come in contact with, I feel it should be my judgment that makes the decision. They refuse to realize that *times have* changed. Boys just don't come home on week-ends at 11:00 anymore. Inflation makes higher allowances necessary. They also feel that putting money into things for my car is ridiculous. I have three sisters who are very quiet and make good grades in school. I make a C+ or B— average. My older sister got A+ all the way through high school so my parents feel that I should do just as well. My teachers feel that I do not apply myself. This is all very true, but why should I stay home and study all the time? I'd be a nervous wreck and very soon I'd crack up. These are just a few of the problems that the parents of many teenagers present. Since they lived in their teens and a few decades have passed, they can't cope with the adjustment that is necessary to be fair to their children today.

Leonard has decided that a grade of C is good enough for him. He wants to have a good time and he does not intend to become a "nervous wreck" over his books. There is no inner searching, questioning, indecision, or self-doubt; it is clear to Leonard that his parents are wrong.

Leonard says that since his parents are not the only people in the world with whom he comes in contact, he has to take other people's opinions into consideration. He does not really say, "I want to be what *I* conceive myself to be," but rather, "There are many *other* people who want me to be something different from what my parents want me to be." Since he immediately talks about staying out late and about his allowance, it seems probable that the "people" he "comes in contact with" are his boy and girl friends—his immediate and intensely meaningful personal community, constructed by him with care, toil, and anxiety. Against this, his parents place the distant and uncertain goals of adult approval and career, but since coercion and punishment by parents have no place in the *Midsummer Night's Dream,* while parental love is guaranteed, Leonard's parents fight a losing battle. Like Kirk, Leonard sees himself not so much an autonomous self, determining what he shall be, but rather as a particle in a field of forces, yielding to the most massive one. He even invokes impersonal powers like inflation and changing times.

Thus, central to the problem of motivation in American culture is the question: What is a person's image of himself? Is his self-image that of a nearly helpless particle in a field of forces or is it that of an autonomous human being?

When the demands on a boy are numerous and unmeasured, so that he sees himself as constantly subject to the will of others; if he is in danger of losing his personal community if he shuts himself off in study; if he lives in a culture that does not value scholarship or scholars and does not guarantee to him the fruits of study though it prods him to indulge his impulses; if a boy can exercise only minimal choice with respect to what he shall do with his life, while at the same time he sees that his father is not content in *his* choice; if, in addition, a boy has misgivings about his own adequacy—then it is a wonder that he ever studies at all. In these circumstances learning, far from being at the core of life, is at its periphery. It is a striking paradox that in a culture where scholarship is in such poor repute, the schools themselves should be increasingly luxurious.

The situation becomes unbearable when "education" is rammed down the throats of those who do not want it. Says sixteen-year-old Lola:

My problem is making good grades and finding the right time to get my homework done. It's very hard to turn aside social activities to get my homework done. It seems as though we go to school until we reach around 21 or 22 and then go into the strange and selfish world to make money or get married and raise a family, sewing and cooking until we die. What is really gained there? All this work doesn't really get us anywhere, it seems. We take ourselves away from the things we enjoy just to do homework and then if you're like me, you turn it in and it comes back with a lousy grade. It seems like it's never-ending. I have tried very hard this year to make good grades, but haven't gotten anywhere.

Of course, in Lola we have a problem peculiar to girls, since ordinarily a woman does not look forward to a career but to raising a family. Furthermore, since in America it is not said that a mother's learning is an inheritance for her children, stimulating and shaping their intellects, Lola does not see why she is in school at all. In any event, children are a distant and, for Lola, a threatening event, while right now, outside the door, are "social activities"—the world of boys and the things "we enjoy."

Since study prevents girls from concentrating on boys, and since the ultimate value of girls' education is especially problematical, it is not surprising that, like Lola, they should, at times, have a violent hatred of schooling. Lucy is another explosive sixteen-year-old:

My main problem right now is homework. In the past two weeks I have learned to hate school and homework. I'd like to know how I can get interested in it again. I used to love it. I've tried to get back in the swing of things as I used to be, but I just can't seem to do it.

Another problem I have to contend with is my social life. Don't get me wrong—I'm not complaining. Say, for two week-ends straight I'll be full with dates; then for the next two week-ends I won't have one single date. I guess every girl goes through that, though. I have this certain boy in mind whom I'd like to go out with, but I guess I'll just have to wait.

Sometimes the teachers don't seem fair to me when I work myself silly on some of their assignments. I will try my best this coming semester, but it seems the more I try, the worse I get. Last report card I made all B's except for French which I made a D in. I guess if I really tried to make it interesting, it would become so eventually.

How do you improve your personality? I am kind of shy when it comes to talking to new acquaintances.

Though all cultures should have ways in which a person can measure his own achievement, we have seen that in America the devices are sometimes lacking, and often the measures— like the so-called rising standard of living—compel standardization and conformity. The function of high school, then, is not so much to communicate knowledge as to oblige children finally to accept the grading system as a measure of their inner excellence. And a function of the self-destructive process in American children is to make them willing to accept not their own, but a variety of other standards, like a grading system, for measuring themselves. It is thus apparent that the way American culture is now integrated it would fall apart if it did not engender feelings of inferiority and worthlessness.

All currents come together in the compositions of two sixteen-year-olds, Leah and Mary. Leah writes:

I do not know whether you would call it a problem or not, but I worry a lot. My main worry is my school work. My education is very important to me and I always strive to do better. To me, my grades are an indication of my ability. Therefore, I try to make as good grades as possible. Up to now I had been doing quite well. But the other day I received a book report on which I got a very bad grade. I don't know how it happened. It didn't seem to me any different than ones I had been getting A's on. Right now I'm afraid to write another book report because I don't know how it will turn out. The same day I got back the book report, a history test was returned and, again, I made an exceptionally low grade compared to ones I had been making. The only explanation I can give is that I was excited over the coming Christmas holidays.

An American girl who is unsuccessful in her studies can try to be successful with boys; but though these are the main paths to self-validation in the high school years, it is next to impossible to tread both of them. Although it is true that in the middle class success with boys is the more glamorous achievement, failures in studies can provide powerful energies for a compensatory courtship drive, a drive which, if successful, can enable the girl who flunks to thumb her nose at her more scholarly but less sexy rivals.

In Mary, however, we have a girl who, having placed courtship in the forefront of her life, finds failure in school hard to take:

> I am a 16 year old girl. One of my biggest problems is to keep my mind on my school work. I go steady and have for two years. My boy friend and I plan on marriage after I graduate. This makes me want my school years to be over in a hurry, thus making my school work decrease and my grades go from bad to worse. I, at one time, had wanted to be a nurse, but now I find that I'm telling myself that I'm not capable. This worries me because I think a woman should be able to get a job at any time in case of her husband dying or the like, but I still am not sure if I want to wait so much longer. Some other big problems are trying so hard to conquer my fault of not being able to make decisions, trying to get along with everyone, not to talk bad about other people, to be fair at all times, and to be an all-around *good* girl.

Since she wants to marry quickly, school becomes unimportant to Mary and her grades drop. As her grades fall, her opinion of herself declines and she begins to think that she lacks the ability to be a nurse or even "an all-around good girl." That is to say, since Mary is turning out "bad" in one way (poor studies), she seems to feel she is going to turn out "bad" in all ways. The fact that children accept the grade system as a measure of the self may turn out to mean that for many sensitive or anxious children being no good at school proves they are no good in any way at all.

SUMMARY

In discussing teen-agers' answers to the question, "What are your main personal problems?" I have rambled, using the responses now to illustrate a trend, now to develop an idea suggested by something written by a particular child. In this way, however, I think I have been able to bring out many of the concerns of teen-agers. I see many of their preoccupations with acceptance, appeal, personality pruning, and conformity as stemming from the great population flux of our country, that makes the personal community so uncertain from day to day that people must use every possible device to guarantee that they will not be alone. This enormous population instability, and the ensuing fact that relationships are never guaranteed, but must be won, is the source of uncertainty in interpersonal relationships, of vicious gossip, and of the hunger for popularity among teen-agers.

Because boys are united in "flocks" by the requirements of their games, they are held together more tightly than girls, and hence the competition among girls for friends is more intense than among boys, and gossip literally runs wild. Meanwhile, as courtship becomes more important to the girls, competition and gossip increase in intensity. What makes the courtship experience particularly tense for girls is that it is the only activity through which they can validate their femininity. Since boys can validate their masculinity in a greater variety of ways, the chase does not have the same sex-validating importance for them. Behind the girls' courtship drive, of course, looms the parental—usually the maternal—image, tirelessly keeping tally of each date. While many girls mention their parents in connection with the courtship drive there is not one boy in my sample who does.

Of course, we can understand maternal concern about courting: as the age of marriage declines, and as girls are permitted to be more aggressive in their sexual advances, the competition for boys grows ever sharper. It is no exaggeration to say that the teen-age American girl lives on a razor-edge of sexual competition. Thus beneath the gaiety of any teen-age party throbs the anxiety of being left out next time, of losing a boy tomorrow that one has today or not getting the right one; of not getting the one you really want, of not getting the popular one, and so on. Such concerns appear much less often in boys' responses.

It is really in the mid-teens that boy's and girl's responses come to resemble one another. Between fifteen and seventeen they both seem to turn inward in self-examination, and they ask themselves, "What am I? What are my capabilities? Is there something wrong with me? How can I change?" Though these questions may have suggested themselves earlier, at the mid-teens they surge strongly into consciousness. Then boys and girls become articulate about their lack of self-confidence, their feelings of inadequacy, their indecision, and many other types of unsureness. I have urged, however, that such feelings are extremely useful to a culture that requires high drive and the ability to work not at what one wants to do but at what one has to do. The person with feelings of inadequacy will readily accept a job doing what he has to do rather than what he wants to do because he is not sure that he really could do well at what he wants to do even if he had a chance to do it; and such a person will drive hard to prove he *is* something.

Thus the answers to the question, "What are your main personal problems?" have enabled us to give a preliminary sketch of the misgivings and anxieties of the troubled teens. Naturally, a question about personal problems does not elicit descriptions of the pleasures of life. What has happened, indeed, is that courtship and friendship—presumably two of the greatest joys of life—are discussed with considerable anxiety. And this is a central paradox of the age—that its pleasures are often negated by a concomitant anxiety, so that love itself, one of the dearest values of our culture, becomes a drive—the courtship drive.

Compositions written in answer to a question can tell us much, but we still must come to closer grips with youth than we can through mere compositions, however sincere. The next chapter, therefore, attempts to examine the problems of youth in their wholeness, through a study of a high school and interviews with about 200 students there.

7: Rome High School and Its Students

kiss
us
we're
sweet 17

SEVENTEEN is 17 . . . isn't everybody?
Of course we know that everybody can't be 17. But SEVENTEEN Magazine lives in such a whirl of girl (girl 13 to girl 20) that sometimes it seems as if everybody who is anybody must be 17 or thereabouts. Because teen-agers are the most powerful, influential, affluential chunk of population today. Twasn't always thus. Back in September 1944, when SEVENTEEN started, a teen-ager was a nobody—with no voice, no status, no jobs, no money, no clothes to call her own, no makeup to call her own, no nothing to call her own. Now she has SEVENTEEN to call her own—which she does regularly, lovingly, gratefully, trustingly, faithfully every month. We practically invented the teen-ager. Certainly we found that forlorn forgotten generation. And you know what they say about finders—*finders keepers!*[1]

IN OUR CULTURE MOST OF THE FEATURES OF ADOLESCENT life are a reverberation of adult life. It is impossible to under-

[1] Advertisement in the *New York Times*, September 5, 1961.

stand why adolescents behave as they do in high school—their most important contact with the adult world, outside of their families—unless we know the shape of high school life. For the high school is not only a place where children spend five or more hours each day for three or four years, but it is an institution run by adults *for the entire community* and, because of this, expresses the demands of the community and the idiosyncracies of the adults who run the high school. This chapter attempts to suggest how adolescent life revolves around the high school, and the manner in which the school, as operated by adults, influences the children as products of their families.

When an institution is studied as a whole one can see the relationship among its parts. It stands to reason that the parts must somehow mesh, for otherwise the institution could not continue. Of course, there will be conflicts within it, but the conflicts will themselves be an expression of the interrelationship among the parts. A high school could not run at all if it did not meet major requirements of the students, and the students could not continue in the school if they did not meet the requirements of the school as conceived by the adults *and* by their peers. This is simple common sense. Thus if Rome High emphasizes athletics, it is because the community and the students want it so; and if the students like football, it is because if they do not they will not be able to endure the environment of Rome High. If Rome High encourages girls to dress in "high fashion" it is because this is what the community wants, and if the girls eschew high fashion they will be wall-flowers. The same considerations apply to scholarship. Community, school, peer group thus become a self-reinforcing system. It is the purpose of this chapter to illustrate how this system works in one community.

Rome is not a strange name in American geography, for as the early settlers moved across the continent they scattered a multitude of Spartas, Athens, Troys, Syracuses, Corinths, and Romes over the land. Some are villages, some became cities, but none approached the grandeur of the originals. Still our ancestors could dream; they read history and in their imaginations future fame sprouted in the tracks of their wagon wheels. Thus the names of ancient greatness are scattered at random across the

United States; and almost everywhere they have become symbols of the gap between reality and aspiration. So I have chosen Rome as the name of the community I have studied; for although *it applies to no city in the United States that actually bears the name,* Rome symbolizes the disparity between reality and hope in the community I discuss.

The Rome of which I speak is a lower-middle-class suburb. Its boys in football costume are *its* helmeted soldiers; there is a special dining room for them in the school cafeteria, special food for them, and all they want of it. In Rome High the athletes are the cultural maximizers, and it is the duty of Mr. Aurelius, the principal, to see that his teams win. Mr. Aurelius is not unique in this pre-occupation with prowess and success in high school athletics but shares it with much of the Rome region, where high school principals, coaches, PTA's, and Fathers' Athletic Associations hover over the players, while scouts from distant universities offer scholarships to Rome's heroes. This does not mean that Mr. Aurelius has no concern for scholarship, but rather that the drive that is maximized in the high school spirit is the competitive sportive one. The most popular males are found in the athletic clique.

This being the case, I shall, in introducing the reader to Rome High, first give a little attention to athletics. After that I take the reader on a one-day visit to Rome High with the Researcher and Lila Greene, a fourteen-year-old freshman. Then we meet Heddie, the sweetheart of Lila's brother Bill, both students at Rome. At dinner at the Greene's we encounter Mr. Greene, Bill, and Lila around the table. Mrs. Greene will not be there because she and Mr. Greene are divorced. Next we go on a double date with Heddie and Bill and the Researcher and her escort. Having become acquainted with Rome High and a few of its average students the reader will meet Chris Lambert, a deviant boy, and through him will learn something of the problems of this type of youth. Finally, because we were able to follow up our study of students now in Rome High with graduates, now freshman at University, it will be possible to round out our picture through joining two of them on an evening at a teen-age dance "joint."

JIM EVANS, AN OUTSTANDING ATHLETE

We begin with a visit by a Researcher to the home of Jim Evans, sixteen years old, a junior, and an outstanding athlete.

When I got to Jim's house he was not there, and his parents were very apologetic, explaining that the basketball coach had called a pop scrimmage, so he could not be there to receive me. They offered me a cup of coffee and a piece of chocolate cake, which I accepted. Their house was modest, I estimate lower middle class or working class. The living room was cluttered with newspapers, coffee cups, etc. Jim's mother was wearing a house dress and her husband wore slacks and a sweatshirt with *Meredith Co.* across the front and back—probably from a company baseball team.

Jim's father said that they've been going to basketball games for ages. Their oldest son is a freshman at ———— on an athletic scholarship, and he played first string basketball all through high school. He has received offers of athletic scholarships from Northwestern, University of Missouri, Ohio State, and others. His mother, who was standing in the dining room ironing, said that it was "amazing how people cater to athletes." She said that when they took their son to ———— the coach met them at the parking lot, carried their suitcases, took them to lunch and on a tour of the University; installed their son in the dorm, et cetera, et cetera, "And all of this while the other kids were standing around not knowing what to do or where to go."

I asked if basketball took much of Jim's time nowadays, and they told me that he has practice every day after school for two and a half hours, games every Tuesday and Friday, and occasional pop scrimmages. But they did not seem to think that this was too much time.

Jim's mother said that the catering to athletes goes on in high school too, but she said also that a teacher told her that if Jim was good at basketball he would be assured of an education. She said that the athletes have a special lunchroom at Rome High, and that they get special food, as much of it as they want. The rest of the kids eat in the school cafeteria and get one serving of the regular fare. If the athlete's grades begin to fall he receives special tutoring from the teachers.

Mr. Evans is a manual worker of limited skill, who has found a way to get his sons out of the little-initiative-and-little-education, low-living-standard rut. Sports readily became a way out for his sons because he himself is athletically inclined. He cannot know, of course, that what a boy on an athletic scholarship gets is a formal misrepresentation of an education.

Jim was not highly articulate in his interviews; we would hardly expect an American boy, tied up in athletics, to be very verbal. Still there is a great deal in his short, ungrammatical sentences.

The Researcher reported the result of his first interview with Jim.

When I arrive at Jim's house, he, his father, and little brother are plastered to the TV set. Jim and I move into the dining room to talk. The TV is going rather loudly; there is a program on in which some guy is trying to get rid of a body—that of his former girl-friend, whom he has just murdered. This makes it rather difficult to concentrate on the interview. It is a suspense-type movie, and I'm as anxious as the rest of the household to see if the murderer gets caught. I explain the project to Jim and we begin:

R: I'd like to talk about your friends—can you tell me if there is a bunch of guys you see a lot of?

J: Yeah. There's Burt Schneiderhof, Pickles Kovac, Dave Platmin, Tom Burke and Ed Laughlin.

R: Who would you say is your best friend?

J: Dave.

R: What do you do together?

J. We go to the show together and double date. We both drive. We double date about every three weeks or a month. We go to the show about once every two weeks. Sometimes I go out on a date alone, but not lately.[1]

---

[1] Actually it took three questions to elicit these answers, but they have been left out in the interest of brevity.

R: Can you tell me something about Dave? What kind of a guy is he?

J: Well, he's President of the Student Council at Rome. He's———.[1] He drives a car. He's got a real nice personality. He's a great guy. He's active in sports. As a matter of fact, we just came from a baseball game—Rome vs. Cliff Heights. We won.

R: What position do you play?

J: I play second base; Dave plays first base.

R: Your father told me you play basketball—did you have a good season?

J: Yeah.

R: He told me your brother plays too.

J. Yeah. He got a scholarship at ———.

R: How's he doing?

J: Real good. He's the best player they got. He helped me a lot with my game.[2]

R: What kind of a guy is he?

J: Oh, he's got a good personality. He goes out with girls a lot. Uh-h-h. We play basketball together and play games and cards at home. We have a lot of fun together.

R: What would you say gives a guy a good personality?

J: A sense of humor, and uh-h-h-h understanding—you know, when a guy can put himself in other peoples' shoes.

R: Do you think looks and clothes have anything to do with it?

J: Oh, yes. I think so. I don't know about clothes; I guess clothes do too—you know, if you dress too shabby or something.

R: What do you think is important about having a sense of humor?

J: 'Cause people like people who are happy-go-lucky and laugh a lot.

R: What do you think is important about understanding?

J: I guess because people like to be understood and like people who understand 'em.

[1] Nationality mentioned.
[2] Interviewer had to ask an extra question to get this information.

R: Who would you say are your next best friends after Dave?

J: There's a couple: Laughlin and Kovac, I guess.

R: What are they like?

J: They're nice guys—they treat you nice. They're good guys.

R: Can you think of an example of a time when you got mad at Dave?

J: Well, like sometimes he wants to go home early Friday night or something and I don't want to go. But I don't get real mad.

R: Is there anything that you and he disagree about?

J: Uh-h-h, well, uh-h-h, we disagree about music. He likes jazz and I like popular music on the radio.

At this point Jim's mother comes in. We shake hands. She is about five feet six, very stocky, with bleached (?) blonde hair. She asks whose bike is parked outside. She's very impressed with my bicycle and drags the whole family out to look. I explain its finer points to an admiring audience but Jim's father is only mildly impressed. His little brother is very much impressed. Jim's mother tells me about the time she got a racer for his older brother and was trying to show him how to ride it. They live on a slight hill. She forgot that the brakes were on the handle-bars and she wound up in the shrubbery at the bottom of the hill. We all laugh.

She asks me if I have my degree yet and I tell her that I'm working on a master's degree in anthropology. When the little one asks what that is she explains that it's the study of evolution and primitive people. She asks me if I have read a book called *The American Indian.* Jim's mother seems to be an active reader. Last time I was over at their house she was reading books on the Civil War.

R: Let's see. Do you and Dave ever argue about music?

J: Yeah. We don't really argue, we just disagree and tell each other we're crazy. You know, friends are bound to

disagree once in awhile. We have lunch together every day;
our gang all eat at the same table.

R: Are most of them active in sports?

J: All of 'em are.

R: Would you say it was a clique?

J: You could say that. There's pretty many of 'em. About
16 or 17. You know, the more popular guys.

R: Are there other cliques around Rome [High]?

J: Uh huh.

R: Can you describe some of them to me?

J: Well, you know, the groups don't mix much. There's
one group of guys that don't go out much on Friday or
Saturday nights. You know, the brains. They're all pretty
smart guys.

Our hero on the TV is smuggling the body out of a hotel
wrapped in a rug. The desk clerk asks him where he's going
and he replies that he is taking the rug out to be cleaned.
It's about 2 A.M. Very tense situation.

J: Of course, there's girls' clicks.

R: What are the girls' clicks like?

J: Well, the most popular clicks are like the boys'. You
know, they're sort of mediocre in grades. And the cutest
girls are usually in the largest click.

[Researcher then turns the conversation briefly to girls
and elicits the fact that Jim went "steadily" for a while. The
difference between going "steady" and going "steadily" is
that the former is more binding than the latter.]

R: What did you do together?

J: We went to parties and to the show. I wasn't driving
then, of course, so there wasn't much to it.

R: Did you notice many changes in your outlook on life
when you started driving?

J: I guess you feel bigger; you know you can date more
when you're driving. I think it's pretty important.

R. Did you make many new friends?

J: Yeah, I notice that anybody that learns to drive becomes more popular, especially with the kids that aren't
driving yet—with the younger kids.

[The Interviewer learns from Jim that he makes $7.50 a
week working and that it goes for shows, dates and "things
like that." He also elicits the fact that Jim helps Dave out
occasionally by driving him to school or to the library.]

R: Is there anything else that you and Dave do for each
other?
J. Not much.

R: How do you feel about sports?
J: I think it makes you enjoy school a whole lot more. I
think everybody should go out for at least one sport. It
helps you to develop your body.
R: How do you think kids in general feel about sports?
J: Most of them like it pretty much. We have a pretty
good attendance at all of our games. We have plenty of
team spirit. And it helps to make you a lot more popular.
Girls look up to you more and other guys envy you more.

It was nearly 9 P.M. and Jim was obviously getting bored,
so I thought it time to conclude the session. As he walked
me to the door he gave his little brother a healthy smack
on the arm, and the little one said, "What are you, some
kind of a nut?"

Athletics, popularity, and "mediocre" grades go together with
inarticulateness and poor grammar. Standing as it does at the
center of lower-middle-class Rome's need to *be* something, the
athletic complex is the natural pivot of social life, school politics,
and the competitive sexual ritual, where a girl measures her
success by the athletes she dates. What is most important in attempting to grasp American social character, however, is that the
athletic complex is a great machine for generating communal
Selfhood. The teams are great hearts pumping Self-substance into
the anemic Self of the community—students and school included.
When you are on a team girls seek you out and boys envy you in

Rome, because when the team wins the communal Self is replenished. In a sense one might say that Jim's poor grades and grammar are ransom for the community's Self. This must be understood in order to comprehend the American phenomenon of the athletic blockhead.

One kind of Self-substance, however, drives out another, for in the process of trying to become a Self through athletics Jim impairs his chances of becoming one through study and learning. On the other hand, if Jim tried this he might never get to college at all because his family cannot afford it. The paradox then is that athletics, the very institution that is antagonistic to higher education, makes it possible for some who might never have had a chance at higher education to accept its counterfeit—the athletic scholarship. In contemporary American schools sports and study have become almost metaphysical opposites—the very place where they should achieve a true unity. If only students with A's and B's were permitted on the teams, the whole character of the relationship between sports and study would change. But the competitive struggle cannot permit this, for the confrontation of defeat is impossible for a weak communal Self.

The central activity of all cultures is always a Self-maximizing machine ("ego-building"), whether it be the ceremonial exchange of necklaces and arm bands as in the famous *kula* of the Trobriand Islands in the South Pacific, the economic competition of businessmen in our culture, or the rat-race to get one's articles and books published in the American academic world.

The reason athletics have such high status is that the teams generate Self-substance to some degree for almost everyone, not just for the athletes. The status of the Self with reference to a team of which one is not a member is peculiar, for though a team rooter experiences a transient enhancement of his Self if the team wins, and some depression if it loses, its failure does not touch him at his core. The rooter is in the unique position of being able to vibrate during the game as if he were a true Self, and to accept team success while insulating himself against the effects of failure. It is true, of course, that the "fan" becomes quite sad when his team is in a losing streak, but his depression is mild compared to that of the members of the team. On the other hand, he can feel exhalted when the team wins. Teams are externaliza-

tions of the communal Self-system, that permit it to expand when
the game is won, but do not cause it to collapse when the game is
lost. Hence their importance in American life—especially in small
communities like Rome.

Though every culture has a Self-maximizing system, it has
made no difference in the history of *Homo sapiens* what the core-
object of the Self-maximizing system was. "Nature" (to anthropo-
morphize "her" for a moment) has never "cared" whether the
maintenance of the Self-image depended on the accumulation of
cowry shells, useless boulders, as on Rossel Island in the Pacific,
arm bands and necklaces as in the Trobriands, or foundation
grants as in contemporary academia. It was all the same to her.
Nature has only cared that the Self-system be *maintained,* because without a Self her creature—without instincts—could not
survive. Communal Self-maximizing systems that are almost
wholly external (such as teams) are contemporary creations;
but we must always expect that when there is no core-object to
be internalized by individuals acting for themselves, they will
find substitutes.

When we return now to Jim Evans we can understand the bio-
cultural pressures on him, and something—though not everything
—of why he is ungrammatical, laconic, and apparently somewhat
dull: his social mission is fulfilled. Looking at his friendships we
notice that they are based in team games, an early form of
juvenile male activity. The narrowing of one's friendships to
team mates in the teens is the persistence into adolescent life of
a pattern that had intense meaning in childhood. Thus the athlete
tends to be a person whose basic adjustment to males has not
changed, whose relation to males continues to be understandable
largely in terms of childhood behavior that was so rewarding that
it has persisted. To be an athlete one must not only be good at
the sport and enjoy it; one must also find association in team
play the most gratifying of all possible associations. The sight of
one's team mate picking up the fast grounder and whipping it to
first; the reassurance felt as the interference mows down the
opponents when one carries the football; the thrill of the blocked
pass as a team mate stops the opposing guard dead in the heat of
a fast basketball game; the comfort of the team mate's face
coming out of the foam in a relay swim, become part of the flesh

and bone of an athlete. He does not readily give any of it up. These are things his team mates *do* for him. Hence Jim's statement that he and Dave, his best friend, do not *do* much for each other cannot be understood entirely in terms of lack of reciprocal solicitude. Actually they could hardly do *more* for each other, collaborating as they do all year in team play. There is something else in the relationship of athletes to one another that Jim does not mention, but which is there all the time—the language. It consists of the endless itemization of games they play together, discussion of the games and athletic meets of others, comparisons of "times"—time for the fifty-yard dash, for the two-twenty, for the quarter mile. Baseball has a fantastic lore and history: batting averages of players back to the early days of the twentieth century, prices paid for players, number of batters struck out, no-hit-no-run games pitched, errors, assists, and so on almost without end. If high schools boys are on the same teams together that is almost all they need from each other. Jim and Dave, however, round out their friendship with arguments about popular music. In this kind of association time is rich and full, but basic problems are not handled. This is the girl friend's job. When the "right one" comes along, association based on externals and on the internalization of team mates is no longer felt to be enough.

It is probably because the athletic life fulfills itself in a never-ending round that Jim can scarcely say more about his friends than that they treat him nice, have nice personalities, or are great guys. However, he likes Dave better than all the rest of his clique, and perhaps it is because Dave has, above all the rest, understanding, a value that Jim esteems so highly. We cannot say more about what Jim means by "understanding," for we have no data.

In this family it looks as if Mrs. Evans, not Mr. Evans, is the imp of fun. It is she who enthusiastically drags the family out to look at the Researcher's bicycle; and it is she who tried to show the older brother how to ride and ended up in the bushes. Mothers as imps of fun are almost nonexistent in my sample of about 400 adolescents, but considering the rapidity of role change in America one could readily predict that mothers are the coming imps! They will have to be if they want to keep up with father!

A DAY AT ROME HIGH

Rome High is by no means entirely dedicated to athletics and fun; it is also an institution of learning. Yet fun looms large in life at Rome High. Let us spend a day there with Lila Greene, a fourteen-year-old freshman. We start at the Researcher's meeting with Lila.

I pick Lila up at her house. When she asks her father for money he says, "What about the ten dollar bill that so mysteriously disappeared?" She smiles, shrugs her shoulders, and says, "O.K., you win." On the way to school she tells me that it was really twenty, but if he's forgotten, "that's alright with me." Lila and her brother Bill are both interested in figuring the angles.

The first class we go to is gym. Lila introduces me to her girl friends—too many for me to catch the names of all of them—and to the gym teacher. Lila undresses and dresses in the shower stall in the girl's dressing room, saying that sometimes they throw girls in there to dunk them. They all like the gym teacher because they threw her in with her street clothes on and she didn't get mad.

The girls are all sharply dressed, except, of course, those who already have their gym suits on. There are mirrors everywhere and the girls are preening themselves in front of them. Lila says, "Most of the girls consist of padded bras and girdles, but they're clever artists; and besides, *what else can you do?*" Lila is not wearing a girdle.

Lila tells me about three girls in this class who dislike her and when I ask why, she says, "Jealous, probably. I make decent grades and have more physical ability and have fair success with boys. One of those girls, I guess, only goes out every three months. I didn't think that was possible. The senior boys were kidding around the other day about senior girls who have never been kissed. I didn't believe it at first." I say, "Oh, it's possible," and she says, "Never? Oh, my!" She asks about my dating habits and says she goes out at least four or five times a month, and was out until 2 A.M. at the backwards dance[1] Saturday. They went for pizza afterwards, and she paid her half of the bill because it was backwards. A couple of girls have asked her whether or not she paid.

Lila notices a boy circling the gym floor running, and says, "He's a nice guy, except he has beady eyes; you can always tell by their eyes." There are NO SMOKING signs everywhere. The boys and girls are separated and do not approach one another. Girls tend to clique up. Class seems to go from ultra-chic hair styles to long mops, with no middle ground. I see two bleached blondes. This gym class contains students from all years.

Gym class is over. Back to dressing room. There *is* a prevalence of padded bras and girdles here—and all of them so young! I ask, "Aren't the fellows disappointed?" and Lila says, "They don't know. Maybe some do, but most are fooled. I wear one once in awhile." One girl, a junior, looks like a high fashion model, bleached blonde.

French class. Mrs. Carling. Class is very crowded. The students get their exams back. Generally the class did well. Lila signals to me that she got A. Most girls wear expensive sweaters. If I had no job I'd have a hard job meeting this standard. I wonder how the less prosperous do. Boys in class all wear slacks but run-of-the-mill shirts. No outstanding marks of wealth among them and no bizarre haircuts.

One girl in the class is Danish. Lila asked her if she spoke Danish and the girl seemed disgusted at this oft-repeated question as she said, "of course." She was pale blonde, wore heavy eye-shadow, little lipstick. Class ring on chain around her neck, another on her hand. Apparently she has stripped her steady of all the tokens of love he possesses. He is hers!

The teacher is wearing a lavender wool dress, four inch spikes, rope beads. She is stocky but not fat, has red hair, and wears glasses; not unattractive. Girls are segregated from boys.

The next class is Home Economics, where the room is a lovely pink with tan upholstered chairs, and is luxurious

[1] A dance where boy–girl etiquette is reversed.

and roomy compared to other rooms in the school. One wall is covered with posters I imagine the girls made. They have to do with hair, skin, weight, posture, grooming. The teacher, Miss Clements, is probably about 45 years old and is tall and bigboned. She is wearing a brown suit of good quality and glasses. Her brown hair is waved back and her lipstick is a little too bright for her age. Her rope beads may be a little frivolous but conform in general to the anticipated appearance of one in her circumstances.

Miss Clements announces that Mrs. Elphin, the special visiting speaker for today, will talk to us about wool. On the wall are posters from Helena Rubinstein cosmetics about skin care, Bobbie Brooks clothing ads, a poster on Facts About Perspiration, and in one corner there is a large, threesided wardrobe mirror, in front of which a student, with the assistance of two friends, has been primping herself since class began. She is wearing a very elaborate oriental type hair-style, piled intricately around her head, and with the help of her assistants she is combing the strays back in place. I am convinced she could not have constructed this by herself; or if she did, it must have taken her hours. She sits down before the speaker begins.

Miss Clements says notebooks are due today but she will understand if some are not handed in on time because today is Monday. Lila passes me a note saying that when the teacher talks so do the students, and the teacher gets mad, shuts up, and so do the students. I say, "Can't win for losing," and Lila agrees. She thinks the situation is very funny.

Mrs. Elphin launches her lecture on wool with a history of British wool, the introduction of wool into our Southwest by the Spanish, the British law against sheep-raising in the Colonies, et cetera. "But to move on to *something more interesting*," says Mrs. Elphin, "we're all interested in our personal affairs, 'How does this relate to me?' Now what sort of things interest us?" Hands wave, and one girl says, "Style." "Yes!" Mrs. Elphin explains that one example of adaptability of wool to style is the way it can be used in dolman sleeves (as in the wool jersey sweater she is wearing) without gathering or bulging. Another advantage is price: it cost a little more per yard, but it comes in extended widths—45 and 54 inches—so you're really *saving*.

Lila passes me a note: it says we have second lunch hour and that her stomach and backbone are one. Same here. I notice she is wearing a purple corduroy jumper and white blouse, both brand new. *This* is why she was wheedling daddy for money this morning, *she tells me*.

Mrs. Elphin drones on: "Now admit it girls, most of us shop in the budget department, not among the higher priced dresses." I wonder! She gives advice on yard goods: "Don't buy a dress if you find the same pattern in the yard-goods department, because soon everyone else will have it and they'll be *dirty, untidy, cheap* people, and you'll be *so* unhappy! Then you'll have to keep wearing it to get the good out of it, and you'll be miserable. However, if you see high priced dresses see if you can duplicate the materials in yard goods because that means it's coming into style."

I notice Lila is wearing a small silver band on her right hand. She says it is because she is one of four girls who go around together. I think we should look into clique symbols.

The lecturer says that wool is good even for summer because it is its own little air-conditioning unit; it keeps out both cold and warm air. One girl says, "I wear wool in summer but I was afraid to say so because I thought everyone would think I was queer or odd or something." If this is so, how did she ever venture into the street so attired? Might not her fellows see her and think her "queer or odd?"

Lila is interested in the lecturer's shoes. We saw a lady with turquoise spikes and Lila commented on them. In French class she was talking to another girl about three inch heels that she wore to the dance. Mrs. Elphin advises us to remember not to *overload* the closet, otherwise our delicate woolens cannot breathe. You should always choose quality rather than quantity. Most girls could get along in school for a whole season with only two good wool skirts, though some girls think they need fifteen, and this is ridiculous. A girl says, "But you'd always look the same," and the lecturer says, "Not if you mix them with blouses and sweaters." The money you save on having fewer skirts can be spent on many sweaters.

The class is getting restless. Lila passes a note: "Next is English class with Mrs. Nasson. There's a tack epidemic, watch before you sit."

One negro girl in the class is very well dressed and well-groomed. She sits with the white girls. Her hairdo is very chic—probably a professional job. Three other negro girls sit in a group by themselves. They are not as expensively dressed or as well-kempt, but certainly they are not messy. One is wearing a going-steady ring on a chain around her neck. She is more high-fashion than the others of her group.

I am introduced to Mrs. Nasson, the English teacher, who reads my credentials to the class. Since we are affiliated with the United States Department of Health, Education and Welfare she announces that I'm working for Kennedy's cabinet! Then she tells the class about their research project for this Spring. She lectures them on the abuse of freedom, saying that stopping by the restroom to smoke when you're on your way to the library is breaking two rules, because you have no intention of going to the library anyway. She says also that speeding is an abuse of the right to drive.

Lila tells me that when I was up front with Mrs. Nasson the boys in back were discussing whether or not to put a tack on my chair in order to teach me 4th hour English culture. Lila says she rescued me in time, by removing the tack. It could have been worse, she says, if she had left the tack there.

The research project is to be entitled "The obligation of freedom; its use and abuse." They are to write 500 words or less. The students think teacher is killing them with work. The essay is to be written either in ink or on the typewriter.

Mrs. Nasson then asks the class, "What if I'm a Communist and get up on a soap box and talk about how the capitalists are rich while I have nothing, and that therefore we should reapportion wealth through the medium of the state?" The class is horrified and seems eager to put her down. Apparently they are terrified of Communism. Then their anger gets lost in arguments about legal ways to silence the teacher [were she such a Communist]. Mrs. Nasson talks about the fact that her husband and father have always felt free to criticize the government, and she and her family are certainly not Communists.

At this point Lila passes me a note: "That's Mildred talking. Mediocre person. The one in the corner is Carl Warren. He's in favor of tacks: one of the ring-leaders of the bunch."

The class gets into a discussion about Miss Pope who, I think, is a teacher in Rome High. Miss Pope has made some comment about reckless teen-age drivers, and the girl next to me grumbles in great disgust, "They always blame it on us." The class, however, agrees that Miss Pope has the right to her own opinion. They decide also that the law must decide whether Mrs. Nasson can speak about Communism or not. Mrs. Nasson wants everybody to read the article "Erosion of individual liberties: current crisis could be decisive" by Marquis Childs, and use it as a reference for their theme. . . .

Lila remarks by note on other students. Eddie Strong is a tack-master. Nellie Burke is smart but not goody-goody. Rob is in the second stage of imbecilic ignorance; heaven knows how he passes! Tim Aupen is very smart, gets good grades, knows what's going on and how to be legally innocent.

Mrs. Nasson reads an outstanding essay from the previous assignment—it surprised her because the boy had been a gold-bricker and procrastinator. She mentions how Woodrow Wilson had died of a broken heart over the failure of the League of Nations and talks about Barney Baruch who is a Jewish man who was advisor to many presidents: he used to sit around on park benches thinking. None of the students had heard of him. These are examples of topics not covered in the essay.

Lila passes a note about Tess Murray: very intelligent; scar on neck; Lila doesn't know how it got there. She is

certain it's one of the reasons Tess, "Just doesn't care.
I wish she'd come out of it. I try to help her, but not much
[can be done]; she's still the same."

There is a poster on the board by Eddie Strong:

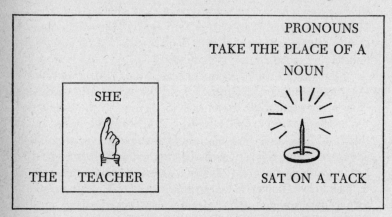

The students are upset because they get off Thursday
and Friday and Mrs. Nasson expects them to prepare an
outline for their paper during those two days. Poor im-
posed-upon kids!

Hour bell rings. Pauline comes up to Lila and says, "I
heard about you going out and getting a drink after the
dance on Saturday night. You silly kid—ordering a Tom
Collins!" I ask Lila if she got it and she giggles and says
yes. She mentions the place.

At lunch in the cafeteria the students are separated into
cliques of boys and girls. The colored students sit apart
from the white and they also are subdivided into all boy
and all girl cliques. At our table I met the six girls Lila
usually has lunch with. They are all rather plain except
Pauline, whom I met in English. She is a very pretty
blonde, with blue eyes. One girl gets the job of fetching
and carrying the cokes and candy bars for the others. I
ask Lila why and she says it's because this girl is a minister's
daughter and they tell her to be a good Samaritan and set
them all a good example. When I look dubious Lila laughs.
Lila tells me everyone cheats in math class *because* Mr.

Snider only tells you how to do the problems *after* they're due, so you don't know how to do them. Also he doesn't give enough time to do them, so they copy from the more inventive students. All the girls wanted to know where Lila got served her Tom Collins. One girl says, "Where? I'll be there." A girl who says she has no desire to drink promptly gets cut out of the conversation. Lila won't tell where she got the drink. She says, "It wasn't something wild, *I just felt grown up,* so I thought I would. I didn't go out to get drunk." Liquor is available at the Greene house; her dad offered me some when I was there last time. Her brother Bill said he'd fix me a highball but wasn't sure how to go about it. I abstained.

Back in the girls' john: there is a large number of negro girls, many of them sad-looking. Cigarette butts are all over the place. Several negro girls are sitting against one wall. The white girls are competing for primping space at the mirrors. The john wall I get to investigate has scribbles of initials: JP plus MK, for example. Also "fuck" and lipstick smears; not as bad as some johns I've seen, by a long shot.

Now in algebra class. I've been mistaken before during the day for a sixteen-year-old, now I believe it: I've just been approached by a young playboy type called Charlie Nelson. I get to sit between him and Lila. A nice colored boy brings me a chair and I thank him; no one else thought of it! Heddie Celine is in here, all amazed to see me. Class chews gum like fiends. A beautiful brunette comes in and Lila introduces us. Lila says to me, aside, "In the hall she's okay, but just look at the insecurity all over her face when she comes in." Lila is very perceptive! She writes me a note asking if Charlie is making me nervous, and I say, "Get serious." She says, "*He* is," and I let the matter drop. But Charlie keeps looking over my shoulder. He asks me if I'd like to join the class, and I say, "Only for today."

The teacher, Mr. Snider, is a broad-shouldered, athletic, blonde, crew-cut, rugged type. Married. Dominance in his whole voice and demeanor—a little bit of beer-gut, it seems.

A note has just been kicked in front of me in the most intricate manner. It gets kicked along the floor, like a piece of scrap paper, to its destination.

This algebra class contains all years. There are hoods and also innocent little freshman boys who seem less worldly than the girls of the same age. There are no *levis* in here but Elvis haircuts are showing up; there seems more attention to fashion on the part of the males. Revision: there is one pair of *levis* in here, belonging to Roger, a singularly unhandsome guy; tall. I ask Lila if he is a hood, and she says, "Um-m-m, I don't know. He goes out with girls for what he can get. I don't know him except by reputation." Teacher is now taking the class grades. Charlie Nelson is so busy trying to read over my shoulder he misses his turn and has to be called on it. He's also unhandsome. Chews gum viciously. Elvis haircut. In and out of his seat constantly. Lila tells me she will give me a story about him later that will make a "bunch of notes."

Mr. Snider is wearing a green, long-sleeved sport shirt, no tie, black wool slacks, tan belt. Looks more like a sport than a teacher.

Celine to the pencil sharpener. Looks sharp today: white blouse, very feminine, purple plaid full skirt, brushed wool. Nylons, black flats. Girls in here run about two-thirds for nylons, one-third for white bobby-sox and bleached tennis shoes.

Sixth hour, Mr. Johnsberg's social studies class. A girl asks if it's true they're all going to Mr. Miller's class next semester. Johnsberg replies, "What does that have to do with what I'm saying?" Girl says, "Nothing—I just wanted to know." She's crestfallen. Johnsberg says, "Yes, it's true, but that doesn't make any difference." But a boy up in front says, "Yes, it does." The whole class is groaning. "We want *you*, Mr. Johnsberg." Johnsberg says gruffly, "Well, I'll miss you too. Now let's get on with it." Big bluffer, he's been touched by this. It is interesting to notice the boys are the loudest groaners in this show of affection.

Girls and boys seem to segregate themselves here as well as elsewhere. In here, a class of all freshmen, the boys fall back on the pattern of slacks, khakis, very ordinary shirts. There is no symbolic display of wealth among them. There seem to be even three or four girls in here who aren't competing in clothing, although they are well-groomed and clean.

Lila and her friend Beatrice, who wears a clique band like Lila's, are giggling. Beatrice won't believe I'm a college senior. Lila tells me most kids have told her I look 16. The top estimate so far has been 18. I show Beatrice my driver's license.

Johnsberg is wearing a gray suit and bow tie, white shirt, black shoes. He makes a very nice appearance before the class. Another teacher passes through the hall wearing a sport coat, tie, slacks. Johnsberg permits all the talk to continue without a word of admonishment. The students are cheating, trading answers to the study quiz right and left, but Johnsberg doesn't seem to care.

The last bell rings and there is a mad rush to lockers and exits. Boys and girls who haven't seemed to know each other all day leave the school hand-in-hand. No one loiters.

We have finished our day at Rome High with Lila Greene, and we have come to know her as a sharp fourteen-year-old, secure in her world. She has many friends, knows everybody, and is at ease in school: there seems to be complete complementarity between Lila and her environment. She has things sized up, and like so many of her fellows, she will get away with what she can. From the standpoint of *this* dimension of her existence, Rome High socializes Lila to the corrupt aspects of the adult world. Of course, this is not *all* of Rome High, but it is a significant part.

SCHOOL'S CONTRIBUTION TO LILA'S CHARACTER

Para-courtship and para-delinquency. Lila is ingenious and thinks the world is to be handled; she seems comfortable in a world where one must "figure all the angles." In this the high school helps her, now in one way, through permissive teachers, now in another, through the students. Let us look at some of the ways in which the high school does its part. (1) Miss Clements tells the girls that "notebooks are due today" but that she will understand if some are not handed in on time because this is Monday. That is to say, recognizing that Friday through Sunday is largely spent in the *Midsummer Night's Dream,* where boy chases girl chases boy, one should not expect work to be accomplished. Actually this is the teacher's recognition that *ceremonial para-courtship* is so intense and so standardized, built-in, and hallowed by the fleeting traditions of twentieth-century youth, that she really ought not intrude upon it with orthodox demands like industry and obligation. In the nineteen sixties, it has become so obvious that para-courtship is a necessary, rigid ceremonial which one must not offend that work and obligation become subordinated to it. How explain, otherwise, the students' complaints at the trifling homework assignments? In a broader context we might say that the development of the pattern of fun, of which para-courtship is but a part, has intruded so far into the orthodox procedures, obligations, and austerities of school, that it has received recognition by the school authorities.

(2) Since what stands out in the minds of many younger adolescents as the most important feature of the independent adult is the right to untrammeled impulse release, hard liquor is the veritable symbol of freedom to them. Everywhere the movement toward independence has its symbol. Alcohol, with its implied narcotizing of the Super Ego, is the liberating fluid for children seeking a taste of the intoxication of total freedom in the age of impulse release and fun. Lila, by drinking a Tom Collins on her date, has herself become the embodiment of adult liberty, and for this she receives suitable recognition and status from her age-mates. When one student dares to say she is not interested in liquor she is cut out of the conversation for contempt of the symbol of independence and "maturity." This incident, and Lila's comment help us understand the importance of such *para-delinquencies* as projections and affirmations of group spirit and solidarity. "It wasn't something wild," says Lila, "I just felt grown up, so I thought I would. I didn't go out to get drunk." Thus Lila has done the thing that is right in the early adolescent world, where to get drunk is wild

and bad, but where it's all right, thrilling, status-enchancing, and group-affirming to obtain an illegal drink occasionally *just to feel grown up.* A child's negation of adult *law* has thus become an affirmation of the condition of being adult. Extracted from the cultural complex by the sharp *Id logic* of adolescence is the generalization that it is adult for a child to violate adult laws in order to follow adult enjoyments. The only originality that I can claim at this point is to have emphasized again that every culture as well as subculture, and every part of the psychic system has its own premises and epistemological method. This was brought out in the examination of the philosophical system of advertising. Adolescents have a philosophical system (with apologies to the philosophers) based on the efforts of the Id to free itself from the restrictions of conscience and of the adult world. The basic postulate of the Id is

> Impulse release is right (Pleasure is truth)

and from this flows, logically,

> What interferes with impulse release is wrong (Pain is falsehood)

Naturally enough, the basic postulate is derived from the adult world where they think they see that

> Impulse release *is* right

All delinquencies have their legitimations, their rationalizations, their logics, and their modes of truth; and within her frame of reference Lila speaks with a sure instinct that makes her a firm member and even a leader of her group.

(3) Everyone cheats in math, says Lila, because they don't like the way the teacher makes the assignments and because he does not give the students enough time. This is another of what we may now call the *conventions of dishonesty (vide* the canons of pecuniary philosophy), the system of rationalizations by which one makes his frauds acceptable to his Self. The psychic function of these modes of thought is, of course, to defend the Self from inner aggression. Socialization to the adolescent culture thus involves an important inner gain: *adolescent culture provides its members with a system of defenses that protects the Self from attack by the voice of conscience.* Who has as much

to offer them? Meanwhile we must bear in mind that these children, through being taught to lie to themselves are learning how to pursue a life of decent chicanery in the adult world. Lila's assessment of Tim Aupen—that he "knows how to be legally innocent"—is culturally resonant. I do not, of course, give adolescent culture all the credit for the canons of dishonesty; this is clear, I think, from earlier discussions. What the adolescent group does is add certain thoughts of its own and lend a generalizing polish and group support to chicanery that makes it easier to absorb the finishing touches of later life. An honest adolescent life could be a crippling preliminary for many phases of contemporary culture.

In Mr. Johnsberg's class the cheating occurs right under his nose. Regardless of whether he approves of it or simply does not care, his students must surely learn that illegality of this kind is not a serious rupture of morals in the eyes of some adults. Given this postulate, we can trust their alert minds to generalize, simply by lopping off the words "in the eyes of some adults."

Consider now the fate and condition of a child who does not cheat either in Mr. Snider's or Mr. Johnsberg's class, who refuses to copy from other children and declines to let them copy from him. He would be more loathsome than the girl who was not interested in drinking. Who could stand against this tide?

Incidentally, Mr. Johnsberg and his wife, who teaches elementary school, are agreed that they "do not want books to interfere with their daughter's social life in high school!"

We have not yet exhausted the means of understanding Lila's surreptitious hand in her father's pocket. Look at the massive stimulation to raise her consumption level Lila encounters in Rome High. Consider, first, the forthright talk of Mrs. Elphin on how to spend money and enhance status. Much of what she said is worth repeating. For example, after giving something of the history of wool she breaks off and says that in order "to move on to something *more interesting*" she will drop the history and discuss style. It is clear as the late sun streaming through the clouds after a dull morning, that style is more interesting than history! On this whole day in Rome High, however, nobody except Mrs. Elphin said anything really close to the students. If Lila did not already know it, Mrs. Elphin, well dressed and the representative of a powerful industry, tells her that history is boring. There, in the comparative luxury of the Home Economics room, 'mid the posters on cosmetics, dresses, and perspiration, Lila learns how to raise social status, how to avoid being linked with "dirty, untidy, cheap people," and how to be happy in an ambient world of tidy, sweet-smelling people and expensive wool! This too is acquiring an identity! What is the prettiest room in the school? The Home Ec room where Lila, a lower-middle-class girl, learns how to consume, to raise her living standard, and to move up in the social scale. This is the room that symbolizes the pressures on Lila to spend; this is where we begin to understand most clearly the compulsion to stick her hand in father's pocket when he's not looking. But it would be wrong to blame the sly hand entirely on the Home Ec class, when the students themselves provoke the drive to competitive display. Consider the following from the record:

1. The girls are all sharply dressed. . . . There are mirrors everywhere and the girls are preening themselves in front of them.
2. Class seems to go from ultra-chic hair styles to long mops, with no middle ground.
3. One girl, a junior, looks like a high fashion model; bleached blonde.
4. Most girls wear expensive sweaters.
5. In one corner [of the Home Economics room] there is a large, three-sided wardrobe mirror in front of which a student, with the assistance of two friends, has been primping herself since class began. She is wearing a very elaborate oriental type hair style, piled intricately around her head. . . .
6. One negro girl in the class is very well dressed and well-groomed. She sits with the white girls. . . . Three other negro girls sit in a group by themselves. They are not as expensively dressed or as well-kempt. . . . One is wearing a going-steady ring on a chain around her neck. *She* is more high-fashion than the others of her group.
7. Girls in here run about two-thirds for nylons, one-third for white bobby-sox and bleached tennis shoes.
8. There seem to be even three or four girls in here who aren't competing in clothing. . . .

The stimulation to spend money on clothes and grooming must be overwhelming for a normal fourteen-year-old lower-middle-class girl; and the school takes this preoccupation for granted. How could Rome High, in the center of a lower-middle-class neighborhood, be indifferent to its yearnings toward status and the high-rising living standard? How could Rome High block the glittering Id of progress? Can we expect Lila, hungering for the group, to sit against the john wall twiddling her thumbs while her peers, glorious in ultra-chic and high fashion, competitively display their cosmetic success? Those mirrors on the wall do not say who is most beautiful of all, but they do communicate to the children that the school supports their strivings toward standards of pecuniary loveliness. There is one girl who has outdistanced the field. She is the girl who, having achieved a coiffure so elaborate that she cannot manage it alone, has two others hovering around her like Nubian slaves, catching the wisps of hair, and shoring up the coils that have broken loose. She might well be Lila's goal, but such opulence is costly, and it is this sort of spectacle that helps to animate the hand that slips in and out of father's pocket in the darkness of his carelessness, fuzzy-mindedness, and nonobsessive attitude toward truth.

SOME CONTRIBUTIONS OF THE HOME TO LILA'S CHARACTER

Lila's father does not seem to object to his cute daughter's efforts to swindle him: when he caught her, it was merely that he had won and she had lost. "OK, you win," she says. But she had really won, for he thought he had given her ten when he had really given her twenty dollars. Meanwhile, there are other aspects of Lila's experimentations with dubious behavior that Mr. Greene does not know about. There is her attempt to get money from Heddie, Bill's girl friend, by selling her pictures Lila had taken of Bill and Heddie doing some heavy necking. Equally ingenious, though not as mercenary, was Lila's effort to blackmail the Researcher into writing a term paper for her. During the Christmas season when Bill took advantage of the mistletoe above the Greene doorway to kiss the Researcher, Lila took a picture of it, and she then threatened to give it to Heddie if the Researcher refused to write the paper. The Researcher solved this problem by staying away from the Greene house until after the paper was due. In the meantime, the picture was stolen from Lila's room.

Now the question arises, have we really encompassed the reality of Lila and her dad? In this context, where Lila is "processed" and socialized by the total environment, it is important for the reader to know that Lila's mother is not in the home but is divorced from Mr. Greene. Mr. Greene, who is often away, tries to do the fatherly best he can for his motherless children. One could well imagine that Mr. Greene, oppressed perhaps by guilt that he has not been able to provide a real home, wants his children to be as happy as he can make them. For many parents one of the ways to compensate a child for deprivation is to "spoil" it, to give it "everything" and to make few demands. The Greene home is pretty, and the children are comfortable. Mr. Greene's giving Lila twenty dollars and not insisting on an accounting may be part of a total pattern of behavior in which, out of desire to make amends and the need to be loved himself, he lets things go, while providing money for competition in the Id-release and consumption patterns. Thus for the family sorrow, i.e., a family with no mother, the father provides money for opiates—the high-rising standard of living and the *Midsummer Night's Dream*—that are insistently advertised. In doing this he gives Lila no moral fibre; for though he enables her to compete, to spend money on clothes and grooming, he presents her also with provocations to cheat. In this way Lila's morals become hostage to the gross national product.

I do not imply that all the little fashion plates in Rome High have become so through the divorce of their parents; the high-rising standard of living means something just a little bit different in the lives of each adolescent. The *miracle of the standard*, however, is that it serves everything, like a "wonder drug." Not religion, but the high-rising standard of living is the "opium of the people"; but it can make the demands for total commitment and unquestioning loyalty and belief that religion does. This is opium number one. Sex is opium number two.

SEX AND THE CONVENTIONS OF MISREPRESENTATION

Lila's knowledge of and dedication to the rituals of sex were obvious throughout the day; but she is no more absorbed in them than most of the other girls. Let us recapitulate the record:

1. Lila says, "Most of the girls consist of padded bras and girdles, but they're clever artists; and besides, *what else can you do?*"
2. Lila tells the researcher about three girls who dislike her, and she surmises that among the reasons is her superior success with boys. Then Lila says, "One of those girls, I guess, only goes out about every three months." She cannot believe that a senior girl has never been kissed.
3. The record reads: Back to the dressing room. There *is* a prevalence of padded bras and girdles here—and all of them so young! I ask, "Aren't the boys disappointed?" and Lila says, "They don't know. Maybe some do, but most are fooled. I wear one once in awhile."
4. In regard to the Danish girl, the researcher says, "Apparently she has stripped her steady of all the tokens of love he possesses. He is hers!"
5. The innocent little freshman boys seem less worldly than the girls of the same age.
6. Lila says of Roger, the singularly unhandsome guy, "He goes out with girls for what he can get."

There is an interesting *moral intricacy* in Lila's comments. She says, for example, that the boys "don't know" that the girls are padded. This can only mean that Lila has set rather strict limits on how far she will let a boy go with her; for if she had not set such limits, and if she did not believe that most of the girls set such limits, she would think that the boys had discovered the deception. Thus Lila is still a little naive and one must assume that this ignorance is at least partly self-imposed. Furthermore, since she despises Roger, who she says, "goes out with girls for what he can get," she must think it wrong for boys to take girls out for sex only. On the other hand, Lila believes she has to make her body more provocative to boys, while at the same time she objects to their reaching for it. There is no doubt that adolescent girls have a carefully worked out and well-understood system of conventions—a kind of pragmatic morality—with which they legitimize their sexual behavior. Among the canons of this morality are *the conventions of legitimate misrepresentation,* as exemplified, for example, in the padded bra complex, summed up in the expression, "what else can you do?" Lila and other girls believe they must pad in order to attract boys in the competitive sexual ritual. Thus misrepresentation, "fooling," and the legitimizing "what else can you do?" are the products of fear—fear of losing out. It is thus important to note that: (1) What is all fun and gaity on the surface has anxiety underneath. (2) The sexual competition of adolescent girls reverberates back on family and school. Family responds with reduction of controls on impulse release; school responds with mirrors, posters, speakers on products to enhance appearance, etc. The response in which institutions adjust to the pathway taken by a particular group may be called *group-institution feed-back,* and the expression implies that the institution *corrects,* i.e., changes its course to conform to the pathway chosen by the group. Where the group got its pathway in the first place has been suggested in earlier sections of this book—it has made its choice in terms of the high-rising standard of living and the *Midsummer Night's Dream.* (3) This competitive anxiety enhances the gross national product, by increasing the sale of padded brassieres.

Meanwhile it is clear that because of the danger of pregnancy and of getting a bad reputation, it is risky for a girl to "let herself go." Contempt for Roger, therefore, derives from the fact that his single-track interest degrades the girl who wants to be liked for herself, that he is a threat to reputation, and that he does not accept the conventions of legitimate ambiguity and misrepresentation.

Girls fear they will not attract boys, and, paradoxically, they fear the boys they attract too well. It is a difficult life to lead, but if one can manage, if one can ski gracefully in and out among the trees on the slippery snows of adolescent purity, one can have a good time!

Out of this double fear, fear of pregnancy and fear of getting a bad reputation, emerges the girls' acceptance of the steady relationship with a rigidly controlled boy; and thus once more the culture, in creating a conflict, provides also an attempted solution.

AGAINST THE GRAIN

Let us turn now to what there was in Rome High on this day that seemed to move in a direction opposed to all that has been described so far—opposed to the *Midsummer Night's Dream* and its legitimization of the illegitimate. Mrs. Nasson stands out most clearly as a force against self-indulgence, goofy thinking, and easy conformity. And she seems a courageous little figure, defending civil rights against convinced conforming conservatism,[1] muddle-headedness, and naked fear. Whether this anxiety is over communism or over fear of not being considered a noncommunist, we cannot know. At any rate the class reaction to the mere idea of communism represents one point at which boys and girls can feel completely in harmony with the adult world. Since adolescent *political conservatism* is compensation for *Id-radicalism*, Mrs. Nasson's apparent open-mindedness is threatening. Firm against the onslaught from the class, she wins a politically liberal and enlightened concession to law and order. She also lectures the class on breaking rules, on dishonesty, and on reckless driving; and she assigns a paper called "The obligation to freedom: its use and abuse." But what chance to take hold do these lessons in the traditional morality have when in so many other classrooms, and in the lunchroom and the restrooms the lessons teach the contrary?

Other more traditional lessons taught, though not necessarily learned, on that day, were by the girl who called Lila a "silly kid" for ordering a Tom Collins and by the negro boy who brought the Researcher a chair. But more important, perhaps, than such isolated phenomena, the general orientation of the

---

[1] In confirmation of teen-age conservatism see surveys conducted in 1960 by the Scholastic Institute of Student Opinion, reported in the *New York Times*, January 9, 1961; and *The American Teen-Ager*, by H. H. Remmers and D. H. Radler. Bobbs-Merrill, 1957.

school toward scholastic performance makes itself felt: Lila respects students who get good grades and she likes to get them herself. Contempt for the "brain" is totally absent in our group from Rome High.

Lila also admires intelligence, and she is perceptive and not without compassion. She worries about Tess, the girl with the scar on her neck, and she senses insecurity behind the mask of the beautiful brunette. That some of her compassion may be of the Lady Bountiful variety, enabling her to feel herself above those for whom she feels compassion, is to be considered, naturally, since Lila obviously has a ruthless side too. At any rate, she is a complex, rather attractive little creature because she has so many possibilities for development in many directions; she has weaknesses and strengths, the one as terrifying as the other is encouraging. The question is, which cultural pressures will win out—those that push her in the direction of being a compassionate, intelligent woman or those that urge otherwise? Possibly they will all win!

Perhaps the best way to finish this introduction to Lila is to quote from an interview with Ed, her steady, who is sixteen and a sophomore at Rome High.

R: Do you date?

E: Yes. As a matter of fact I have a date Saturday night.

R: Can you tell me something about the girl?

E: Her name is Lila, she is a freshman and she will be fifteen in ———. She is a very good student, she is smart. She is a very nice girl and has a very nice personality.

R: Can you tell me where you are going?

E: We are going skating; she *tricked* me into going ice-skating. I like roller skating better.

Before ending our day at Rome High we must take note of the fact that boys and girls separated themselves in all classes and even in the cafeteria—a phenomenon that is by no means universal in American high schools—and that there was no hand-holding and so on during school hours. This restraint is more or less standard in the Rome area. Thus the students have made the decision that school is not a rendezvous. The only person who seems to forget this is Charlie Nelson. Immediately after school, however, hands say what eyes may have said during the day. As the researcher remarks: "Boys and girls who haven't seemed to know each other all day leave the school hand-in-hand."

We have been observing at Rome High, studying Lila Greene, a pupil there, seeing the school partly through her eyes, partly through those of the researcher, and very much through my own, and have been attempting to understand the relation between Lila's character and the school. In the next section we meet Bill Greene's sweetheart, Heddie Celine; then we shall meet Bill, have dinner with the Greene family, and talk further with Lila.

HEDDIE CELINE

Heddie Celine, fifteen years old and a sophomore at Rome High, was not born in this country but came here in late childhood. After necessary introductions and explanations of the study, the interview with Heddie started a little stiffly with a question on girl friends, but Heddie kept reverting so insistently to Bill that the researcher took the hint and turned the conversation in the direction desired by Heddie. Twice Heddie broke off in the middle of a discussion of her girl friends to refer to the Greene family's new house: "Oh, by the way, Bill moved. You should see his house; he has a white phone, his sister has a pink one, and his father has a green one." And again, "I love the way Bill's house is fixed: it has wall-to-wall carpeting. It's *all* fixed beautifully, but I like his room best." Finally the researcher asked,

R: Are you by any chance considering marriage to Bill [age 18 years]?

H: (Smiling, almost shyly) Yes. We've already talked about the house and what he plans to do. He's going to be either a draftsman or an electrician. He tried sheet metal but he didn't like it, and I think he should be happy in his job. The only real problem is that he wants to live in the sticks, and I don't know about that. He doesn't want to live in Rome—he just can't stand Rome.

R: Does your mother know about this?

H: (Almost whispering) No. She even objects to me wearing the [going steady] ring on my left hand. Tom wanted to give me an engagement ring for Christmas, but we're afraid.

R: Do you have a lot of trouble with your mother?

H: Not really. We're pretty good buddies. The other day, for example, I wanted a smoke very bad, so I said I was going to the powder room. This was at Burgess's [department store]. I told her I was tired and wanted to rest a minute. So she said, "Do you have your own cigarettes or do you want to borrow one?" I didn't know she even knew. She said, if I had to smoke, not to be smoking in corners; but we both agree that I can't smoke at home—my father would never give in. Oh, by the way, you said you wanted Bill's phone number. (Gives it to me.) If his sister says something smart, ignore her. She'll probably think it's me. She's the most aggravating girl I ever met—a typical freshman. Oh, by the way, remember when we were talking about Shirley? Her hair is getting light again, and of course she *can't* understand why. She's reading *The Life of a Prostitute*. She's a real bright girl. (Deprecating tone.)

R: Let's get back to your parents for a minute: Do you think they're really strict?

H: Well, they're thoroughly ——[1]. I take that back: my father's part ——, and very stubborn. They're very old-fashioned. They didn't get married until they were 24 and 25. They wouldn't understand if they knew we'd made plans. You *should* interview Bill. He's had a rough life. His mother and father are divorced. The father favors the girl and the mother likes Bill. So Bill was living with his dad and his father sent for Lila. So now Bill has to buy all his own stuff and Lila gets everything. It just isn't fair.

R: Have either of you been serious about anyone before?

H: Well, Bill had an affair with this one girl, but he wouldn't marry her soon enough to suit her, so she married some other guy. She was married and didn't tell Bill for

[1] Name of country of birth.

two weeks. Then all she said was, "He didn't move fast enough."

R: What do you mean, "affair"?

H: Well, I don't think he was that mad about her. He soon figured out that he didn't like her that much, but it hurt him to think that she'd do that to him. After that he didn't want to get serious again, so he took a lot of different girls out. I got tired of waiting around, so I told him I didn't want to go out with him anymore; and I called him stubborn because I'd been chasing him for months, but of course, he didn't know that. Then he got his senior ring and I was at his locker one day admiring the ring and playing with it. I said it was pretty and started to hand it back but he said I could keep it. I was very thrilled by this. That was in May [and it is now December. Heddie and Bill have considered themselves engaged since the end of June.] We'd been going together for about four months then. Then the next day he came over and told me about this other girl and said that if I wanted to give his ring back he'd understand. But I said that that was all in the past and had nothing to do with us.

R: What do you think would happen if you told your mother about the engagement?

H: She'd do anything she could to keep me away from him. She might even take me out of Rome High.

R: Has she ever done anything drastic before?

H: Well, there was one fellow—I wasn't serious about him, though. She said to tell him I couldn't associate with him any more. I didn't want to hurt him, so I told him something else—I don't remember what. But he was kind of a hoody character. [Hoodlum-like.]

R: Can you tell me something about the hoods?

H: Most of them go to school because they have to. Most of them go to the Broken Dish that's run by this crabby old woman. They sit around and curse and smoke. Even if their locker won't close they have to curse about it. I try not to smoke in the girls' room any more—not since I go with Bill. I leave my cigarettes in his car. Then I have one at lunch and try to wait until I get home. [Mrs. Celine comes in.]

Mrs. C: Were you telling her about the hoods, Heddie?

Did you tell her your father was all for shipping you back to
————when you were running around with that bunch?

H: (With a wry grin) Well, I guess I'll tell you about the
barbecue. The fellows I invited chased the party crashers
down the alley with broken bottlenecks. The next day my
father asked, "Why all the broken glass in the alley?" I told
him I didn't know a thing about it. Most of the parties were
necking parties.

R: Why did you leave that group?

Mrs. C: Her father was really going to send her back.

H: I just got tired of that crowd. So did Buzz and Kim.
Some say Kim is a hood because she is planning to get married now, at 16.

Mrs. C: Maybe so. She's much too young.

H: (Indignantly) She knows what she's doing. She's
known Ralph since she was 10.

Mrs. C: By the way, someone else was here to interview
you the other day but you weren't home. The Kotex Company is running a survey of teen-agers. I said you weren't
due again for almost a month. The woman said if you'd
be coming up within a week she'd have left some samples
of a new product for you.

H: You did have to tell her the truth, didn't you? Now
I'll have to buy some.

R: Do you think there are a lot of teen-age marriages at
Rome?

H: Yeah, but most end up in divorce.

Mrs. C: Watch yourself, Heddie!

Heddie goes to the kitchen for a minute. Comes back as her
mother starts to tell me her troubles.

Mrs. C: I had more trouble raising her than her three
brothers together. I'd rather have four boys any day.

H: I feel unwanted.

R: How long have you been going on dates?

H: Since I was 14, but I picked up fellows at the Rome
show [movie theatre] before that. I even went steady with
one.

Mrs. C: A hood. He was a real beauty. Jean used to say,

when people asked him, that he didn't have a sister. That's how proud he was of you, Heddie.

We discuss Jean's last New Year's Eve party, which went on all night, but most of the kids there were already out of school.

R: Any juicy gossip from school this time?
Mrs. C: Take it with a pinch of salt.
H: Nothing exciting. Just Shirley and her hair that she doesn't know what's happening to it. Oh, by the way, Bill's very much worried about his father's heart. I wonder whether Mrs. Williams is peeping out of her blinds again. Bill and I sometimes sit and talk [in his car] and then we goof around [pet] for her benefit. She keeps telling my mother all sorts of things, and if she doesn't stop I'll tipi her house.[1]

Proto-adolescence and Early Marriage. In attempting to understand Heddie's drive toward early marriage we ought to begin with her home, where she does not seem to have had much respect. Rather early she started picking up boys at the local movie, she associated with hoods, and in general behaved so badly that her parents were ready to send her back to the old country, where, under a stricter social regimen, she could be reconstructed. Heddie's conduct seems related to the pain of being a second-class person in her family. But when she went too far, she wheeled about and, in a *flight into redemption,* pursued Bill. Now, at fifteen, she is determined to marry him as soon as it is legally possible. Meanwhile she still flouts her parents through her secret engagement. It is, perhaps, in this context that we can understand the exhibitionistic petting under Mrs. Williams' window: she represents the flouted parents. The flight into redemption is symbolized by Heddie's control of her smoking: she *tries* now not to smoke in the girls' rest room (a breach of school regulations) and *tries* to wait for a cigarette

---

[1] To "tipi" a house means to spread toilet paper over the trees, hedges, et cetera. This prank is almost universal among high school students in the Rome area. It can be a gesture of affection as well as of hostility. It is also a Halloween prank.

until she gets home. Meanwhile she imprisons the dangerous cigarettes in her beloved's car—Bill will protect her against herself. It is in terms of her need to redeem herself that we can fathom her cruel scapegoating of Shirley.

While Heddie's flight into redemption is an outcome of her unique experiences, it is also a consequence of the emergence, in our culture, of the *proto*-adolescent girl as a leader in Id expression. It is she who provokes the fourteen- to sixteen-year-old boys as they hang back. Padded to accentuate the immature breasts, dressed tightly in provocative clothes, loaded with "grooming," tirelessly teasing and insinuating, she has assumed leadership in the Coca-Cola bacchanals of proto-adolescence. Since paradoxically, however, society will punish her if she performs her part too well by actually going off the deep end, she escapes the danger by a flight into redemption. The years between twelve and fifteen thus become a critical period in the sexual cycle of girls in our culture. We have made this child the prime solvent of the traditional restrictions on all that would hamper the delirious release of impulse. It is a serious responsibility, but she has hurled herself into the work with the pathetic yet joyous blindness of childhood. This too is a kind of maturity, for is not maturity a capacity to shoulder the burdens of society? For her historic task the proto-adolescent girl needs, therefore, all the freedom and independence we can give her. That in the process she becomes hostage to the gross national product is irrelevant, for after all, you cannot make an economic omelette without breaking some human eggs. This is elementary.

Here fathers, as imps of fun, can play an important role too, for as they become less the embodiment of Super Ego and yearn more for the overt love of their children, they become foils for the reawakening of the Oedipus Complex at adolescence, when the sexuality of the young breaks out in a resurgence of the repressed attraction to parents of the opposite sex. The stimulating effects of contact with the beloved imp-father become transferred to the boys in school.

Bill is an ugly duckling in his family too, for although his mother prefers him, he lives with a father who prefers and spoils his proto-adolescent daughter Lila. Thus Heddie and Bill, through holding each other dear, can effect a *mutual meta-*

morphosis, each becoming a swan in the other's eyes, muting each other's pain. Early marriage would offer no economic diffi-culties for Bill, since being lower-middle (or upper-working) class he could, even at eighteen, get a manual job with good pay.[1] Marriage would solve Bill's immediate problems as well as Heddie's.

In summary: Heddie comes from a family of foreigners, who are rather orthodox and traditional in their moral outlook. For some reason Heddie has been peripheral in her family and has felt unwanted. In earliest adolescence she rebelled through loose, "hoody" behavior, utilizing against her family an American lower-class deviant pattern. But when she was further rejected by the family and threatened with trans-shipment to Europe, she re-formed. Now that she is fifteen the role of Bill in her life is made possible by the fact that he, as a working-class boy, will be able to get a fairly well-paid factory job early, and by the fact that early marriages are, in general, more acceptable in contemporary culture than in the past. One remembers also, that marriage is easier nowadays because of installment credit and the decline of saving and parsimony as moral values. Playing their parts also are the institutionalization of the high school as the site of adolescent courtship and the emergence of the proto-adolescent girl as Id-leader. In the background is the hidden assumption that "if it doesn't work out," Heddie and Bill can be divorced.

In closing this introduction to Heddie, I would like to em-phasize that I do not consider Heddie and Bill's particular ex-perience the explanation of the origin of early marriage in contemporary American culture. What I do wish to make clear, however, is that early marriage, once accepted as a cultural form, serves, like any other cultural form, a variety of emotional needs. As a matter of fact, if it did not, it could not endure.

We will understand the relationship between Heddie and Bill better, however, after we have a chance to study Bill.

BILL GREENE

Bill was a reticent respondent, often giving the Researcher the impression of hostility, loneliness, and apathy. Since many of

[1] The growth of automation, however, will surely alter this.

his answers were short or not germane, I shall omit a great deal of what he says and shall condense his three interviews without indicating where one starts and another ends.

At the outset the Researcher remarks:

> Bill is working on algebra when I come in. I notice he has a very orderly desk, good posture, and good light. Apparently he believes in good study habits. I have to wait for him to finish a problem. Lila comes in and sits gaping at me. [This was before the trip to Rome High, and Lila had never seen the Researcher before.]

> B: She wants to interview me. Get lost. Maybe if she wants to interview you she'll come over to see you.
> L: I don't want to be interviewed, I just want to hear the questions she asks you. (After he glares at her for awhile she finally leaves.)
> R: How old is your sister?
> B: About 14, but I don't know.

Researcher admires the room divider he has constructed, made of white rope and beautifully finished wood. Bill says he remembered seeing one like it somewhere and built it from memory. He shows me the workmanship on his stereo set, which he built himself. The cabinet, which he designed himself, has room for bookcases and record storage and covers the lower half of one wall.

> B: It's a pretty expensive hobby, but I go to discount houses and get things wholesale. I have a tube tester. I guess they think I run a TV shop or something. It's better than soaking my father for the money.

He is wearing *levis* and a plaid shirt. Attitude of apathy.

> R: Tell me more about your hobbies.
> B: I like to draft, but I don't know if that will be my occupation. I'll either be a draftsman or an electrician—probably *whichever one I fall into first.*

R: What else do you do for kicks in your spare time?

B: Between Heddie and school, not much. My spare time is limited.

R: What do you do when you are with Heddie? When you take Heddie out, where do you go?

B: Well, bowling, swimming, theatres, drive-ins, Teen Town.[1]

[There now ensues a complicated discussion of the rise and fall of this Teen Town, a demise due, apparently, to inability of the Rome community to manage it.]

R: How come?

B: I don't know. I guess Rome wanted to run it and be big wheels. They promised big games and stuff if they let Rome run it. I think there was some other angle. Of course, in Rome everyone has an angle. My father belonged to the PTA and they wanted a tape recorder. Dad worked for an outfit that would give it at cost. Everyone was looking for his angle. After that he wouldn't have anything to do with it.

R: Do you have what you would call a best friend?

B: Well, I used to bum around with a bunch of guys until I met Heddie.

R: What made you stop?

B: I don't have time. You know, you get to an age where you'd rather bum around with a girl than the boys. Once in a while we go on double and triple dates.

R: Don't you ever have problems you would like to talk over with a boy?

B: I talk them over with Heddie.

R: What if it's a big problem, or a problem about Heddie?

B: If I had a problem that big I'd need professional help. I don't want to talk to the boys around here because they're just as stupid as I am. I never came up against such a problem. I don't know, I can't visualize a problem that big because I haven't experienced any.

---

[1] A Teen Town is a recreation (usually dance) hall operated for teenagers. Some are run by commercial outfits, some by churches, YMCAs, communities, etc. The one Bill is referring to was run by the YMCA.

R: Who did you talk to before you went with Heddie?

B: Well, that has to do with the problem. When parents have kids growing up, they don't remember how it was when they were kids. I'm old enough that I really don't remember, but probably I talked to my family. Then when I got to an age when I couldn't talk to them, I talked with whoever I bummed with. Otherwise you can let it eat inside of you until you find your parents aren't so stupid after all.

R: What is this stage when you can't talk to your parents?

B: Everybody goes through one, and when you come out of it you find out that parents can be wrong, but they have much more experience too. Then when they're wrong you find out why they're wrong and you remember it, and you don't fuss about it. Most parents, the first time they're wrong, try to get around admitting it. They hate to see the kids grow up and admit they're old. Parents aren't perfect.

Bill's parents have been divorced for seven years and his mother remarried.

B: Mom's been married five times, but my father was the first and I guess she's spent all this time trying to get over him. After the third guy I got fed up and left. He turned out to be a not-so-good guy. He sold Mom's furniture and pocketed the money. Mom said she'd had enough and went to ———. She earned a lot of money being the only ———[1] around. That's when I made my trip. Then she married this guy; then she came back here without the guy and got married again.

R: Do you know anyone you would like to model yourself on?

B: No, I don't know any millionaires. No, I was just teasing. I don't think so. I think a person shouldn't mold himself after someone else. You can't take someone else's place, so you should make the best of your own self. I read about that somewhere—trying to be what you're not. It's silly. I

[1] Her occupation.

don't think you'd ever be successful. You might have that same destiny anyway, but probably not. I want to make the best of myself.

R: Have you ever copied anyone, done what they did?

B: Oh, I might borrow a good joke from someone, but I try not to copy too much. I don't have any one person I copy after. There are about 30 different people.

R: Who?

B: I was waiting for you to ask that. I don't know, off-hand. I guess *whoever could do a job better than me.* I'd learn how he did it and take a lesson from him. Then I'd learn how to do it better the next time.

[There ensues a discussion of school, of Bill's having once stayed away from school for a day, and of his once having been "thrown out" of a class. Then he drifts into a discussion of his school performance.]

B: In my freshman year they put me in general math. I didn't like it so I didn't do the homework except in class, so I went from B plus to F, but I passed. The teacher was my counselor. In algebra I went from D plus to an A. In geometry I got a C plus. The teacher said I could do A work if I would buckle down, but I didn't. I did my running around then. That was in my junior year. I sure wasted that one. I wasted the other two too. So, I'm wasting this one too.

R: Would you change if you had it to do over again?

B: Hm-m-m-m. I haven't seen the final outcome yet; that is, what happens when I go out looking for a job. I'm not stupid enough to think I could change like that (snaps fingers). I'd need will power and I don't know how much I have.

As I am leaving Bill catches me under the mistletoe, and Lila takes a picture; I did not see her in time. Bill is angry about the picture. Lila promises not to tell Heddie and to give me the negative.

Resignation and the Instinct of Workmanship. Veblen called the tendency to do things well the *instinct of workmanship* and while we no longer consider that there is such an instinct, it is well to take note of the significance of the traditional values of excellence and usefulness for Bill and other adolescents. Usefulness stands in contrast to "bumming around" or "messing around" with. The latter two may mean anything from associating with friends to institutionalized collaborative idleness, like driving around in a car with friends, bowling, going to hangouts, et cetera, but they usually suggest diffuse time-killing activity engaged in with friends. In the interviews with adolescents "bumming around" and "messing around" appear so frequently that one derives from this a strong sense of empty lives in which most spare time is devoted by boys and girls to avoiding constructive work, school work especially.

Bill is puzzling. His room is a model of orderliness, and he has done very good things with tools. He seems immediately like a boy with a strong "instinct of workmanship"; yet his school work is poor, he feels he has frittered away the high school years and that he is still doing it. He doesn't think much of himself (the "standard inferiority complex" of American adolescents). "I don't want to talk to the boys around here," he says, "because they're just as stupid as I am." He says he wastes his time and that he doesn't know whether he will ever have enough will power to change. On the one hand, we see in his room a fine, self-confident capacity for work with tools and a good sense of design and arrangement; on the other hand, evidences of self-depreciation are painfully present. His underlying feeling of powerlessness is expressed in the prediction that "I'll either be a draftsman or an electrician—probably *whichever one I fall into first.*"

Bill's real dream emerged one evening in the following interchange between him and the researcher:

R: If you could be anything in the world, what would you be?

B: (Long pause) Anything? Would I be successful in it?

R: Yes. Let's assume you would be.

B: (Long pause) I don't know; there are drawbacks in

everything; and I don't want something I'd be miserable in. Why did you ask me that?

R: You wanted me to ask you an interview question.

B: But I didn't think it would be anything like that. Oh, I guess an electronics engineer or something like that. I guess a Ph.D. in electronic design would be the best.

The researcher evidently challenged Bill on an agonizing subject, and Bill's efforts to master his pain and anxiety appear in his attempting to avoid the question: in the long pauses, in his saying that everything has drawbacks and in a heavy lightness of manner in answering the question; even in giving a speculative answer he wants to be assured that he will not fail in the speculative occupation. Bill's response enables us to understand better his resignation and his inability to pick a model for himself: any meaningful choice would cause too much suffering. Thus in answering the researcher's question about a life model he constricts his choice narrowly within the sphere of craftsmanship to "whoever could do a job better than me."

But he does not know who that might be, and the model would serve only until Bill learned "how to do it better." To pick a person after whom to model one's self is an aggressive act of will, and Bill is much too anxious and passive to do it. But there is another deep vein running through Bill's character that prevents modeling; that is the vein of cynicism.

Everybody has an angle, says Bill, and everybody thinks you are working an angle even if you aren't. Furthermore his mother had five husbands and since she threw them all away, men cannot be much good. In addition his father prefers Lila to him. What male is worth modeling himself after? Boys are stupid; parents are only so-so, and when you reach a certain age you can't talk to them.

Such a combination of attitudes—self-depreciation, resignation, and cynicism—can readily add up to mediocrity or failure in school, where Bill is under pressure to do not only the things that come naturally, like drafting and electrical work, but also the things that come hard.

All I Have to Sell Is Labor

(A fanciful construction of an interview with Bill Greene twenty years after.)

Bill is working for *Spacetime Inc.*, manufacturers of space-time equipment. Ninety-five per cent of the company's operations are "defense" contracts; *Spacetime* is one of 9000 subcontractors on Project Spacetime for exploring the outer limits of our own universe in order to discover whether other than direct great circle trajectories may be found to vital parts of the Communist world. Bill is a member of the new phantom élite—the technicians who help the technologists, who are the real élite because they are college-trained.

An interviewer from University's Labor Economics project is ushered into the Greene parlor. University has a $2,000,000 grant from the Department of Defense for the purpose of studying the problem of why workers shift jobs. The project is phrased, "socio-psychological determinants of worker commitment," and is the same problem University has been working on for the past thirty years. The interviewer is a graduate student working at $4.00 an hour, equivalent to $2.00 an hour at 1960 prices. His pants are a little frayed. He has had 5 weeks' intensive training in interviewing, which included such things as "how to get rapport with the interviewee," how not to use big words, how to concentrate on what the "interviewee" is saying, how to draw him out, et cetera. He is to obtain the "interviewee's" confidence by carefully explaining the objectives of the project and assuring him of anonymity. He has a small tape recorder, which he does not conceal from Bill.

Bill's house is small but Heddie keeps it nice; it is a picture-book house and Bill and Heddie own it. They have only fifteen more years to pay off on the mortgage. It has things like wall-to-wall carpeting, a pink phone in the kitchen to contrast with the pale green of the walls, and a portable color TV in their daughter Marge's room. Of course, there is a large console TV in the little parlor and a radio dial in the kitchen that can tune in on the house radio while everybody else is watching TV.

The lad from University goes through a considerable number of questions like: What things in particular do you like about the work you do at *Spacetime?* What things do you dislike about it? Is there any job with *Spacetime* that you would like better than the job you have now? And so on. At last he comes to the question: If you had it to do over again what job would interest you?

There is a long pause. The silence is intensified by the swish of the tape through the machine as it records silence. Bill looks a little depressed; he seems almost to be submerged by the ballooning upholstery of the chair in which he is seated. In the seconds that pass along the whispering tape he thinks back to his days at Rome High; his quandary about himself and what he should do; his feeling that he was stupid; his knowledge that his father, having provided him and his sister with a home like this one, had no money to send him to college; his intuition that it wouldn't have been any use anyway; his long sensuous evenings with Heddie that were so much more gratifying than study. Deep inside of him there is suddenly a transient pain, the twinge of shame that is a consequence of the almost conscious awareness that somewhere along the line he has let himself down, and he cannot face that. At this point, where there is a brief inner blush, he raises his head, laughs a little in an embarrassed way, and says to the interviewer, "Now that's kind of a tough one. I never really did think about that. But considering my education and . . . and everything else, why yes, I guess I would go in for technician. Wherever you go you can always get a job somewhere as technician; so it's steady and it pays good. It's kinda interesting too—always something new coming up. Yeah, I guess I'd go for technician if I had it to do over again. Hell, all I've got to sell is my labor!"

Later, back in his hotel room, the interviewer dictates into the machine, "Number 455 is very strongly committed to technician as an occupation."

Erosion of the Capacity for Emulation. In Bill we can see something of the widespread process of what I shall call the *erosion of the capacity for emulation,* loss of the ability to model one's self consciously after another person. When Veblen spoke of emulation he was thinking of material goods and the associated ceremonials of status validation, and there is no doubt that in this respect the spirit of emulation persists in our culture in all its primordial strength. But what I have in mind when I speak of the erosion of the capacity for emulation is not emulating a person with respect to his property, but rather emulating his *properties*. Culture depends on this latter potentiality, for it is in great degree through *Homo sapiens'* strong inherent potential for the emulation of properties that the moral qualities of culture have been maintained, and *Homo sapiens* has relied heavily on this mechanism to educate the rising generations. But when cynicism, resignation, and passivity enter life the first makes all emulative choice of properties seem vain, and passivity and resignation sap the will necessary to the emulative decision. But positively, in order for a morally sound emulative choice to be made there must be present some faith in one's self; a certain amount of naive optimism and a certain quantity of will. When these are lacking life readily becomes a series of moment-to-moment choices dominated, especially in adolescence, by Id and status cravings. In this the pecuniary world (as witness advertising and Mrs. Elphin, the "lady in wool") is usually ready to cheer the adolescent on. We can now understand better why the walls of Bill's room are covered with stereo equipment and not with pictures of inventors, for what interests him is *the things invented and not the qualities of the inventors;* and he himself says he does not want to model himself on anyone. In this case rejection of all human models is simply the obverse of inability to emulate any model.

One thing remains, and this seems strong in Bill: the desire to do a good clean job and to better his performance. Bill retains much of the "instinct of workmanship" and it is "natural" that it should appear in a boy who plans to be a draftsman or electrician; it is the "true instinct" of the man who works with his hands. What will happen to it when Bill lands a job in an industrial system that values quantity over quality is not problematic: his cynicism will be confirmed and intensified, so that he will have no attachment to his job beyond his pay and seniority, and little involvement in his occupation.

In many respects Bill is culturally an ideal young man, for he has some characteristics that are necessary to our economy. For example, if he tried to emulate heroes he would have their ascetic qualities too, and these are poison to consumption. If, instead of being cynical, he had high moral expectations he would not put up with chicanery and with the type of dishonesty represented in so much of the pecuniary system. As it is now, he will tend to say, "So what? That's the way it is; everything has an angle; you are in this world to be took." If he really had confidence in his own abilities—did not think he was stupid, did not expect to work at the first thing he "fell" into—he would insist on having the kind of job he really needed for his Self, thus frustrating industry in its effort to put him in the job it needs. Given ten million boys like this the economic system would fall apart. There is, however, one thing wrong with Bill— his "instinct of workmanship." Once in a job where "good enough," rather than "good as you can make it," is the criterion for performance, he may become disgusted; not so much, perhaps, because he cannot stand to do worse than he is able but because "good enough" deprives him of the only measure of worthwhileness remaining to him and leaves him no better than the next guy. Nor is he any worse—and herein resides the paradox, for the very factors that depreciate excellence also maximize security. Being no worse than the next guy, he cannot be fired. The decline of the value of excellence (what Veblen called the "instinct of workmanship") is another revolution in our time; but it has its compensations.

Bumming and Messing Around. I have defined bumming and messing around as institutionalized collaborative idleness engaged in with friends, and have pointed out that this fills the gap in time left by school, minimal study, and attention to eating, sleeping, et cetera. In early high school years messing and bumming around are done largely with members of the same sex, but, as Bill says, "you get to an age when you'd rather bum around with a girl than the boys." Since one does the same thing when bumming with a girl as when bumming with boys— bowling, swimming, theatres, drive-ins, Teen Towns—the tie with the boys is easily fractured. At this age and in this social class the only significant difference between the two types of bumming is sexual; the monosexual group can give so little to hold its members, at this age, that once sex becomes important early friendships among girls and among boys become tenuous. But there is a further factor—implied in Bill's remark that boys are as stupid as he is—and that is the inability of boys to really cope with one another's deeper personal problems. On the other hand, even if a girl does not really know what is going on inside a boy, the institutionalized feminine view of males will do a great deal for him. According to this view, all males are little boys who need mothering and need to "feel superior" and "show their masculinity." Once even a stupid female has got hold of the notion that people need mothering and an opportunity to feel superior, she can do a great deal with almost *any* human being. Her task with a boy is all the more necessary and easy since the male group rejects weakness. In this way bumming and messing around with a girl takes on a quality of bumming and messing which males do not have. At this point the *Midsummer Night's Dream* needs a feminine touch.

This section started with a trip to Rome High with Lila Greene, a fourteen-year-old freshman. In the course of the day we came to some understanding of her and of the school. Then we were introduced to Heddie, sweetheart of Lila's brother Bill, and then we met him. Through these encounters we have, perhaps, come to a somewhat deeper understanding of the problems of adolescents than that developed in Chapter 6. Now we shall look at two abridged reports of dinners to which the Researcher was invited at the Greene's.

DINNER AT THE GREENES

Both dinners were badly cooked, Mr. Greene and Lila collaborating to make them so. At one of the dinners Cornish rock hens were served (this was Mr. Greene's idea).

Excerpts from record of the first dinner

Mr. Greene and I, under his stimulus, discuss the recipes for various alcoholic beverages, while Lila listens attentively, and Bill sits in his room, which is just off the kitchen, doing homework and making no effort to join the group in the kitchen. When dinner was served Bill came to the table

only at the last minute. Mr. Greene tells mildly risqué jokes
he had recently heard, while Lila hangs on every word,
studying me to see when I laugh. Bill eats in silence,
showing little interest in the conversation. After dinner he
goes immediately to his room to study.

While I was doing dishes with Lila she brought up a
number of topics. [Some of them are not included in this
discussion because the focus is on family relationships.]

Lila has family problems. She doesn't know what to do
about asking advice or permission on things because if she
goes to her father she thinks she's cheating her mother and
vice versa. So usually she winds up talking to the guidance
counselor instead because she wants to be fair to both her
father and mother and doesn't know how to go about it. She
says that's where she picked up the idea that you find
psychology very helpful in dealing with people—from the
guidance counselor.

She asks me if I've ever been in love and about herself
she says, "There's this boy in Minnesota—I've tried and
tried and can't get him out of my mind. I go out a lot but I
still think of him." I suggest she write to him, but she says
she doesn't know what to say—how to "keep it light." I tell
her I'll think about it and see what I come up with. She
looks grateful. I think that in her eyes I am no interviewer
but rather an adult female. She has no other since she isn't
living with her mother any more. Both children seem to be
very lonely, and Bill reacts with resentment and Lila with
pleas for friendship. [It will be noticed in the course of
these dinners that Bill is not reacting with resentment only,
but also with his technique of pursuit by retreat.—J. H.]

Father came in to ask me if I'd like a highball, but I tell
him no, that I'm going to talk to Bill for awhile.

Lila asks Bill to come and put the dishes away, but although he comes out of his room he just stands around and
does nothing and then leaves. His whole manner during
dinner and when I first came to interview him was one of
resentment covered by apathy. I'm almost certain he resents
his sister's intrusion [into his relationship with the Re-
searcher] by asking me to dinner, talking with me afterward,

and asking me to come to school with her. I think these kids are fiercely competitive and jealous of every scrap of attention.

At the door [as the Researcher was preparing to leave] the father nails me under the mistletoe. I didn't even look for it at this late date. Lila was expecting Bill to do this; he looks surprised, dad looks pleased.

Excerpts from record of the second dinner

The scalloped potatoes are excellent and I mentioned this to Lila, who beamed proudly, but when she went to the kitchen to bring in dessert Bill said that I shouldn't be fooled by her—Heddie made the potatoes half an hour before I got there. Mr. Greene is responsible for the Cornish hens and says that maybe if I come for supper often enough, one of these days they'll get the whole thing coordinated. He offers me a highball before dinner, which is excellent, but a little heavy on the whiskey. There is little conversation going on during the meal, but Lila tells me a joke after her father leaves the table. The joke is as follows: This little Mexican swam over to the United States and when he got there the first person he saw was a giant Texan. So he said to the Texan, "Gee, señor, you are so big; you must have a very big penis." The Texan agrees and the little Mexican asks if he can see it. The Texan shows him, and the Mexican says, "Gee, señor, you must have very big balls." The Texan says yes, and the little Mexican asks if he can feel them, so the Texan says yes, and the Mexican stands on a chair to reach up. Then he says, "All right, señor, hand over your money or I jump." Lila thinks this is the perfect robbery.

Before dinner was served I went to Bill's room, which is just off the kitchen, and he talked about his new physics project which is the construction of a theremin. His father had remarked that seventy dollars seemed an ungodly price to pay for such an insignificant instrument, but now Bill tells me that it only costs fifty-four dollars and his father paid

only half. *This whole family seems to take delight in con-
tradicting the statements of the others.* Bill tells me that in
addition to putting this model together he has to learn to
play it for physics, but Lila says he only had to put it
together. Apparently before my arrival there had been a
heated discussion about the theremin: Lila had been wheedling her father with the argument that since he paid half
the cost of the theremin she was entitled to play it half the
time, provided he gave her permission. But he says, leave
it up to Bill—if he doesn't want her to play it she shouldn't
pester him. She pouts and stomps off into the kitchen.

Meanwhile, back in Bill's room, I compliment him for
his cleverness with electronics. When I express interest
in the theremin he unscrews the case to show me the inside. Then we discuss the amplifier of his stereo set and he
opens this for me too, using a great deal of time and energy
to do it. As I sit on the floor looking at all the wires he
says, "I hope you realize this is hard work, and that I
wouldn't do this for just anyone." I acknowledge that I am
aware of this and that I appreciate very much what he is
doing.

Lila comes in and Bill becomes just as surly as he can get.
He deliberately delays going in to supper and says very
little at table. Lila gets up to get dessert, saying it's going
to be a surprise. Bill winks at me, pokes his head around
the corner, comes back and tells me that dessert is ice
cream with whipped cream and nuts and a cherry on top,
thereby spoiling Lila's surprise, of course. He says he
thought about grabbing the whipped cream and spraying
her with it, but decided against it. It's a good thing, because Lila has just changed clothes, and is wearing short
shorts and matching blouse, which she is beginning to fill
out rather well. I think she is aware of this.

I am getting ready to interview Bill when Lila returns
and starts firing questions at me. First we discuss religion
and Lila tries to force me to admit the existence and power
of God and the need of man for God. From the nature of
the questions she throws at me in the course of the evening
I'm sure they were planned in advance.

[Lila asked many questions, not giving the Researcher, who obviously, being a guest in the house, had no right to "turn her off," much chance to talk to Bill, who withdrew almost entirely from the conversation. Lila's questions covered many topics, including the following: technology and progress; Russia and dictatorship; capitalism; socialism; prejudice. Questions are mostly of the following character: "What do you think of capitalism?" "Well, what about socialism?" "Do you believe prejudice enters into our ideas?"] Presently Bill leaves the room for a minute, comes back, and says, "Are you still at it?" but he doesn't seem angry. Lila suggests he play the record I brought (Shorty Rogers, "Afrocuban Influence on Music"). Lila has been heckling me because I had forgotten it for over a month. Bill picks it up, hits her lightly over the head with it, and says, "I dub you Sir Knothead." Lila says, "You will note the clever way I get this reproduced in beautiful hi-fi, because he can't deny *you* the use of his record player." Bill glares. The record plays in all its savage glory and Lila gyrates with tribal enthusiasm, while her brother looks at her as if she's out of her mind. She says, "You can just *feel* the emotions. I'm very interested in studying emotions. If you can work on one kind of emotion, then you can work on any other. For example, if I say to you, 'Don't smile,' because I want to see your dimples, you will try very hard not to smile and will wind up laughing, of course, and I will see your dimples." She tries this and I resist, but it finally works and she calls Bill's attention to my dimples.

[Lila steers the conversation around to styles and grooming, and says] "I'm letting my hair grow out. I want it long because it's more efficient like yours. You can wear it real long, either way. So then I'll be efficient like you (smirk). What do you think of movies?"

The record player is now playing a drum solo by Shelley Mann (my record) and Lila is beating time on the chair arm. Bill says, "I suppose you think you're a bongo player. I have sad news for you." Lila says, "I bet with a little practice I could play bongoes as well as he (Shelley Mann) does. Well, maybe not as well but quite adequately." Bill says, "I have more sad news for you." Lila says, "Just give me the opportunity and I can do anything I want to" and Bill remarks to me, "If she keeps that up she'll be something she didn't plan to be, a lunatic." To which Lila replies, "Well, it's true. Give me a recipe and I can cook anything. Just show me how and I will do anything." Bill throws a small cork at her. Bill is especially sensitive to what he calls "speech impurities" and trips Lila up on this quite frequently.

Analysis of these observations starts quite naturally with Mr. Greene, Id-boy and imp of fun when he is not working hard to provide for his children. His way of relating to the Researcher is by repeatedly offering her highballs, discussing recipes for alcoholic beverages with her, telling slightly risqué jokes, and by trapping and kissing her under the mistletoe—all in front of his children. Listening and watching with intense concentration is the fourteen-year-old Lila. What more natural than that Lila should tell a sex joke too, feel that alcohol is the way in which males and females relate to one another and that taking a drink is a symbol of being grown up? A smart little man victimizing a vain and stupid one by playing on his weaknesses seems a likely theme for a joke told by Lila. Considering also her hostile, competitive relationship with her brother, the castrating theme would also give her pleasure. Cheating in Rome High and obscenities on the walls of the girls' dressing room find their obvious place in all of this: family and school form an uninterrupted mutually supportive relationship.

It makes sense for Lila to wait for her father to leave the table before she tells her joke, for it seems natural to us that Mr. Greene, while telling risqué stories in front of his children should not want them to tell similar ones. It is part of the same *logic of impulse:* I may drink but my young children may not; I may have sexual intercourse but my young children may not; I may tell sexy jokes but my children may not; I may smoke but not my children, et cetera. I know of no culture where such a total division is attempted between impulse release patterns in children and impulse release in adults. Among my friends the Pilagá Indians of Argentina, children of all ages attempted or had intercourse with one another, played sexual games, listened to and told sexual stories, and smoked if the adults would let them have tobacco (which was very rarely, because there was so little). Older children did not go near the beer fiestas because this was for older men, not because it was "immoral." Thus, since the Pilagá have no impulse logic according to which children are excluded from the impulse release patterns of adults, when children engage in them they need not do it surreptitiously and are not made to feel immoral.

On the other hand, neither can we have our children drinking and promiscuous, for the whole pattern of impulse regulation in Pilagá society is different from our own. The point I wish to stress is that in our society the constant awareness of parents engaging in apparently free impulse release while children are supposed to be controlled places an enormous strain on children's impulse regulation, and creates subterfuges, shams, and guilt. The discontinuity between child and adult behavior in this regard is disappearing, however, not only because it is difficult to maintain but because the world, including the parents, offers no rewards for self-restraint and no satisfying substitutes for indulgence.

Here is the place to take passing note of Lila's interest in God and religion. Her combination of selfish pragmatism and verbal interest in God occurs sporadically in the two hundred interviews we have with run-of-the-mine adolescents of all ages. It is reminiscent of the earliest religious forms, when religion was divorced from ethics; and in the adolescent internal economy it seems to serve the function of somehow putting the adolescent back in touch with the orthodox tradition while making no ethical demands. Of course, Rome, being close to the fundamentalist regions of the country has some seriously religious youngsters.

Not only is there no mother in the Greene home, but the *maternal qualities* are absent. The cooking is dreadful and though Mr. Greene gives his children a good home, there is little parental tenderness, if for no other reason than that he is always on the go. Since, furthermore, Bill is resentfully withdrawn, and he and his sister are constantly badgering each other,

they seek warmth outside: Lila by dating and by clique relations, Bill in his relationship to Heddie. When we realize that
Lila could have learned how to cook or that Bill, recognizing the
need for decent food for his sister and especially for his busy
father who works hard to give his children a nice place to live,
could have learned to prepare meals instead of giving almost all
his spare time to fixing up his room, to hi-fi, and to his sweetheart, we can understand that warmth has almost departed from
this house. This emphasizes once again the milieu from which
come a competitive, exploitive, gregarious Lila and a resentful,
withdrawn, self-questioning, woman-seeking Bill. To repeat a
conclusion drawn many times in this section, Rome High is not
merely a "high school culture"; the adolescent group is not just
a "group culture" handing on attitudes and behaviors as simple
"pressures from the group"; rather the school and the adolescent
group cultures are constantly renewed by the needs of children
who want desperately what the school and group cultures have
to give.

We have visited the Greene home, seen the members together,
gotten an idea of how they treat one another and a young
feminine guest, and obtained further insight into the relation
between the adolescent, school, and home. Each adolescent home
is different from every other, of course, and I certainly do not
mean to suggest that what upsets us about adolescents is created
by broken homes. All homes, intact or broken, make contributions
to adolescent culture, and to the culture in general. There is a
constant interplay between each family and the culture at large,
one reinforcing the other; each unique family up-bringing gives
rise to needs in the child that are satisfied by one or another
aspect of the adolescent-and-school-culture. But this is the nature
of *culture*—it is a mine, a deep pool, a complicated and rich
universe out of which each person takes what he needs, as *he
becomes the culture*. If culture was not this way it would fall
apart.

A DOUBLE DATE

Now we are ready to go on a double date with Bill and Heddie.
The purpose of discussing it is to present another dimension of

adolescent relationship. Obviously Bill and Heddie are not going to act on the double date with the Researcher as they would with other teen-agers, so that although we can learn something from it, we cannot believe that behavior on this double date is entirely spontaneous. A very important feature of it, however, is the gossip of Heddie and the Researcher. The latter's conversation with Heddie tells us a great deal about gossip, about the people Heddie gossips about, and about Heddie herself.

As usual I shall abridge the report in the interest of brevity: the process of arranging the date and getting together is left out, and we start with the Researcher's description of Heddie and Bill's clothes. The reader is asked to refer again to the advertisement for *Seventeen* at the begining of this section.

> Bill wore a dark charcoal wool suit with narrow lapels, white shirt, conservative tie, black slip-on shoes, white crew sox. He looked well-groomed; appropriate for the occasion. It was miserably cold but Bill wore no overcoat. Heddie looked very attractive in a cherry-red wool dress, new short hemline, designed to compliment a good figure; high-fashion black spikes, a dark mouton jacket, which differed from the run-of-the-mill in its cardigan front. She dressed in what I considered expensive clothes. I *could* afford this wardrobe on my salary, if I considered it essential, but how does this non-working, 15-year-old daughter of lower middle or upper working class family afford it?
>
> On the way to the show we passed the ———— restaurant and Heddie said she wanted a menu from there because she's collecting menus. One place charged her $1.50 for one, and she thought that took nerve, but she paid it.
>
> On the way to the show Ned [the Researcher's escort] and I wondered what our chances were of getting there at all, for although some of the roads were still icy Bill refused to go less than 40 mph anywhere, including the curves. Bill and Heddie talked about grades. It seems he did very well in his *practical* (i.e., vocational) subjects this time, two A's in drafting and such. Heddie sits close to him with left arm around his shoulder, head resting on his shoulder. Both are very quiet. Bill announces we are going to see

Please Turn Over at the Odeon.[1] When we get to the show it seems we'll have to wait an hour for seats because we're late. So back to the car, which, joy of joys, won't start. Heddie says this is typical.

Heddie says they were parked on a lonely barricaded road called "Lovers' Lane" once not long ago and found the car wouldn't start and they didn't know what they were going to do, as this was a rather embarrassing place to send for a tow truck. Finally some husky boys came along and helped them. Heddie thought this was pretty funny too—a million laughs, this girl.

We go back to the show, it's now 8:20, and wait for it to begin. In a couple of minutes Heddie notices two orange-blond young ladies, painted like what she pictures shady ladies to be. As she remarks, neither one looks more than 15 or 16 even with all that makeup. Heddie hates bleached hair: it looks tough, she thinks. One is smoking a cigarette, blowing smoke as if she were a steam engine—mighty blasts, not vapor trails, and Heddie thinks this hilarious. I ask her if Lila treats her hair and Heddie says she does, that she's getting sloppy and letting the roots show. I *thought* so. Heddie tells me that Lila's steady [remember Ed, the roller-skating boy] is a real mess. Bill more or less declines comment on his sister, but Heddie continues. She thinks Ed looks like an undertaker. He knew Lila about four years before they started going steady. When she took him to the backwards dance at school apparently his appearance didn't pass the test because he wasn't appropriately dressed. He wore a light blue coat that came half-way to the knees and dark blue slacks. (Poor guy, that was the greatest when *I* went to high school!) He acted like an undertaker too; he said "Hello" in a monotone and didn't mix with the others well.

Heddie is leaning against Bill because, she says, she's tired and there's no place to sit while waiting. Every once in awhile he asserts his strength by pulling her arm until

[1] A "high class" theatre close to an upper-middle-class section, attended also by upper-uppers, and costing twice as much as neighborhood movies or drive-ins.

she is almost sitting down. The man in front is staring and Heddie says to me, "Do you ever feel the whole world is staring at you?" When Bill gives no indication of stopping she laughs it off.

Show time. We're almost trampled. As soon as we're seated Heddie gets up to call her mother.

She checks to see if I'm sitting with my legs tucked under me, because she wants to sit that way. Decides it will be acceptable to do so and does. Bill puts his arm around her but presently withdraws it as she becomes engrossed in the picture. Her bubbly laugh, so continuous in the car and lobby is almost non-existent here. Bill chuckles at the sexy innuendos in the picture but Heddie rarely laughs. One line about the heroine celebrating her seventeenth birthday by contracting with a scout to go to work as a call girl strikes her as funny. She is very eager to pick up any allusions to her age group; more so, apparently than Bill, who seemed more concerned with identifying with the sex ambitions of the young man. Once Bill takes Heddie's hand very gently and tenderly.

We go back to the car and Heddie says to talk very nicely to it and maybe it will start. She tells Bill the trouble is that he gets mad and gets profane but that loving words would have more effect on it. But the car refuses to start. Bill takes Heddie's good silk gloves and uses them to wipe the windshield. She's not happy about this but laughs it off.

By the time the tow truck got there it was already 11:45 and Heddie and I decide it would be better to postpone having pizza to next time. Bill is determined on pizza but we talk him out of it by setting a specific time next week. He tells me a long story about the heavy schedule he has next week at school but under Heddie's influence he can "make time for it." I would surmise that Heddie was eager to get home because of her parents and that for *that* reason Bill was just as eager to keep her out.

I ask Heddie if she knows why Lila doesn't wear lipstick, and Heddie says, "I think she thinks she has natural beauty. But Liz Taylor she isn't." I say that I didn't mean she was unattractive but that I was curious about this and thought that maybe Lila had mentioned why she didn't use lipstick. Heddie says, "She just thinks she's hot even without it. She's a mess, don't you think so, Bill? Hope you don't mind me saying things like that." Bill assures her he doesn't care one way or another. He's totally indifferent to his sister.

Heddie wants to tell me something confidential, so I lean forward to let her. It seems Lila spent the night at Heddie's house once. Lila had been bragging that she was a 35½ inch bust but that part of it was her broad back. Heddie didn't believe that, so when Lila had gone to bed Heddie got up and looked at her bra tag—32A. Heddie thought this was hilarious.

Its hard to catch conversation between Heddie and Bill in the car with Ned and me in the back seat, but Heddie and Bill seem to be discussing her mother. He says, "Yeah, but you let her talk you into things. . . . Now whose influence is *that* talking? It's your mother's, isn't it? Well, isn't it? If you care so much about me couldn't you take my side once in awhile?" Heddie laughs, brushes his cheek with hers. "Well, see if you can't make her see it my way now and then, okay?" I couldn't hear Heddie's reply, but Bill seems satisfied.

Heddie kept heckling me about my declining years and once or twice was wistful about my extra privileges that came with advanced years. [The Researcher is 22.] She mentioned that Jean was going with a 20-year-old who ordered a pink lady at Smather's. The waitress said, "You *are* 21, aren't you," and the girl said, "No, darn it!" and started crying. It seems she couldn't lie because she was a Baptist. Heddie thought this was funny because Baptists aren't supposed to drink either, so why one scruple and not the other?

I think they saw me more as an old friend rather than as a snooper.

Heddie was dying for a cigarette so I gave her one. She had asked Ned for one but he didn't have any. I think she was surprised that I had some. She imitated the smoking technique of the orange-blond at the show and we laughed.

Bill was not in the car at the time. He disapproves of her smoking but permits it. It impresses me that Heddie smokes in the manner of an adult who finds smoking pleasurable, not in the compulsive inept manner of many girls her age who smoke to show off.

Let us imagine Bill and Heddie, dressed to the outermost limits of their own and their families' pocketbooks, standing at the center of concentric ripples extending to the outermost fringes of the world. There is on the backs of Bill and Heddie more money than the average Hindu sees in a year—$69 by a recent estimate.[1] Thus Heddie and Bill have meaning in a world-wide context. In order to bring Bill and Heddie to this pitch of consumption a number of things had to happen. First, we had to deprive the rest of the world in order to pamper ourselves. This was done not by seizure as in the days of military conquest, but simply by contriving to keep our goods at home. Second, we had to create an insatiable home market. Finally, we had to develop an insatiable character structure. In this sense *Seventeen* magazine has put its finger on the truth that teen-agers feel they have "no nothing," for it is this feeling that creates insatiability. The sources of this are in the constant sensation of being chosen and rejected, in the experience of having no way of proving one's worth definitively, and in not having any absorbing goal except fun. Every adolescent in our culture goes through this, but in addition, every family makes its own contribution to the basic sources of *the feeling of being empty handed,* bereft, abysmally poor, *no matter what the material circumstances.* All youth ask themselves the questions, "What have I got?" and "Will I hold my own?" To these questions the clothing industry answers, "You've got *us!*" and *Seventeen* burbles to the girls, "You have *Seventeen!*"

Meanwhile, this precarious balance or, rather, this tendency to slide downhill, is aggravated by a gnawing discontent and competitiveness that leads the youth—very especially the girls— to attack one another. Heddie's attacks on Lila are merely special cases: Lila's date, she says, looked and talked like an undertaker and was inappropriately dressed. Heddie peeks at Lila's bra to

[1] *New York Times,* August 25, 1961.

see whether it really is 35½, and relays the juicy fact that it is only 32A to the Researcher, her confidante; Lila "just thinks she's hot even without" lipstick; the roots of her dyed hair are showing. What is especially significant here is not so much the gossip and hostility but the trivial criteria with which they are preoccupied, the smallness of the mind that would get up at night to check the size of a brassiere. From the standpoint of the total culture in which these children live, the criteria are *momentous*, however. We must understand also that Lila and Bill are cultural paragons. If girls do not wear lipstick and if boys like Ed go around in old style instead of new, and if all the Heddies across the land date in old clothes, the economy falls on its face.

This brings us to menu-collecting and the Odeon, both of which are merely different aspects of the maximization of consumption. The Odeon deserves particular attention because it is high class and therefore has a special appeal to lower-middle-class children. Waiting in the little lobby of the Odeon is a special experience because the lights are very bright, and people can get a good look at one another. You have to be able to "make the grade" there, so you had better be dressed "appropriately, and act accordingly. Bill, however, seems to have forgotten how to behave and has set a man to staring at him; but Bill's clothes probably passed (at least the Researcher said so). Heddie continues sensitive to the protocol of the situation, looking to see how the Researcher sits in the theatre—legs drawn up. She would not have done it if the Researcher had not. Every step must be watched, every move planned, for on the move of a limb, the quality and timing of a smile, the exact timbre of a laugh, on the way one says "Hello" (never do it like an "undertaker"), or on the precise manner of blowing smoke—all quite apart from the clothes one wears—depend one's holding one's own or losing it. Such are the canons of adolescent conduct in the Era of Impulse Release and Fun. Just to give this sensitivity a name, let us call it *hypervigilance for etiquette cues.*

The extent to which clothing, cosmetics, and sensitivity to the correct trivia are *an integral part of the Self* in our culture must not be underestimated, and at the risk of seeming to labor the obvious I must spend just a little more time on it.

The drug-taking, wine-drinking, knife-wielding horrors and

despairs of the New York male juvenile delinquents are notorious throughout the country, but probably less is known of the thousand or so young girls who, attached to gangs, are considered a major cause of many gang outbreaks. Recognizing that one of the basic components in the character of the gang girl is the feeling that she is nothing, Martha S. Lewis, a group worker attached to the New York City Youth Board, was attempting to alter this feeling through a program of rehabilitation in 1960. Important in her approach was what she called her "charm clinic." I quote from a *New York Times* article on the subject:

> Tonight she says she wants to talk [to the girls] . . . about several "charm clinics" that she needs their help on . . . she feels they need to know something of self-respect. On coming evenings, she proposes, perhaps they would like to have a beautician show them how to do their hair, to learn table manners and decorum, and finally to conduct a real fashion show. Some look startled and immediately say they aren't sure they can come. Others look at their dowdy clothes and laugh noisily at the idea of a fashion show for them. . . .
>
> At the "charm clinic" on manners, a dozen girls show up. . . . Though Miss Lewis has not shown them how to dress, they wear uniformly neat blouses and skirts and high-heeled shoes—as though agreed upon among themselves. Their manners are something else . . . "in whatever situation you're in," Miss Lewis calmly continues, "if you know the correct thing to do, you can feel comfortable at all times."[1]

The fact that Miss Lewis sees the problem of these girls in *her* way, as a member of her social class is, of course, of first importance. But Miss Lewis's approach must be right in some ways, for *unless these girls learn to do the right thing in externals they will never be accepted by nondelinquent girls*. Miss Lewis, aware of this, states the rule: "If you know the correct thing to do, you can feel comfortable at all times." This means that if the girls know the correct trivia they have a better chance of "making it" with the nondelinquent girls than if they don't.

Please Turn Over, the movie that Heddie and Bill chose to see,

[1] *New York Times Magazine*, July 10, 1960.

is a typical "heart-warming, utterly hilarious" British movie about a seventeen-year-old girl who writes a best-selling novel. The gimmick is that since it thinly disguises the personalities of her perfectly moral family, while making them all sexually corrupt, the family is disgraced and the house is mobbed by the curious. In the book—and vividly portrayed in the movie—the father carries on an affair with a gold-digger, the mother sleeps with the uncle (begetting the novelist heroine), and the family doctor seduces his patients. In this artistic context the absorbed interest of Bill and Heddie can be readily understood. Thus the movies abet the adolescent culture. Of course the décor of the picture is upper middle class, and Heddie can take lessons from the interiors, the clothes, the gardens, the automobiles, and so on.

Now we ought to study the relation between Heddie and Bill. During the evening Heddie engaged in *molding* and *binding* her future husband. For example, when she tells Bill to talk nicely to the car (whose name is Heddie) she is teaching Bill to control his temper and to use loving words instead of profanity when he wants something. On the other hand when she "laughs off" his jerking her arm and his using her gloves to wipe his windshield she is binding him by *the gentle art of acquiescence*. At this time in their love career she is acquiescing in his aggressiveness; when they are married she will probably not put up with it. She *gentles* him too when, because she pays more attention to her parents' wishes than to his, Bill becomes petulant and she soothes him by rubbing her cheek against his. Here she does not acquiesce in his wishes, but rather *narcotizes the issue*. Thus molding, binding, and gentling Heddie schools herself and her consort, preparing them both for life in a little house. Bill flails around in a blind sort of way, while Heddie, supremely conscious every moment of the time, softly makes a human being.

These two are visibly in love, which means that they recognize that they have the right to expect tender and yielding behavior from each other. Whatever doubts they may have about having something and holding their own, those misgivings have not undermined their feeling of having the *right* to demand love and of being able to *give* it. Both Bill and Heddie feel *lovable*—this they have not given up; and the ability to retain and to entertain that feeling must be a fundamental ingredient of Selfhood.

There is much tenderness between Bill and Heddie and a remarkable ability on her part to adapt to the nagging, resentful personality of her sweetheart. At this stage there is already a certain domesticity in their relationship. Meanwhile the culture, i.e., Heddie's family, is opposed to their being together and they have no place to go—a major complaint of teen-agers—so they park on Lovers' Lanes. The world around, lovers have trysted illicitly in "the bush." In the jungles of South America, on the atolls in the Pacific, whether in the Old World or in the New, it has been the same. Generally they are not despised for it or bothered by the police. Everywhere the "bush tryst" has been the adolescent's way of subverting the adult order, when it has been against him, and everywhere acceptance of the "bush tryst" has been, one way or another, the adult way of coming to terms with sexuality of the young. The "bush tryst" is an expression of the rule according to which *a person will drive to fulfill a role once he has the capacity for it, provided always that he is interested.* If society prevents him he will do his best to subvert it. In the old days boys and girls contained themselves and bush trysting was at a minimum, but that was before the era of impulse release and fun, before the attack on inhibition became so terrifyingly successful, before fathers were expected to be playful imps.

In the analysis of the double date, as elsewhere in this book, I tried to show that every event reflects the cultural configuration. So, in talking about clothes, I pointed out that the fact that Bill and Heddie have more money on their backs than the average Indian sees in a year is a consequence of our position in the world economy, of the character structure produced by this economy, and of our own domestic social organization, particularly the family. I pointed out that the trivia on which Heddie's gossip focused are really momentous in terms of the configuration—in terms of the consumption needs of the economy and of what is important to Heddie and her peers. I argued that what weaknesses exist in adolescent character structure are aggravated because one is so often attacked by gossip. At the Odeon we saw the lobby as an arena where people took each other's measure, not with gladiatorial weapons but with clothes, grooming, and decorum; and the movie *Please Turn Over* was seen to fit with the sexual orientations of the configuration[1] and with the sexual interests of Heddie and Bill. In the theatre the Researcher sat with her legs drawn up on the seat, and Heddie, aware that this might not be the thing to do, checked with the older college girl before daring to do it herself, for Heddie remembered that this was not a neighborhood joint or a drive-in where you paid sixty cents and got a double or triple feature, but a high-class "theatre" attended by high-toned people, where you paid a dollar twenty-five for only one picture. Heddie's concern about this led us to reflect further that in the absence of more important criteria of worth, trivia loom as the measure of what is right and not right.

Finally, we perceived that the values of tenderness and yield-ingness and the capacity to deem one's self lovable have survived in both Heddie and Bill; and this is precisely where they should survive—in the relation between a boy and girl who are planning to marry.

CHRIS LAMBERT, A STRANGER

Jim, Lila, Bill, and Heddie are more or less average, seeming to fit relatively well into the milieu. But not all adolescents find the milieu congenial and some deviate from it sharply, often looking with contempt on the others. The religious girl who rejects smoking and sex; the boy who wants to be a poet-philosopher; the girl who is already far along in a career as a musician—all are deviants, nonconformists to the standard adolescent regimentations. It is not possible to study all of these refractory characters, so I have selected one, Chris Lambert, seventeen years old and a senior, because he is just emerging from a group life much like that of the rest of the high school and which he has rejected because he found it empty. Thus in Chris, who has been through and rejected what others still cling to, but who has not yet found himself, we have a person in whom to study some of the problems of the nonconforming adolescent. Both of Chris's parents had more than a college education but

[1] The fact that *Please Turn Over* is a British picture merely suggests that the British are in this respect very much like us.

there are individuals like him in the sample whose parents are working-class people, too.

Chris is tall, wears a crew cut and a car coat. We meet in the hall of University as I am returning from The Hole with a few cups of coffee. He accepts one of them and we sit down in Room Z. He stretches out his legs, drinks his coffee, and smokes a lot of cigarettes, speaking fast and with many slurs.

I explain something about the project—that we are trying to learn something about the lives of today's young people; and that we hope to get to talk to others through our original respondents.

C: I can refer you to every type of individual. I was once in a Y group that we organized. It broke up when the charter ran out. That was in the freshman year. In the sophomore year it was the biggest and strongest group, it had about 16 members. Some have moved now.

R: Are you still together with some of them?

C: Oh yeah. We are still in a group. Most of us have split up into sub-groups. In the sophomore and junior year we got together at somebody's home and played poker. Some of us would just sit and discuss.

R: Did you play for money?

C: Uh-huh. Oh yeah, that's what killed me. After you play for a half a year—you start with a half cent, then a cent—it gets bigger and bigger, that's what killed me. But just getting together with the boys was not satisfying. We still have friendly relations.

R: What was missing?

C: Some boys were dating—they missed out on stag parties. Now everybody is a senior and dating.

R: What do you mean, "they were missing out?"

C: In the junior year these individuals collected at people's houses on week-ends. It was all right for the time I was young. It was interesting; it meant new experiences for me. We would play poker in one room or talk: whether it was philosophic, I don't know; or we would listen to records—progressive jazz, folk songs, classical music. Constantly there were people who would go from one room to another getting tired of poker. Some of the time I played poker; many of the parties were at my house. When I got in the group I invited Alex over, he brought another friend of his. Slowly but surely I was looked upon as a member of the group. I wanted to be a member.

R: Did you invite them for that purpose [to play poker]?

C: Yes, that was the major reason I think. But Alex and I both realized at about this time last year that playing poker was senseless and an almost useless waste of time. You can get more done with one or two people—your mind is not your own when you are with anybody else, especially with a group. Your mind is influenced if you are with somebody else, you are prevented from reasoning although reasoning would be faulty alone or with others. In my sophomore year I tried to see the use of life. Man has one thing, his mind and the ability to acquire knowledge. That is necessary; in fact, it is the only thing in life, the only purpose of my life. I would like to go into theory of nuclear physics [in college], evolution of man; history, especially of the development of the arts and of man. I would like to know enough to compose and paint but *because I am compelled to go on in society and make money* I will be hindered in these wishes. I spend some time with close friends but we are still isolated individuals. This year I have not done a thing; I feel I have not accomplished anything.

R: Can you explain what you mean by "close friend"?

C: Alex and I have always been close friends. I feel attraction and affection for Alex; he concerns me. He's had a definite influence on my life, and at the same time I acted independent of him.

R: Can you illustrate that?

C: Take Saturday, for example, he drove me over for the College Boards and we had lunch together and then went to the Art Museum and then home and he invited another individual. What I mean by friend is not just associates. I have only two or three friends. The boy I came here with today is an associate, a nice fellow, but I don't consider him a friend. Do you understand the difference?

R: Yes. Can you tell me about your friends?

C: You know Alex. Let's talk about him. I was attracted to him and he was attracted to me. We have the same interests; we are the same with respect to our outlook on life in general, I suppose. He is interested in folk music. I don't know much about it. He has read more widely than I, and I respect his ability as a thinker. He opened new concepts to me.

R: Can you tell me more about your outlook on life?

C: It has a lot to do with thinking. I can think openmindedly; it appeals to me. I appreciate it if one can see something at the same time grotesque and beautiful.

R: For example?

C: Art, for instance. In modern art the abstraction may or may not be apparent; the meaning is there or not. Some people give it no credit and say the artist is foolhardy. They have no basis for judgment—kids my own age I'm talking about. Alex doesn't have one either, so he only says, "I like it or I don't like it." Alex and I will never have enough knowledge. If I could learn now or in the future everything learned before me, I would have a basis to come a little closer to what everybody calls truth. I am a strong believer in the universe of truth.

Second interview

R: I meant to ask you what it meant to be "missing out" because of dating in the group you were associating with.

C: We might all go down town or to somebody's house, but the person who had a date wouldn't be included; they would have no desire to be [because of the date]. But it wasn't consistent: one night they'd have a date and another night they'd be with the boys.

R: I wonder whether boys' friendships fall apart when they start dating.

C: Not necessarily. We included one boy who went steady for two years. That's something I look down on. It's superficial—a person going steady connects himself with something—with a person. The irony is, they aren't connected at all, except by this token, like a ring. It definitely limits a person. A date—one can have one, but you don't have to go steady. It's ridiculous and not necessary at all. Of course a lot of people do it. The kids around me go steady all the time. They go with a girl a certain time; then they break up and are no friends any more. They don't break up peacefully. It's silly in the first place. It has all kinds of repercussions. That's what convinced me.

R: What do you mean?

C: There are no permanent repercussions. If you want one person, fine; but it limits you timewise, and consequently your independence. I always looked at it that way. Same with marriage, incidentally, although there is more worth in it. It is almost necessary.

R: How so?

C: Some boys say they will never get married but they were never out from home in the world with nobody. I have been away and worked. I worked on a farm twelve to thirteen hours a day—from 5 A.M. til 7:30 P.M., often. On a good day especially, I would go home and sleep; and if you do that for three months you get lonely. You ride a tractor with nobody to talk to. You hear the roar of the motor; you just sit there with your thoughts. Those kids have not been away from home.

R: Do you remember we talked about what you would like to do, and you said you would like to study a lot more but you would have to go out and work?

C: Sure. *I'll just be another person.* I can't go to college all my life. I just hope to get into the line of work that I like. I have no idea what that would be—probably some engineering.

R: What do you find so attractive about engineering?

[Chris then explains his interest in science and mathematics.]

R: Is that why you like engineering, because it combines all of these?

C: Yes. But it is too limited. What happens to your reading, art, foreign languages, classical languages, history? That's what I mean—it is impossible to do all this. I talked to a professor of architectural engineering because I want to do some liberal arts when I go to the school of architecture. Well, he said it takes 5 years to get a degree in architectural engineering.

R: Is that normal?

C: (Shakes his head) Four years. Most students do not play around in other fields. They get their limited training, get into a special field, have a special income, *and die. I will be just like them.*

R: So you don't expect a solution?

C: No. Oh, I could find a solution. If I could find enough money to support me—maybe make a pile of money. But that is all wishful thinking. I'm not hopeful yet but I'll go on fighting it though and not give up. I will be trying as long as I have interest but I won't succeed I know.

R: You said Alex had a definite influence on you—how do you feel about your relationship with him?

C: I couldn't care less. What do you mean by my "relationship" with him? I respect him well enough: if you know a person you aren't impatient with his defects. Alex is not very patient: he is nervous and this has caused him a lot of trouble. He wants to express himself. Sometimes he'll go out and paint and get frustrated because he is not a good artist. I can understand this, knowing Alex. I don't care much.

R: Is he a model for you in any respect?

C: He is a model in respect to my becoming more scholarly—I mean more diligent. I want to catch up but I can't do it as rapidly as I would like. *Since I was born I've been wasting my life.* People have been awarding me but it's foolish because I do not accomplish anything. You hear about these people—Nixon and Kennedy—they are always in the limelight but they haven't accomplished more than I have. They have only experienced more. I owe more as models to Leonardo da Vinci, Newton, James Joyce. They and I have needs and individual ways of satisfying them; that's what people say Christianity is—it only depends on people's needs. I say it to my Mom all the time, but I can't get it into her head. "All right, Mom," I say, "you do what you want and I'll do what I want." There was a lot of violent misunderstanding between my parents and me. We couldn't be farther apart; but at the same time we are close.

R: I get a feeling for what you mean, but could you give me some illustrations? In what areas does that come up?

C: As far as I am concerned, I do what I want. If we disagree I respect their opinion. *Where I am dependent,* I give in where I must. My parents' ideals and my ideals are distinctive [i.e., different]. My parents cannot think open-mindedly as myself.

R: Where does that come up?

C: Religion, for one thing. Mother is a devout Christian; I more or less scoff at it.

R: Can you give me another example?

C: I don't know—I don't have much to do with my parents. They are concerned when I get in [i.e., what time]. I got used to the idea: I'd tell them nothing about what happens to me, and they don't tell me what happens to them. I don't like the feeling of dependence; but then, *I feel I'll be dependent all my life.*

R: On what?

C: I don't know. Money, for one thing, and society; the nature of things; the environment—of course, man tries to get away from his environment.

R: You said you did not have much to do with your parents.

C: Mother has always been overly concerned—that's my opinion.

R: You said although you have so many differences you are close at the same time. What did you mean?

C: I'm not the rationalist to say I'm going away. I don't hate my parents; I don't hold them in utter contempt. I respect them for their position in life, that's all.

R: What's that?

C: They have grown to be what they are. They know more, although not as much as they should. We are a middle class family. [Chris now gives a number of details about his family that cannot be repeated because of the need to protect his identity. His rather long talk emphasizes further his feelings of distantiation from his family, includ-

ing his invalid younger brother. He continues.] I used to be
a sensitive kid. Things would hurt my feelings. For awhile I
had a real inferiority complex. That was in the fifth or sixth
grade. I have never been close to my family. My moods
exhibited themselves in various manners. In ninth grade I
started to form my opinion on life: I stopped studying and
started learning. Learning involves patience and persever-
ance. Studying does that too, but in seventh and eighth
grade I got E's and F's. After that I studied but I didn't
learn. Learning constitutes enough knowledge and conclusions; being studious merely means written data, mem-
orization and then discarding them.

R: When you talk about the inferiority complex you
had, what do you mean?

C: I had no connections to the world, and I cared. I don't
have connections to the world now, but I don't care. I
realize I never will have but I couldn't care less. From first
grade through eighth grade I was a sensitive individual; I
didn't know my capacities, my physical strength and mental
prowess. My worst time I had in fifth and sixth grade: I
had no connections with the world and no strong family
life by my own choice. My grades suffered in the sixth and
seventh grade. There were several circumstances surrounding this. I was stimulated—have you got that so far?

R: I wonder. . . .

C: Then I was getting good grades and I found out my
capabilities—*that was my tie to the world,* all I needed. I
studied; I worked hard; I did neat homework assignments.

R: What was it that stimulated you?

C: First, my mother was a great influence—she told me
I could do it. I needed confidence. A teacher tutored me
during the summer. In Boy Scouts I passed the Morse code
merit badge—it was awarded me because I memorized the
code in the shortest time ever. Of course, I was elevated by
the badge. In school I decided half-heartedly to do some
homework and suddenly that became an obsession. Up to
the eighth and ninth grades I wasn't connected to any person. I didn't know what friendship was; even though I tried
acquaintanceships they failed for one reason or another.

R: Can you think of a reason?

C: The reason was mostly due to me—my own personality. I didn't understand people; I didn't know how to handle them—*I was too anxious to know people to take time out to learn.* In ninth grade *I decided to prove myself socially—if I could do one thing I could do another thing.* I did no studying and got bad grades. I gained some acquaintances but these were superficial; I learned about people a great deal and have been learning ever since, and the more I learn the choosier I get—who are friends, acquaintances, enemies, and who are just contemptible. Some people I regard with contempt and just don't deal with them.

I disregarded everything else in my life. My grades were quite good although not as good as before. Previously *the grades were my attachment to the world;* then *getting along with people became an obsession.* I then decided during the first summer on the farm that I wasted my life. That was *proving* myself physically—I never worked harder.

So when I came back from the farm I resumed my studies —ignored people; but I decided I was missing something. I found I wasn't learning. Since my sophomore year I have taken it to task to learn rather than study. Now *I let things happen*—I do not seek them as far as people are concerned.

R: What about knowledge?

C: I still seek it. It is an obsession. You know that— basically people have to find themselves. I was lucky. I *got* my philosophy. Most people are messing around, not learning, and these are the most confused. They don't identify themselves with life. If I find a person like that and he becomes pestiferous, I knock down his guard. I don't talk behind their backs because that way you may cut your own throat.

R: What do you mean by pestiferous?

C: (Holding out his arm, making an embracing motion) Trying to be chummy.

R: When do you think you cut your own throat?

C: There is a girl up at school who got pregnant and had to get married. Her parents are respectable and she is respectable. Her friends are respectable and they will be hurt. It is now a known fact that she opened her mouth and took one individual into her confidence. It is not widely known, but I know about it and I shouldn't. That is why I say don't trust anybody; don't say anything if it would hurt. People will open their mouths. I got a reputation for not opening my mouth, so I know a great deal of what happens all the time.

R: You mean that people confide in you because they think you will keep it to yourself?

C: They realize I will keep it secret. If it came to testifying against one of my good friends I would not do it. I would rather perjure myself.

Chris and I start a brief conversation on this, and it appears that he would really not want to make false statements in order to cover up for his friends, but rather that he would either refuse to testify or make statements that would confuse the issue or mislead the prosecution. At one point he said, "I can always take the First Amendment" but I pointed out that the Fifth Amendment protects a citizen against self-incrimination only.

During the interview, when occasionally I put my pen aside and rubbed my right hand when it grew tired and hurt me from continual writing, he would notice that smilingly. Otherwise he was very serious and involved in what he said. Occasionally his pessimism seemed combined with a somewhat blasé attitude. Now, however, as we get up and leave the room, he smiles and we start exchanging the conventional Merry Christmas wishes. He is "friendly" and exhibits a genialness which seems to contrast rather incongruously with the disposition he so recently showed toward the world.

A BRIEF INTRODUCTION TO THE STUDY OF CHRIS LAMBERT

> *Dans notre société tout homme qui ne pleure pas à l'enterrement de sa mère risque d'être condamné a mort.*[1]

There is something about Chris Lambert that irresistibly reminds one of Meursault, hero of Camus' *The Stranger,* for since Meursault never developed any feeling for anybody, he became unconnected with life and so let things happen to him. Marie, his mistress, was the aggressor in sex and when she proposed it was "all the same" to Meursault (*cela m'était égal*); they would marry if she wished; he would say the same to any other mistress. Meursault's relationship to Raymond, the petty underworld character who was the cause of his committing the senseless murder, was equally passive: Meursault accepted Raymond's first invitation to visit because it saved him the trouble of preparing his own supper. Everything just happened to Meursault— even his homicide and execution. In this oceanic estrangement from life Meursault tells the truth out of inability to sense that it makes any difference. Only when he is found guilty of murder and sentenced to death does he start to think; from which one derives the lesson that some men must be sentenced to death— and *know* it—in order to be compelled to think.

Whoever, like Meursault, cannot mourn his dead mother, whoever, after the funeral, goes to a comic movie with a new mistress, has no feeling for his mother; and the reason that a person who does not weep at his mother's funeral may be condemned to death is that he is so disjoined from life that he will let almost anything happen to him because "it's all the same."

ANALYSIS OF CHRIS LAMBERT

Chris Lambert fits one stereotype of adolescence. Remote from his parents, although he does not hold them in "utter contempt"; hating dependence of any kind, so that he looks on almost any human association as threatening; distrustful and contemptuous of others as well as of himself, he makes grandiose identifications which cause him to be even less self-confident and to feel he is wasting his life (for he is not yet approaching the achievements of Leonardo, Newton, or Joyce). He feels lonely and isolated

---

[1] "In our society, every man who does not weep at his mother's funeral is in danger of being condemned to death." Albert Camus, *L'Étranger.* Edited by Germaine Brée and Carlos Lynes, Jr., Appleton-Century-Crofts, Inc.

because he is distrustful and fears involvement; and he fears involvement because he is distrustful and because involvement requires some accommodation to others. It is better, then, to let things happen to him than to make them happen.

Already the fear of being just like everybody else and hence dying to his Self ("I'll just be another person") casts its shadow on his future. Even the classic torment of thinking of what he would do if he had to testify against a friend assails him. Chris is of the United States but he is also of the modern world. He would, perhaps, be more at home in New York or Paris or Tokyo, where his kind accumulate, than in Rome where there are few like him.

There is an echoing of Meursault in Chris: his passivity, his willingness to let things happen to him, his disconnectedness, his lack of involvement, are all reminiscent of Camus' hero. Yet Chris is different too, because he does not say *cela m'était égal*, for things *do* make a difference to Chris; and he is thinking *now*, whereas Meursault did not think until it was too late. Chris no longer does things, as Meursault did, just because he had "nothing else to do" (*je n'avais rien à faire*), thereby getting himself into insoluble difficulties.

Integration in the Boys' Group. When Chris was younger he spent an enormous amount of time playing poker, but as he grew his problems became so big that they could not be "solved" by that narcotic. Adolescent culture the world over is held together by rituals and ideas expressed in endless round. Adolescents and young men among the Pilagá Indians spend their leisure drinking *yerba maté*, primping and preening in preparation for the evening courting dances, joking about sexual affairs, and talking about sorcery. Ritual and talk affirm the unity of the age group, and all societies have some way of achieving such an affirmation. The contents of the ritual and talk always reflect age-group and cultural interests. Obsession with impulse release and fun, with being "grown up," et cetera, provide the ceremonial components and ideology of much of contemporary adolescent social integration, and in this context poker seems an obvious choice. Money, competition, adult-like behavior, are all contained in poker. But it has no ideology. Eventually poker fails boys like Chris; for others it endures for life. But as long as

poker served an integrating function for Chris's group, it kept
them from girls. So important was poker to Chris that he felt
that boys who preferred to go out with girls "missed out." This
is a typical reaction of early male adolescence to the pressure
from the girls—the boys' group is so satisfying that boys hesitate
to leave it by dating. Chris was reluctant to go steady because it
would have taken him away from the boys and because it would
have meant giving up some independence. Paradoxically, meanwhile, he gave up the boys' group, he says, because one cannot
think independently in a group.

Independence.   In view of the fact that for most of the world
independence was for millenia an *outlandish* idea, we ought
to have another look at it. For most of his time on earth *Homo
sapiens* shunned independence, for cooperation with others
and the ensuing dependence on them was the only way to
survive. Even today millions outside our country cannot understand our bumptiousness in this regard. When, however, dependence is no longer perceived as contributing to survival it
becomes a lost, even a contemptible value. Nowadays in our
culture, dependence has taken on a special meaning to adolescents because in the family dependence imposes impulse restraint; and an adolescent's desire to be independent rarely
implies more than the appetite for doing what he pleases. Parents' anxiety or anger is then felt as "unfair," absurd, backward,
and hampering. When one reflects on the basis of many adolescent complaints and recalls the meaning of "independence" and
"backwardness" in the history of Western thought, the true
significance of many of these adolescent claims becomes really
threatening. For the adolescent demand for independence often
has a kind of mindless infantile egoism about it that is worlds
away from earlier meanings. It has been fostered by the philosophy of permissiveness in child-rearing and by the consequent
erosion of the capacity for gratitude in an Id-oriented culture.
Lack of self-confidence is another source of the wish to be independent, for when one has many self-doubts, almost any concession to another person seems to make inroads on an already
precarious autonomy. Meanwhile, continued dependence and
parental blocking of impulse release intensifies adolescent self-
doubt, while surreptitious impulse indulgence causes guilt and

self-depreciation. Sealing one's self off from all emotion can therefore become the solution for the adolescent who stands tormented between his impulses and parental disapproval.

The capacity to yield to the wishes of others—to give up being "a hog on ice" as John Whitehorn once put it—obeys an inner law, which is simply that the capacity to yield is related to personal autonomy. A person who has no self-confidence may lean happily on others, while one whose self-confidence is merely shaky may feel strongly a need to stand on his own feet (which often means stepping on other people's toes). Obsession with independence is related to the anxiety that one has nothing or that one may not be able to hold one's own. In this context, independence, aloofness, is an expression of the fear that one may lose out if he falls under somebody's control through love, friendship, gratitude, or intellectual dominance. Such a desire to be free shades imperceptibly into *the fear that one may not be able to escape,* and thus blends with those nightmares of man in our time, wherein he is trapped by faceless enemies, accused of nameless crimes, and shot as he sweats in his sleep.

In view of the almost endless sources of the will to independence in *our* time, it seems senseless to invoke the American Frontier to explain it: there is much here and now to make men wish to be free. The drive, however, is not the same as that which animated the Founding Fathers and the thousands who drove their carts across the Continental Divide, for theirs was born of strength; ours is the product of many weaknesses. What unites the independence drive of 1760 with its rachitic contemporary great-great-grandchild is merely a word. What Chris Lambert feels is not the heartbeat of old heroes, but the frightened pulse of his own epoch.

Rejection of the commoner cultural criteria of Self-measurement—grades and acceptance by others—has made Chris a stranger. There was a time in his life when he needed to get grades and to be accepted by others (it "became an obsession"), but he "couldn't care less" for these now, even though his grades are good. Knowledge and identification with the artistic and scholarly traditions of our culture are what count for him, and connectedness to the common world is of no importance. Chris's inner struggle could hardly have been expounded better in the

Buddhist Suttras: the alternation between involvement and detachment and the ultimate determination to "walk alone like a rhinoceros,"[1] accepting not the involvements and the measurements of the everyday world, but seeking rather union with a greatness outside one's Self. This is the spiritual pilgrimage of Chris; it is probably the pilgrimage of many sensitive, introspective, intelligent adolescents.

Thus Chris is part of history: he stands on sand at the edge of an ocean of thought that rolls to his feet from China, India, and Greece. He has reached it by ways known only to him, for the experiences he has had no one can quite repeat. And every adolescent will come to the primordial ideological sea of the culture along the pathways of his unique experience—if he does not fall asleep, narcotized on the way by the purple vapors of *The Dream*, or dulled by too much misery. If he is well off, like Chris, he may inwardly debate the problems of his Self: of detachment versus involvement, of learning versus studying, of the humanities versus science. But if he is not affluent and yet not stultified by suffering or narcotized by *The Dream*, he may ruminate on opportunity versus deprivation, on poverty versus riches, on degradation versus dignity.

Now we ought to try to pierce the veil and enter the *Midsummer Night's Dream* of impulse release and fun.

TIGHT-PANTS TEEN-TOWN (T-P-T)

THE
NEW
AMERICAN

TEEN-AGE TEMPO!

They play records at ear-splitting
volume.
Tie up the telephone for hours.
Today's teen-agers are spirited,
inquisitive, wonderful.[2]

[1] From the *Suttra Nipata*. Edited and translated by Coomara Swamy. London: Trübner & Co., 1874.

[2] Advertisement for Standard Oil (Indiana), in *Life*, September 22, 1961.

Preliminary Note. Tight-pants Teen-town where the Researcher went with Sam and Tony, recent graduates of Rome High and now freshmen at University, is a commercial dance hall, catering to teen-agers from the Rome region, who come by hundreds to dance there several nights a week. A narcotizing machine for putting the powers of inquiry to sleep, the frenzy of T-P-T contrasts sharply with the introspective, searching moodiness of Chris Lambert. Sam has just broken with his girl Kate. Alone, Sam had accumulated enough money to buy Kate a diamond engagement ring and to finance a real wedding with trimmings. Sam had already spent a great deal of money and the wedding day had been fixed, when Kate broke the engagement. Dazed, Sam was ready to quit University even though his scholastic rating was high. A first step in getting a grip on himself was a trip to T-P-T, where, 'mid blasting rock 'n roll and high school girls whirling in tight pants, he could put his sensibilities to sleep for awhile. The record follows:

Dionysus and Coca-Cola

I asked Sam how he was feeling about Kate and he said he was feeling a lot better and that he'd talked to her on the phone without getting all excited and upset. As far as he could tell, they were "finished."

The T-P-T is about 20 minutes from Tony's house on a relatively untravelled road. We parked and went in.

It is perhaps best to begin with a description of this joint. There is one large hall with a high vaulted ceiling, about 50 by 30 feet, with a small stage at one end. It's done up in a rather rustic fashion with deer heads and moose heads on the wall. This forms the long axis of a T-shaped floor plan. The short part of the T is divided into a bar and a small restaurant. No liquor was behind the bar, and the kids could buy only soda and ice cream there. Apparently the place is run by private interests who hold teen-towns on Wednesday, Friday, and Sunday nights and use it as a regular bar on other nights, when they do not admit kids under 21. The admission price is $1.00 per person, and as you enter your wrist is stamped with a rubber stamp in the shape of a star so that if you should leave for any reason you may re-enter without having to pay again.

The main hall was very crowded. I'd estimate there were between 250 and 300 kids there. On the stage was a five-piece band consisting of an electric guitar, a bass violin, drums, and alto and tenor saxophones. Music was exclusively rock and roll, very loud and very fast. This was one of the first things that struck me, for in my teen-town days the music was usually half fast and half slow, for slow dances. Here in the T-P-T they played only one slow dance and that at the very end.

Tony, Sam, and I stood in a corner looking the situation over, joking about who would hold the other guys' coats in case any trouble started: there were a lot of rather tough looking characters standing around, complete with black leather jackets and belligerent expressions. I didn't notice any of these guys dancing.

Most of the boys were dressed in khakis and short-sleeved sport shirts with letter-jackets or windbreakers. The girls wore either very tight skirts or very tight pants and blouses. The boys stood around the sidelines admiring their backsides. Sam and Tony and I stood with them and discussed the various fine points of various of these backsides. Occasionally Tony's face became positively lecherous as he studied one girl or another.

The band was pretty terrible, we all agreed. What annoyed me particularly was the electric guitar, which would occasionally produce about a 60-cycle note that rattled my teeth, the windows, and the floor. The place was very dark.

The procedure is generally for two boys to pick out a couple of girls that are dancing and cut in on them, each one taking a prearranged partner. After a couple of minutes Tony and Sam decided to dance but they could not decide which couple to approach. Sam is only about 5'7" and feels uncomfortable dancing with a girl taller than he. Every time Sam and Tony would see a potential "cut-in" they would argue about who got whom. Sam protested that

Tony always wanted the prettiest girl and that he got stuck with the dog. At last about 10:30 Tony saw a girl he knew and persuaded Sam to take her partner. That was the last we saw of Tony until we left at 11:15. He and his girl just simply disappeared, as we later found out, into the parking lot.

This left Sam in an unfortunate position because he now had no one to cut in with. He couldn't use me because I hadn't the nerve to try to dance with any of those girls. It wasn't that I was afraid of them;[1] it was just that I didn't understand the steps they were using. So Sam had to prowl around the sidelines trying to find girls who were sitting by themselves. Finally he found one and led her out on the floor. I was surprised to see she was about three inches taller than he. She was blond, pretty, slender, and wearing toreador pants that she must have painted on. I kept wondering how she ever got out of the house with them on—how she got by her parents with them on, for I don't see how they could possibly have approved of them: they were flesh-colored chino and unbelievably tight. Anyway, Sam had only one dance with her, as she didn't seem terribly interested in him. So after that dance he prowled around some more until he found another partner.

The music was very frenzied, very erotic, almost hypnotic. In front of me there were about 200 kids wildly jumping up and down, flinging each other around the dance floor. I had the feeling many of them were dancing improvised dance steps. In front of the stage was a semi-circle of about 15 girls who were doing what I thought at first was some kind of cheer-leading routine. They were facing the stage with their arms extended above their heads, making rhythmical "Allah-be-praised"-like gestures toward the band. They would raise their arms above their heads and bend from the waist until their hands touched the floor, then return to an upright position, all in time to the music.

Sam was dancing again so I got up and walked into the

[1] The Researcher is an unusually handsome youth with an "adequate masculine record."

bar and had a coke. In there was a group of about six girls
and boys. One of the girls was demonstrating some kind of
contortionist trick, which she bet the boys couldn't do.
They couldn't, and the girls laughed heartily at the boys.
Standing at the bar were three tough-looking guys and two
girls. The guys were obviously trying to snow the girls and,
from what I could hear, were bragging about how much
they could drink. One guy said he had had five bottles of
beer the night before without feeling a thing. Then they
tried without success to talk the girls into going downtown
with them.

I went back into the hall, found Sam, and the two of us
started to look for Tony. At last we found him in the parking lot sitting in the car with a girl. Since we didn't want to
disturb him we went back into the hall.

I asked Sam how the girls got to this place, since it was
so isolated, and he said that they come in cars in two's and
three's. He complained that this made picking them up
rather difficult since they are pretty hard to separate.

Sam found another dancing partner—one of the two girls
sitting on a bench—and danced a couple of numbers with
her. He seems to be a pretty good dancer and pretty fast.
He gets out there and slings the girls with the best of them.
Tony, on the other hand, is much subtler. In fact, he hardly
moves at all. He just grabs the girl in his arms and gently
sways back and forth with an ecstatic look on his face. The
girls seem to like it very much. Anyway, the last dance was
a slow one, so I asked Sam's partner's friend to dance. She
said, "O.K." and we moved on to the floor and began to
dance, standing about a respectable two or three inches
apart. She closed this distance up quickly, and in another
minute her head was on my shoulder. I said, "What's your
name?" "Barbara, what's yours?" I told her my name and
said, "Where do you go to school?" "Oakton [High]. Where
do you go to school?" "University." "Oh," she said, and we
danced for a few minutes quietly. She asked me what I
studied and I told her. She said, "Do you know that tall,
dark-haired guy, Tony?" "Yes." "He disappeared with my
girl-friend," she said. "Here they come now," said I.

The dance was over. The band began to put away its instruments, and, since Tony was back, the three of us stood in a circle talking with the three girls. [They joked around and then said goodbye.]

On the ride back Tony and Sam tried to talk me into buying some beer but I refused, without offending them. I asked Sam why he enjoyed going to that place and he said that it was the only way he could meet girls, and I asked him why he hadn't become acquainted with any of the girls at University. He said he didn't know; he didn't have any of them in his classes. I couldn't understand why he should have such difficulty meeting girls at University. At the T-P-T he didn't seem to be too shy and yet the reverse seems to be true at University. I suspect that both Sam and Tony feel ill at ease with girls they think are more mature than high school girls. I sense that their predicament is that they aren't old enough to go to bars and to participate in the kind of things that adults do, while at the same time they feel somewhat uncomfortable doing the things high school kids do. The guys that come from upper-middle-class backgrounds, who do not have jobs and who belong to fraternities and date sorority girls, don't seem to have this problem and seem perfectly content doing the things their peers do.

[When T-P-T closed before midnight Tony, Sam and the Researcher went to a pool parlor,[1] played a few games, and went home.]

ID-LEADERSHIP

The fourteen-to-sixteen-year-old girl as the Id-creature, having a good time, dancing to erotic music, bending in adoration of the players, whirling magnetic buttocks in skin-tight pants and skirts, "closing the gap of respectability" between herself and her totally strange partner, is almost, though not quite, a revolution in our time; for after all, Helen of Troy and Juliet were also quite

---

[1] It is necessary to add, for the benefit of New Yorkers, Chicagoans, and other denizens of urban sinks of iniquity, that in most of the United States pool parlors are not dens for "hustlers" and other mad-dog types, but are respectable, pop-drenched hangouts for good clean teen-agers.

young. But in T-P-T there is no love; the hall is commercial, the contacts are transient (almost anonymous), the phenomenon is a mass one, and sensuality is merely a good time, having lost the aesthetic trappings of romance. Since many boys and girls have come here because they are lonely and unsatisfied, misery once more makes its contribution to the gross national product, for the $1.00 admission and the Coca-Cola and ice cream consumed are calculated in the GNP. Though some may lose their loneliness here, it can only be intensified for others: the impersonal, supermarket-package-like stamp on the wrist and the sensation of being alternately accepted and rejected by one boy or girl and then by another intensifies the feeling of impersonalness, anonymity, and loneliness.

What is narcotized by a good time in the throbbing semidarkness? First is the interest in thinking. After all the act of choosing and rejecting in T-P-T is purely hormonal. And in the second place, the inner problems are narcotized. Sam is a good example.

Surely these barely sexual, proto-adolescent girls have wrested leadership in the rituals of Id-fun from the boys, for they make the biggest display. Without their provocations things could not move so fast: where there is no meat, hungry dogs will not salivate! Today, in the era of impulse release and fun, the freshly-sexual girl is the goad that breaks the reluctance of the lagging teen-age boy, hanging back because he likes team play, poker, bumming, and just "the guys"; and here in T-P-T she "processes" him swiftly and rather impersonally for early marriage alignment. She herself acts under a double goad—her own impulses and the competition for boys.

ID AND SOCIAL CLASS

But why do Sam and Tony have to come here? What of the girls of University? Why can't Tony and Sam find girls there? After all University is much more of a courting pavilion than Rome High. There is a self-imposed austerity in the latter whereby boys and girls seem scarcely to know one another during school hours, whereas in University they sometimes walk hand in hand, lounge between classes in intricate convolutions on the broad lawns, occasionally arm-around each other in the corridors

—et cetera, et cetera. What then of Tony and Sam? Their central difficulty is social class, for most of the girls in University are upper-middle class and hence recoil from a working-class boy like a high-caste Hindu from the shadow of a pariah. In India caste pollutes; in Rome, class does. But in addition to what might be called the intangible person-repellent exuviae of class in University, there are the more concrete phenomena of social structure—the fraternities and sororities which, open largely to upper- and upper-middle-class students only, exercise a powerful directive force on dating, liquor consumption, dress, and conduct. He who has fraternity brothers has all the dates he wants right from the start, carefully graded and classified as to looks, stacking, necking, and so on. A fraternity is a kind of Sears Roebuck catalogue of females. If one can imagine Sam and Tony as pellets in a pinball game, one can see that they are ejected from the University dating system by the rigid rod of class measurement and propelled to the far outskirts where they bounce around in a random way, like a pellet in a pinball machine.

ANOMIC ACQUAINTANCE AND THE EROSION OF PREFACE

In most societies the introduction of boys and girls to one another is accomplished through a *preface* of some kind. Perhaps a go-between intercedes, or the boy waits beside the path or at the spring where she gets her water, or perhaps there is an exchange of letters. Such prefaces lend a certain ceremonial propriety to a new acquaintanceship, affirming the dignity of the participants, giving the ultimate meeting a quality of fitness and social solidity—in the jargon of anthropology, affirming society's acceptance of the relationship. Even the Pilagá Indian courting dances, which are very free youthful associations, are socially recognized, and the rendezvous that are consummated at the dances have usually been foreshadowed by some previous communication. Furthermore, everybody knows that the dances are being held and where. The dances are affirmations of the importance of sexuality, courtship, marriage—and of the individual as a known, named, socially significant object.

But T-P-T itself is scarcely known to the parents of the Rome region and the meeting of the overwhelming bulk of the children is a collision, without preface, affirming only the importance of anonymity, transitoriness, and fun. There is no intermediary, nobody takes account of the contacts, except, sometimes, the children themselves. No dignity is enhanced and the connection has no solidity. The meetings at T-P-T are *outside the formal social system*, in contrast to most of the relationships established through the fraternity and sorority. T-P-T is a mechanism for accentuating the anomic, nonsystemic aspects of culture. Since anomic acquaintance, that is, a meeting without preface, has become a major mode of transient association over a large portion of the world, we ought to listen to an American interpretation of it by Susie Muller, a respectable seventeen-year-old senior at Rome High.

S: You can't meet anybody by staying home all the time or not going out. These girls who say they never got married because they never met any eligible man—this isn't true. If they only stepped out of their house. . . . ! If you go out of your house and drop your purse and a fellow picks it up for you, you can get to meet him; or when a fellow opens the door for you, you can meet him this way—you don't have to be introduced to a fellow just to talk to him or to get to know him. You meet somebody every day if you bump into him, or if you sit next to him on a bus or at a counter somewhere and you start talking to him or he will start talking to you. And that way you meet more people and the more fellows you meet the better you can make up your mind.

R: When would *you* start talking to a fellow?

S: Well, on a bus you can't do this; but say in a restaurant, I could ask "Pardon me, do you have a match?" Or if the place is crowded you could say, "Pardon me, is this seat taken?" Haven't you ever had somebody talk to you like this?

R: What are some of the other ways in which you could start talking to a strange fellow and get to meet him?

S: Oh, you could accidentally step on his foot in the bus or something (laughs). I don't know, it just comes naturally to people, I mean. You can start a conversation and say, "Haven't I seen you somewhere before?"

[Susie has something important to say about the enjoyment of life, too.]

R: You know, a lot of people wonder about kids, whether most of the time kids enjoy life, what do you think?
S: Yeah, I think they enjoy life.
R: What makes you think so?
S: Because we are always having a good time. Maybe I shouldn't say always, because we're not always having a good time. People my age. . . . I think life is just opening for us; we are starting; we are getting new interests; we meet new people; we just see what life is all about. We have problems, responsibilities—we are just learning how to have fun—it's just as if you were opening a new frontier when you are my age.

DO KIDS ENJOY LIFE?

T-P-T is a wild, physical affirmative answer to this question and, indeed, negative answers are extremely rare among our teen-agers. As Susie says, at this age, "we are just learning how to have fun—it's *as if you were opening a new frontier. . . .*" For most teen-agers in our culture the purple vistas of impulse release are the new frontier and the greater the number of acquaintanceships, the greater the fun. Hence my gloomy comments on T-P-T do not imply that I think that the kids are not having a good time, as they see it, for I believe they are. What I meant to emphasize was T-P-T's narcotizing functions, its anomic aspects, and the Id-leadership of the young girls, a new frontier in impulse expression.

In interpreting T-P-T I used a very fierce expression, "where there is no meat, hungry dogs will not salivate," because I wanted to make clear the degradation implied in our culture by such flamboyant provocation. It goes hand in hand with anomic acquaintanceship, the erosion of preface, and the obsession with the "new frontier." The degradation derives from the fact that the girls convert themselves into mere "backsides." Turning their buttocks to the boys, the girls are really saying, "We know that there is nothing much to *you* except the capacity to rut at the sight of our fannies." And the boys confirm this by staring. It is a relationship of mutually reinforcing metamorphosis, the boys and girls reducing (i.e., degrading) one another exclusively to their sexual components. We may note, in passing, that referring to the less-than-pretty girls as "dogs" is also a degradation—more of the boys than of the girls.

But suppose boys and girls merely sat and talked? Suppose there were no anomic acquaintanceship and that Preface was still lord of the social relationships of boys and girls, what would happen to the GNP? Would as many girls buy as many pairs of toreador pants, as much cosmetics, as many coiffures and padded brassieres? The gasoline to drive to T-P-T would not be bought, and the band would not be hired nor the hall rented. Would as much Coca-Cola be drunk and ice cream eaten if not for T-P-T and its thousands of duplicates across the country? If we assume that T-P-T's gross income from the teen-agers is about $1500 a week (for three nights a week), and that there are about 50,000 T-P-T's in the United States, that represents 75 million dollars a week. It stands to reason we cannot do away with such institutions.

Let me now revert for a moment to the Standard Oil (Indiana) advertisement at the head of this section (page 262). This ad, affirming in true pecuniary burble, that the teen-ager is "wonderful," et cetera, is accompanied by a full-page color picture of a creature, clearly human because of its hands and feet, lying supine on what appears to be a bed. We cannot see the head or torso, however, because a record album (98¢–$6.00) supported on the raised thighs, blocks vision. Study of the hands holding the record (where the head might be expected to be) reveals that they are feminine—long-fingered, delicate, and white—and examination of the pants shows that they are slim-jeans and must therefore be on a female. In the pecuniary view, therefore, *The New American* teen-ager is symbolized by a delicately nurtured, otiose, upside-down female listening to popular music and, we must add in the interest of pecuniary completeness, burning up the family gasoline ("to keep up with the teen-age tempo of your household, your car needs the best") when she gets off her back. The reader can scarcely fail to recognize that this picture represents the way Standard Oil (Indiana) conceives the *wonder* in wonderful. The point to be made is that when such an image is made to represent what is wonderful in teen-agers, industry is supporting the view of the teen-ager as merely a pleasure-seeking creature.

I have said that the teen-age girl has snatched Id-leadership from the boys, and in this ad we see that, with characteristic genius, Madison Avenue represents Id (i.e., self-indulgence) as a girl. I leave to my psychoanalyst friends the deeper interpretation of an advertisement that shows only the divaracated lower anatomy of a young girl. Meanwhile, Standard Oil and Madison Avenue cooperate even further ("laying it on the line," so to speak) in helping us to understand the pecuniary view of, interest in, and hope for the American adolescent. The copy presses breathlessly on:

> And nobody knows better than you [parents] . . . that their lives revolve around the car. Shopping safaris, football games, dances and dozens of other "musts" keep the family bus humming.

I have spoken of pecuniary philosophy; let us call this *gasoline spirituality*. Is Standard Oil wrong? Can a billion dollars lie?

It will be recalled that I said that T-P-T generates a need for gasoline because the children have to drive out there, and that therefore T-P-T is a must because of its economic contribution. Standard Oil declares that our reasoning is correct. It underscores our essential rightness also in the demi-breach presentation of the picture.

A Note from the Diary of Professor Lügner

Today I observed that my bow-wow "Little Treasure" (*Schätzlein*) has two stupid adolescent male friends who do not seem yet to know the difference between nubile (*mannbar*) and nonnubile females. This error can be extrapolated to humans under certain conditions. The whole issue, of course, is that in dogs we deal with a genetic base, whereas in humans we deal with the phenomenon of culturally transmitted mass misrepresentation. Dogs are bound by biology; humans can soar on the wings of conventionalized misrepresentation (*übliche falsche Darstellung*).

It has been suggested by Slokony-Zymonov that "in Western culture maturity is merely the capacity to mislead and avoid being misled."

Setting aside for the moment Slokony-Zymonov's argument, we may come to grips with the problem of "mass misrepresentation," for in T-P-T we seem to see nymphs who are not nymphs, but who represent themselves as nymphs to boys who do not perceive them as nymphs but almost act as if they were. The point is that most of these girls will get into their cars when T-P-T closes and go home with other girls, telling their parents, when they arrive, that they have been to Jane's house to study, to the library, or to the movies—also a mass misrepresentation. The episode over, the pseudo-nymphs melt chastely into the frame and brick foliage of Rome and its surrounding suburbs, drink perhaps a glass of milk, and go to bed. The boys whom they provoked understand and do not rage against the girls who have seemed to misrepresent themselves as lovers for the night. This, I think, is the general sort of thing that Lügner was talking about when he wrote his famous diary. For what we, indeed, are "dealing with" in T-P-T is "conventionalized misrepresentation," and everybody there understands this. Of course, some of the girls, like Tony's, for example, do fade, late twentieth-century sylphs, into the forest of parked cars, there to engage in a misrepresentation of love, but that too is conventionalized, and the rules are well known by pseudo-nymph and pseudo-satyr. But according to Slokony-Zymonov the capacity to misrepresent and to avoid being mislead by the misrepresentation of others is considered maturity in Western culture. If true, it is a terrible indictment. In the present situation it would mean that the girls who best wiggle and resist, and the boys who do not press the girls too hard and do not get angry when the girls resist, are the most mature. In some way this reminds us of the philosophy of Lila Greene. Slokony-Zymonov may be right, even though he was an embittered, exiled Pole sitting in Canton in 1692, darling of the Emperor K'ang Hsi and court pet. Meanwhile, I think he should have added another sign of maturity—the capacity not to care if you are misled.

A thread of misrepresentation seems to run dark and strong through many of the relationships Tony and Sam have to other boys and even to each other. It was partly cut out of the transcript in the interests of brevity and continuity, but must now be restored.

MISREPRESENTATIONS IN THE RELATIONSHIP OF SAM AND TONY

1. We got to Tony's house, honked, and he came running out to meet us. He said that another fellow called earlier and asked him what he was doing tonight and asked Tony if he could join us. Tony said yes but the guy never showed up and Tony was very angry. He apparently did not like the guy very much in the first place, nor the idea of his coming along, but was very angry when he did not show up.

   Misrepresentation: (1) Tony's letting the boy come along though he did not like him. (2) The boy's promising to come and not appearing.

2. On the way [to T-P-T] we talked about Mike Schurz. Sam and Tony don't like Mike too much. They think he is kind of a wise guy and that he is conceited. They criticized his devotion to his car and the amount of time he spends slicking it up.

   Misrepresentation: Sam and Tony profess friendship for Mike but dislike him and criticize him behind his back.

3. Every time [Tony and Sam] would see a potential cut-in they would argue about who got whom. Sam protested that Tony always wanted the prettiest girl and that he got stuck with the dog.

   Misrepresentation: Since friendship implies mutual solicitude, selfish competition over which girl shall be chosen by which friend is a contradiction, and was felt to be so by Sam. Hence the relationship between Tony and Sam is misrepresented by both of them.

4. As we walked [into the pool parlor] a guy asked Tony how he had done with the girl he was with last Friday.

This made Sam angry, because it seems that Tony told Sam that he was going to the library that Friday and not that he was seeing a girl. Sam tried to find out who the girl was but Tony wouldn't tell him. Tony had gotten out of the house by telling his mother that he was going to the library.

5. It has already been mentioned in the text that when Tony picked his girl he disappeared with her for the rest of the evening. This was contrary to agreement and left Sam high and dry. Furthermore, Tony's disappearance made both the Researcher and Sam anxious because, since Tony had complained of being somewhat sick to the stomach when they started out, they feared he might be ill somewhere.

It should not surprise us that the relationship of these boys to other people and to one another is shot full of deceit and negation of the traditional morality of friendship, because in the first place much of so-called adult friendship is the same, and in the second place anyone who has even begun to explore adolescent friendships—monosexual or heterosexual—soon finds out how much misrepresentation there is in them. Meanwhile, the reader, I am sure, will agree that Sam behaved very "immaturely" by showing anger at Tony's deceptions and at the competition between him and Tony for the best-looking girls.

We must now ask the question that has by this time become routine: Is all this misrepresentation necessary in order to swell the gross national product? At first the question seems stupidly evil; but is it not at least plausible to suggest that if, instead of merely pretending to be pure sex the girls were really so, there might not be a general drop in the consumption level among adolescents? In terms of a widely accepted psychoanalytic theory of sublimation, it seems plausible that if boys and girls were permitted complete sexual experience, instead of an abortive one, the T-P-T's might disappear. Where reality replaces the imitation, it seems unlikely that there would be as much wild dancing and as much consumption of Coca-Cola and ice cream because, according to the theory, the sexuality would be too engrossing. A review of the relationship between sexuality and consumption—consider, for example, declining ancient Rome, and all other centers of high debauchery and consumption—fails to support such plausibilities, however, and I therefore conclude that since consumption shows no tendency to decline in the presence of sexual indulgence, the elimination of misrepresentation (i.e., the substitution of reality for illusion in adolescent sex life) in the sexual relationships between boys and girls would be no direct threat to the gross national product. It would therefore seem that honesty in sex relations would not be immediately dangerous to Western Culture. Hence, it is possible to abandon misrepresentation and become honest; not, of course, through promiscuity, but simply by eliminating abortive provocation.

There is one grave difficulty, however; and it pivots on the words *direct* and *immediate,* for though there may be no *direct* threat to the GNP if honesty dominates in interpersonal relations (in the broadest sense), there may be an *indirect* one, because of the tendency for honesty, once started, to become a juggernaut, flattening all corruption before it. That is the rub, for misrepresentation in interpersonal relations, though having no direct effects on the GNP, affects it indirectly, and must be continued if a pecuniary economy is to survive. To have a dishonest pecuniary system it is necessary to have a dishonest interpersonal one. Every businessman of unexacting scruples knows that if honesty breaks out in one dimension of society it may spread with mortal consequences to others. Consider the devastating effects of the investigation of the rigged TV quiz shows: immediately on the heels of the Van Doren case, inquiry spread to payola.[1] And this has been followed with paralyzing swiftness by the drug hearings,[2] the punishment of the electrical companies and their executives,[3] Mr. Minow's attack on bad TV programs, and President Kennedy's public declaration that since the steel industry was making more money than the aver-

---

[1] In the remote possibility that this book may live for ten years and even be translated into a foreign language, it is necessary to explain that *payola* is the practice whereby the person who chooses the records during broadcasts of popular music is paid to promote a particular number.

[2] The Congressional investigation of high pricing and misrepresentation of drugs.

[3] For engaging in monopolistic practices.

age for industry, steel could not justify a price increase. Were honesty—the representation of things as they are rather than as we want people to believe them to be—to become a habit, it would threaten the very foundations of Western Civilization. Having learned well from adults, however, American adolescents are no present threat, as the present data show. There is yet one danger—the Peace Corps, for if thousands of young Americans, having lived among the rags, the disease, the destitution (and the dishonesty and greed) of the underdeveloped nations, should return to the United States fired with a burning reformer zeal, there is no telling what honesties they might perpetrate. Some of these young people might some day become Congressmen, perhaps one or two might rise to President! The possibilities are so appalling one wonders whether we should let the Peace Corps continue; or at least, whether we should not recruit members from corporation executives displaced by mergers, instead of from students. We have been sending the underdeveloped countries our surplus food and obsolete munitions, why not do the same with our surplus and obsolete executives?

SUMMARY

Give an anthropologist any problem and he will tell you it cannot be understood unless the "whole situation" is taken into account. This generally makes his "more sophisticated" colleagues in other disciplines turn away in silence because they "know" that most situations, particularly in our culture, are "too complicated" to be grasped in their entirety. "Too many angles," of course, is what makes most people turn from understanding:

> the international situation
> domestic politics
> local politics
> how much they pay above the real price
>   on installment purchases
> the nature of the universe
> advertising
> their own children
> ADOLESCENCE

We must not be bamboozled by the unnumbered crowds of Those Who Turn Away. Fundamentally everything is incomprehensible, and great religions have been built on this premise. They, too, have their fundamentalists, as, for example, those who read nothing but the Bible.

This chapter, therefore, flies in the face of what Professor Galbraith has called the "conventional wisdom." I have tried to arrive at some understanding of Lila, Heddie, Bill, Chris, and of adolescence in general through considering Rome as a whole. Naturally, in one chapter one can only suggest the lines of inquiry and the kinds of connections that exist between family, school, child, community, and *the world*. "Rome High and Its Students," however, comes after several chapters on American culture, so that it does not stand alone, depending for understanding on its few pages only. I have had to lead up to Rome High through our socioeconomic system, our phantasmagorical advertising, a discussion of parents and children, and a previous chapter on teen-agers. And the task is not yet done, for our adolescents must be understood also in terms of their elementary school years and in terms of what will happen to many of them in old age.

Rome High is committed to two contradictory orientations: fun and scholarship. The athletes, given prominence in the town newspapers, fed in a gladiatorial dining room, and given special coaching in studies, set the pace of social life. But athletics are not fun only. Athletics are a kind of community Self, generating Self-substance for everybody, and it is this dimension of athletics that accounts for its peculiar position. And this, in general, is much of the problem of fun, self-indulgence, and impulse release in Rome High. It is important for this community that its girls learn how to dress and spend money, for this is a way to mobility upward. This, too, is communal Selfhood. And it is critically important that Rome's young women get married off fast: they are a drain on their families, the jobs they get will not be much if they do not go on to college, and the competition for husbands is keen. Putting brakes on para-courtship is problematic when a community is confronted by this situation, and the school must make allowances—not pushing for promptness in handing in assignments, for example, and not requiring much homework. The *exigent* rituals of para-courtship, with its accompanying demands in dating, shopping, telephoning, primping, impose *exiguous* demands in scholarship. It is a simple question of balance in any culture: what is *exigent* in one dimension imposes what is *exiguous* in another. Attendance at games is also of critical importance. But if the girls must be unencumbered and caparisoned cosmetically for the chase, the boys must be left free to be chased and to chase. Both are cheered on by the gross national product which, in an autarchic economy geared to ever higher profits and living standards, needs the adolescent billions. These conditions are reflected in the Home Economics room, the countless mirrors, the expensive costuming, the posters, and many other things.

But there are other important aspects of the integration of life in Rome and Rome High. We are in the era of the *Midsummer Night's Dream* when the cultural demands for epic deeds of consumption lie upon us all, and where the "grand old morality" would be merely an impediment to impulse release and to getting along in business and interpersonal relations. This is reflected in the school's sloppy attitude toward cheating and in the students' enthusiastic response to it; it is reflected in Mr. Greene's carelessness about money and his daughter's willingness to exploit it. And the importance of taking the surreptitious drink is a reverberation of adult impulse indulgence and the fact that the adult world hastens the children on. What more natural then that getting a drink on the sly should be a measure of being "grown up"? In this environment the unspoken mottoes of adolescence are

> Pleasure is truth
> Pain is falsehood

In a culture with an ethos of impulse release and fun, where slovenly morality is institutionalized, but where, paradoxically, the protests of the remnants of the adult Super Ego render the culture absurd by attacking adolescent taboo-breaking, the adolescent group acquires a transcendent power over its members by legitimizing all para-delinquencies (all taboo-breaking), providing the adolescent with a support and a kind of conscience that enables him to confront the preposterous adult world. This para-conscience that exists side by side with a tattered "real" conscience derived from the ragged family Super Ego, exercises an enormous attractive power over the peer group, making adolescent life especially cozy and close. If there is indeed such a thing as an adolescent culture, its basic power derives from its capacity to counteract the adult Super Ego.

Meanwhile, adolescence has its own *conventionalized misrepresentations*, particularly in what pertains to its abortive sexual life. But we must remember that these misrepresentations are related in part to adult stimulation to early marriage. Paradoxically the adults, while goading the girls into sexual competition, savagely condemn the girl who slips out of line. Adolescents themselves, however, turn upon one another viciously in sexual matters and let one another down in interpersonal relations. On the other hand, there is much long-standing friendship among them. Much of this friendship is expressed in bumming and messing around, by both boys and girls, for the adult world has not provided anything more significant for them to do. Magazines, movies, TV, radio, and Home Ec engulf the adolescent in inducements to self-indulgence, to the degree that it is largely through mutual participation in impulse release that the friendships of adolescents reach their fullest expression: much more time is spent just "having fun" or talking about "fun" than in anything else. Since friendship and love have no meaning unless cemented by some agony, adolescent friendships often tend to evaporate without pain.

Rome High has emphasized scholarship so successfully, and it has come to have so much meaning in this community that is mobile upward that it is possible, veritably in the teeth of fun, to get high grades and not be looked upon with disdain. Another feature of the school that goes against the grain of enjoyment are those teachers with high standards of scholarship and democracy. Committed though they are to impulse release and fun, the students at Rome High yet respect such orientations. Thus the school reflects the division within the total culture between hedonistic mindlessness and austere intelligence; between frightened, often compensatory conservatism and courageous liberalism.

In our study of Lila, Bill, Heddie, and Chris we had an opportunity to look into the effect of the Rome milieu on individuals. We came to understand Lila's almost amoral pragmatism, her empty home life and her *flight* into the group; her brother Bill's deep feelings of inadequacy, resignation, and cynicism, and his *flight* into Heddie's arms; Heddie's outcasting from her family and her *flight* into redemption; and Chris' feelings of estrangement and his *escape* into independence. Flights into something are all escapes from something else and they lack the quality of spontaneous full-hearted choices. In this way, life itself becomes a second choice, and its pleasures too often are anodynes for pain. This is man-in-culture—or, at least, man in *our* culture.

8: Golden Rule Days: American Schoolrooms

INTRODUCTION

SCHOOL IS AN INSTITUTION FOR DRILLING CHILDREN IN cultural orientations. Educationists have attempted to free the school from drill, but have failed because they have gotten lost among a multitude of phantasms—always choosing the most obvious "enemy" to attack. Furthermore, with every enemy destroyed, new ones are installed among the old fortifications—the enduring contradictory maze of the culture. Educators think that when they have made arithmetic or spelling into a game; made it unnecessary for children to "sit up straight"; defined the relation between teacher and children as democratic; and introduced plants, fish, and hamsters into schoolrooms, they have settled the problem of drill. They are mistaken.

EDUCATION AND THE HUMAN CONDITION

Learning to Learn. The paradox of the human condition is expressed more in education than elsewhere in human culture, because learning to learn has been and continues to be *Homo sapiens'* most formidable evolutionary task. Although it is true that mammals, as compared to birds and fishes, have to learn so much that it is difficult to say by the time we get to chimpanzees what behavior is inborn and what is learned, the learning task has become so enormous for man that today learning—education—along with survival, constitutes a major preoccupation. In all the fighting over education we are simply saying that we are not yet satisfied—after about a million years of struggling to become human—that we have mastered the fundamental human task, learning. It must also be clear that we will never quite learn how to learn, for since *Homo sapiens* is self-changing, and since the *more* culture changes the *faster* it changes, man's methods and rate of learning will never quite keep pace with his need to learn. This is the heart of the problem of "cultural lag," for each fundamental scientific discovery presents man with an incalculable number of problems which he cannot foresee. Who, for example, would have anticipated that the discoveries of Einstein would have presented us with the social problems of the nuclear age, or that information theory would have produced unemployment and displacement in world markets?

Fettering and Freeing. Another learning problem inherent in the human condition is the fact that we must conserve culture while changing it; that we must always be *more* sure of surviving than of adapting—*as we see it.* Whenever a new idea appears our first concern as *animals* must be that it does not kill us; then, and only then, can we look at it from other points of view. While it is true that we are often mistaken, either because we become enchanted with certain modes of thought or because we cannot anticipate their consequences, this tendency to look first at survival has resulted in fettering the capacity to learn new things. In general, primitive people solved this problem simply by walling their children off from new possibilities by educational methods that, largely through fear (including ridicule, beating, and mutilation) so narrowed the perceptual sphere that other than traditional ways of viewing the world became unthinkable. Thus throughout history the cultural pattern has been a device for binding the intellect. Today, when we think we wish to free the mind so it will soar, we are still, nevertheless, bound by the ancient paradox, for we must hold our culture together through clinging to old ideas lest, in adopting new ones, we literally cease to exist.

In searching the literature on the educational practices of other civilizations I have found nothing that better expresses the need to teach and to fetter than the following, from an account by a traveler along the Niger River in Africa in the fourteenth century:

> . . . their zeal for learning the Koran by heart [is so great that] they put their children in chains if they show any backwardness in memorizing it, and they are not set free until they have it by heart. I visited the *qadi* in his house on the day of the festival. His children were chained up, so I said to him, "Will you not let them loose?" He replied, "I shall not do so until they learn the Koran by heart."[1]

Perhaps the closest material parallel we have to this from our own cultural tradition is the stocks in which ordinary English upper-class children were forced to stand in the eighteenth century while they pored over their lessons at home. The fettering of the mind while we "set the spirit free" or the fettering of the spirit as we free the mind is an abiding paradox of "civilization" in its more refined dimensions. It is obvious that chimpanzees are incapable of this paradox. It is this capacity to pass from the jungles of the animal world into the jungle of paradox of the human condition that, more than anything else, marks off human from animal learning. It is this jungle that confronts the child in his early days at school, and that seals his destiny—if it has not previously been determined by poverty—as an eager mind or as a faceless learner.

Since education is always against some things and for others, it bears the burden of the cultural obsessions. While the Old Testament extols without cease the glory of the One God, it speaks with equal emphasis against the gods of the Philistines; while the children of the Dakota Indians learned loyalty to their own tribe, they learned to hate the Crow; and while our children

---

[1] Ibn Battuta, *Travels in Asia and Africa*, London: Broadway House, Carter Lane, 1957, p. 330. (Translated and selected by H. A. R. Gibb, from the original written in 1325–54.)

are taught to love our American democracy, they are taught
contempt for totalitarian regimes. It thus comes about that most
educational systems are imbued with anxiety and hostility, that
they are against as many things as they are for. Because, therefore, so much anxiety inheres in any human educational system
—anxiety that it may free when it should fetter; anxiety that it
may fetter when it should free; anxiety that it may teach sympathy when it should teach anger; anxiety that it may disarm where
it should arm—our contemporary education system is constantly
under attack. When, in anxiety about the present state of our
world, we turn upon the schools with even more venom than we
turn on our government, we are "right" in the sense that it is in
the schools that the basic binding and freeing processes that will
"save" us will be established. But being "right" derives not so
much from the faults of our schools but from the fact that the
schools are the central conserving force of the culture. The Great
Fear thus turns our hostility unerringly in the direction of the
focus of survival and change, in the direction of education.

Creativity and Absurdity.   The function of education has never
been to free the mind and the spirit of man, but to bind them;
and to the end that the mind and spirit of his children should
never escape *Homo sapiens* has employed praise, ridicule, admonition, accusation, mutilation, and even torture to chain them
to the culture pattern. Throughout most of his historic course
Homo sapiens has wanted from his children acquiescence, not
originality. It is natural that this should be so, for where every
man is unique there is no society, and where there is no society
there can be no man. Contemporary American educators think
they want creative children, yet it is an open question as to what
they expect these children to create. And certainly the classrooms
—from kindergarten to graduate school—in which they expect
it to happen are not crucibles of creative activity and thought.
It stands to reason that were young people truly creative the
culture would fall apart, for originality, by definition, is different
from what is given, and what is given is the culture itself. From
the endless, pathetic, "creative hours" of kindergarten to the most
abstruse problems in sociology and anthropology, the function
of education is to prevent the truly creative intellect from getting
out of hand. Only in the exact and the biological sciences do

we permit unlimited freedom, for we have (but only since the Renaissance, since Galileo and Bruno underwent the Inquisition) found a way—or *thought* we had found a way—to bind the explosive powers of science in the containing vessel of the social system.

American classrooms, like educational institutions anywhere, express the values, preoccupations, and fears found in the culture as a whole. School has no choice; it must train the children to fit the culture as it is. School can give training in skills; it cannot teach creativity. All the American school can conceivably do is nurture creativity when it appears. And who has the eyes to see it? Since the creativity that is conserved and encouraged will always be that which seems to do the most for the culture, which seems at the moment to do the most for the obsessions and the brutal preoccupations and anxieties from which we all suffer, schools nowadays encourage the child with gifts in mathematics and the exact sciences. But the child who has the intellectual strength to see through social shams is of no consequence to the educational system.

Creative intellect is mysterious, devious, and irritating. An intellectually creative child may fail, for example, in social studies, simply because he cannot understand the stupidities he is taught to believe as "fact." He may even end up agreeing with his teachers that he is "stupid" in social studies. Learning social studies is, to no small extent, whether in elementary school or the university, learning to be stupid. Most of us accomplish this task before we enter high school. But the child with a socially creative imagination will not be encouraged to play among new social systems, values, and relationships; nor is there much likelihood of it, if for no other reason than that the social studies teachers will perceive such a child as a poor student. Furthermore, such a child will simply be unable to fathom the absurdities that seem transparent *truth* to the teacher. What idiot believes in the "law of supply and demand," for example? But the children who do tend to *become* idiots, and learning to be an idiot is part of growing up! Or, as Camus put it, learning to be *absurd*. Thus the child who finds it impossible to learn to think the absurd the truth, who finds it difficult to accept absurdity as a way of life, the intellectually creative child whose mind makes him flounder like a poor fish in the net of absurdities flung around him in school, usually comes to think himself stupid.

The schools have therefore never been places for the stimulation of young minds. If all through school the young were provoked to question the Ten Commandments, the sanctity of revealed religion, the foundations of patriotism, the profit motive, the two-party system, monogamy, the laws of incest, and so on, we would have more creativity than we could handle. In teaching our children to accept fundamentals of social relationships and religious beliefs without question we follow the ancient highways of the human race, which extend backward into the dawn of the species, and indefinitely into the future. There must therefore be more of the caveman than of the spaceman about our teachers.

Up to this point I have argued that learning to learn is man's foremost evolutionary task, that the primary aim of education has been to fetter the mind and the spirit of man rather than to free them, and that nowadays we confront this problem in our effort to stimulate thought while preventing the mind of the child from going too far. I have also urged that since education, as the central institution for the training of the young in the ways of the culture, is thus burdened with its obsessive fears and hates, contemporary attacks upon our schools are the reflection of a nervousness inherent in the school as a part of the central obsession. Finally, I argued that creativity is the last thing wanted in any culture because of its potentialities for disruptive thinking; that the primordial dilemma of all education derives from the necessity of training the mighty brain of *Homo sapiens* to be stupid; and that creativity, when it is encouraged (as in science in our culture), occurs only after the creative thrust of an idea has been tamed and directed toward socially approved ends. In this sense, then, creativity can become the most obvious conformity. In this sense we can expect scientists —our cultural maximizers—to be socially no *more* creative than the most humble elementary school teacher, and probably less creative socially than a bright second-grader.

COMMUNICATION

Much of what I have to say in the following pages pivots on the inordinate capacity of a human being to learn more than one thing at a time. Although it is true that all the higher orders of animals can learn several things at a time, this capacity for polyphasic learning reaches unparalleled development in man. A child writing the word "August" on the board, for example, is not only learning the word "August" but also how to hold the chalk without making it squeak, how to write clearly, how to keep going even though the class is tittering at his slowness, how to appraise the glances of the children in order to know whether he is doing it right or wrong, et cetera. If the spelling, arithmetic, or music lesson were only what it appeared to be, the education of the American child would be much simpler; but it is all the things the child learns *along with* his subject matter that really constitute the drag on the educational process as it applies to the curriculum.

A classroom can be compared to a communications system, for certainly there is a flow of messages between teacher (transmitter) and pupils (receivers) and among the pupils; contacts are made and broken, messages can be sent at a certain rate of speed only, and so on. But there is also another interesting characteristic of communications systems that is applicable to classrooms, and that is their inherent tendency to generate *noise*. *Noise,* in communications theory, applies to all those random fluctuations of the system that cannot be controlled. They are the sounds that are not part of the message: the peculiar quality communicated to the voice by the composition of the telephone circuit, the static on the radio, and so forth. In a classroom lesson on arithmetic, for example, such *noise* would range all the way from the competitiveness of the students, the quality of the teacher's voice ("I remember exactly how she sounded when she told me to sit down"), to the shuffling of the children's feet. The striking thing about the child is that along with his arithmetic —his "messages about arithmetic"—he learns all the noise in the system also. It is this inability to avoid *learning the noise with the subject matter* that constitutes one of the greatest hazards for an organism so prone to polyphasic learning as man. It is this that brings it about that an objective observer cannot tell which is being learned in any lesson, the *noise* or the formal subject matter. But—and mark this well—it is *not* primarily the message (let us say, the arithmetic or the spelling) that constitutes the most important subject matter to be learned, but the noise! The most significant cultural learnings—primarily the cultural drives—are communicated as *noise*.

Let us take up these points by studying selected incidents in some of the suburban classrooms my students and I studied over a period of six years.

THE REALM OF SONG

It is March 17 and the children are singing songs from Ireland and her neighbors. The teacher plays on the piano, while the children sing. While some children sing, a number of them hunt in the index, find a song belonging to one of Ireland's neighbors, and raise their hands in order that they may be called on to name the next song. The singing is of that pitchless quality always heard in elementary school classrooms. The teacher sometimes sings through a song first, in her off-key, weakishly husky voice.

The usual reason for having this kind of a song period is that the children are broadened, while they learn something about music and singing.

It is true that the children learn something about singing, but what they learn is to sing like everybody else, in the standard, elementary school pitchlessness of the English-speaking world —a phenomenon impressive enough for D. H. Lawrence to have mentioned it in *Lady Chatterly's Lover*. The difficulty in achieving true pitch is so pervasive among us that missionaries carry it with them to distant jungles, teaching the natives to sing hymns off key. Hence on Sundays we would hear our Pilagá Indian friends, all of them excellent musicians in the Pilagá scale, carefully copy the missionaries by singing Anglican hymns, translated into Pilagá, off key exactly as sharp or as flat as the missionaries sang. Thus one of the first things a child with a good ear learns in elementary school is to be musically stupid; he learns to doubt or to scorn his innate musical capacities.

But possibly more important than this is the use to which teacher and pupils put the lesson in ways not related at all to singing or to Ireland and her neighbors. To the teacher this was an opportunity to let the children somehow share the social aspects of the lesson with her, to democratically participate in the selection of the songs. The consequence was distraction from singing as the children hunted in the index and raised their hands to have their song chosen. The net result was to activate the competitive, achievement, and dominance drives of the children, as they strove with one another for the teacher's attention, and through her, to get the class to do what they wanted it to do. In this way the song period on Ireland and her neighbors was scarcely a lesson in singing but rather one in extorting the maximal benefit for the Self from *any* situation. The first lesson a child has to learn when he comes to school is that lessons are not what they seem. He must then forget this and act as if they were. This is the first step toward "school mental health"; it is also the first step in becoming absurd. In the first and second grades teachers constantly scold children because they do not raise their hands enough—the prime symbol of having learned what school is all about. After that, it is no longer necessary; the kids have "tumbled" to the idea.

The second lesson is to put the teachers' and students' criteria in place of his own. He must learn that the proper way to sing is tunelessly and not the way *he* hears the music; that the proper way to paint is the way the teacher says, not the way he sees it; that the proper attitude is not pleasure but competitive horror at the success of his classmates, and so on. And these lessons must be so internalized that he will fight his parents if they object. The early schooling process is not successful unless it has accomplished in the child an acquiescence in its criteria, unless the child *wants* to think the way school has taught him to think. He must have accepted alienation as a rule of life. What we see in the kindergarten and the early years of school is the pathetic surrender of babies. How could it be otherwise?

Now, if children are taught to adopt alienation as a way of life, it follows that they must have feelings of inadequacy, for nothing so saps self-confidence as alienation from the Self. It would follow that school, the chief agent in the process, must try to provide the children with "ego support," for culture tries to remedy the ills it creates.

Hence the effort to give recognition; and hence the conversion of the songfest into an exercise in Self-realization. That anything essential was nurtured in this way is an open question, for the kind of individuality that was recognized as the children picked titles out of the index was mechanical, without a creative dimension, and under the strict control of the teacher. Let us conclude this discussion by saying that *school metamorphoses the child, giving it the kind of Self the school can manage, and then proceeds to minister to the Self it has made.*

Perhaps I have put the matter grossly, appearing to credit the school with too much formative power. So let us say this: let us grant that American children, being American, come to school on the first day with certain potentialities for experiencing success and failure, for enjoying the success of their mates or taking pleasure in their failure, for competitiveness, for cooperation, for driving to achieve or for coasting along, et cetera. But school cannot handle variety, for as an institution dealing with masses of children it can manage only on the assumption of a homogeneous mass. Homogeneity is therefore accomplished by defining the children in a certain way and by handling all situations uniformly. In this way no child is directly coerced. It is simply that the child must react in terms of the institutional definitions or he fails. The first two years of school are spent not so much in learning the rudiments of the three Rs, as in learning definitions.

It would be foolish to imagine that school, as a chief molder of character, could do much more than homogenize the children, but it does do more—it sharpens to a cutting edge the drives the culture needs.

If you bind or prune an organism so it can move only in limited ways, it will move rather excessively in that way. If you lace a man into a strait jacket so he can only wiggle his toes, he will wiggle them *hard.* Since in school children are necessarily constrained to limited human expression, under the direction of the teacher, they will have a natural tendency to do with exaggerated enthusiasm what they are permitted to do,

They are like the man in the strait jacket. In class children are usually not permitted to talk much, to walk around much, to put their arms around each other during lessons, to whistle or sing. But they are permitted to raise their hands and go to the pencil sharpener almost at will. Thus hand-raising, going to the pencil sharpener, or hunting in the back of a song book for a song for the class to sing are not so much activities stemming from the requirements of an immediate situation as expressions of the intensified need of the organism for relief from the five-hour-a-day pruning and confining process. This goes under the pedagogical title of "release of tension"; but in our view the issue is that what the children are at length permitted—and in-vited—to do, and what they therefore often throw themselves into with the enthusiasm of multiple pent-up feelings, are cultural drive-activities narrowly construed by the school. In that context the next example is not only an expression by the children of a wish to be polite, but an inflated outpouring of contained human capacities, released enthusiastically into an available—because approved—cultural channel.

ON HANGING UP A COAT

The observer is just entering her fifth-grade classroom for the observation period. The teacher says, "Which one of you nice, polite boys would like to take [the observer's] coat and hang it up?" From the waving hands, it would seem that all would like to claim the title. The teacher chooses one child, who takes the observer's coat. The teacher says, "Now, children, who will tell [the observer] what we have been doing?"

The usual forest of hands appears, and a girl is chosen to tell. . . . The teacher conducted the arithmetic lessons mostly by asking, "Who would like to tell the answer to the next problem?" This question was usually followed by the appearance of a large and agitated forest of hands, with apparently much competition to answer.

What strikes us here are the precision with which the teacher was able to mobilize the potentialities in the boys for proper social behavior, and the speed with which they responded.

One is impressed also with the fact that although the teacher could have said, "Johnny, will you please hang up [the observer's] coat?" she chose rather to activate all the boys, and thus give *them* an opportunity to activate their Selves, in accordance with the alienated Selfhood objectives of the culture. The children were thus given an opportunity to exhibit a frantic willingness to perform an act of uninvolved solicitude for the visitor; in this way each was given also a chance to communicate to the teacher his eagerness to please her "in front of company."

The mere appearance of the observer in the doorway sets afoot a kind of classroom destiny of self-validation and actualization of pupil–teacher communion, and of activation of the cultural drives. In the observer's simple act of entrance the teacher perceives instantly the possibility of exhibiting her children and herself, and of proving to the visitor, and once again to herself, that the pupils are docile creatures, eager to hurl their "company" Selves into this suburban American tragicomedy of welcome. From behind this scenery of mechanical values, meanwhile, the most self-centered boy might emerge a *papier maché* Galahad, for what he does is not for the benefit of the visitor but for the gratification of the teacher and of his own culturally molded Self. The large number of waving hands proves that most of the boys have already become absurd; but they have no choice. Suppose they sat there frozen?

From this question we move to the inference that the skilled teacher sets up many situations in such a way that *a negative attitude can be construed only as treason.* The function of questions like, "Which one of you nice polite boys would like to take [the observer's] coat and hang it up?" is to bind the children into absurdity—to compel them to acknowledge that absurdity is existence, to acknowledge that it is better to exist absurd than not to exist at all.

It is only natural, then, that when the teacher next asks, "Now who will tell what we have been doing?" and "Who would like to tell the answer to the next problem?" there should appear "a large and agitated forest of hands," for failure to raise the hand could be interpreted only as an act of aggression. The "arithmetic" lesson, transformed by the teacher, had become an affirmation of her matriarchal charisma as symbol of the system.

The reader will have observed that the question is not put, "Who *has* the answer to the next problem?" but "Who *would like to tell*" it? Thus, what at one time in our culture was phrased as a challenge to skill in arithmetic, becomes here an invitation to group participation. What is sought is a sense of "groupiness" rather than a distinguishing of individuals. Thus, as in the singing lesson an attempt was made to deny that it was a group activity, in the arithmetic lesson the teacher attempts to deny that it is an individual one. The essential issue is that *nothing is but what it is made to be by the alchemy of the system.*

In a society where competition for the basic cultural goods is a pivot of action, people cannot be taught to love one another, for those who do cannot compete with one another, except in play. It thus becomes necessary for the school, without appearing to do so, to teach children how to hate, without appearing to do so, for our culture cannot tolerate the idea that babes should hate each other. How does the school accomplish this ambiguity? Obviously through competition itself, for what has greater potential for creating hostility than competition? One might say that this is one of the most "creative" features of school. Let us consider an incident from a fifth-grade arithmetic lesson.

AT THE BLACKBOARD

Boris had trouble reducing "12/16" to the lowest terms, and could only get as far as "6/8". The teacher asked him quietly if that was as far as he could reduce it. She suggested he "think." Much heaving up and down and waving of hands by the other children, all frantic to correct him. Boris pretty unhappy, probably mentally paralyzed. The teacher, quiet, patient, ignores the others and concentrates with look and voice on Boris. She says, "Is there a bigger number than two you can divide into the two parts of the fraction?" After a minute or two, she becomes more urgent, but there is no response from Boris. She then turns to the class and says, "Well, who can tell Boris what the number is?" A forest of hands appears, and the teacher calls Peggy. Peggy says that four may be divided into the numerator and the denominator.

Thus Boris' failure has made it possible for Peggy to succeed; his depression is the price of her exhilaration; his misery the occasion for her rejoicing. This is the standard condition of the American elementary school, and is why so many of us feel a contraction of the heart even if someone we never knew succeeds merely at garnering plankton in the Thames: because so often somebody's success has been bought at the cost of our failure. To a Zuñi, Hopi, or Dakota Indian, Peggy's performance would seem cruel beyond belief, for competition, the wringing of success from somebody's failure, is a form of torture foreign to those noncompetitive redskins. Yet Peggy's action seems natural to us; and so it is. How else would you run our world? And since all but the brightest children have the constant experience that others succeed at their expense they cannot but develop an inherent tendency to hate—to hate the success of others, to hate others who are successful, and to be determined to prevent it. Along with this, naturally, goes the hope that others will fail. This hatred masquerades under the euphemistic name of "envy."

Looked at from Boris' point of view, the nightmare at the blackboard was, perhaps, a lesson in controlling himself so that he would not fly shrieking from the room under the enormous public pressure. Such experiences imprint on the mind of every man in our culture the *Dream of Failure*, so that over and over again, night in, night out, even at the pinnacle of success, a man will dream not of success, but of failure. *The external nightmare is internalized for life*. It is this dream that, above all other things, provides the fierce human energy required by technological drivenness. It was not so much that Boris was learning arithmetic, but that he was learning the *essential nightmare*. *To be successful in our culture one must learn to dream of failure*.

From the point of view of the other children, of course, they were learning to yap at the heels of a failure. And why not?

Have they not dreamed the dream of flight themselves? If the culture does not teach us to fly from failure or to rush in, hungry for success where others have failed, who will try again where others have gone broke? Nowadays, as misguided teachers try to soften the blow of classroom failure, they inadvertently sap the energies of success. The result will be a nation of chickens unwilling to take a chance.

When we say that "culture teaches drives and values" we do not state the case quite precisely. One should say, rather, that culture (and especially the school) provides the occasions in which drives and values are *experienced in events* that strike us with *overwhelming and constant force.* To say that culture "teaches" puts the matter too mildly. Actually culture invades and infests the mind as an obsession. If it does not, culture will not "work," for only an obsession has the power to withstand the impact of critical differences; to fly in the face of contradiction; to engulf the mind so that it will see the world only as the culture decrees that it shall be seen; to compel a person to be absurd. The central emotion in obsession is fear, and the central obsession in education is fear of failure. In order not to fail most students are willing to believe anything and to care not whether what they are told is true or false. Thus one becomes absurd through being afraid; but paradoxically, *only by remaining absurd can one feel free from fear.* Hence the immovableness of the absurd.

In examining education as a process of teaching the culture pattern, I have discussed a singing lesson, an arithmetic lesson, and the hanging up of a coat. Now let us consider a spelling lesson in a fourth-grade class.

"SPELLING BASEBALL"

The children form a line along the back of the room. They are to play "spelling baseball," and they have lined up to be chosen for the two teams. There is much noise, but the teacher quiets it. She has selected a boy and a girl and sent them to the front of the room as team captains to choose their teams. As the boy and girl pick the children to form their teams, each child chosen takes a seat

in orderly succession around the room. Apparently they
know the game well. Now Tom, who has not yet been
chosen, tries to call attention to himself in order to be
chosen. Dick shifts his position to be more in the direct
line of vision of the choosers, so that he may not be over-
looked. He seems quite anxious. Jane, Tom, Dick, and one
girl whose name the observer does not know, are the last
to be chosen. The teacher even has to remind the choosers
that Dick and Jane have not been chosen. . . .

The teacher now gives out words for the children to
spell, and they write them on the board. Each word is a
pitched ball, and each correctly spelled word is a base hit.
The children move around the room from base to base as
their teammates spell the words correctly. With some
of the words the teacher gives a little phrase: "Tongue,
watch your tongue, don't let it say things that aren't kind;
butcher, the butcher is a good friend to have; dozen,
twelve of many things; knee, get down on your knee; pocket,
keep your hand out of your pocket, and anybody else's. No
talking! Three out!" The children say, "Oh, oh!"

The outs seem to increase in frequency as each side gets
near the children chosen last. The children have great
difficulty spelling "August." As they make mistakes, those
in the seats say, "No!" The teacher says, "Man on third."
As a child at the board stops and thinks, the teacher says,
"There's a time limit; you can't take too long, honey."
At last, after many children fail on "August" one child gets
it right and returns, grinning with pleasure, to her seat. . . .
The motivation level in this game seems terrific. All the
children seem to watch the board, to know what's right
and wrong, and seem quite keyed up. There is no lagging
in moving from base to base. The child who is now writing
"Thursday" stops to think after the first letter, and the
children snicker. He stops after another letter. More
snickers. He gets the word wrong. There are frequent signs
of joy from the children when their side is right.

Since English is not pronounced as it is spelled, "language
skills" are a disaster for educators as well as for students. We

start the problem of "spelling baseball" with the fact that the spelling of English is so mixed up and contradictory and makes such enormous demands on the capacity for being absurd that nowadays most people cannot spell. "Spelling baseball" is an effort to take the "weariness, the fever, and the fret" out of spelling by absurdly transforming it into a competitive game. Over and over again it has seemed to our psychologist designers of curriculum scenery that the best way to relieve boredom is to transmute it into competition. Since children are usually good competitors, though they may never become good spellers, and although they may never learn to *spell* "success" (which really should be written *sukses*), they know what it *is,* how to go after it, and how it feels not to have it. A competitive game is indicated when children are failing, because the drive to succeed in the *game* may carry them to victory over the *subject matter.* At any rate it makes spelling less boring for the teacher and the students, for it provides the former with a drama of excited children, and the latter with a motivation that transports them out of the secular dreariness of classroom routine. "Spelling baseball" is thus a major effort in the direction of making things seem not as they are. But once a spelling lesson is cast in the form of a game of baseball a great variety of *noise* enters the system, because the sounds of *baseball* (the baseball "messages") cannot but be *noise* in a system intended to communicate *spelling.* Let us therefore analyze some of the baseball noise that has entered this spelling system from the sandlots and the bleachers.

We see first that a teacher has set up a choosing-rejecting system directly adopted from kid baseball. I played ball just that way in New York. The two best players took turns picking out teammates from the bunch, coldly selecting the best hitters and fielders first; as we went down the line it didn't make much difference who got the chronic muffers (the kids who couldn't catch a ball) and fanners (the kids who couldn't hit a ball). I recall that the kids who were not good players danced around and called out to the captains, "How about me, Slim? How about me?" Or they called attention to themselves with gestures and intense grimaces, as they pointed to their chests. It was pretty noisy. Of course, it didn't make any difference because the captains knew whom they were going to try to get, and there was not much of an issue after the best players had been sorted out to one or the other team. It was an honest jungle and there was nothing in it that didn't belong to the high tension of kid baseball. But nobody was ever left out; and even the worst were never permitted to sit on the sidelines.

"Spelling baseball" is thus sandlot baseball dragged into the schoolroom and bent to the uses of spelling. If we reflect that one could not settle a baseball game by converting it into a spelling lesson, we see that baseball is bizarrely *irrelevant* to spelling. If we reflect further that a kid who is a poor speller might yet be a magnificent ballplayer, we are even further impressed that learning spelling through baseball is learning by absurd association. In "spelling baseball" words become detached from their real significance and become assimilated to baseballs. Thus a spelling game that promotes absurd associations provides an indispensable bridge between the larger culture, where doubletalk is supreme, and the primordial meaningfulness of language. It provides also an introduction to those associations of mutually irrelevant ideas so well known to us from advertising—girls and vodka gimlets, people and billiard balls, lipstick and tree-houses, et cetera.

In making spelling into a baseball game one drags into the classroom whatever associations a child may have to the impersonal sorting process of kid baseball, and in this way some of the *noise* from the baseball system enters spelling. But there are differences between the baseball world and the "spelling baseball" world also. Having participated in competitive athletics all through my youth, I seem to remember that we sorted ourselves by skills, and we recognized that some of us were worse than others. In baseball I also seem to remember that if we struck out or muffed a ball we hated ourselves and turned flips of rage, while our teammates sympathized with our suffering. In "spelling baseball" one experiences the sickening sensation of being left out as others are picked—to such a degree that the teachers even have to remind team captains that some are unchosen. One's failure is paraded before the class minute upon minute, until, when the worst spellers are the only ones left, the conspicuousness of the failures has been enormously increased. Thus the *noise* from baseball is amplified by a *noise* factor specific to the classroom.

It should not be imagined that I "object" to all of this, for in the first place I am aware of the indispensable social functions of the spelling game, and in the second place, I can see that the rendering of failure conspicuous, the forcing of it on the mind of the unchosen child by a process of creeping extrusion from the group, cannot but intensify the quality of the essential nightmare, and thus render an important service to the culture. Without nightmares human culture has never been possible. Without hatred competition cannot take place.

One can see from the description of the game that drive is heightened in a complex competitive interlock: each child competes with every other to get the words right; each child competes with all for status and approval among his peers; each child competes with the other children for the approval of the teacher; and, finally, each competes as a member of a team. Here failure will be felt doubly because although in an ordinary spelling lesson one fails alone, in "spelling baseball" one lets down the children on one's team. Thus though in the game the motivation toward spelling is heightened so that success becomes triumph, so does failure become disaster. The greater the excitement the more intense the feeling of success and failure, and the importance of spelling or failing to spell "August" becomes exaggerated. But it is in the nature of an obsession to exaggerate the significance of events.

We come now to the *noise* introduced by the teacher. In order to make the words clear she puts each one in a sentence: "Tongue: watch your tongue; don't let it say things that aren't kind." "Butcher: the butcher is a good friend to have." "Dozen: twelve of many things." "Knee: get down on your knee." "Pocket: keep your hand out of your pocket, and anybody else's." More relevant associations to the words would be, "The leg bends at the knee." "A butcher cuts up meat." "I carry something in my pocket," etc. What the teacher's sentences do is introduce a number of her idiosyncratic cultural preoccupations, without clarifying anything; for there is no *necessary* relation between butcher and friend, between floor and knee, between pocket and improperly intrusive hands, and so on. In her way, therefore, the teacher establishes the same irrelevance between words and associations as the game does between spelling and baseball. She amplifies the *noise* by introducing ruminations from her own inner communication system.

CARPING CRITICISM

The unremitting effort by the system to bring the cultural drives to a fierce pitch must ultimately turn the children against one another; and though they cannot punch one another in the nose or pull each other's hair in class, they can vent some of their hostility in carping criticism of one another's work. Carping criticism is so destructive of the early tillerings of those creative impulses we cherish, that it will be good to give the matter further review.

Few teachers are like Miss Smith in this sixth-grade class:

The Parent-Teachers Association is sponsoring a school frolic, and the children have been asked to write jingles for publicity. For many of the children, the writing of a jingle seems painful. They are restless, bite their pencils, squirm in their seats, speak to their neighbors, and from time to time pop up with questions like, "Does it have to rhyme, Miss Smith?" At last she says, "Alright, let's read some of the jingles now." Child after child says he "couldn't get one," but some have succeeded. One girl has written a very long jingle, obviously the best in the class. However, instead of using "Friday" as the frolic day, she used "Tuesday," and several protests were heard from the children. Miss Smith defended her, saying, "Well, she made a mistake. But you are too prone to criticize. If *you* could only do so well!"

In our six years of work, in hundreds of hours of observation in elementary and high schools, Miss Smith is unique in that she scolded the children for tearing down the work of a classmate. Other teachers support such attacks, sometimes even somewhat against their will.

"For many of the children, the writing of a jingle seems painful" says the record. "They are restless, bite their pencils,

squirm in their seats. . . ." What are they afraid of but failure?
This is made clear by Miss Smith's angry defense of the outstanding child as she says to her critics, "If only *you* could
do so well!"

In a cooperative society carping is less likely to occur. Spiro
says of the *kibbutz*:

> . . . The emphasis on group criticism can potentially en-
> gender competitive, if not hostile feelings among the chil-
> dren. Frequently, for example, the children read their
> essays aloud, and the others are then asked to comment.
> Only infrequently could we detect any hostility in the
> criticisms of the students, and often the evaluations were
> filled with praise.[1]

But in Miss Smith's class, because the children have failed while
one of their number has succeeded, they carp. And why not?
However we may admire Miss Smith's defense of the successful child, we must not let our own "inner Borises" befog our
thinking. A competitive culture endures by tearing people
down. Why blame the children for doing it?

Let us now consider two examples of carping criticism from
a fifth-grade class as the children report on their projects and
read original stories.

> Bill has given a report on tarantulas. As usual the teacher
> waits for volunteers to comment on the child's report.

> Mike: The talk was well illustrated and well prepared.
> Bob: Bill had a *piece of paper* [for his notes] and teacher
> said he should have them on *cards*. . . .

> Bill says he could not get any cards, and the teacher says
> he should tear the paper the next time he has no cards.

> Bob: He held the paper behind him. If he had had to
> look at it, it wouldn't have been very nice.

> The children are taking turns reading to the class
> stories they have made up. Charlie's is called *The Un-
> known Guest*.

[1] Melford Spiro, *Children of the Kibbutz*. Harvard University Press, 1958,
p. 261.

"One dark, dreary night, on a hill a house stood. This house was forbidden territory for Bill and Joe, but they were going in anyway. The door creaked, squealed, slammed. A voice warned them to go home. They went upstairs. A stair cracked. They entered a room. A voice said they might as well stay and find out now; and their father came out. He laughed and they laughed, but they never forgot their adventure together.

Teacher: Are there any words that give you the mood of the story?
Lucy: He could have made the sentences a little better. . . .
Teacher: Let's come back to Lucy's comment. What about his sentences?
Gert: They were too short.

Charlie and Jeanne have a discussion about the position of the word "stood" in the first sentence.

Teacher: Wait a minute; some people are forgetting their manners. . . .
Jeff: About the room: the boys went up the stairs and one "cracked," then they were in the room. Did they fall through the stairs, or what?

The teacher suggests Charlie make that a little clearer. . . .

Teacher: We still haven't decided about the short sentences. Perhaps they make the story more spooky and mysterious.
Gwynne: I wish he had read with more expression instead of all at one time.
Rachel: Not enough expression.
Teacher: Charlie, they want a little more expression from you. I guess we've given you enough suggestions for one time. [Charlie does not raise his head, which is bent over his desk as if studying a paper.] Charlie! I guess we've given you enough suggestions for one time, Charlie, haven't we? [Charlie half raises his head, seems to assent grudgingly.]

It stands to reason that a competitive system must do this; and adults, since they are always tearing each other to pieces, should understand that children will be no different. School is indeed a training for later life not because it teaches the 3 Rs (more or less), but because it instills the essential cultural nightmare fear of failure, envy of success, and absurdity.

We pass now from these horrors to gentler aspects of school: impulse release and affection.

IMPULSE RELEASE AND AFFECTION

The root of life is impulse, and its release in the right amount, at the proper time and place, and in approved ways, is a primary concern of culture. Nowadays, however, in the era of impulse release and fun, the problem of impulse release takes on a special character because of the epoch's commitment to it. This being the case, teachers have a task unique in the history of education: the fostering of impulse release rather than, as in past ages, the installation of controls. Everywhere controls are breaking down, and firmness with impulse is no part of contemporary pedagogy of "the normal child." Rather impulse release, phrased as "spontaneity," "life adjustment," "democracy," "permissiveness," and "mothering," has become a central doctrine of education. It persists, despite protests from tough-minded critics from the Eastern Seaboard. In this sense education, often attacked for being "soft," is, as so often the case, far ahead of its detractors. Hardboiled critics of the educational system concentrate on curriculum. The teachers know better; the *real*, the persisting subject matter is noise.

How can a teacher face the whelming impulse life of children and yet discharge the task this period of history has assigned her? How can she release children's emotions without unchaining chaos? How can she permit the discharge of impulse and yet teach subject matter? How can she permit so much *noise* and not lose the message? Were they alive, the teachers I had in P.S. 10 and P.S. 186 in New York City, where we had to sit rigid and absolutely silent with our hands behind our backs or clasped before us on the desk, would say that chaos does prevail in many modern classrooms and that the message *is* lost. But then, each age has its own criteria of order, and what seems reasonable order to us nowadays might look and sound like chaos to them.

In our research on this problem in suburban classrooms it became necessary to develop a rating for noisiness (not noise).[1] It is a problem whether at certain times classrooms committed to impulse release can be said to have *any* social structure. Indeed, the pivot of order can scarcely be, as under more traditional discipline, the teacher but must become the pupil. As a matter of fact the extent to which order in any logical sense can be present in the midst of impulse release is problematic. As one reads the observations that follow, one should bear in mind that these are not delinquents or disturbed children tearing the social structure from its hinges, but nice suburban boys and girls who are merely being given their heads. We are concerned, meanwhile, not so much with what the children do, but rather with the absurdity inherent in the situation; with how the teacher manages to prevent chaos while, in a sense, encouraging it; with how she controls impulse while indulging its release. The first example is from a second-grade classroom with 37 children. Rather full excerpts are taken from one typical day, and very brief materials from a day a month later.

> The observer[2] arrives in the classroom at 12:45 and remarks, "As has been the case in past observations, the *noise rating was 2.*" The record continues:

> There are about seven children walking around, apparently doing nothing. There are about nine children sitting on the floor on the left side of the teacher's desk. Teacher is passing back some papers the children worked on yesterday. She says, "If you missed more than one of the questions on the board, it means that you either aren't reading carefully or that you aren't thinking enough. Betty, will you sit over here, please. Thank you."

This teacher, like most of the teachers in the area, uses "honey" and "dear" a great deal. Some examples recorded on this day are:

[1] Very noisy, "mild uproar," 3; somewhat noisy, 2; a little noise, 1. Quiet, 0. Tending toward bedlam was rated 4. These ratings were established by creating the conditions experimentally in my own classroom and accustoming my students to use of the rating scale.

[2] Unless otherwise stated, observers are always students trained by me.

(1) Could you talk a little louder, Johnny dear?

(2) I'll have to ask you to go to your seat, honey.

(3) Honey, where were you supposed to go if you didn't have your paper?

(4) Bill, I think George can do that by himself, honey,

(5) Susie, honey, what's the name of it?

(6) It's up here, dear.

The record continues:

1:10. The reading period is over. Children return to their seats. Teacher begins to write four words on the board. As she does this the talking and moving around the room increase to a mild uproar. *Noise rating 3.* Teacher says, "May I have your eyes this way please? Bill, will you and Tommy please watch?"

1:20. "May I suggest that the people in John Burns' group, instead of doing this work with the vowels, read in *The Friendly Village?*"

1:40. Teacher is sitting at desk. Children seem to be busy at work. Everyone seems to be doing something different. *Noise rating has dropped to 2.* Fifteen out of 34 of the children present are not doing the assigned work. Most of the children in this group are doing absolutely nothing in the line of school work. Some are merely staring into space; some are playing with rubber bands, hankies, etc.

1:56. Presently there are 10 children out of their regular seats and seated in the rockers at the bookcase, at the library table, or just aimlessly walking around the room. Two girls in the back of the room are showing each other their scarves. There is a great deal of foot shuffling; everyone looks as if he is preparing to go home. Teacher comments, "Boys and girls, we do not go home at 2 o'clock, so please continue with your work. Doug, may I talk to you a minute?" Doug goes up to teacher, who says, "We're going to let you stay 5 minutes after school because of this talking."

A month later the record reads:

12:40. When the teacher reprimands the children, her voice in all instances is soft, almost hesitant. She informed me [the observer] that when she scolds she wants the children to feel she is disappointed in them. I can see how the sad tone of her voice would convey this message.

12:50. Teacher says, "May I have you in your seats, please?" During the collection of papers the *noise rate had increased to 2*, and 12 people were out of their seats.

1:04. Teacher returns and says, "Annie, would you sit down honey, and get busy. Whose feet are making so much noise?" One child says, "Pam's!" and teacher says, "Pam, that's very annoying, please don't." Observer remarks, "It's odd that this small noise should bother Mrs. Olan. I didn't even hear it." Teacher says, "Doug, will you turn around, please? Billy, do you understand the process—how to do it? I thought maybe Jimmy was helping you. Stephen, are you finished? Murray and Mickey! Boys and girls, let's tend to our own work, please." [At this point the observer remarks, "Watch it, Mrs. Olan, just a little bit of authority is creeping into your voice!"]

1:55. Five minutes before recess. Teacher says "Put your work away quietly." She sits back and with a completely expressionless face waits for the five minutes to pass. The number of children out of their seats increased to 17. Three boys were bouncing balls on the floor; one was throwing his against the wall of the cloakroom; three children were killing each other with imaginary guns.

The absence of nightmarish qualities is what repels us most in these observations. The children seem to be so at ease. Competitiveness and fear of failure seem minimal, and the only thing left seems to be absurdity—the absurdity of trying to teach subject matter, or, perhaps, of being in school at all. Everything seems to be subordinated to impulse release and fun. I have said that fun is a clowning saboteur; here we have it. In her own sweet, human way Mrs. Olan is chopping at the roots of the old system, but the children hold the hatchets. Of course, it is exhausting; in any one and a half-hour observation period Mrs. Olan was fre-

quently in and out of the room, sometimes for as long as ten
minutes. Who wouldn't be? Her withdrawal naturally resulted in
increased noisiness, and she had to work at getting the sound level
down when she came back. The social structure does not quite
break down, because Mrs. Olan creates an affectionate atmosphere; because, by expressing disappointment rather than anger
she makes the children feel evanescently guilty and afraid of
losing love, and because the children's egos are remarkably firm.
They seem to have an inner strength that does not permit the
social structure to fall apart; and Mrs. Olan manipulates this
strength with a kind, maternal skill. Lest old-fashioned readers
argue that the social structure *has* fallen apart, I will point out
what does *not* happen: the children do not fight or wrestle, run
around the room, throw things, sing loudly, or whistle. The boys
did not attack the girls or vice versa; and the children did not run
in and out of the room. They did not make the teacher's life
miserable. All this happens when the social structure *is* torn down.
What this does to the subject matter, of course, is evident.

Let us now look at some parts of an interview with Mrs. Olan.

> In this day and age, she says, the children have more ten-
> sions and problems than when I first taught. In the one-
> room schoolhouse in which I first taught the children came
> from calm homes. There was no worry about war, and there
> was no TV or radio. They led a calm and serene life. They
> came to school with their syrup pails for lunch buckets.
> Children of today know more about what is going on; they
> are better informed. So you can't hold a strict rein on them.
> It is bad for children to come in and sit down with their
> feet under the seat: you have to have freedom to get up and
> move around. When they do this they are more rested and
> have a greater attention span. . . .
>
> Children need to enjoy school and like it. They also need
> their work to be done; it's not all play. You must get them to
> accept responsibility and doing work on their own.

Technological drivenness creates the problems and the needs
that Mrs. Olan feels she has to meet in the children. To the
question, "What would you say is your own particular way of
keeping order in the classroom?" she says:

Well, I would say I try to get that at the beginning of the year by getting this bond of affection and a relationship between the children and me. And we do that with stories; and I play games *with* them—don't just teach them how to play. It's what you get from living together comfortably. We have share times—that's the time a child can share with the teacher; and he gives whatever he wants to share: a bird's nest he has found; a tadpole that he and his dad got. Sometimes he may simply tell about something in his life— that his grandmother fell down and broke a leg and is not at home. ... These are the things that contribute toward this discipline. Another thing in discipline: it took me a long time to learn it, too—I thought I was the boss, but I learned that even with a child, if you speak to him as you would to a neighbor or a friend you would get a better response than if you say, "Johnny, do this or that." If you say "Mary, will you please cooperate, you are disturbing us; we want to finish our reading," rather than just giving a command, they feel they are working with you and not just taking orders.

Mrs. Olan has a philosophy: love is the path to discipline through permissiveness; and school is a continuation of family life, in which the values of sharing and democracy lead to comfortable living and ultimately to discipline. If you produce a comfortable atmosphere through affectionate sharing, she says, the children will "cooperate." And her children do cooperate in producing that *quality* of order obtained by *that kind* of classroom management. But it is not the order educators of an earlier generation had in mind. It is the order of the imp—the order of impulse release and fun—with just enough old-fashioned order so the class does not completely disintegrate and achievement scores are somehow maintained. Sometimes they are not.

A motto for this kind of school would be "Discipline and knowledge through love." One for an earlier generation of public schools would be, "Discipline and knowledge through disciplined competition."

Love is very, very important to Mrs. Olan. She continues:

With primary children the teacher is a mother during the day; they have to be able to bring their problems to you.

They get love and affection at home, and I see no reason not to give it in school.

If you have the right relationship between teacher and child or between parent and child he can take harsh words and the things you say in the right spirit; and if you don't have that bond of affection he just doesn't take it.

To Mrs. Olan, mother of a twenty-one-year-old son, second-grade children are pussy-cats, and you quiet them as you do kittens. For example, in answer to the question, "Do you think the children tend to be quieter if the teacher is affectionate?" she says:

If a teacher has a well-modulated voice and a pleasing dis-position her children are more relaxed and quiet. Children are like kittens: if kittens have a full stomach and lie in the sun they purr. If the atmosphere is such that the children are more comfortable, they are quiet. It is comfortable living that makes the quiet child. When you are shouting at them and they're shouting back at you it isn't comfortable living.

Observation has made clear that Mrs. Olan is no "boss," but lodges responsibility in the children. She clarifies the matter further:

It means a great deal to them to give them their own direc-tion. When problems do come up in the room we talk them over and discuss what is the right thing to do when this or that happens. Usually you get pretty good answers. They are a lot harder on themselves than I would be; so if any punishment comes along like not going to an assembly you have group pressure.

As the interviewer was leaving Mrs. Olan remarked, "My children don't rate as high [on achievement tests] as other chil-dren. I don't push, and that's because I believe in comfortable living." *Noise* has indeed become subject matter.

As a result of the idea that elementary school teachers should be affectionate parents, tenderness has become a defense against the children's impulses; the teacher awakens affection and makes her children fear the loss of it if they behave badly. In this way one array of feelings—affection, fear of losing it, and guilt— becomes a containing wall against another.

From where comes the belief that teachers should be parents? The answer is from the circumstance that our children *do not have enough parents,* because parents are unable to do all that has to be done *by* parents nowadays. Two technologically driven parents are not enough for technologically driven children, and technological drivenness has made the two-parent family obsolete. The school teacher who acts like a parent is society's answer to the obsolescence of the two-parent family. It is the unheralded socialization of parenthood; it is the culture's feeble remedy for the anguish of being a parent.

While woman teachers seem repeatedly to control children's impulses through affection and fear of loss of it (like almost any middle-class mother) an interesting question is, "What does a male teacher do in this kind of school?"

In the classroom Mr. Jeffries, now principal of his school, takes the role of one type of contemporary middle-class American father: a puckish imp-of-fun, buddy of the boys and sweetheart of the girls, he addresses the latter with endearments and uses nicknames and diminutives for the former, as he pats them on the head or puts an arm around their shoulders. His room is a rough-and-tumble, happy-go-lucky, brink-of-chaos sort of place. Mr. Jeffries calls it a "rat-race" and says, "We get tired and ready to drop by the time it is over." Let us have a look at Mr. Jeffries' classroom:

11:05. The class is having a reading lesson. Teacher says, "Galapagos means tortoise. Where are 300-pound turtles found?" A boy says, "In the zoo," and Teacher says, "Where are they native in this country?" A girl says, with a grimace of disgust, "We saw them in Marine Land in Florida. They were slaughtered and used for meat. Ugh!" John has raised his hand and Teacher calls on him. "We saw one in Wisconsin about the size of Bob's head." Teacher says, "That's pretty big!" and the class laughs.

Teacher asks, "What was Douglas [a boy in the story] doing on the island? Have you ever been scared, John?" "Yes," replies John. "So have I," says the teacher, and the class laughs. Teacher says, *"That's what I like about buddies."*

11:25. Teacher says, "Let's read the story silently." He says to a girl, "Do you mind putting your beads away for the rest of the morning instead of tearing them apart?"

The room is now very quiet. He walks around the aisles as the children read.

Mr. Jeffries obviously runs a democratic classroom, and his pupils are spontaneous and effervescent. He tells them he is a buddy; he is no aloof figure, pretending to invulnerability, but like the children, he is capable of fear; he is "scared" *with* them. He is right down there on the floor with the kids, so to speak; like a contemporary American daddy, he has levelled the distance between himself and his children. Yet by command he can suddenly get quiet when he wants it, though rarely for long.

A week later we are at a grammar lesson:

10:15. The class is discussing types of nouns. Teacher says, "If I had lots of Ritas, she'd be a type. Maybe we're lucky we have only one." Class laughs. A girl raises her hand and Teacher says, "What is it, honey?"

10:25. The room has grown noisy during the lesson and Teacher says, "Can't hear you, Shirley. You're not going to find out a thing by looking in that direction." His voice has risen, getting louder in order to be heard above the classroom noise.

10:40. Clatter is increasing. Eight or nine pupils are walking around the room. One boy throws a paper wad at another. Four pupils are at the pencil sharpener. Noise grows louder but teacher ignores it.

10:45. Teacher says, "It would seem to me that in the past five minutes you haven't accomplished a thing; you've been so busy wandering around." This creates complete silence. Then two boys stand to look at neighbor's work. Another goes to Teacher's desk to get help. Teacher and he confer. Noise is louder now.

10:55. Two boys raise hands. Two others stand next to teacher. One girl pats his back as he bends over. She giggles.

11:00. Teacher, "O.K., put language books away, please!" He giggles as a girl asks him a question. Pupils put books in desks. Teacher: "Take a couple of minutes here. Girl with the blue hair, get up. Stretch a bit." Loud laughter from the class. Teacher: "Get up and stretch." Most of the class stands. Two boys continue writing at their desks. A boy and girl push each other. The smallest boy in the class stands alone and looks on as two girls wrestle.

At the end of this observation period the observer wrote, "I feel that the pupils are truly fond of Mr. Jeffries. They enjoy laughing together; not *at* somebody, but *with* each other." Though we might question the last in view of the joshing, buddy-buddy jokes at the expense of Rita and Bob, there seems no doubt that Mr. Jeffries is a love object and that everybody has a wonderful time. Frequently the noise gets so loud that Mr. Jeffries has to shout and the students cannot hear. When children are pushing and wrestling, Mr. Jeffries ignores it. Suddenly, absurdly, even though he has permitted disorder and noise he may scold the children for not accomplishing anything. The following week, during a hilarious and noisy arithmetic lesson, when the children can barely hear what is going on, a girl takes a boy's paper, tears it up and throws it into the waste basket; but the teacher laughs, the class pays no attention, the paper is fished out and taped together, and the lesson continues.

One day five weeks later, Mr. Jeffries was sick and a substitute was on duty. The room was in its usual noisy state when the principal walked in and stood in the back of the room for a few minutes. No change took place in the class. The principal bent over one of the little girls, embraced her, whispered something to her, then turned to the observer and said, "Fine bunch of gals here," and left. Thus, in his own behavior the principal expresses the emphasis on impulse release. Teacher, principal, children, and community are one continuous cultural system.

As the school year entered the last month, evidence began to appear that impulse release and noisiness had reached a point beyond the endurance of the children, for the children, particularly the girls, began to *shush* the class.

10:40. The children have just finished singing. Teacher says, "Get paper, eraser, pencil." There is a loud buzz at this command, and a girl says, "What's the paper for?" Teacher says, "Now don't go wild just because you sang. Your pencils don't have to be so sharp." Observer notes that a bunch of kids is storming the pencil sharpener as Teacher says this. Someone *shushes* the class. Teacher says, "Fill this out the same as yesterday." He passes the sheets out very carefully, dropping the correct number on the first desk of each row. "Today's date is the eighth of May," says Teacher. "Sorry you're so noisy. Don't open your books till I tell you. Just fill out the first page. This is a reading test." The class reads in silent concentration.

11:01. The test is over. Teacher starts to issue instructions for the next activity and a girl says to the class, "*Shush!*"

11:06. A girl goes to the Teacher's desk for help in spelling. He spells a word aloud as she writes, leaning on his desk for support. A girl walks by John and smacks him playfully. He gets up, walks by her, smacks her on the back soundly and sprints away. Teacher says, "I notice that most of you have finished your papers promptly. I'm very pleased. Now devote your time, the next 15 minutes, to your spelling." A girl says, "*Shush!*" There is a loud buzz. Observer notes that this *shush*ing has occurred several times today, only from the girls.

These observations underscore a point made earlier, that in this kind of class responsibility for maintenance of order has shifted, the children determining the controls. In the last observation, their efforts to hold the social structure together become audible; but throughout the term, the teacher's interest in order is so slight, he so often ignores the racket in his room that order would have disappeared entirely had not the children tacitly set their own limits.

It wasn't until two years later that we talked to Mr. Jeffries, now principal of this school, about his theories of classroom management. His passionate involvement in teaching and in children easily won the interviewer.

At the very beginning of the year, says Mr. Jeffries, he expands the boundaries of his own family to bring his sixth-graders close:

The very first day, I introduce myself to the children and tell them about myself. I use my family a great deal. I talk about my boy and about my daughter. I tell them about certain of my experiences, just to give them an understanding that "here is an individual."

In this way he begins to draw closer to the children. He becomes almost one with them. Speaking of himself, he says,

They know the teacher's a friend with whom they can exchange jokes and banter. But if the teacher says, "Come on, we must get to this or that," they say to themselves, "We must do it." Maybe they say, "He's a good Joe, he's a guy, so let's get the job done."

Mr. Jeffries is like Mrs. Olan in that he sees himself as working out the criteria for classroom management and discipline with the children in a democratic way, and he lets the children set their own punishments when they get into serious trouble, like fighting in the school yard. Mr. Jeffries' long explanation of how he goes about letting children set their own rules cannot be reproduced here, but what it amounts to is that he guides the children in the course of discussion to acceptance of his ideas.

We have seen that Mr. Jeffries' room is a buoyant, noisy, brink-of-chaos sort of milieu. "You can't hold children in a tight rein," he says, "no more than you can hold a racehorse in a tight rein. A racehorse needs freedom and so does a child." If you hold in a child in class he'll somehow break loose and "stomp" on somebody, just like a racehorse that breaks out into the spectators. Children are "God-given individuals" and have a right to get up and walk around whenever they please. As a matter of fact, he says, since in this way they may find their way to an encyclopedia or a map, mobility is closely related to creativity. To Mr. Jeffries "a quiet classroom is a dead classroom" where "the children are not thinking or are afraid to think." A stranger, he says, walking into his room might think it a "riot" or that "Mayhem was being committed," but he simply would not understand the basic thinking behind Mr. Jeffrie's management. Furthermore,

A classroom with affection can be an awfully happy and joyous one. A quiet classroom may be an awfully fearful situation for someone.

Love, demonstrativeness, freedom, mobility, creativity, noisiness, and thoughtfulness all go together as Mr. Jeffries sees it. As a matter of fact, he is afraid of quietness and restraint.

In such classrooms the contemporary training for impulse release and fun is clear. There the children are not in uniform but in the jerkins and gossamer of *The Midsummer Night's Dream;* it is a sweet drilling without pain. Since impulse and release and fun are the requirements of the classroom, and since they must be contained within the four walls, the instrument of containment can only be affection. The teacher must therefore become a parent, for it is a parent above all who deals with the impulses of the child. In these circumstances male and female teachers adopt roles natural to the contemporary American parent. The classroom atmosphere becomes erotized as the children receive their first lessons in how to live in the "friendly," "relaxed" climates of the contemporary bureaucracies of business and government.

In these classrooms subject matter has a difficult time, for the noisiness and the low level of order make concentration problematic. Always *noise* is more important than subject matter; but in the era of impulse release and fun subject matter has trouble in surviving at all. Meanwhile, in these middle-class schools, the children's egos display remarkable firmness: they do not admit true chaos in spite of provocations to it. It is obvious that the classroom of fun and impulse release must remain a middle- and upper-class phenomenon, for the children's underlying controls are still strong enough there.

Today our emphasis on impulse release, spontaneity, and creativity goes hand in hand with culture-weariness, a certain tiredness and disillusionment with impulse restraint, and a feeling that the Self has been sold down the river. In these circumstances permissiveness has invaded many phases of work with children, so that in some schools there is a great relaxation of controls, the essential nightmare is impaired, and the teacher most highly regarded is the one who lets children be free. Of course, it is the *adult* Self that is really straining to be free; and when Mr. Jeffries says that a child held in tight rein may break loose and "stomp" on somebody, the racehorse tearing at the halter is his own inner Self.

It is hard for us to see, since we consider most people inherently replaceable, that there is anything remarkable in a parent-figure like a teacher showering the symbols of affection on a child for a year and then letting him walk out of her life, to be replaced next year and the next and the next by different children. However, this is almost unheard of outside the stream of Western civilization; and even in the West it is not common. As a matter of fact, the existence of *children* willing to accept such demonstrations is in itself an interesting phenomenon, based probably on the obsolescence of the two-parent family. The fact that a teacher can be thus demonstrative without inflicting deep wounds on *herself* implies a character structure having strong brakes on involvement. Otherwise how could the teacher not go to pieces? If she became deeply involved in the children in her classes she would have to give up teaching, for the hurt inflicted on her as she lost her beloved children each year would be too severe. It must be, then, that the expressions of tenderness imply also, "So far and no farther"; over the years, children must come to recognize this. It is a kind of mutual conspiracy of affectivity in which children and teacher hold themselves aloof, neither giving nor demanding more than the tacit rules permit. If this were not so children would have to be dragged shrieking from grade to grade, for they would become too deeply attached to teachers. This is one of the first lessons a child has to learn in kindergarten or the first grade. From this regular replacement-in-affection they learn that the affection-giving figure, the teacher, is replaceable also. In this way children are drilled in uninvolvement: they are affectively weaned from the social system. Meanwhile they learn the symbols of affectivity; that they can be used ambiguously, and that they are not binding—that they can be scattered upon the world without commitment. Classroom demonstrativeness is a phantom commitment on which no one can collect.

The reader should not imagine I am "against" affectionate classrooms. They are a necessary adjunct to contemporary childhood and to the socialization of parenthood at this stage of our culture. They are also an indispensable training ground for the release of impulse and for the buddy-buddy relations of contemporary business, government, and university.

A FINAL NOTE ON LEARNING AND CREATIVITY

In some areas of modern education theory (especially inside the heads of my education majors) democracy, permissiveness, originality, spontaneity, impulse release, learning, thinking, and adjustment to life are all mixed up together, so that, without any historic perspective at all, students come to me with the conviction that criticism of permissiveness is an attack on democracy itself. They have not been taught that the schoolrooms in which the originators of our American democracy received instruction were places of strict discipline. During the eighteenth and nineteenth centuries, when England was creating the industrial revolution and adding to her great literature, schools were anything but models of permissiveness. Although German schools have been among the most "authoritarian" in Europe, Germany was one of the most creative nations in the West—and also, before Hitler, a great political democracy. China is unparalleled in the tyranny with which schoolmasters ruled, yet China has given the world great poetry, drama, painting, and sculpture. France is one of the most turbulent and creative democracies of modern times, yet her classrooms are strict—much stricter, for example, than those of Czechoslovakia.[1]

What, then, is the central issue? The central issue is love of knowledge for its own sake, not as the creature of drive, exploited largely for survival and for prestige. When knowledge is loved for itself, *noise* is at a minimum and never endangers the subject matter. Creative cultures have loved the "beautiful person"—meditative, intellectual, and exalted. As for the creative individual, the history of the great civilizations seems to reveal little about creativity except that it has had an obstinate way

[1] For these remarks on contemporary European classrooms I am deeply indebted to Professor David Rodnick's observations on the spot.

of emerging only in gifted individuals, and that it has never appeared in the mass of the people. Loving the beautiful person more we might alter this.

SUMMARY

The twentieth century is the period in history when man has at last set himself to thoroughly investigate the process of learning; his study has produced an enormous mass of literature. *Homo sapiens* has finally come consciously to grips with his most essential evolutionary task; for as his culture swept him on he discovered that he was moving rapidly in the current of new knowledge but yet had no efficient way of understanding its full implications or communicating its enormous mass to his children.

As he acquires new knowledge, modern man becomes perplexed by the fact that old ideas and preoccupations bind; that in the process of teaching his children he acts in ancient ways, fettering mind and spirit. But while acknowledging that this hampers the capacity to move, man is yet afraid that unchaining the young intellect will cause overthrow and chaos. Meanwhile culture, which must be impressed upon the young mind so that traditional ways will not be thrust aside by youthful rebellion or new ideas, has to have obsessive power, and convey its antagonisms and sympathies during learning. Thus education is burdened with the weight of cultural anxieties and hatreds to the degree, indeed, that what it *loves* is often obscured, and originality is thrust aside.

Children everywhere have been trained to fit culture as it exists; and to the end that they should not fail to fit, man has used the great ingenuity of which he is capable. As a device for teaching what was necessary and preventing deviation, education became an instrument for narrowing the perceptual sphere, thus defining the human condition of being absurd; of learning to be stupid; of learning to alienate one's Self from inner promptings.

Turning to the contemporary school we see it as a place where children are drilled in cultural orientations, and where subject matter becomes to a very considerable extent the instrument for instilling them. This comes about, however, not only because school, as the heartbeat of the culture, naturally embodies and expresses the central preoccupations, but also because schools deal with masses of children, and can manage therefore only by reducing them all to a common definition. Since it is in the nature of things that the definition should be determined by the cultural preoccupations, school creates what I have called the *essential nightmare*. The nightmare must be dreamed in order to provide the fears necessary to drive people away from something (in our case, failure) and toward something (success). In this way children, instead of loving knowledge become embroiled in the nightmare.

In this situation a modern trend to make school the habitat of impulse release and fun is an expected development. It is a therapy for the cultural obsession—educators' expression of their own disenchantment with the cultural nightmares—and they have made the trend synonymous with democracy itself. That a vital democracy can be the product of a disciplined and intelligent population only; that disorder and laxity are poison to democracy, they naturally cannot see because they are just as obsessed with destroying the nightmare as an older generation was with creating it.

9: Pathways to Madness: Families of Psychotic Children

THERE ARE MANY ROADS TO INSANITY AND OUR CULTURE has probably trod them all. It is difficult to find in any other society a form of madness, or a pathway to it, that cannot be duplicated by us. The opposite is not true: that all cultures have developed as many forms of psychosis or found as many ways to attain it as we. In this we are secure in our riches. We are as highly developed in psychopathology as in technology.

Psychosis is the final outcome of all that is wrong with a culture. Coming to intense focus in the parents, the cultural ills are transmitted to their children, laying the foundation for insanity.[1] The parents, blinded by their own disorientation, confusion, and misery, sometimes half mad themselves, make dreadful mistakes; but only an observer who sees these with his own

[1] I am, of course, aware of the fact that nowadays many in the psychiatric professions no longer want to "blame" psychosis on "bad parents." There is no question of "blame," but rather of fundamental causation. Meanwhile, considering my own research, and the mass of good case history material pointing to the basic pathogenic role of parents, I see no reason for changing the "old-fashioned" psychiatric position with respect to etiology. The really new dimension to be added to the old theories of etiology is the role culture plays in *consolidating* the disturbance in the child once the foundations have been laid by the disturbed parents.

eyes can really know exactly how the tragedy was prepared. How can a parent who is psychologically blind perceive what he did to his child? How can he remember twenty, or even four years later exactly what occurred? How can he recall for a psychiatrist his innumerable acts, especially since most people are unaware of what they are doing? What I have to say in this chapter about the development of psychosis derives from about 500 hours of direct observation in the homes of families that had a psychotic child.[1] (In both families described in this chapter, the psychotic child is living away from the home.) Since each family story is condensed from between a hundred and two hundred pages of notes, they are bare summaries. They are, nevertheless, sufficient to sustain a major argument of this book, that culture is a unified whole, even unto psychosis and death.

THE PORTMAN FAMILY

THE CULTURAL ILLS

Every family in the United States is somewhat different from every other, the difference consisting in the manner in which each develops its own version of the general cultural configuration. A family's culture—its variant of the general culture—always contains something that makes for tranquility and well-being, and something that makes for anxiety and misery. Every family has its special enjoyments, variants of the general cultural modes of enjoyment, and struggles with its *own peculiar* versions of the *general* causes of misery. In a family that has produced a psychotic child, however, there is always more suffering than contentment. Much of it comes as a consequence of the disaster; some of it was there before. It is difficult to tell, after the event.

In the Portman home the outstanding cultural ills are lack of involvement, impulsiveness, insincerity, a struggle for dominance and an emphasis on strength to the exclusion of tender-

[1] Fuller presentation is to be found in my "L'observation naturaliste des familles d'enfants psychotiques," in *La psychiatrie de l'enfant*, vol. IV, I (Presses Universitaires de France), Paris, 1961.

ness. These will appear as the reader follows the record of my observations, but first I shall give sketches of the personalities of Mr. and Mrs. Portman.

MRS. PORTMAN

I chatted for many hours with Mrs. Portman during my week's stay in her home, but I did not try to get beneath the surface since she was guarded. She told me that since she was a spoiled child she did not want to spoil her children. She believes people are dishonest, exploitive, jealous of the rich, and hostile to snobs. Sexual restraint is right before marriage, she says, but now she seems to resent her husband's prudishness. Though she protected him in talking to me, I nevertheless got the impression that she felt he was pretty insensitive.

At thirty Mrs. Portman doesn't seem to be interested in much outside of her immediate household, and on the surface she seems rather content with her comfortable suburban life, the comics, and Ann Landers.[1] The Portman house is one of several thousand identical ranch-type houses all around it. Mrs. Portman told me that she will buy a product because it is sponsored on TV by a star she is fond of, and that she was hoodwinked by an encyclopedia salesman, who made her believe that as a prominent person on the block (which she is not) she would receive an encyclopedia free just for signing an affidavit endorsing it. Her husband managed to extricate the family before it was too late.

Mrs. Portman's feeling for her children—Pete, age sixteen months, and Belle, age five weeks—lacks intensity and depth. Psychotic Mimi, four years old, not now living at home, weighs on Mrs. Portman's mind, yet she treats Belle as she did Mimi, and she does not know what happened to make Mimi psychotic at the age of three. Somewhere within her, though, may be a feeling that she was somehow responsible, for she repeatedly told me about the terrible things her friends do to their children, yet "mentally" they are perfectly sound.

When a woman like Mrs. Portman gives birth to a so-called "good baby"—one that does not cry—she may accept this

[1] A syndicated news column of advice on love and family affairs.

quietness without question and leave the baby alone. "I didn't have to go in to Mimi at all," she told me. Since many, even in the psychiatric profession, until recently have been unaware of the terrible effects on young children of mere isolation, it would be expecting too much of Mrs. Portman to change, even though at five weeks Belle is a healthy, noisy baby. "After the first child," she remarked to me paradoxically, "you harden yourself to their crying." Mrs. Portman's inability to relate to a young child is so great that when, just before my departure, I advised her strongly against leaving Belle too much alone while awake, she said, "Oh, you mean I should hold her a little while before I give her her bath?"

Mrs. Portman is what clinicians call a "sub-clinical" case—a person recognized as having a potential for pathogenic behavior but superficially well-adjusted. Mrs. Portman is comfortable with her friends; she likes to visit neighbor housewives and to talk on the phone. She has a good sense of humor and is not dull. She is rather careless in personal appearance and in her housekeeping, and though she tries to adhere to baby-care schedules she changes them around constantly to suit her own sudden plans for the day. She is forgetful too, and somewhat confused: once she started to give Belle a second bath just after completing the first.

It is really only in relation to her children that a visitor for a week can come to understand how this woman, apparently so "well adjusted," can produce[1] a psychotic child. This fact is central to understanding why, in general, apparently "lovely" parents may have a disturbed child. There are some parents about whom one says, "They are such charming, intelligent, *nice* people, they could not possibly have made their child psychotic. It must be constitutional." "Constitution," "inheritance," can be excuses for cases badly understood. *An infant organism cannot prosper on the culturally valued façade; it makes no difference to a mind dying from lack of social stimulation that its mother is popular.*

---

[1] It is my impression that in contemporary clinical practice the sophisticated view is that given a constitutional predisposition to psychosis, it will not emerge without contributory environmental (parental or other) conditions. This view merely reflects good biological theory in general.

On the first day of my visit to the Portman house I made the following note:

> She deals with Pete and Belle in a dead-pan way. It is not a dissociated face; but the expression does not change.

When Mrs. Portman was not feeding or cleaning her children—activities in which she limited herself almost entirely to the necessary operations—she went to them only when they cried, and she left them when they had stopped. Leaving Pete alone was legitimized as teaching him independence. Mrs. Portman's response to Belle's crying was sometimes deliberately timed, so that if the baby stopped in ten minutes by the clock Mrs. Portman felt relieved of obligation. Belle was often left to cry, however, much longer than ten minutes, with no move from her mother, who saw the situation as a struggle between her will and the baby's.

Whenever Belle or Pete cried I tried to make a note of it, but, of course, since I did not carry a notebook[1] I probably missed some spells. At any rate, of the 26 times that Belle cried her mother failed to go to her in 14 of them. I was also able to record six periods when the baby was awake but silent and alone. When Pete cried his mother responded promptly, picking him up and sometimes kissing him, asking him what the trouble was, or giving him something she guessed he wanted. Her rare play with him seldom lasted longer than a minute, and the words she spoke during it carried the *meta*-communication, "I'm uninterested!" Since she played with Pete only when he was upset, it is clear that the purpose of it was to quiet him. When he screamed she became humiliating and sometimes violent. Pete could not yet talk.

Mrs. Portman's life with her babies was so patently joyless one could not but wonder why she had them. She took care of them in a businesslike, though anxious, sometimes even grim, way, though there were some kisses and tenderness too. Belle was force-fed and Pete avoided the forcing only by acrobatics. A strong, firm, rather large baby, alert, intelligent, and generally able to carry out what he set himself to do, he had

---

[1] At the Portman's I had a notebook in the room where I slept and would go in there from time to time to make quick jottings.

great *élan vital* and a good appetite. "Mastery" was well developed, as they say in the trade, so that his mother's continued reliance on baby food and her persistence in feeding him rather than letting him feed himself had no relation to his real capacities. Feeding the children was complicated during my stay by delays caused by Mrs. Portman's oversleeping and schedule manipulation, by her forcing solid foods on the baby, and by her reducing its feedings from seven to five. Forcing solids was related to Mrs. Portman's planned reduction of feedings also, for according to Mrs. Portman, when a baby has solid food it can go longer between feedings.[1] Shifting feeding and sleeping schedules around always results in complications, but in Mrs. Portman's case matters were made worse for the children by her tendency to get mixed up.

Mrs. Portman, in spite of having had three children, usually commented in an irritated or disgusted way on her children's excreta. To Pete she once said, "You smell, you stink." She calls him a "human garbage pail" and keeps the garbage bag and other refuse in his high chair when he is not in it.

In sum, we see in Mrs. Portman some of the least attractive aspects of our culture—its tendency to produce self-centered, impulse-dominated, detached, confused parents, who, therefore, cannot separate the primordial demands of their infants from their *own*. The pathologically ramifying effects of this will be seen when we review some of the observations. Meanwhile let us have a look at Mr. Portman.

MR. PORTMAN

Mr. Portman is divided within himself. On the one hand, he believes in the importance of being violent and tough; on the other, he feels himself a weak, helpless, but rather amusing chip on the ocean of life. He has a great admiration for what might be called pecuniary heroism—the strength and courage to come out on top in economic difficulties, and that is why he admires and reveres his boss.

Though you should avoid a fight as long as possible, said Mr.

---

[1] There is no well-controlled clinical evidence that babies fed early on solid food are healthier than others who are not.

Portman, you must be prepared for one if it is forced on you. That is the way he wants Pete to be. Toughness embraces a great deal in Mr. Portman's thinking: hard bargaining, physical fitness, laughter at Pete's minor injuries, insensitivity to "hard-luck stories." Inner commitment to toughness, however, comes out also in stubbornness and in callousness to his wife's needs. At home, fixing upon an idea, he becomes quietly unshakable; meanwhile, at work, he seems to be unassertive. Like his wife, Mr. Portman was also spoiled as a child: for fourteen years it was believed that he had a dangerous heart condition, and he was treated delicately and kept away from participation in sports.

Mr. Portman is fearful. He has worked for the same boss for years, has never requested a raise, and will not take a vacation or ask for a day off, even though he often works Sundays. Unremitting work, meanwhile, keeps Mr. Portman away from home and the emotional demands of his wife and children. Mr. Portman feels exploited at work and deprived of just credit for what he does—he feels tossed around, a leaf in the storm. But Mr. Portman is intelligent, is better informed than his wife, and he admires cleverness. He thinks himself smarter than the Boss, but thinks also that the Boss merely uses this to get more out of him than he pays for and that he doesn't even give him verbal credit for what he accomplishes. "I'm the fall guy for the Boss," he says.

The one intimate matter about which Mr. and Mrs. Portman were willing to talk to me frankly was Mimi. Mr. Portman said his wife destroyed the child by humiliation—by "treating her like a monster"—while to him Mimi was "like a doll." Mrs. Portman says that her husband would not recognize that there was anything wrong with Mimi until the psychiatrist's diagnosis. Anger and guilt over Mimi are just below the surface. Meanwhile husband and wife are doing the same things to Belle that they did to the first child. Mr. Portman ignores the baby, but things are different with Pete, for he "eats him up," sometimes kissing him with his mouth open wide. When he plays with Pete it is usually very violent: he lifts him up in the air, rolls him around on the floor, and hits him hard with his fist in the abdomen. Mr. Portman is training his son to be tough and violent and to care only about him.

Toughness, violence, insensitivity, and stubbornness are thus joined in Mr. Portman to fearfulness and a feeling of exploited helplessness. Of course, even though Mr. Portman is little at home, these characteristics must affect his children, but their impact must be particularly strong on his wife, contributing to her apathy toward the children.

Thus the culture of the Portman family contains, but in a distorted or extreme way, the characteristics I have emphasized as important in American culture as a whole: wooly-mindedness, toughness, detachment, humiliation, fear of exploitation, yielding to impulse, independence, violence, pecuniary motivations, the achievement drive. It is largely a joyless house now, and one perceives there little of other dimensions of American culture— tenderness, generosity, kindness, and compassion.

Let us now review some of the direct observations of the family. I start with the problem of time.

THE PSYCHO-BIOLOGY OF TIME

In primitive cultures, where babies are usually fed in harmony with their spontaneous hunger and schedules do not exist, clock time is not interposed between mother and child to complicate their lives: the baby gets food when it is hungry and its mother has no need to watch the clock and count bottles. Though a schedule can be a convenience for an American mother running a busy, heavily furnished home, if she is a Mrs. Portman, impulsive, confused, and somewhat unable to put herself in her baby's place, a schedule can become a monster, creating chaos and misery. Mrs. Portman would get up late, shift schedules around, forget. The result was that Pete and Belle often were fed either too late or too soon; and if babies are fed this way they become hard to handle, scream, mess up their feeding, and anger the mother. Time is a psycho-biological experience, for it has something to do with the mother's *mind* and has indirect effects on the *children's* organisms. Let us look now at some of the observations of Mrs. Portman's difficulties with time.

2:22:14[1]

Yesterday Mrs. Portman was off schedule, having gotten up
at seven thirty. So the children's feeding time was pushed
around quite a bit. Having decided to delay Belle's feeding,
she left her in the crib, apologizing to the baby by saying,
"Don't be angry." Even though Belle was crying, she left her
there, but the crying increased in intensity, until, although
Mrs. Portman had planned to delay the feeding another half
hour, she went in and gave the baby the bottle anyway.

2:24:16

All day yesterday Mrs. Portman was worried about her upset
schedule. Once she counted through the number of bottles
she had in the refrigerator to see if she had one for each of
Belle's feedings.

2:50:13

Today[2] Belle was crying at 6 P.M., and Mrs. Portman said
to her, "It's not time for you," and left her in the carriage.

5:92:13

Today Mrs. Portman is dominated by the idea of getting
Pete a haircut. It seems that every day she gets up possessed by a particular idea. For example, yesterday she was
dominated by the idea that she wanted to get over to
Marilyn Muntz's house. Then everything became organized
around going over to Marilyn's. Today it is getting Pete a
haircut. The first day I was there her behavior was mobilized
in terms of rearranging schedules because she had gotten up
at 7:30 and had thrown everything off. This morning when
Pete was whimpering because he had not had his breakfast
Mrs. Portman said, "He acts like a real starvation case. You
can't be *that* hungry—it's only half an hour past your feeding time."

---

[1] Second day, page 22, line 14 of the record.
[2] The two preceding transcriptions refer to the first day of my stay, i.e.,
"yesterday"; this one refers to the second day.

7:140:5

At 5:25 the baby is crying hard while Mrs. Portman is preparing the bath for Pete, and she calls out, "All right, Belle."
She put Pete into the bathtub and held Belle on her lap for
a short time while she read the comics. Then she said to me,
"As long as she's up, why waste the time?"—the idea being
that although it was still a bit early for Belle's feeding, she
might as well take advantage of the baby's being awake to
feed her. It would appear that she looks upon merely holding Belle as a waste of time. At 5:50 P.M., she starts feeding
Belle.

7:141:9

She scolded Belle for clamoring so much and then not
finishing the bottle. When she started to feed the baby it
was crying paroxysmally. She began with cereal but quickly
gave up because the baby choked and continued to cry. So
she gave her the bottle and the baby stopped.

"Don't be angry," says Mrs. Portman to her hungry, screaming
baby; "It's not time for you," she says, as she leaves Belle out in
the carriage; "You can't be *that* hungry," she says to Pete, "It's
only half an hour past your feeding time." And as she reads the
comics, her baby held briefly on her lap, she gets the idea that
"As long as she's up, why waste the time?" so she might as well
feed the baby. Apologies and scoldings addressed to babies who
cannot understand, and an inappropriate connection between
wakefulness, time, and feeding ("As long as she's up . . . etc.")
are consequences of confusion and insensitivity. *Thus a pathogenic mother's disorientation in time affects her babies through
action on their psycho-biological systems:* since their feeding
schedules are pushed around by their confused mother, their
hunger is driven to a fierce pitch, and they become anxious and
hostile; or they are fed when they are not hungry.

BABIES AS PRIVATE ENTERPRISE

In our culture babies are a private enterprise—everybody is in
the baby business as soon as he gets married. He produces his

own babies; they are his; only he has the right to a say-so in their management; they cannot be taken from him without due process of law; he has the sole responsibility for their maintenance and protection. He has the right to expand his production of babies indefinitely and curtail it whenever he wishes. As long as he takes care of his young children the outside world has no right to cross his threshold, to say "No" or "Yes" about anything he does with his children. Pinched off alone in one's own house, shielded from critical eyes, one can be as irrational as one pleases with one's children as long as severe damage does not attract the attention of the police.

In other words, there is minimal *social regulation* of parent–child relations in our culture; this is, above all, what makes lethal child-care practices possible. In a primitive culture, where many relatives are around to take an active interest in one's baby, where life is open, or in large households, where many people can see what a mother is doing and where deviations from traditional practice quickly offend the eye and loosen critical, interested tongues, it is impossible for a parent to do as he or she pleases with his children. In a literal sense, a baby is often not even one's own in such societies, but belongs to a lineage, clan, or household—a community—having a real investment in the baby. It is not private enterprise. The almost total absence of the *social regulation* of parent–child relations in our private-enterprise culture is a pivotal environmental factor accounting for Mrs. Portman's behavior.

Shut a young mother up alone in her house and you have immediately one condition for the development of behavior that may be harmful to her child—not only because of the well-known ignorance of baby-care of contemporary mothers, but especiall because, shielded from all public correction, her own problem can run wild in her dealings with her children, and unawares she does them harm. If Mrs. Portman failed to feed her baby at all she would be quickly bundled off to a psychiatric hospital, but she can do many dubious things before that happens. We have seen how she has distorted the feeding *rhythm;* let us now look at the mechanics of feeding.

THE WAR AROUND THE MOUTH

It seems a reasonable assumption that *the more conflict revolves around biological functions like eating, sleeping, crying, and elimination, the greater the tension of the baby,* because the conflict hits him, literally, where he lives. While such conflicts develop in other cultures, no culture other than our contemporary one has transformed all of them into battlegrounds. In our culture eating, sleeping, crying, eliminating, and play have become struggles between parents and children, reflecting the more general cultural orientation toward struggle and survival. Only in the most miserable of families is everything a fight, but in most homes one or another biological function becomes involved in conflict at some time during the first three years of life.[1] In those primitive cultures where struggle does develop between parent and child around a biological function, it tends to be postponed until weaning which, of course, is the commonest, the worst, and often the only function-centered battle in primitive cultures. If you want to train a child for maximal survival-strain, convert biological functions into a battleground. The psycho-biology of this is very simple: since the biological functions are the basic means of survival, if they are made the scene of conflict the organism will tend to remain in a latent state of mobilization for survival struggle. In the Portman home Mrs. Portman made feeding a battle between her and her children, and we shall see the extreme state of mobilization to which she had brought them.

Mrs. Portman was trying to cut down Belle's feedings to the cultural standard of three a day, and, on advice of her pediatrician, was giving solids because the baby could go longer between feedings. Belle detested this, and with great determination mobilized her tiny forces against it, while her mother, with equal determination, overpowered her and shoved the food into her mouth. With little variation from day to day, the feeding pattern was as follows: Standing up to avoid the onslaughts of Pete, Mrs. Portman would hold Belle in her left arm, the baby's right arm

[1] The reader should check this by glancing through some of the excellent material in a book like *Infant and Child in the Culture of Today* by Arnold Gesell and Frances Ilg. Harper & Brothers, 1943.

pressed against Mrs. Portman's abdomen so it could not move, while Mrs. Portman's left hand held down the baby's left arm. Now, with a baby spoon, Mrs. Portman pushed food into Belle's mouth, but Belle pushed it out with her tongue. Mrs. Portman would then scrape it off the baby's face with the spoon and shove it back. For every mouthful that Belle finally swallowed, Mrs. Portman had to do this five or six times. If Belle's arm got loose the baby would wave it in front of the oncoming spoon, but as soon as her mother gave her the bottle the arm would drop. As the shoving continued the baby would try to turn its head away but Mrs. Portman was able to partially control this by stiffening the muscles of her left arm. Meanwhile, the baby's entire body would grow stiff and arched *in a state of maximum counter-mobilization against the invasion.* As soon as the bottle was substituted for the shoving process, the baby relaxed. Let us now look at the record.

5:86:40

I shall dictate first on the 9:30 A.M. feeding. As usual the mother stood in the corner of the kitchen cabinet holding the baby in her left arm. Mrs. Portman remarked to me that, "It would probably be easier to feed her if I could sit down." But, of course, she can't sit down because Pete, true to his usual behavior, clamored and tugged at his mother while she fed the baby. Very often he goes for the baby's feet. Mrs. Portman did as she usually does, shoveling the food into the baby's mouth, putting it in several times more than would ordinarily be necessary for one spoonful because the baby pushes it out so often. Belle also tried to turn her head away, and used her left arm vigorously to try to fend off the food. The interesting thing is that Mrs. Portman did not pinion the baby's arm this time until late in the feeding and then for but a short time. Mrs. Portman said that Belle tugs so hard to get it loose (her arm) that her mother felt she ought not to hold on. Somewhere in here Mrs. Portman said that she was aware that the baby didn't like cereal. I said, "Belle is certainly running a fast interference with that left arm," and Mrs. Portman said, "What do you mean?" When I said, "Well, she seems to be trying to keep the food away," Mrs. Portman indicated that she didn't think so. But when Belle tried to jerk the arm loose as her mother held it, Mrs. Portman said, "I guess she is trying to run interference with that arm." When Mrs. Portman gives the baby the bottle the arm immediately drops.

My remark about the "interference" did not change Mrs. Portman's behavior.

I have been told from time to time by pediatricians and others that they have seen many mothers engage in similar behavior. To this there are several replies: (1) In many cases such forced feeding probably is a contributing factor to later disturbance; (2) Were the observations as detailed and continued as mine? (3) Was the mothers' behavior as extreme as Mrs. Portman's? (4) Were the children observed by the pediatricians upset and starved by disoriented manipulation of the feeding schedule so that forced-feeding was just *one more* pathogenic influence? (5) Compelling a baby to *reject* food when it is supremely mobilized to *take it in,* because its feeding has been delayed and it is famished, makes the forcing particularly bad in Belle's case.

Since Mrs. Portman says she fed Pete in the same way as she feeds Belle, and since at sixteen months she still feeds him and gives him baby food, we have an excellent opportunity to see a later development of an early pattern; to see how an older child solves the problem he has had since infancy. The material I shall take from the record gives us a full-length picture of the characteristic delay and insensitivity, while including also some of the juggling that Pete invented in order to block the attacking spoon. Now, however, he no longer resists solid foods but tries rather to slow the rapid shoveling which often does not give him a chance to swallow.

3:53:26
(This morning, Mrs. Portman, having gotten up at 6:15 to feed Belle, complained repeatedly of fatigue. She said she had been forgetting to take her vitamins. Pete has also been up since 6:15.)

At 7:25, with a great feeling of relief, she grabbed the newspaper and dashed back into bed. As she lifted the paper she uncovered some food and Pete responded to it, but his mother said, "Oh, you can wait until eight o'clock, can't you?" and she got into bed. Pete went into the kitchen and began to play very noisily with the pots. At 7:57 he dragged a huge copper-bottom saucepan in to his mother in the bedroom and she said, with remarkable insight, "What are you bringing me that for, is that a hint?" After his mother made the insightful statement Pete returned to the kitchen and played on the floor with the pots again for about ten minutes. He put them inside of each other and put the cover on the top pot. He also made drinking movements, holding a pot up to his mouth and pretending to drink. He put one of the pot handles into his mouth, dropped the pot covers on the floor, and when he threw one of the pots into the living room his mother cried, "Hey!" He brought the pot in to his mother, and she said, "Hi!" At about eight o'clock Mrs. Portman got up and came into the kitchen to make breakfast for Pete. She was very sleepy so took the wrong cereal, mixing it with milk which she warmed in a cup. Just before this she put Pete in the high chair and he began to scream and bang furiously and then to bite his wrists and the backs of his hands. There was a tremendous amount of this this morning, even after Pete had been fed. He banged, screamed repeatedly, sometimes with anguish in his face and sometimes almost without expression, and a great deal of the time he was biting the backs of his hands. Now, just before she gave him his breakfast Mrs. Portman got his three empty cereal boxes from the closet and placed them on the shelf of the high chair in front of Pete, and proceeded to feed him from behind them. What the child was doing here was interposing these moving boxes between himself and the spoon as his mother tried to feed him. I was amazed at the way she was able to maneuver among all those boxes, and I complimented her on her expertness. She replied, "Well, I'm glad there's something I'm good at."

(Having finished feeding Pete, she left him in the high chair while she and I had breakfast.)

As we ate Pete kept clamoring and screaming. There was a tremendous amount of this. Sometimes his mother imitated him; in general she has gotten hardened to his scream-

ing, it seems to me, and now tends to ridicule it. I think
it is important that she half imitates it and half makes fun
of it, and then tells him it's of no importance—that he
should just go ahead and scream.

I think it is apparent from these events that one can be *trained*
to irrational stubbornness and need not be born that way; that one
can learn to perceive even an act of succor, like feeding, as a
threat; that the irrational minutiae of feeding can transform even
the idea of food into a nightmare, so that what should be a most
inviting situation becomes tangled in a web of irrelevant, terrifying associations. The idea of survival becomes in this way built
nightmarishly into one's flesh and bone, surging at one's very
lips.

Pete not only blocks food with boxes; he holds it in his closed
mouth, covers his mouth with his hands, and even spits food back
into his mother's face.

I have been at pains to emphasize the relation between Mrs.
Portman's confusion and detachment on the one hand, and the
character of her relations with her children on the other, because
I want to show that characteristics that are widespread in our
culture can, when present in extreme form, have seriously pathogenic outcomes: although we can by no means say that Pete and
Belle are mad, they are obviously feeding problems. Meanwhile,
it is important to notice other *ramifying consequences* of Mrs.
Portman's behavior. For example, Pete, in the anguish of his
hunger and rage, turns his anger against himself, biting his own
hands instead of his mother's. It would not be far-fetched to
suggest that when I observed Pete, feeding time already gave
him a feeling of rage, fear, and depression. Twenty years later
he might wonder why every time a meal came on the table he
would become angry and depressed. Nor would his wife understand why this happened, and why he sometimes sat there sucking his wrists. Finally, let us consider the natural history and
the consequences of his screaming. Because his mother regularly
delays Pete's meals he screams and since this upsets his mother,
because she does not know what to do about it, nor even why it
occurs, she ends up humiliating Pete, adding further to his
anguish.

Whether it be the chirp of a nested fledgling, the faint squeak of a new wolf pup, or the cry of a human child, the *cry* of the young of warmblooded animals is one of the fundamental biological functions of organisms from birds to man. Readily learned by females in lower animals, direct and adequate maternal response to the cry is usually fairly well installed by the time of the first litter or brood. In humans, on the other hand, the cry becomes enmeshed in a tangle of culturally determined inhibitions and impulses to action. We have just seen how Pete's screams lead to the uniquely human phenomenon of humiliation; how his cry causes Pete's mother to *withdraw* from him, while in all other warmblooded animals the cry of the young *brings* the mother. Let us therefore explore further the distortion of the warmblooded message in the Portman house.

CRYING

Some of the most critical problems in child development arise as a consequence of the fact that a human infant of a few weeks cannot directly approach its mother, nor readily cling to her. The anthropoid young entangles its fingers in the abundant hair on its mother's abdomen and readily clings there. Only when the differences between a newborn *Homo sapiens* and the newborn lower mammals are put together with the enormous variation in motivation in *Homo sapiens* as parent, do we have the conditions for the creation of a Mrs. Portman; for *she* must make the approaches to her child since it cannot come to her nor cling to her at five weeks. Nor, since she is not an American Indian, can she strap her babe on her back in a cradleboard or bundle it like an Eskimo in her parka.

But other cultural factors are involved. Since Mrs. Portman is a modern American middle-class mother she alone is responsible for the daily care of her children, for there is not, as in many primitive cultures, some relative around to assist her. *Thus there is no extended social responsibility for daily care.* Striking *material considerations* are at issue also. The fact that Belle can be placed in any one of four rooms while her mother is in another separates mother and child, not so much because of the distance between them but because of the fact that the mother is usually doing something in one room that is incompatible with her going into the room where her baby may be at the moment. Each room—kitchen, bedroom, bathroom, and so on—in an American middle-class home tends to be dedicated to particular activities, so that if a person leaves a room his activity there ceases automatically. This is not the case in many primitive and peasant dwellings, for there is only one room and most necessary routines are carried on there and often at the same spot on the floor. Mrs. Portman thus confronts a material paradox faced by millions of American mothers living under the same high-rising living standard, though, as we shall see, she deals with the problem in her idiosyncratic way. In each room Mrs. Portman has to manipulate different material objects. In the kitchen, for example, are the stove, the automatic washer and dryer, and the radio. As a matter of fact, most of the time when Belle cries her mother is busy manipulating something in the kitchen. Thus the high-rising living standard places a mother squarely between her baby and her possessions; places the baby squarely between her mother and her mother's possessions; places the possessions squarely between the mother and the baby. Let us then look at the tug Mrs. Portman's wall-to-wall carpeting exerts on the maternal tie.

5:95:36

Now when Mrs. Portman picked Belle out of the carriage and changed her the baby kept on crying in a paroxysmal way[1] for a long time. After each scream she would suck in her breath with a spasmodic, hiccough-like sound, and she kept this up for a very long time, making her mother anxious. Mrs. Portman, however, left the baby outside in the carriage in order to vacuum the rug. She apologized to the baby for leaving her there, but, she said, she had to vacuum the rug. All the time Mrs. Portman was vacuuming, the baby was crying. Belle cried for twenty minutes until Mrs. Portman finished. Then she went to her, saying, "I can't stand it. Okay, you're the winner—Belle's the winner."

---

[1] Babies cry in three stages: (1) light complaining or *whimpering;* (2) full-scale crying; (3) extreme or paroxysmal crying, in which there is a sharp, gasping intake of air after each vocalization. Mrs. Portman often responded only to Belle's paroxysmal cries.

In view of the introduction to this section, the record speaks very much for itself. Something else may be added, however. A living room rug is not merely a piece of furniture; as a component of the standard of living it is expressive of phantom selfhood, internalized by Mrs. Portman and tens of millions of other Americans. Mrs. Portman is, perhaps, extreme in that she permitted observance of the carpet ritual to take precedence over paroxysmal crying. In Veblen's terms, Mrs. Portman is an exponent of conspicuous consumption engaged in the ceremonial validation of the family's status, and she let this need to affirm status interpose itself between herself and her baby. It is, perhaps, in her inability to make the decision in favor of the baby and against the rug that we see Mrs. Portman's unique lethal variant of the culture pattern.

There is one more point to be underscored—the fact that Mrs. Portman sees responding to Belle's crying as capitulation to the baby. If a mother experiences her own positive response to her child's cry as a defeat, it is by that token also a humiliation for her. Mrs. Portman's calling Belle "The Boss" therefore is something more than a tender mother's harried but joking acknowledgment that she is bound by the new life. In that context also her anger with Pete's screaming is not only an expression of irritation with herself and with the mere persistence of the noise, but a reaction to the requirement that she surrender. Let us have a second look at Pete's crying.

RETREAT FROM CRISIS

If one is alienated from one's Self, so that one is inwardly roleless, and estranged from others, so that it makes no difference whether one withdraws or mixes with them, then one lets others define one's role, for whatever one does, it is all the same. One is a stranger to one's self and estranged from others. Furthermore, since decisions are difficult for an alienated person, it gives some orientation to existence to have others tell one what to do. The only condition to be laid down is that the role-definers not be persistent to the point of irritation. Mrs. Portman is alienated from her children and from herself, and she reacts by drawing into a shell from which she is dragged by Pete, who, in his own extremity, forces his mother into maternal gestures.

I have pointed out that Mrs. Portman's solicitude never failed when Pete cried. She would go in to him, pick him up, kiss him, try to divine what he wanted, give him something. Though it is true she sought him thus only when he cried, he at least got that from her. But when he screamed his mother withdrew, even though these were his times of greatest anguish. Sometimes his screams angered her to the point where she slapped him; often she humiliated him; sometimes she seemed merely to dissociate, retreating into a shell. Once she asked me whether it would be all right to slap him on the mouth to silence him, but I did not answer. These maternal retreats are the most dramatic events in the Portman house, and illustrate the fact that a person like Mrs. Portman, certainly through no fault of her own, cannot tolerate strong feeling, with its attendant drama. She is simply unequal to crisis; to have to face it is unendurable. Being "spoiled" as a child—combined with whatever else happened in *her* childhood —has not equipped Mrs. Portman to deal with the intense, emotional suffering of babies. Let us now look at two instances of *retreat from crisis.*

3:71:1

I returned at 4:45 P.M., to find Marilyn Muntz in the house. Marilyn is a vivid, "outgoing," intelligent, intrusive type of woman, often considered "warm." She says that when she and her husband were courting she could never get a rise out of him, so she used all kinds of devices, like threatening to break off, for example, just to get a response. (A "response-hungry" dame!) Well, the main point is that when I extended to Pete the little teddy bear I had brought him, she immediately snatched it out of my hand and began to play with Pete, using the bear in a very vigorous, almost violent, very vivid and very amusing way. She kept it up for a long time and he was delighted. Suddenly she had to leave, and Pete got very upset, screaming, crying, and pointing to the door where she had left.

(Before I go on with the story I have to mention Mrs. Portman's response to my remarks on the danger of involving children too deeply in play when you know you have to leave.)

She said, "I do the same thing to her children. I suppose she's getting back at me for what I do to her children when I'm at her house." Well, at any rate, after Marilyn left, Pete just stood there and screamed, while his mother looked detached and even dissociated. Pete screamed, his face anguished, his fists clenched, obviously in terrible pain. Several times she made seconds-long attempts to interest herself in interesting him in some distraction. She tried weakly to play with him as Marilyn had done. She sang with him; she got his toy telephone and talked with him. She sounded hollow and distant and her efforts were always very short-lived; she preferred to talk to me. At last she went into the kitchen to call her husband, but Pete hung around her, screaming. Once off the phone she took him into the living room and sang songs with him, beating time holding his arm, and he started to smile and quieted down. She was holding him close on her lap.

Mrs. Portman simply does not now have the emotional resources to cope with primordial anguish, and when her baby forces it upon her she seems to experience a kind of emotional panic. As she flees inward, casting up desperate defenses behind, she appears bored, cold, and insincere—"just not there"; what we see from the *outside* is a frozen, aloof attitude. As Pete stands there screaming, his mother can only be detached, so that as she plays with him her voice sounds icy with ennui. At last she is able to take him on her terms—after having left him for awhile. But Pete's position as the defenseless-one-in-anguish, who is met by the indifference of his mother, is humiliating: he has cast himself emotionally upon her only to be treated coldly. Her detachment, however, is not complete or final: his continued crying at last and at least brings *something*, and this *expectation* of something—this "reward"—is the pellet of comfort which, over and over again, will cause him to place himself in a similar position. Again and again when he presses the lever of anguish he will receive a pellet of comfort. In this way Pete is learning to place himself in what *we* observe to be a humiliating position, without his or his mother's knowing it.

All of us, I am sure, know people who seem to put themselves repeatedly in a position to be humiliated. Such experiences as Pete's enable us to understand how a child *learns* to "like" humiliation and then, in later life, continues to put himself in a position to be humiliated. As a baby such a child understands nothing of humiliation, except, perhaps, that that particular type of *situation* gets him some "reward"—a bit of comfort, a kiss, or a cookie. After awhile seeking that kind of situation becomes automatic, a "habit." Later, much later, perhaps, such a child learns that to get rewards in this way is to be looked down on—that contempt for him is always implied by whoever rewards him and that he has to pay in *self*-contempt for the rewards he gets through assuming the humiliated position. Yet by that time it is too late to change; all such a person knows is that he is driven repeatedly to seek the "pleasure" of humiliation, and that having obtained it he experiences a frightful mixture of satisfaction and inner degredation. Thus, the unbelievable state of learning to like humiliation is nourished by the hungry swallowing of pellets of comfort; and if one does not take them, one has nothing.

When one visits a family for a week one has a chance to see not only how a parent deals directly with his children, but also how he reacts when outsiders intervene. This is often more revealing than the round of daily activities in the family.

One day I went with Mrs. Portman to get Pete a haircut.

5:107:30

When the barber asked Mrs. Portman how she wanted the hair cut she turned and asked me, but I gave no opinion. The barber kept asking if she wanted a crewcut. She looked at me, but I said nothing. A second barber came over and said it would be good for Pete to have his hair cut very short in back and a little bit long in front. She looked at me and I said nothing, so she said okay to the barber. Pete sat quietly enough in the chair while they put the little piece of paper around his neck and the big sheet around his body. But as soon as the barber approached him with the vibrating electric clipper Pete began to cry and tried to get out of the chair. One barber was not enough to hold him, so the other held Pete's head while the first clipped the hair. All the time the child was crying wildly with fear and trying to escape.

During the entire operation this continued—the two men holding Pete and the child crying pitifully. Mrs. Portman looked on with expressionless face. Her major concern was whether his hair would be the right length. As she talked to me about this she smiled and laughed, giving no sign that she was disturbed by what was happening to Pete. When it was all over she said she thought the haircut was good, but made no comment about Pete's crying or about the men holding him down. Then Mrs. Portman asked me to drive over to the shopping center so she could buy some rubber pants for Pete. So I drove over and she got out and left me alone in the car with Pete. Actually he had not completely stopped crying as we left the barber shop. Perhaps I should say that he had stopped, but that you still had the feeling he had not been "cried out." So as soon as she got out of the car he began to cry again and continued until his mother came back.

This is another example of retreat from crisis—when Pete needed his mother most she simply was not there. She did not go up to him and hold his hand, or say to him, "It's all right darling, Mummie is here and they won't hurt you," nor did she comfort Pete after it was all over. Mrs. Portman gave no sign that she was at all moved by what her child was going through.

6:115:34

In order to get a clearer idea of Mrs. Portman's reaction to yesterday's barber shop episode, I said to her today, "They sure had to hold him down yesterday." And she replied, "That was mild. Some of them hold their breath. Some of them kick the barber, and always are careful to kick them in the groin. You feel like you've been through the wringer after a thing like that. It seems that women can take that sort of thing better than men."

Here Mrs. Portman is saying, "These dangerous children hurt barbers. They make it so difficult for barbers that after watching what babies do to them you feel as if you've been through it yourself—all wrung out." Such *inversion of the actor* suggests a new interpretation of Mrs. Portman's frozen response to Pete after the teddy bear incident, for it now seems that her attitude toward Pete's tantrum may have been that her son had no feeling for her; that he was trying to lord it over her, trying to extort a response. At any rate, the more withdrawn a person is from others the less he is able to perceive who is actor and who is acted on; the less he is able to understand who is doing what to whom. This is a *loss of the transitive sense*.

PATHOGENIC METAMORPHOSIS

Extreme detachment from others is one possible interpretation of Mrs. Portman in the barber shop. Another is that unconsciously she feels Pete is a kind of monster. We can readily understand that a mother with few emotional resources might come to feel that her child's emotional needs are a monstrous drain on her, becoming ever more terrifying as the child, gradually discovering that there is little to be had, intensifies its demands, and the mother defends herself by becoming more and more detached, and even angry and downright humiliating.

I have called the process of converting a child mentally into something else, whether it be a monster or a mere nonentity, *pathogenic metamorphosis*.[1] Mrs. Portman called Pete "a human garbage pail"; she said to him, "you smell, you stink"; she kept the garbage bag and refuse newspapers on his high chair when he was not in it; she called him Mr. Magoo,[2] and never used his right name. Thus he was a stinking monster, a nonentity, a buffoon. By secondary transformation, she had unconsciously changed the monster that might exhaust or devour her into a mere garbage pail, an obese, half-blind Mr. Magoo, a nameless nothing. Once he is magically degraded, even further detachment from Pete is legitimate, for who could love a monster, a nonentity, a buffoon?

Let us turn again to Mr. Portman. Since he wasn't around much there is not a great deal to say about how he treats his

[1] See J. Henry, L'observation naturaliste des familles d'enfants psychotiques, in *La psychiatrie de l'enfant,* 1961. Vol. IV, Paris.

[2] Mr. Magoo is an animated cartoon character with an enormous belly and toothpick legs. He is half-blind and his goings-on are simply hilarious.

children. Continuing the pattern he followed with Mimi, he rarely went near Belle and never asked about her, but he liked to keep Pete beside him at the table and played with the child before leaving for work in the morning and at night when he came home. With the goal of making Pete tough and athletic, his play was always more or less of a rough-house: Mr. Portman would growl (like a monster!) and roll and heave Pete around. Sometimes he would give the child a kind of tigerish, devouring kiss with yawning mouth. Extracts from the record follow:

2:48:1

Stretched out in the big leather chair in the living room, with Pete on top of him, Mr. Portman "ate Pete up," opening his mouth wide and pressing it against the child's face. Pete loved it. Then Mr. Portman played a little ball with him. Next he swung him around like a dumbbell, like a bar-bell, and like a pendulum. Mr. Portman rolled Pete up on his own (Mr. Portman's) back and, on all fours, rode Pete around. Then he rolled Pete over on Pete's back, held him tight, and rubbed his fist hard into the child's belly several times. He exercised Pete's legs; he crawled on all fours and growled fiercely at him. It went on and on and the child loved it, got terrifically excited, smiled and laughed. It was obvious that Mr. Portman was intentionally giving the child a work-out, toughening him, etc. Mr. Portman said to me that one must be careful with Pete because he is so big for his age people expect him to behave like a three-year-old.

3:62:10

Before Mr. Portman left this morning he was not so rushed that he did not have time to punch Pete twice in the belly. This was too much for Pete, who, though he smiled, went away from his father.

6:116:3

This morning at 7:10 I went into the living room where Mr. Portman was playing with Pete. He held him on his lap; he crawled around on the floor with him. He growled at him; he made playful biting movements at his arm, putting the child's arm in his mouth. He held him on his lap. Pete en-

joyed this very much, as evidenced by his smiling and coo-
ing.

The difference between Pete's experiences with his mother and
father could hardly be more dramatic: joyless (funless), detached
acquiescence alternating in the mother with icy boredom and
humiliation; intense, interested bodily collision in the relations
between imp-of-fun father and son. Here roughness and toughness do the work of love: Mr. Portman expresses his love for
his son through throwing him around, punching him in the belly,
and imitating a devouring animal. Pete cannot fail, therefore, to
associate love with physical violence: to love a person is to throw
him around, wallop him, and symbolically chew him up—in
other words, to have fun. Pete tries a baby version of this on
Elaine, his little playmate next door. Thus the toughness-love-
violence combination, so common in our movies, is here built
into the child's flesh and bone through the basic biological mam-
malian function of play. My impression of Mr. Portman was that
only through violent play could this rather withdrawn man bring
himself into contact with Pete. But he is not interested merely in
enjoying and having fun with his son; he wants also, he says, to
toughen him, strengthen him, make him a man. So, while
father fires him, mother freezes him, and Pete is caught in the
cultural paradoxes expressed through his parents.

Mr. Portman's roughhousing probably makes Pete more difficult for his mother to handle; and Mr. Portman's coolness to her
contrasts so with his involvement in Pete that she might take
out her resentment on the child. Thus emotional illness is the
result of what is done to the child by his parents, motivated by
their relationship to each other; and, if the child does not become
psychotic very early, the outcome of its experiences with its
parents is heavily affected for health or illness by school and
play group.

When Pete is a little bigger he will probably have toy pistols
and cowboy chaps; his father will be proud, when Pete is about
eight years old, to buy him his first real football togs. His toy
box, mostly a collection of odds and ends now, will probably
sprout soldiers, tanks, and artillery, and he may have a toy
missile that actually goes off. As he matures he will enjoy guns,

prize fights, football, hockey, Western movies, movies of gangsters and war, and stories of murder and robbery in the "funnies." So he will make his contribution to the gross national product. *Violence is a natural resource.* More valuable than the iron of Mesabi (which is nearly exhausted) or lead and zinc (which are drugs on the market), violence is inexhaustible and constantly increases in price—a better investment by far than diamonds!

Should Pete and Belle turn out to be badly disturbed children, it will not be *only* because their mother made them ravenous by delaying and mixing up their schedules and then shoved the food into their mouths; or *only* because she humiliated them; or *only* because she played with them while hating it. Nor would their sickness be due *only* to the fact that she was emotionally absent when needed most; or *only* to the fact that in general she was a rather confused sort of woman. And so on. Madness or mere wretchedness are never due to one factor alone.[1] As a matter of fact, much of what we have seen Mrs. Portman do to her children can be seen in exotic cultures also, where, however, the children are not psychotic. But we never see it *all* wreaked on *one* child in the *same* culture. Emotional illness, particularly psychosis, is usually the result of violation of the organism in many ways—particularly of the basic biological functions.

SUMMARY OF THE PORTMAN CASE

I do not know whether Belle and Pete will become psychotic, but both of them are already serious feeding problems, and the anguished rages of Pete are warning signs. It is impossible to foresee the swiftly ramifying malignant consequences of seemingly minor quirks in "nice" parents. Coming together in *lethal* form in Mr. and Mrs. Portman, widespread American personality characteristics such as shallowness of involvement, confusion

---

[1] There is probably one exception to this, for it is likely that complete isolation of the child during the first year of life, so that it sees an adult only when cleaned or fed, is probably *sufficient* to create infantile autism of one type.

and vagueness, a tendency to read life off in terms of a dominance–submission struggle, a tendency to sacrifice tenderness to strength, and a tendency to humiliate others, have produced a dreadful, unplanned and unintended but nevertheless pathogenic entanglement of parents and children that has the quality of destiny and tragedy. In this state, isolated from public view, husband, wife, and children live out their secret misery. Babies are private enterprise in Western culture and so are misery and dissolution.

We have seen that in unpredictable ways a disoriented, confused mother has lost her way in time, and that this, together with her lack of connectedness to her children and her determination to dominate, have created a great "War Around the Mouth" that has converted her infant, who yet fights with feeble weapons, into a feeding problem, and her older child, who fights now with more ingenious and stronger ones, into a stubborn juggler. By pressure on her babies' fundamental biological apparatus she has mobilized them for pathologically maximal resistance to threats to their survival. Thus time, feeding, crying, and play have become subject to complex, pathogenically extreme motivations rooted ultimately in the cultural configuration.

Of course, Mrs. Portman does not accomplish all this without assistance from her husband who, while providing more than adequate financial support, seriously weakens his role as husband and father through emotional withdrawal and simple physical absence from the home. At the same time his violent but brief affectionate encounters with Pete must leave the child hungry for his return and an even more difficult problem for the mother.

Mrs. Portman, meanwhile, has so little capacity for involvement, so little empathy for an immature organism, that she engages more in the mechanical operations of motherhood than in rich expressions of it. Driven to attempts to extract from his harassed mother more than she has to give, Pete merely forces her deeper into her shell—into insincere demonstrations and massive withdrawal—when he needs her most. Alienated from herself and others, when crisis strikes Pete's mother seems sometimes unable to tell who is suffering—Pete, herself, or the person who hurt him. Finally, in order to defend herself more, in order to extricate herself further from her predicament, she converts Pete, in fantasy, into a monster and then into a nothing. This is part of her *delusion of extrication*.

Thus emotional disorder in children is the product of underlying, culturally determined psychological conditions, different in all parents, but ramifying hideously into a multitude of behaviors and feelings, until the entire psychic apparatus of the child is invaded by the cancer of emotional illness.[1]

These matters will be examined further in the following section on the Ross family.

THE ROSSES

Ancestor worship puts in every man's mind the certainty that when he is dead people will revere him; and the kinship systems of primitive people, with their compelling social relationships, guarantee that one will never be deserted as long as one lives. Contemporary man suffers from the certainty that when dead *he will mean nothing to everybody*, and from the anxiety that even while alive he may come to *mean nothing to anybody*. For this reason he allocates his emotional resources to those to whom he wants to mean something, and he is torn between his commitments to them and the demands of those who want to be significant in his life but who are not important to him. In our society the absence of formal regulation of mutual commitment turns friendship, love, and parenthood into a jungle of competing claims. With *abundant emotional resources*, one can be relatively sure of a personal community, for one has much with which to bind other people; otherwise, it is difficult, for then one is emotionally stingy and every heartbeat is a major investment. In the Ross family we have a configuration of *emotional and pecuniary parsimony*, a massive *im-*

---

[1] While clinical theory and practice assume the existence of an "x," some constitutional factor in emotional disorder, it is only the die-hard genetic determinists who ignore the crucial importance of environmental contributions. The assumption of an environment–constitution transactional system is simply good biological theory.

poverishment of life, particularly that of four-year-old Georgie, who calls himself "Georgie nobody."

I stayed a week in the Ross home, sharing a room with Georgie and sleeping in the bed once occupied by Joseph, the psychotic older brother, now in an institution. Though because of a long week-end I had an unusual opportunity to be with the family, I spent much more time alone with Mrs. Ross than with her husband because he was away week-days at the office.

Lucy Ross is intellectual. She is a liberal, reads best-sellers, and has a broad interest in religion, education, and music. On the other hand she listens only to popular music on the radio and is devoted to bridge. She helps support the family by teaching part-time and working part-time for her husband. Whereas Mrs. Portman was a "spoiled child" and "had everything," Mrs. Ross was thrust aside as a child and had nothing. Through Mrs. Ross's feeling toward life runs a deep current of disappointment: "We wanted filet mignon," she says, "and we ended up with hot dogs."

Having male children was an "obsession" with Mrs. Kvorak, Mrs. Ross's mother, who pushed her daughter aside when sons were born; and when Daniel, the older son, died, she would not speak to her daughter. Mrs. Kvorak was found hemorrhaging on Daniel's grave when Lucy was still a child, and it was Lucy who later saved her from suicide by turning off the gas. When Mrs. Kvorak gave birth to Ben, the second son, Lucy was ignored in favor of this beautiful and talented boy. The claims of maleness were too strong, so Lucy starved on the limited and lopsided emotional resources of her mother.

At thirty Mrs. Ross is a pretty woman, but she says her mother is beautiful. Her father, though a man of some education, was never able to get work at anything but common labor on coming to America; and though he is sensitive and scholarly, he is a disappointment to his dominating wife who belittled and finally badgered to death his intellectual activities—writing that was never published and discussion groups with people of his own low status. Mr. and Mrs. Kvorak controlled their children through psychosomatic symptoms: the father would vomit "at the sight of a button" and the mother would get diarrhea.

But Mrs. Ross admires her father and used to side with him and Ben against her mother.

The Kvorak family was hard hit by the Great Depression and, says Mrs. Ross, she has been dependent on social agencies most of her life. Thus the socioeconomic system has almost stood on its head for Mrs. Ross. She has a long history of emotional and material deprivation; and if she feels, as I shall show, that she will get only the garbage of life, she comes by that feeling by birthright. All of this underscores the difference between her and Mrs. Portman.

Deprivation has continued for Mrs. Ross into the present, for though her husband, in contrast to her father, earns a good income, the cost of keeping Joseph in a psychiatric hospital is so high that they have big debts and, in addition, have become dependent for a portion of the cost on a private charitable agency. Meanwhile, the Rosses live in a typical, well-kept, contemporary middle-class suburban community, their nice-looking little house surrounded by a small carpet of yard overflowing into the yards and affairs of their neighbors. The garden of the Ross family, however, is planted with the flowers and shrubs their neighbors have thrown away. Living in such a neighborhood the Rosses can maintain the appearance so necessary to Mr. Ross's business, his status as officer in one of the national businessmen's clubs and pillar of the church. Hardly anyone knows that his garden was scavenged by his wife—and the ones that know don't count much.

Thus Mrs. Ross has long been under degrading economic pressure and, like many in contemporary culture, has wanted the "better things of life" as defined by the high-rising living standard, but has had to settle for clothes bought degradingly at rummage sales, for garbage, leavings, and cast-offs. Masking humiliation, meanwhile, stands the little house. Many of the extreme feelings Mrs. Ross has about food have to be seen in terms of her lifelong but losing battle to preserve economic and psychic integrity. Her fear of social workers and agencies, and her excrutiating sensation of being treated like a being without personality are related to the callousness of the eleemosynary institutions she knows so well. Her long-standing depression has, nowadays, a further source in Joseph's psychosis and removal from the home, and his memory absorbs much of her meager personality reserves.

Mrs. Ross's life is punctuated by little triumphs, like beating a traffic ticket; with agonies of small suspense, like the fear of being discovered in a rummage-sale dress by an acquaintance; with minor feelings of entrapment, as when her butcher tries to get her to buy more meat; and with woeful feelings of personality dissection, as when she goes to the psychiatric clinic and is "stared at" by the clerks. Childhood experiences, financial insecurity, and the realization that she did the wrong things with Joseph make her a person with little feeling of autonomy who says she is unsure of herself. Indeed, to Mrs. Ross to be "carefree" means literally merely to be able *to think* of the time, before Joseph's illness and departure, when she was sure that her way of bringing up a child was right. Now she feels "on the outside looking in" when she is with other mothers.

Whereas Mr. Kvorak is quiet, sensitive, financially unsuccessful, and dominated by an acidulous wife, Mr. Ross is a determined success, resolved not to let a woman get the upper hand. Intelligent, responsible in an economic sense, often pleasant, he is also a man of contained rage, indifferent to Georgie, often sullenly uncooperative and not up to many simple household chores—a child rather than a father in the home. He resents his wife's cleverness and his anger gathers at the slightest sign that she might somehow diminish him. The effort to neutralize such an explosive mixture is very taxing on Mrs. Ross.

Joseph was still around when Georgie was born; his bed was still in Georgie's room when I was there and that is where I slept. Georgie's birth was a depleting experience for his mother, for he was born after several miscarriages and a stillbirth. When I saw him he was a skinny, sad, and cross-eyed little four-year-old, and he walked around constantly sucking his thumb and holding his penis, often doing both at the same time. He was hard to understand because his articulation was muddled, and he was often unintelligible to his father though not to his mother or to me. He had some tendency to act up, particularly when he was being dressed, but on the whole he was remarkably acquiescent with his parents. On the other hand, he liked to give orders to kids his own age and his mother was worried

about this. She told me not to let him order me around, because
then he would try to lord it over her.

Considering Mrs. Kvorak's attitude toward boys and the fact
that Mrs. Ross hated her brother Ben, one might expect Lucy
to be harsh with Georgie, but although she was harsh with
Joseph, she was not with Georgie. Her attitude toward him
was one of gently sustained distance, fluctuating in long, slow
waves from rather lively, almost warm interest, through anxious,
tender, but rather remote solicitude when Georgie was sick,
to abstracted caressing, and finally, to an occasional bizarre
punishment. Through Mrs. Ross's relations with Georgie ran
her pervasive depression, and though she was reasonably protective, I felt that she discerned Georgie through a mist, dimly,
and that he was like an intruder in her life. Her feeling for
Georgie was like a Maine island summer that is neither cold
nor warm, and periods of sunshine are interrupted by fog. One
must be prepared for many and ambiguous weathers, and one
can never tell when the fog will come, or if a day that starts
hot and bright will not soon be cold and dim. Though on a
Maine island there are days when the sun is unmuddied by fog,
this seems never to be true between Mrs. Ross and Georgie. It
cannot be, for Mrs. Ross is in anxious and guilty mourning for
Joseph and preoccupied with managing her husband; and she
never recovered from being pushed aside.

Obviously *knowledge* and *intellect* are important in the Ross
family. Indeed, one of Mrs. Ross's regrets is that she pushed
Joseph too much in this respect. The struggle for *dominance*,
to which I have referred previously, might naturally be expected in the Ross household, not only in view of Mr. Ross's
drive, but also in consideration of the fact that Mrs. Ross,
given her early background, must have a strong inherent contempt for males. It was Joseph and Georgie's bad luck to
be born to a woman whose childhood experience included
an ineffectual father, and two brothers vastly favored above
herself by a domineering mother. *Responsibility* is lopsided
in the household, for as far as Mr. Ross is concerned it
seems to mean largely financial responsibility; as for his wife,
she seizes on one central idea in a rather obsessive way—her
husband's capacity to shoulder the responsibility for taking care

of Joseph. Like most people the Rosses value social *status*, and their sense of not being treated as *equals* by social agencies is very painful. Finally, living in an era of impulse release and fun the Rosses, while yearning for the *good things of life*, are compelled to be *parsimonious*. Thus, the Rosses are beset by value paradoxes, and whereas for many people drives and values open a way to a decent life, for the Rosses they are a trap. One might say that *in a pathological family the value system of the culture is a deadfall.*

FOOD AND THE SELF

Georgie lives in an atmosphere of material and emotional constriction, where emotional and material resources seem to be sucked up and held back, and where food seems to be relinquished to him rather than given. Let us start the study of the record with observations on food.

No matter how miserable, there is scarcely a culture where people have not managed to work out a distinction between foods of high and foods of low status, and where food does not become associated with the Self image. Perhaps the best-known examples of this come from the area of the rice "psychosis" (obsessive preoccupation with rice)—South China, Japan, the Philippines, and much of southeast Asia. Wherever this obsession prevails, status[1] is measured by the amount of rice in the diet, and those who cannot afford it daydream about it, while their daily reality is the degrading sweet potato. On the other hand, before the Communist revolution, the populations of some villages in North China were divided into status classes depending on the amount of wheat in the diet, for in more northern China wheat, not rice, was the prestige food. In such places one absorbs a Self-image with his food; with every mouthful he takes the peasant is reminded of who he is—of where he stands on the status ladder. Mrs. Ross's melancholy, "We wanted filet mignon and we ended up with hot dogs," is not so much a re-

[1] The reader can gain some appreciation of the class significance of this from reading Junichiro Tanizaki's novel of the Japanese upper middle class, *The Makioka Sisters.* In it all the characters receive weekly injections of vitamin B against beri-beri, the characteristic illness of people depending too much on polished rice.

flection on what is intrinsically good in food, as a comment on her feelings of self-depreciation.

In all cultures the values and conventions associated with food are as much a part of eating as the food itself. In contemporary America, for example, food should be fresh and abundant, and it must be served according to a certain etiquette. Large quantities of it should be pressed repeatedly on guests, and it should always be of the best quality. If food is not abundant, if one has constantly to eat leftovers, and if etiquette is repeatedly violated, one feels spiritually diminished, because of the significance to the Self of such violations of the food value system. Above all, food must be wasted, for to hoard it, to use up the last speck, is a violation of the value of the inherent graciousness of waste. Since to waste no food implies a massive distortion of the Self, for a socially mobile person to waste nothing is degrading.

All of these violations occurred in the Ross household. To these must be added Mrs. Ross's peculiarity of favoring rotten produce, for in my trips to market with her I never saw her select really sound fruit or vegetables. In the summary of the Ross family I remarked that in view of Mrs. Ross's lifelong depression, her anxiety, guilt, and depression over Joseph, and her need to use great circumspection and effort to contain her husband, she had only what was left over of herself to give to Georgie. In such a context, it seems to me, one should not overlook the possible symbolic significance of the fact that in the week I spent at the Rosses only one major dish was prepared from fresh food, while all the rest were leftovers, and that in front of me her husband called her "Leftover wife." The obvious significance of all this can only be that she had only the leftovers of her Self to give.

And now for the record.

Left-overs

2:30:27

Because his church organization buys meat from a certain wholesale butcher, Mr. Ross is able to get meat and frankfurters wholesale. Mrs. Ross mentioned a beef brisket that she had gotten there wholesale, saying she cannot buy it retail because the price is so high. It was this that served as the basis for our meals. Last night we had it barbecued and today we had it left over and barbecued in sandwiches, together with canned beans.

4:58:4

Lunch was leftover salmon salad, leftover wax-bean salad, bread, butter, and milk.

4:73:1

When Mrs. Ross said we were going to have leftover salmon and leftover beans for lunch, Mr. Ross said, "Leftover wife."

6:121:3

Mrs. Ross said she was going to make over the made-over leftovers, and she told me not to look at what she was doing. She took some leftover spinach and mixed it up with cracker meal, cream, and egg, and fried it in pattys. It didn't taste bad, but after all, one has to eat anyway.

It cannot have escaped the good housekeepers among my readers that it isn't very economical to add cream, egg, and cracker meal to old spinach, and that there are much better ways to save money than by buying canned salmon (even tuna fish is cheaper). At a somewhat different level: Does one save, in the long run, by giving exhausted spinach to a skinny four-year-old?

Parsimoniousness and Pathogenic Democracy. Mrs. Ross hated to throw anything away, and she would use any human being around for a kind of food bank. I quickly discovered that an offer of food might be just a way of preventing it from going to waste:

2:29:17

She asked me whether I would like some ice cream, and I said, "Are you going to have some?" and she said, "Well," pointing to the box, "there's no room in the refrigerator for this, and I'm not hungry. I don't want to throw anything

out." I said, "Okay, I'll eat it." At table this evening she
took more bread than she could eat, and so she tried to
get Georgie to eat it, but he would not.

Sometimes I left the table hungry, but that was no problem,
for with a more than adequate expense account,[1] I could always
slip away for a meal or a snack. On weekends and holidays the
Rosses got up late, and Mrs. Ross took advantage of this to put
the whole family on two meals a day, even though it might be
a three-day holiday week-end. I was always awake early,
holiday or no holiday, so that I was famished by the time
breakfast went on the table:

3:46:11

We had scrambled eggs for breakfast, and Mrs. Ross dished
them out in such a way that there was nothing left in the
pan. Since breakfast was quite late I was hungry, and I
left the table hungry.

4:56:20

I did not have enough to eat for lunch today because I
felt that there would not be enough to go around; and
that is the way it turned out. I held off so that the salmon
and the salad would be finished by the Rosses, because
I knew that I could get away to a restaurant and have
something to supplement the meal.

If, as Mrs. Ross says, she likes to take advantage of late
sleeping on holidays to save a meal a day, that might be mere
parsimoniousness; but to put skinny little Georgie, who she
knows is underweight, through the same regimen is pathogenic
stinginess. Meanwhile, the Rosses ate while Georgie slept. They
sometimes had a snack before going to bed, though Georgie
never got even a glass of milk; and one evening, after having
told Georgie that "dessert will be later," they sent him off to
bed with no dessert while they had strawberries and cream.
Mrs. Ross said that Georgie had gained weight since he started
nursery school, where, apparently, they serve an abundant hot
lunch. Since Georgie was skinny when I knew him, he must

---

[1] Of course, I offered to pay for my room and board, but Mrs. Ross would
not accept.

have been a concentration camp case before he enrolled! School was begun on the advice of the agency caring for Joseph.

I can understand that Mrs. Ross, having made up her mind to economize on food, should just prepare a limited amount for each meal, but to treat Georgie with the same even-handedness as she treated the adults is *pathogenic even-handedness.* She served a couple of ounces of citrus fruit and juice every few days, and Georgie got no more than anybody else—even when he was sick. Eggs were a rarity, being kept even-handedly from Georgie just as from the rest of us. Such *pathogenic equality* or *pathogenic symmetry, in which everybody is treated the same, regardless of whether he is sick or well, thin or fat,* derives from a *pathological insensitivity to crucial differences.* It is democracy gone to seed.

Mrs. Ross's even-handedness could, however, be subordinated at times for her husband. The strawberries and other nocturnal snacks are typical.

It is worthwhile spending another few lines on the concept of *pathogenic symmetry,* for most of what has been written about disturbed children dwells on the extent to which they are treated differently from other members of the family. It would appear to me, however, that there is an equal chance of a child's becoming ill because his parents, failing to take account of important conditions, treat the child the same as everybody else.

The Problem of Scale. Emotionally ill people tend to lopsidedness when they should be balanced and to balance when they should be lopsided. They ignore big differences and exaggerate trivia. For example, since he was so thin Georgie should not have been fed in the same way as his parents. In some disturbed people the whole problem of scale or size is unmanageable, so that almost anything can become distorted out of proportion in a phantasmagorical way. Mrs. Ross's brother-in-law's cake is a good example of the exaggeration of a trivium —pathological mountain-making! Let us buy it, study it, watch it grow old, and finally become an item deductible from the Ross income tax!

4:58:6

(Mrs. Ross's brother-in-law was to come to the house, and since he was expected to bring a potential customer for

Mr. Ross, she bought a cake when we went to the bakery. When the brother-in-law could not come the Rosses were left with the problem of how to handle the cake.)

It is interesting that the cake bought three days ago for the brother-in-law is still standing around. Mrs. Ross said to me at one point, "You see how much we like cake." In this connection I am reminded of the fact that she said to me that her husband is getting very heavy, but she thinks he has to eat. When I asked her what she meant by that she said, "Well, some people have to smoke, and some people have to drink, and my husband has to nibble."

6:102:46

(Fifth day of the cake)

Mrs. Ross said this morning, "How are we going to handle the matter of the cake? Can we take it off our income tax?" I said, "Yes, I think you can, because it was going to be used to entertain a customer"; and Mr. Ross said, "Yes, it is a good idea"; and as far as I could see both of them decided that the unused cake would be taken off the income tax. It is interesting that they have just left the cake in the box to quietly become stale.

8:128:47

(Seventh day of the cake)

The cake that was bought seven days ago is still on the kitchen cabinet. It has not been eaten or given away. Why they don't give a piece of it to Georgie at least is very puzzling.

We all make mountains out of mole hills; the only difference between *pathological mountain-making* and the exaggerations of most of us is the size of the mountain and its character. When we say that making a veritable financial incident of this dollar-and-a-quarter cake is bizarre, we arrive at that conclusion by putting together the fact that except for one evening snack with a neighbor, the cake was untouched, that it was not offered to Georgie, and that the Rosses decided to deduct it from their income tax. We take into account also the fact that the Rosses were so overwhelmed by the minuscule cake that they had to resort to the giant machinery of government to reassure themselves. Thus in pathological mountain-making a person is overwhelmed by a *monster trivium* from which he tries to *save himself* by using a *giant power* (like government) that is *bizarrely disproportionate* to the dimensions of the actual threat. Pathological mountain-making is the opposite of pathological even-handedness, for the former makes mountains out of mole hills and the latter makes mole hills of mountains or acts as if they were not there.

Considering the fact that Georgie's problem of underweight is "not there" and that the problem of the cake *is*, we can say that pecuniary considerations have caught the Rosses in their grip, for both the cake incident and the underfeeding of Georgie are related to money, although in an obsessive, irrational, and indirect way. Thus, though we can by no means say that it was "just money" that created the cake incident and the underfeeding of Georgie, the pecuniary structure of our society is a *vehicle* through which the family pathology is expressed. In this, again, the difference between the Rosses and the rest of us is a matter of quality and degree only, for after all, we all act foolishly because of money, are penny-wise and pound-foolish, allocate our money in the wrong ways, become anxious about money when we should not, fail to be provident when we should, et cetera. This *pecuniary syndrome* has simply fallen like a brick wall on the Ross family.

Pathogenic As-ifness. Man-in-culture is a dissembler: he acts as if he likes something when he does not; as if he believes something when he does not; as if he is telling the truth when he is not, et cetera. Americans have the reputation for acting as "sincere" friends when they are not, and advertising is presented as if it were the truth and often it is not. It would not seem far-fetched to propose that psychopathology in a family is directly proportionate to the amount of "as-if behavior" present. In psychopathology not all as-if behavior is of the relatively simple kind I have mentioned. Much of it is due to disorientation. For example, Mrs. Portman seemed to act as if she were on a relatively strict schedule, but she was not; she acted as if it was not Pete who was suffering in the barber shop, but the barber; she talked to her children as if they knew what she was talking about, and so on. Mrs. Ross feeds Georgie as if he needed to lose weight instead of gain, and treated the dollar-and-a-quarter cake as if it were a financial incident. Let me give one more example of this kind of as-ifness.

I had repeatedly suggested to the Rosses that we go out to dinner at the Ford Foundation's expense, so on the holiday week-end Mrs. Ross suggested that we go to a restaurant. After a late breakfast she took us to a very modest place, where we arrived about three in the afternoon.

3:39:2

> When we adults ordered, Georgie said very pathetically "I want my dinner." No dinner was ordered for Georgie because Mrs. Ross was going to share hers with Georgie. So she ordered a rib-steak, which cost, I think, $1.15.[1] It was a very thin sliver of meat, broiled, and she gave some of her meat and potatoes to Georgie. Mr. Ross gave him nothing. The adults each had a salad, which we ate while Georgie sat there eating nothing, but he did not complain. At last, when food was given him from his mother's plate he played with it a little, filling up mostly on bread and butter. Mrs. Ross showed considerable anxiety about his not eating the food she had given him from her plate, and told him that if he was not going to eat it she would take it back. He ate a few pieces and left the rest and she ate what was left over. Meanwhile Mr. Ross and I ate our swiss steak and mashed potatoes. Tea was ordered for Georgie, but even after many spoonfuls of sugar had been put into it he refused to touch it, so his father drank it. I paid the bill and tip.

It is important to note first, that on this day Georgie had only one "meal"—breakfast. The midday "meal" was this one, and at night he had watermelon. That is all.

Although Mrs. Ross knew I was going to pay she acted as if *she* were, ordering one dish for herself and Georgie in order to

---

[1] It is very important that the reader remember what my financial situation was. I repeat that the Rosses had been informed by me that I was well-supplied with funds by the Ford Foundation. When I took the Portmans out to dinner they picked a "high class" restaurant with wonderful food. It is simply a matter of difference in family attitudes toward expenditures.

save money. It is important to note that it was ordered as if it were *hers*—not *theirs*—and it was made clear that she was giving something of hers to the child. Naturally, if he did not eat it, she should take it back and eat it herself. In regard to Mr. Ross, his behavior was no different from that at home: if Georgie is sitting with him at the kitchen table with no food on his dish Mrs. Ross has to tell her husband to serve his son after he has served himself. Usually, however, this is not necessary because Mrs. Ross serves both of them. In the restaurant she was merely serving Georgie—an action for which Mr. Ross has no responsibility just *as if* the meal were being served at home.

Thus the meal in the restaurant is a study in *as-ifness*: everything takes place as if it were something else. Such pathological extremes of as-ifness are merely special phases of the average cultural *as-ifness* we encounter in advertising and elsewhere. One might say that advertising simply exploits the ability of the ordinary citizen to live in an as-if universe. Everybody knows we often act toward people as if we like them when we hate them; as if we trust them when we know they are hypocrites; as if we believe them when we know they are lying, and so on. We are all very much alike; it is only that pathogenic parents are crazier.

Let us examine the restaurant incident further. Since Georgie was not told that his mother would share her food with him, he naturally concluded that he would get nothing. "I want my dinner," he said, anxiously. Meanwhile his parents sat there eating salad, in *pathogenic unawareness*, while Georgie had nothing, though he likes salad. The fact that he got no salad drove home the fact that the meal that his mother and he were to divide was hers, not *theirs*. We come finally to the sharing: How must this have looked to Georgie? His mother, after taking food from her plate and putting it on Georgie's—taking food away from herself to give it to him—threatens to take it back and eat it if he does not. Surely if she was ready to eat it if Georgie did not, he must conclude that when she gave it to him in the first place she was taking the food out of her own mouth. How could Georgie eat his mother's food when she was actually telling him, in a wordless message, "You're taking the food out of my mouth." How then could Georgie eat without either being afraid or feeling guilty for having deprived her? The result was as we have seen: he toyed with the food given him by his mother but ate only bread and butter, until she took the food back. Pushing the matter to its logical conclusion: Georgie and his mother entered into a conspiracy in which, by mutual understanding, she would act as if she were proffering food and he would act as if he did not want it. In this way they could maintain a phantom relationship which, at any rate, was, perhaps, better than none for Georgie, and definitely better than none for Mrs. Ross, who needed to maintain the delusion of motherhood in order to stay alive.

ON BEING A PHANTOM

> *What spurs me on [to kill Caligula] is not ambition but fear, my very reasonable fear of that inhuman vision in which my life means no more than a speck of dust.*[1]

Since Mr. Ross is getting fat while Georgie is skinny, since Mrs. Ross is comfortably rounded though not stout, since Mr. Ross "has to nibble" while Georgie never nibbles or even asks for food between meals, we can say that Georgie *acquiesces* in the family pathology. This acceptance of relative starvation, of acquiescence in the role of a phantom child, is the *thither* side of that conformity which is expected of us in contemporary culture: in order to retain a little, we give up much. Georgie acquiesces in the misrepresentations in his family and in his family's failure to feed him adequately, because he has learned that refusal to acquiesce to a phantom life would be worse than being a phantom. Let us look at a consequence of refusal.

5:82:16

(At dinner Georgie screamed for attention but got none. Then there was no dessert, because Mrs. Ross said it would be eaten "later." But "later" never arrived for Georgie, and he knew that the strawberries that were to be eaten later were in the refrigerator. Georgie was also prevented from

---

[1] Cherea in Act II of *Caligula* by Albert Camus. *Caligula and Three Other Plays*, New York: Alfred A. Knopf, 1958, page 22.

going outside because his mother so enjoys watering flowers that she wants to be alone when she does it. After she returned the following occurred.)

Georgie was sitting in one of the chairs by the window in the living room and his mother tried to hug him, but he drew away, and then took the edge of the curtain and shoved it over her face. At the same time she tried to hug him, but he resisted, and kept rubbing the curtain over her already covered face while she was trying to hug him, until she at last got up and walked away. Then he ran screaming after her, but she did not pick him up. As she left, she said, "Georgie has a way of spoiling my hair."

So she wouldn't even acknowledge that he had affected her inwardly; he had only spoiled her hair. Even when the child seems to cry out, "I will *not be a phantom;* I will not accept the appearance of love for love itself," his mother transforms the anguish into a mere prank—thereby negating it. Meanwhile, even as she distorts the communication, she signals, by walking away and by refusing to pick Georgie up when he runs screaming after her, that she understands it. In response to Georgie's revolt against being treated like a phantom his mother says that he merely ruffled her hair; but she signals by her actions, "Protest too openly and you will be a lonely phantom. Now, at least, you have company, your spectral mother."

After this incident Georgie watched TV while his parents looked at old photographs. Among them were many of Joseph—none of Georgie.

5:83:8

So while Mr. and Mrs. Ross and I were looking at photographs Georgie was watching TV. The general theme of their looking and talking seemed to be "Oh, the good times we used to have!" There were many deep sighs from Mrs. Ross over the photographs of Joseph, particularly when I would say, "What a beautiful child!" She would say, "Oh, he was beautiful," and would sigh very deeply. Meanwhile there was no response from Mr. Ross to any of the photographs of Joseph. The pictures to which he seemed to respond most frequently were those of his wife and sister, of whom he said, she is "well stacked."

Georgie is a phantom in this house because his father is almost unaware of his existence, and because his mother, who has few personality resources to begin with, is engrossed in holding his father and is deeply involved in Joseph. Georgie and his brother are in a state of *phantom sibling rivalry*, for from behind a dark curtain Joseph, though absent, exercises a spectral influence on Georgie; symbolically, he still sleeps in his bed in Georgie's room. Corporeally he is gone, but the air is thick with his presence. Since so much of Mrs. Ross's energies go into saving to maintain Joseph, it would not be far-fetched to surmise that she feels that whatever Georgie eats is taken from his brother, and in this way, from her. Joseph is an open wound in his mother, and every time she serves food she must say to herself, as she inwardly weeps, "I could be giving this to Joseph." Feeding others, all she can give is ambivalence.

Before closing this section it is necessary to talk a little about pathological acquiescence again. Reluctant acquiescence is inherent in the life of *Homo sapiens*, of man-in-culture. Man acquiesces out of love but mostly out of fear. Acquiescence is part of the pattern of dissembling. Terror has been one of the commonest instruments for obtaining acquiescence, for people who have refused to acquiesce have been tortured and put in concentration camps. But there is also a "softer" terror that merely imprisons the soul. Without threat of tangible rack or prison a child can be terrified merely by the implication, conveyed to him through innumerable soundless messages, that if he does not acquiesce in being what his parents want him to be he will be in grave (though unnamed) danger. The difference between ordinary and pathological acquiescence is simply in the extent and quality of the acquiescence demanded, in how much and what kind of renunciation of the self are required. Intuition alone guides us in deciding whether the acquiescence is average or pathological, for we have no objective measures of it. But since Georgie seems to be a kind of phantom child hovering on the fringes of his family, I have called his renunciation of Self—his becoming "Georgie nobody," as he says—*pathological acquiescence.*

I have said also that such pathological acquiescence is the *thither side* of conformity, because it is the ultimate reach of conformity, in that whereas much conformity as we know it is merely socially patterned defect (to use Fromm's expression), pathological acquiescence is a bizarre suicide of the soul. It is, for example, like sawing off one's own head.

In international politics suicidal acquiescence is called *appeasement,* and its fundamental instruments are terror and illusory promises. Whenever suicidal acquiescence occurs frightfulness is presented together with an illusory promise of gratification, in order that the person (or nation) may stifle its sense of humiliation and alienation by presenting the promise to itself in a vivid and satisfying way. One might say that in suicidal acquiescence illusory promises of gratification stand forth in the blinding glare of frightfulness. But it is simple logic (or, rather, the simple logic of the feelings, which is never really simple) that a gratification offered by a wielder of terror must be illusory, for whoever uses terror has no intention of gratifying anything but himself. Whoever intends to be frightful cannot possess the ability to gratify; all he can do is make people enjoy humiliation.

The Rosses do not terrorize Georgie overtly, yet his acquiescence is evident. The fear that has been communicated to Georgie derives partly from impalpable threats of abandonment that manifest themselves in poor feeding, weak maternal interest, and, in the case of Mr. Ross, an almost—but not quite—complete turning away. The satisfactions, such as they are, are the continued, though meager, feeding; the gestures of parental warmth; and above all, his parents' continued *presence.* There are, meanwhile, several more tangible threats in Georgie's background: (1) The disappearance of Joseph. It is interesting that the social agency urged that Joseph's bed remain in Georgie's room, because if the bed were taken away, Georgie might feel that he would go next. (2) The fact that Mrs. Ross is away a good deal of the time teaching or helping her husband in the office, and that during these periods there have been two women who came in to take care of him, but who have since been sent away. (3) Georgie used to spend the afternoons at the Rudigers, friends of the Rosses, and have his supper there. They made such obvious efforts to absorb Georgie into their own family, however, that on the advice of the social agency, Georgie was taken away from them. They "drowned him in love" and insisted that he love them. I was able to see for myself that they still continue these attitudes.

When one speaks to adults of terror they tend to think of it in terms of obvious instruments—air raids, concentration camps, beatings. It is difficult to understand, perhaps, that for a young child fear of abandonment can be an overwhelming terror, freezing him or turning him into waxen acquiescence. Catatonia is the thither side of freezing; waxy flexibility is the thither side of acquiescence. Both are forms of schizophrenic change, well known to us from the literature of psychosis. They are fear manifest, transmuted into bodily tonus and stance; visible expressions of terror without gratification.

Of course, a child does not reason it out—so much acquiescence for so much gratification; so much consent for so much parental presence. But gradually, by feeling his way, he comes to believe that if he acquiesces in the roles and metamorphoses prescribed for him, his parents will not leave him. Perhaps the reality of Georgie's sensation of impending desertion is illustrated best by a dream his mother had, in which she saw him taken away from her forever. The rain was pouring down, and there, in a departing bus, was his little face pressed against the glass. Whether one interprets this dream as a wish fulfillment or as an expression of a real fear that he would be taken away—as the social agency wanted to do—the issue is the same: the persistence in Georgie's life of threats of separation. When one considers the indifference of his father and the abstraction of his mother, what could one expect in the child but a *sensation of impending abandonment?* This is *Georgie's* image of frightfulness. Thus if his mother perceives him through a mist, so does he perceive his parents through a mist of fear.

I have said that suicidal acquiescence carries with it an illusory promise of gratification, but where is the illusory promise in Georgie's case and what is the nature of the suicide? The illusory promise is that his parents will be with him and the suicide is the immolation of his Self. For obviously these are but phantom parents, even as Georgie is a phantom child, and obviously what is dying is Georgie's Self. He is the best witness of this, for he already calls himself, "Georgie nobody."

The Function of Reminiscence. Besides thinking of Georgie as a phantom, I have thought of him also as a visitor who happened to stay for breakfast. What has made me think of him in that way is the fact that he never figured in his parents' reminiscences.

Since memories are a family's folklore, reminiscences about the happier moments of life affirm and stabilize the family, for the recollection of pleasure actualizes past solidarities and mutes whatever threatens the present. When a family is miserable happy reminiscing becomes an idyllic quasi-life, narcotizing pain and lending the appearance of validity to real life. When Roquentin, the miserable hero of Sartre's *Nausea*, discovered that the past did not exist for him, he almost went mad. Previously, Roquentin says, the past to him "was another way of existing" and "each event, when it had played its part, put itself meekly into a box and became an honorary event." When Roquentin made his discovery he was overwhelmed by "an immense sickness," and through the rest of the book we find him insisting that he really does exist.

Up in the attic, in a carton ten times too large for its contents, the past of the Rosses sloshed around, a miscellaneous flotsam of snapshots, certificates, letters, and greeting cards. With or without the box the Rosses spent many hours reminiscing about themselves and Joseph. Since Georgie was never present in these conversations about the past, he naturally could not quite exist in the present: the rituals of recall affirmed the existence of husband, wife, and absent child only. Thus great literature suggests to us "the law of reminiscence": *whoever does not exist in memory does not exist at all.*

The following are excerpts from conversations about the past.

4:56:29

Mrs. Ross was very depressed this morning and talked to me in a very depressed way. But as soon as her husband came home she perked up tremendously, and was really quite gay. One of the things that made her gay was reminiscing about courtship days again. They told, for example, how her husband, in courting her, had to travel along the longest bus line in town. Once, after taking her home, he got on the bus to go home to his own house, but fell asleep in the bus and was not awakened until it reached the end of the line, and when he got another bus he did the same thing all over again at the other end of the line. In reminiscing about their courtship days they were very sweet to each other, and she leaned against him and nuzzled his shoulder.

5:83:24

As we looked at the pictures there were reminiscences of the honeymoon—how wonderful it had been—of trips to Florida, to Wisconsin, and to the beach.

5:85:13

Mrs. Ross was in a mood for reminiscing again. She spoke about her high school prom dress—how she had needed a strapless bra but that the family didn't have the money to buy one. So her mother got an old bathing suit and dismantled it to make a strapless bra. She said to her husband, "I never told you what I was wearing under my prom dress. You never knew what I was wearing under my prom dress." And he said, "At that time I never got under your dress."

6:116:30

They used to dance the "dirty boogie," a very sexy dance, openly until the principal of the high school noticed it and forbade it. I can't get over the extent to which they hark back to their high school days, which were, apparently, among the happiest in their lives.

It is often true that a woman who feels somehow dead inside will marry a violent man because he is the only kind that can make her feel alive and arouse her sexually. I would guess that this was Mr. Ross's attraction for his wife. Since high school and courting days were very sensual they are still tremendously important to the Rosses, and repeated rekindling through reminiscing keeps the fires burning. The tragedy of Joseph and the gradual improverishment of their lives make it difficult for them to find periods to reminisce about much except courtship and the first years of marriage. As Freud once put it, "they are marooned in time" by the tragedy of their lives. But they are also compelled to make the past exist; it is a powerful life substance, a kind of lymph, which they share between them, and from which Mrs. Ross draws vitality even as she gives it.

In addition to tales of happier days there are stories in which Mr. Ross is a family culture hero. Narration of these gives him stature and validates his masculinity. In addition to being a pecuniary hero, he is also like Greatheart in *Pilgrim's Progress*, holding off the lions and the giants grim that would harm the family. Sometimes Mrs. Ross told me these tales as we chatted, sometimes she and her husband recalled them together, in an exchange of life-stuff. There was a story of how Mr. Ross had personally handled his wife's traffic ticket in court and gotten her off with a suspended sentence; a tale of how he had invigorated the Men's Club at the church; and an account of how he had gone "straight to the top of the company" when his wife had signed a document without reading the fine print. These stories of Perseus and Andromeda and the labors of Hercules replenish family narcissism, a restoration the family sadly needs.

Though it was almost always Mrs. Ross who made the advances to her husband, although she had to watch her every step to prevent him from raging, and although there was one nasty, long-drawn-out quarrel between them while I was there, there was warmth too. Between them and Georgie, however, the ground was cold and poor.

CEREMONIAL IMPOVERISHMENT

In all cultures occasions of *social climax* require emotional demonstrativeness, almost by decree. Arrivals and departures (including birth, which is an arrival, and death, which is a departure) are such occasions. So are initiations, the first word spoken, the first steps taken, birthdays, and even illness, depending on the culture. Social climaxes are ritualized. Sometimes the emotional demonstration itself is a ritual, as when two Kaingáng Indians meet after a long separation and for about half an hour ritualistically deny that they have been angry at each other because of the separation. In other cases, a ritualization seems so much a part of a usual activity that it is recognizable as a ritual only on comparing the activity in one culture with that in another. In our culture a good example is the bath of a middle-class child: the toys, the wash cloth, the fun, the chatter, the splashing, and the final engulfment in the large cocooning towel are not perceived as a ritual until one sees children being bathed in other places.

The biosocial function of social climax is that by compelling social recognition of children it convinces the children they are real. *What convinces* Homo sapiens *that he exists is not that he thinks, but that other people think, that they think of him, and that they express this thought in social relations with him.* In our culture the parent who is close to his child does not need to be compelled to social climax by cultural ordinances, for, as Fromm would say, he likes to do what he is supposed to do. But a withdrawn parent, feeling the compulsive quality of these rules, will often provide the ambiguous ghost of a climax.

In contrast to the social climax is all the rest of the young child's day in our culture, for between kissing on getting up and having fun in the tub and in bed before turning out the light, there are no ritualistic prescriptions, unless the child is going to school. Then, of course, his departure and return are social climaxes too. During the remainder of the day, the parents must create the occasions for warm contact. It will be remembered that Mrs. Portman created none, but left it up to her children to do it by crying. Once infancy is past, the child's cry is not "for attention" but is the expression of the *strong innate need to be reminded that he exists.* A withdrawn person, if he gives any warmth at all, releases it largely on occasions of social climax, whereas one who is really in contact with a child will pour it out not only at social climax, but will also create occasions for warmth. In a withdrawn person, even social climax is distant or ambiguous.

Let us now consider a few examples of social climax in the Ross household.

Separation and Reunion.   Every culture defines separation and reunion in terms of a dramatic plot. In our culture ritualization of the daily departure from and return to the family is probably related to the fact that the family is isolated, so that every time a father comes home from work or a child from school his reception is a thankful, ceremonial reincorporation; and whenever he leaves, it is a kind of anxious severance. For this reason every ordinary person in our culture knows well how to play his role in this drama of wounding and healing, of deprivation and replenishment; and nice people, ordinary people, average folk are expert arrivers and departers, farewell-sayers and welcomers. The arrivals and departures, the farewells and the welcomes of disturbed people are saturated with ambiguities: the welcome is cloying or barren or merely ambiguous, and so with the farewell.

The following is a good example from literature:

> Anny came to open the door in a long black dress. Naturally she did not extend her hand or say hello. I kept my right hand in my coat pocket. To get over the formalities, she said quickly and sulkily, "Come in and sit down wherever you please, except in the chair by the window."[1]

Let me now give an example from a meeting of Georgie and his mother.

6:121:19

I drove Mrs. Ross to the nursery school after five to call for Georgie. He was already in the school station wagon. Apparently they were going to drive him home because Mrs. Ross came so late. When she saw Georgie she did not kiss him at once and he did not try to kiss her, but when he was in the back of my car and she was seated in front with me, she turned around and kissed him.

By placing the seat between herself and Georgie, so that she could not easily touch him, and so that twisting around to kiss him made it uncomfortable, Mrs. Ross expressed the distance between herself and her child even better than she could have with an abstracted air or a far-away look. But other points are at issue here also. Since she arrived very late—so late, indeed, that it was assumed she was not coming and the school was preparing to drive Georgie home—one would expect some indication of anxiety about being late, some apology or explanation

---

[1] From *Nausea* by Jean Paul Sartre.

to Georgie, and a special effort to handle *his* anxiety and disappointment. On the contrary, what we find is that just when *more* demonstrativeness might be expected, there is less of it. This is the phenomenon of *pathogenic unavailability* at critical moments to which I called attention in the relationship between Mrs. Portman and Pete.

Let us look at one more example of a reunion.

6:124:22

When Mr. Ross and I got home Mrs. Ross was sitting on the walk at the side of the house weeding. She looked very depressed, and when Georgie brought to her the toy tank his father had bought him she said, with an abstracted smile, "Oh, that's wonderful." Some time later I saw her kissing and hugging him on his feet, but with a rather distant smile on her face. Georgie played for quite a long time around her, pushing his tank very gently in and around the flowers and earth, often very near her, as she kept weeding.

If we again ask ourselves why Georgie has become so acquiescent, we can see that this is a mother who is always just out of reach, so that it might seem to Georgie that if he does anything to disturb her she may vanish altogether.

Going to bed is a departure, for the child has to leave the adult world for the night. Children's bedtime rituals in our culture ease the transition for adults and the children; they are partly a form of bribery to coerce the child into giving up the adults, partly a last warm contact for the parent. They are a medicine, healing what wounds to feelings a child may have sustained during the day, and they remind him again that he exists for his parents, and that therefore everything is fundamentally all right.

Georgie was sometimes kissed when his mother put him to bed; more often he was unceremoniously placed in his crib, which remained unmade the whole time I was there with the exception of the day they had guests. Though Joseph was read to before turning in, Georgie's bedtime was a blank. On the rare occasions when his father put him to bed Georgie was merely set down. Georgie was acquiescent at bedtime: only once did he get up and roam around, and that was the evening guests were

there. He never asked for a bedtime drink and never complained
that he was hungry—and his parents never offered anything. The
next extract from the record starts with a bath and follows
Georgie to bed.

2:21:22

Mrs. Ross took Georgie into the bathroom, stripped off his
clothes, with no objection from him, ran the water in the
tub, and poured *Rinso* detergent into the water. In the tub
Georgie had his duck, which fell on its side—it won't float
standing up—and, I think, one boat and another on the edge
of the tub that he did not put in the water. Mrs. Ross
donned an apron and knelt beside the tub, right down on
the hard floor, and mopped Georgie off. The whole thing
took about five minutes and Georgie remained fairly quiet
while his mother held him in a firm grip. Then she took a
large towel saying, "We will show Dr. Henry how we wrap
you in a cocoon." She picked him up out of the tub in the
towel and wrapped it around him, first standing him on
the toilet seat and then putting him into his crib. He was
all covered with detergent suds and she did not rinse them
off. Then she laid him down in the crib and rolled him
around, and he lay there sucking his thumb. I believe he
complained that he was cold.

To bathe a child in a laundry detergent is to say wordlessly that
he is a batch of dirty laundry; not to rinse him off is to drive the
point home, for many detergents have claimed that rinsing is
unnecessary. The impersonal, "home-laundry" character of the
bath was not followed through, however, for Mrs. Ross did
treat Georgie like a human being when she took him out of the
tub. When he was put to bed, however, she left him there without kissing him good night and without covering him, though
he was cold.

The deritualization of bedtime, and the *general poverty of
child-centered rituals* in the Ross house is another aspect of the
impoverishment of Georgie's life. Any *decay of ritual* represents
a *decay of culture,* and by that token the culture of the Ross
family is in a state of decay. One of the first things that happens
when a primitive culture starts to fall apart under the impact of

the West is that the ceremonial systems disintegrate; this leads to internal disorganization, loss of values, and interpersonal atomization. The *relationship* of Georgie to his mother is therefore in a state of decay.

If Georgie is magically *metamorphosed* and degraded by being treated as laundry, he is maintained as an infant by being obliged at the age of four to sleep in a crib. He is a kind of "quick-change artist." The only thing he is unable to do is to completely disappear!

Let us now witness some separations and reunions of Georgie and his father.

2:5:18

I noticed that Georgie did not go near his father this morning and vice versa, and that Mr. Ross did not kiss Georgie goodbye. Mr. Ross reminds me of Mr. Langly[1] in his habitual behavior: his dedication to TV, his tendency to fall asleep, and the fact that the child has to make overtures to *him*—he does not make overtures to the child.

1:15:25

Georgie and I were in the backyard when the father drove up to the curb, and Georgie went running out to him, saying, I think, "Daddy, daddy!" Georgie ran to him, but it seemed to me that the only point at which the father and child made contact was when Georgie touched his father's extended hand. The father did not pick him up and Georgie made no effort to be picked up.

3:38:6

The father is watching TV and did not get up to say goodnight to Georgie or to kiss him goodnight.

4:66:45

At 8:30 A.M., Georgie was up and his father came in to say goodbye and, after saying goodbye and smiling, he walked out without touching the child.

---

[1] The father in another family included in this research on the families of psychotic children.

In contact with his parents, Georgie is *pathologically wary:* vigilant for what is expected of him, he does not ask for much. He will, for example, run to meet his father, but lacking a signal he will not fling himself at his neck. Sucking his thumb, Georgie will lean against his father, a favorite position, but will not crawl on him. Rather he waits, in *pathological forbearance* for the hand to stroke him, and if it does not he does not try to compel it. Georgie carefully avoids (*pathological avoidance*) violating the invisible borders of parental withdrawal. In this way he escapes disappointment, but he also pushes his isolation further: having been taught wariness, he makes it easy for his parents to withdraw. In Georgie we see an extreme of *protective insulation* against pain, of which I have spoken in Chapter 6. Of course, it is no real protection, for the pain only grows worse, until one weeps in one's dreams for people one cannot have.

Protective insulation, a syndrome made up of wariness, forbearance, and avoidance, is a psychic mechanism of our time. Present in most of us in "normal" form, it protects against emotional rebuffs and enables us to carry on an emotional life, relatively free from acute pain. A sick person either has no protective insulation, so that he flings himself on everyone, or he has too much, so that ordinary people cannot make contact with him. What he learned at home is excessive (*pathological*) for the world at large. To use a metaphor from economics, a person who is pathologically insulated has no imports, is incapable of exports, and has lost his gold reserve!

CLOSENESS AND DISTANCE; ABSENCE AND ABSTRACTION

Though Georgie and his mother were seldom in close contact,[1] he did get some warmth from her. There was, however, little that was spontaneous in their relationship and contacts that were not decreed by social climax were usually cool or distant. Aside from Georgie's illness on the seventh day of my stay, when his mother held him a great deal, the morning of the fifth day was the closest time Georgie and his mother had together as long as I was there.

[1] See Appendix A for the analytical table of warm, distant, and mixed contacts.

5:73:22

I heard Mrs. Ross and Georgie singing together. I think one
of the songs was "Mary Had a Little Lamb." When I came
out I found him sitting on her lap feeding her—as Georgie
said, "fooding" her. They were both having an awfully good
time, and she nuzzled him and, I think, kissed him. It was
a very pretty picture and one which, if recurring again and
again, would give the impression that there was a very
warm relationship. Georgie went into the living room, his
pajamas having been taken off by his mother. He flopped
down on the davenport naked, and his mother came in to
dress him and she nuzzled his body with her face and sang
to him very cheerily.

What we see more often in the relation between Mrs. Ross
and Georgie is not absence of warmth but meagerness; not
absence of contact but infrequency; not absence of contact but
absent-*mindedness;* not absence, but abstraction. The following
is a paradigm:

1:19:11

(After supper Georgie was at loose ends, wandering around
in the living room sucking his thumb.) Georgie took a little
book of mazes and brought it to his mother, and she tried
to participate in play with the mazes while dividing her
attention between the mazes and TV. So there was Mrs.
Ross, not really interested in the book, and the TV helped
to divert her attention even further. She never really attempted to show him how to thread his way through the
mazes.

One might argue that since the advent of TV, Americans are
better trained in divided attention than any Western population
and this incident is simply a case of the general cultural plague.
With Georgie, however, Mrs. Ross was *fundamentally* of divided
attention, and TV was merely another occasion. Always she was
far away—even, I believe, in her warmest moments—and that
is why Georgie was a phantom.

PATHOGENIC METAMORPHOSIS AND THE PLEASURES
OF HUMILIATION

Without a Self *Homo sapiens* is nothing. Revolutions erupt not from starvation and misery alone, but from humiliation also, for it attacks the Self, and an intact human being smolders beneath it. It is incredible how much poverty a people will stand as long as they are not humiliated; and the polemical literature of rebellion combines hunger with humiliation. The Declaration of Independence is unique in revolutionary literature because it speaks of humiliation but not of physical misery. Unless one can be taught that benefits will accrue if one accepts humiliation, he will fight it.

In contemporary society the Self dies a little bit at a time. Surrounded by visible expressions of the high-rising living standard and reminded constantly of his good status position a man can gradually forget that he is alienated from his Self (except, of course, that his dreams will not leave him alone). The slowly immolated Self that gives no conscious trouble is the interred reality for man in our culture, and he "gets along" with his socially patterned defect. A person who becomes psychotic, however, has had his Self destroyed brutally and completely.

Since getting to like humiliation is central to our time, it is important to understand how the process can be started in childhood. We have seen something of it in the Portman family, and I shall go more extensively into it here. I start with a record of one of Mr. Ross's homecomings.

4:78:47

When Mr. Ross came home he played with Georgie for about fifteen minutes. Georgie wanted to play catch with two balls at once, but when this didn't work out they played with one, a large, soft rubber ball. Catch developed into a game in which Mr. Ross bounced the ball off Georgie's head. That is to say, he would throw the ball to him gently and Georgie would stand there as if to catch it, but 95% of the time the ball landed on his head. Georgie seemed to enjoy this and so did his father. After about five or ten minutes of this they played another game. Georgie wanted to climb up on a sort of wall attached to the stoop, so his father lifted him up by his hands and set him on the wall a couple of times, and each time he picked him off and set him down he kissed Georgie on the belly. He did this about three or four times. I had the feeling all the while Mr. Ross was playing with Georgie that he was treating him as if he were a strange, non-person object. At last, after not more than fifteen minutes of totally desultory play with Georgie, Mr. Ross went into the house and sat down in the living room, reading.

A child who has learned to think of himself as nobody is not likely to be insensitive to the fact that his father treats his head like a wall. Georgie knows that a way to keep his father interested is to distort himself; and in a ball game, what could be more intriguing than to transform one's head into a wall? If, by the magic of a self-destructive metamorphosis Georgie can bind his father for only ten minutes, it is a huge gain. The Observer did not perceive who invented the trick, but that is unimportant. What is important is that *father and son conspired* to make the child a wall, or, at least, a buffoon. Georgie is skilled in extorting recognition of his existence from his father by distorting himself: eating paint and drinking filthy soapy water were two other tricks I observed.

To play ball and be a wall, to be kissed repeatedly on the belly instead of on the face like a human child, is better than not to play and not be kissed. To have one's existence recognized as a wall or as a clown is better than not to have one's existence recognized at all. This is the process of learning the pleasures of humiliation, of learning that humiliation can be rewarding. Teaching Georgie to enjoy humiliation was largely the father's responsibility. In this sense, we might say, Mr. Ross took much responsibility for his son's moral upbringing, for the capacity to sustain humiliation is an ancient virtue in our society, a quality that nowadays divides nice people from obstreperous ones. Mrs. Ross humiliated Georgie less, though, as we have seen, she played an important part in teaching him how to be a phantom. The following example is another instance of how a child learns the pleasures of humiliation.

For breakfast Mrs. Ross gave Georgie *Krinkles,* banana, and milk, and set him in front of the TV. When he had eaten, he took the box of *Krinkles* into the living room but dropped it on the floor, spilling a lot of the little pellets on the rug. Mrs. Ross gave no indication of annoyance, though Georgie looked very unhappy. She got a broom for him and picked the box off the floor. Georgie, however, used the broom, not to sweep up the *Krinkles,* but to spread them all over the floor, for the broom was too huge for him to manage. Georgie also walked on the *Krinkles.* All of this irritated his mother, so she told him to get the vacuum cleaner out of the closet, which he did. The vacuum cleaner, an upright one, was taller than Georgie, and being rather heavy, was not easy for him to maneuver. Using the cleaner was made even more awkward by the fact that the tubing was long and cumbersome. Mrs. Ross sat in the living room and told Georgie to clean up the *Krinkles* with the vacuum cleaner. She had him pick up the *Krinkles* one at a time with the long attachment that is usually used for very narrow surfaces, like, for example, the edge of a baseboard. She sat there quietly watching him, completely expressionless, while he picked up the *Krinkles,* which were about the size of beans, one by one. Georgie developed the idea of placing the sole of his foot on a Krinkle so that it would stick, and then he would vacuum it off the sole of his foot. This amused his mother so much that she laughed heavily, and covered her face with her hands. She stopped this foot trick, however, because it was slowing things up. She sat doggedly in her chair and pointed out to Georgie every single *Krinkle.*

The whole operation took about half an hour. A couple of times Georgie wanted to stop, and said, "Now you do it," but she said, "No, you do it." He did not seem upset, but went about the work carefully and automatically until he had finished. Later in the day he took the *Krinkles* and again dropped them on the floor, but this angered his mother so that she picked him up and stuck him in the kitchen, saying very harshly, "You can't have the box any more." She put some *Krinkles* into a bowl and left Georgie in the kitchen crying. She closed the door and just left him there.

The trouble with Georgie was that since he enjoyed his mother's undivided attention for half an hour after spilling the *Krinkles* the first time, he wanted to repeat the performance. Since she, by sitting there in amused fascination, showed she was having a good time, how could he imagine that she would not enjoy a second performance?

I do not mean to suggest by these examples that Georgie knows he is being humiliated. I think that what he consciously knows in these and similar cases is pleasure and that the pain of self-immolation is dissociated. There are many in our culture so trained in the pleasures of humiliation that all their lives they naturally place themselves in a position to be humiliated whenever they can, for humiliation has become a joy. On the other hand, since Georgie calls himself "Georgie nobody" he must feel that something is wrong, that something has been, perhaps, destroyed.

In this house there is a problem of asymmetrical commitment —a problem of who is to get what from whom; of who is to be autonomous and who is to abandon his Self; of who is to be corporeal and who is to materialize only in metamorphosis. I think it can be seen now that Mr. Ross is to be a culture hero while Georgie is to become "nobody"; that his father is to be fat while Georgie is skinny; that the affections of father and mother are for each other much more than they are for Georgie, and that Georgie is to exist in shadow as long as his mother remains so deeply committed to Joseph.

If one were to look at this situation in terms of classical biology, one could cite the so-called "competitive exclusion" principle, according to which related organisms living off the same environmental resources will compete for them in such a way that only the best adapted to the competitive situation will survive. In the psycho-biology of a pathogenic family there may be also, however, a form of pathological cooperation. In the Ross family the most obvious cooperator is Georgie, who does it by acquiescing in almost everything required of him, whether it be that he be undemanding of food and attention, or that he be a phantom, a wall, a buffoon, a nobody. In this way Georgie has worked out a paradoxical, and, in the long run, self-destructive solution for himself, for while, on the one hand, acquiescence does obtain some recognition of his existence, it is so small and distorted that he gradually becomes misshapen and diminished, thereby enabling his parents to withdraw more.

DELUSIONAL EXTRICATION AND THE LOGIC OF NONEXISTENCE

From a somewhat extreme point of view, much that happens to Georgie can be understood as a consequence of his parents' efforts to extricate themselves from the condition of having him, and in terms of a family philosophical system that postulates the nonexistence of Georgie. Let us start with the latter.

If it is postulated that a child does not exist, then a number of consequences follow necessarily. For example, the child does not have to be fed; his bed need not be made; one need pay him no attention nor reminisce about him, for certainly there can be no memories of what does not exist. When one goes with him to a restaurant one need not order for him, for although he came along, he is not there. Furthermore one does not say goodbye to the nonexistent when one leaves for work, nor does one greet it when one returns. Things do not follow this pattern rigidly in the Ross family, particularly because his mother has some affection for Georgie. Nevertheless the postulate of nonexistence puts the family tragedy in an intenser light. Only a madman would interpret the postulate literally, for a child's simple corporeal existence obtrudes itself insistently on reality. After all, a real child must be fed and he refuses to be materially annihilated merely by the crazy logic of nonexistence. But one can get around this by compromising with the brute flesh and by creating a delusion about the child. I have called this the *delusion of extrication*—a delusional system that seems to enable one to delusively extricate one's self from a situation by creating a fantasy about it. The function of the delusion is to save one from the full realization that he is in a situation he would rather not be in. Having created the delusion, he then acts as if it were the reality. The partial feeding of Georgie, the distant parental smile, the abstracted kiss and finger-tip greeting, the bath in Rinso, the metamorphoses of Georgie are all expressions of delusion and compromise.

Delusions of extrication are common enough in our culture. Think only, for example, of the advertising man who detests the work while imagining it a vehicle for his creative genius: *he* is not an advertising man, he is a creative artist. Enormous numbers of Americans participate in similar delusions. In a society where most people work at what they have to do rather than at what they want to do, work is denied and even home becomes a kind of delusional reality—not in the sense that it does not really exist, but rather in the sense that it becomes magnified into the *only* reality, while work becomes a kind of phantasm. The fairy-book way in which many American homes are furnished, so that every inch of space is elaborated into some kind of moonshine—figured and filmy draperies, strange-looking little animals, weird shapes on the walls, exotically tapestried and convoluted furniture and lamps—is an expression of the somewhat delusional nature of the American home, halfway between reality and fantasy. Even the home machinery is fey. The function of the American home is to deny the existence of factory and office: it is a concrete expression of the logic of nonexistence wrapped up in delusional extrication.

SUMMARY OF THE ROSS CASE

Let us start with Mr. Ross. Here is a man who has calmed down since the early days of marriage, but whose capacity for rage still lies within him like a poised tiger. Mrs. Ross says he used to be very violent; and I could still see, by the way she handled him, and by his ready surges of anger that never quite erupted because she acted swiftly, that she still had her problems with him. Since he is an insensitive, self-centered man, signs of affection had to come first from his wife, and she had regularly to get up and lead him to bed by the hand from the living room couch where he had fallen asleep watching TV. She talked so intensely to me about how important it was that he continue to support Joseph that I got the impression that she was at particular pains to keep him content because he might suddenly decide to stop contributing to the hospital bill. She always seemed nervous about her husband, but he never gave me the impression of being that way about her.

But Mrs. Ross had heavy burdens besides this. Thrust aside

by a mother who cared only about boys and was ready to die when she lost a son, Mrs. Ross has suffered from a lifelong depression. If Joseph or Georgie had been girls instead of boys it might have been better for them. Meanwhile she was so wrapped up in Joseph, so worried about her husband, that she had little left over for Georgie, little to give him to prove he existed. As a matter of fact by failing to feed him adequately she seemed to emphasize his nonexistence.

Born into a family where the emotional resources had already been heavily committed, Georgie was a kind of visitor who had stayed for breakfast, a phantom child. His parents never talked about him in my presence and were remote in their contacts with him; even when physically present, they were emotionally unavailable. The parsimony and the emotional improverishment in the household fell most heavily on Georgie because, being immature, he was least able to bear it. Unlike most American families the Rosses were not child-centered, because their child had never quite gotten into the family, but rather was made to hover on the edge of it. His bed was never made; he was never offered a snack. Under these circumstances Georgie had become remarkably acquiescent at home, matching in his childish compliance with his parents' demands on him the pattern of compliance forced on *them* by the social agency that had taken responsibility for the family, and by all the economic circumstances with which they compromised. Georgie had learned to accept and even to cooperate in the metamorphoses and humiliations visited upon him because this was the only way he saw to stay within his parents' ken.

Really, it would be hard to say that anybody really possessed anybody in the Ross family. A narcissistic father, a depressed and far-away mother wrapped up in an absent child, while the one at home has been so trained to pathological wariness and protective insulation that even direct reaching out to him does not encounter him fully—three shades in search of substance!

CONCLUSIONS

In this chapter I have tried to show that there are many roads to madness, that it is an extreme expression of the cultural configuration—the ultimate consequence of all that is wrong with a culture, and that it is largely the result of the confluence in the child of lethal cultural influences mediated to the child through his parents. I could not give an exhaustive demonstration of these propositions in a single chapter, but I have tried to suggest their probable truth, using material from cases with which I am personally familiar.

The Rosses and the Portmans are good people. Liquor never crosses their lips; the fathers are decent, hard-working, law-abiding, and the mothers are intelligent, moral women. As angry as I may have sometimes sounded here, I really liked and respected the Rosses and the Portmans and practically all of the families with whom I stayed. They are nice people, likeable people, but they are inwardly miserable and confused and need psychiatric help. And because they are this way they often do not know what they are doing to their children; certainly when I tell them, on the eve of my departure, they show little comprehension. Many of us, when we are upset and confused, tend to lose our bearings and "bite people's heads off." But when parents are disturbed all of the time, let their children look to their heads! or to their souls! for the parents may not know for years what they are doing to their children.

The Rosses and the Portmans are quite different from each other, yet both have produced a psychotic child and there is serious disturbance in the younger children. Since the family cultures of the Rosses and the Portmans are distinct from each other and the problems of the parents are different, the nature of the disturbance in the children is diverse. But in spite of variation there are similarities also. In both, the parents are withdrawn from the children and engage in what I have called *delusional extrication* and *pathogenic metamorphosis*. They construct delusional systems around their children which somehow enable them to half believe the children are not present, and they imaginatively convert the children into nonhuman objects. Massive humiliation is present in both families, and there seems little doubt that it is constant in all psychosis that develops largely on a nongenetic base, for humiliation, since it saps the ability to believe in one's Self impairs perception. Inwardly such a person always asks, "Is this rock indeed a rock; this chair a chair? How can I, who am nothing, perceive anything?" Thus humiliation erodes the capacity to learn, and one who has suffered massive doses of it cannot believe the ground is firm beneath his feet.

In no family is it possible to predict safely how the children will turn out unless we have a veritable inventory of what the parents do to them and for them—and even then it would be a brave guess! Knowing the Rosses or the Portmans even fairly well, one could not foresee that Georgie would fight a lonely battle by acquiescing in becoming a phantom, or that Pete would scream, hit his mother, juggle boxes, and bite his wrists. Nor could one who knew only the parental personalities in the Ross and Portman homes predict that they would be expressed in such very *specific* things as forced or inadequate feeding, disrupted schedules, bathing in Rinso, pathological wariness and constant thumb-sucking, masturbation and garbled speech.

On the other hand, it is probable that where children have become psychotic the following are fairly constant features of parent–child relations: (1) humiliation and metamorphosis; (2) delusional extrication; (3) mutual withdrawal; (4) massive ambiguities and distortions in communication; (5) unavailability of the parent when most needed—flight from crisis; (6) the children are regularly compelled to fight against what they want most. This produces a Belle who pushes the food out of her mouth, or a hungry Georgie who refused to accept food from his mother's plate.

But the central issue is to know exactly what is done: *one form of abuse alone does not make a child mad.*[1] *It is an accumulation of miseries, backed up always by disorientation in the parents.* An abused child will become emotionally ill, but he will not be psychotic unless his parents are disoriented—adrift in time, unable to tell actor from acted on, easily thrown off by new situations, never sure that they mean what they say, mixed up in speech, forgetful, etc. Nor will a mixed up or even psychotic parent produce an insane child if the child is loved—if he is permitted to be a child and not a garbage pail or a phantom. He may be mixed up, but he will not be mad.

And what are the prospects for Georgie and Pete? There is no

[1] Saving, of course, that most destructive of all abuses, isolation.

question but that both of them will continue to be badly disturbed; but the life-chances are better for Georgie than for Pete, because Georgie's parents are not as disoriented as Mrs. Portman. On the other hand, Pete's father loves him, even though he expresses it in a somewhat extreme and distorted way. It is unlikely that either child will become psychotic, but they will have a hard life. Mrs. Ross is the only one who is seeing a psychiatrist. They all should.

PART THREE

❧ ❧

INTRODUCTION

The book is now almost finished. I passed from the institutional structure to an interpretation of the lives and loves of parents and children, seeking to understand their vicissitudes as consequences of the institutional matrix. In this final section I deal with one phase of human obsolescence—its ultimate stages in old age homes run by public and private agencies. I do not discuss the problems of the older worker or the discarded executive, but rather deep aging, the final years and days before the end. It will be seen that just as the relations of parents to children and those of adolescents to one another are determined by the system, so does the system inescapably define how the aged shall be viewed and treated. It could scarcely be otherwise.

10: Human Obsolescence

THIS CHAPTER IS ABOUT THREE HOSPITALS FOR THE AGED: Municipal Sanitarium ("Muni San"), Rosemont ("Hell's Vestibule") and Tower Nursing Home.[1] Though Muni San is supported by public funds, Rosemont and Tower Nursing Home are private, profit-making institutions. Tower is comfortable and humane, Rosemont is inhuman, and Muni San is somewhere in between.[2] Taken together these three institutions give a good picture of the kinds of fates that await most of the people who become sick and obsolete in our culture.

MUNI SAN

Although Muni San has a vast number of beds, this study concerns only one part of it—a ward containing around a hundred patients and having male and female sections. For these patients there were a registered nurse and about a dozen attendants spread

---

[1] The names Muni San, Tower, and Rosemont have been arbitrarily chosen and have no reference to any actual institutions that may bear the names.

[2] They were studied by trained graduate nurses under my direction.

over three shifts. A doctor made regular rounds and patients were bathed twice a week. Linens were changed when the patients were bathed or were incontinent. The patients were adequately fed and kept clean, though it often took the help a long time to get around to it. Although Muni San does what it can within the limits of a penurious budget, the patients suffer psychologically from the impersonality and vastness of the setting.

A NOTE ON THE SOCIAL CONSCIENCE

Public institutions for sick "social security paupers"—those who have no income but their social security checks—are ruled by the social conscience; that is to say, obvious things that readily excite conventional feelings of right and wrong are taken account of within the limits of miserly budgets, but everything else is slighted. For example, an institution may have plenty of medicine and an abundance of sterile gauze, but the medicine is often administered by ignorant persons and the gauze contaminated by ill-trained aides. Bedding, even when sufficient, may be dingy grey because of penny-pinching on soap and bleach. Food may be adequate but distributed in assembly-line fashion and eaten within obligatory time limits. Every bed may have a thin blanket sufficient for the regulated temperature of the institution, but if the heating breaks down or the staff decides to open the windows when the outside temperature is freezing, the patients are unprotected. Thus, were the social conscience to inquire whether the inmates had enough of what they need, the answer would be "yes," and the social conscience, easily lulled by appearances and small expenditures, would sleep on.

Always interested more in outward seeming than inner reality, always eager not to be stirred or get involved too much, always afraid of "pampering" its public charges and more given to the expression of drives than of values, the social conscience cannot be stirred to a concern with "psychology" unless some terrible evil, like juvenile delinquency, rages across the land. Hence, the spiritual degradation and hopelessness of its obsolete charges seem none of its affair. The social conscience is affected by things having "high visibility," like clean floors, freshly painted walls, and plenty of medical supplies, rather than by those having "low visibility," like personal involvement. A nurse in a mental hospital once put it to me this way: "When you go off duty they can tell if you've got a clean dressing room, but they can't tell if you've talked to a patient." In an institution for obsolete social security paupers the supervisor can tell whether or not a patient has been bathed but not whether the aide who did it spent a little extra time bathing the patient as if he was a human being rather than something inanimate. Since too many minutes devoted to being human will make an aide late in getting her quota of patients "done," they are washed like a row of sinks, and their privacy is violated because there is no time to move screens around or to manipulate the bedclothes in a way that preserves the patient's sense of modesty.

In many primitive societies the soul is imagined to leave the body at death or just prior to it; here, on the other hand, society drives out the remnants of the soul of the institutionalized old person while it struggles to keep his body alive. Routinization, inattention, carelessness, and the deprivation of communication— the chance to talk, to respond, to read, to see pictures on the wall, to be called by one's name rather than "you" or no name at all— are ways in which millions of once useful but now obsolete human beings are detached from their selves long before they are lowered into the grave.

THE NATURE AND CAUSES OF STILLNESS

As one enters a public hospital for the aged the thing that first impresses him is the stillness. It is natural that a tomb for the living should be silent, and since those who work in such a depressing atmosphere need something to sustain them, the wards present the paradox of a tomblike hush pervaded by the rasping throb of rock 'n roll music:

> The patients in the first section sat quietly by their neatly made beds except for one bedfast patient. There was no conversation between patients. The windows were frosted over. The radio beat out rock 'n roll. One man was reading. The rest of the ambulatory patients were just sitting.

These patients are not silent because they are too sick to move but because hospital "life," as we shall see, does something to them. But let us continue on our way.

Two men were sleeping and two were reading, one with his back to the ward. One sat in a chair at the end of his bed, just sitting. A third sat in a wheelchair holding his urinal, which he used as a spitoon. One patient walked through on his way out of the ward. That was the only activity on this section.

The first section of the men's ward was still, with the exception of the rock 'n roll. By this I mean that there was absolutely no activity. Mr. Bergstrom and Mr. Xavier were not on the ward.

Mr. Erik was sitting dressed on the side of his unmade bed. Mr. Quall sat in his chair by the window, facing the wall.

Mr. Anison lay propped up in bed watching Elsie, an aide who had come in and started to mop. She moved his bed, pulling and pushing it as she cleaned without a word to him.

"Noisy" patients who get into animated discussions are put into "noisy" sections, or are moved from place to place until they find patients who will not respond to them, and so settle down. One day the observer

asked the head nurse if there was a way of telling which patient was in which bed according to the chart in the hall. She took me out and showed me how and explained that it was often inaccurate because patients were moved frequently.

Since arguments among patients interfere with the smooth functioning of the hospital, the sensible thing is to interrupt communication between them and thus nip all possible disputes in the bud—or before the bud. Unruffled routine requires also that improbabilities be controlled and hence that all patients be perceived and treated as identical. In these circumstances the elimination of patients' individuality is first accomplished by dropping names:

The aides worked silently, speaking to the patients only to make requests such as "turn over," "sit down," and other remarks connected with the work at hand. The patients did what they were asked to do. The radio was playing rock 'n roll.

The aide Elsie walked over to Mr. Gratz who was sitting by his bedside table in a chair. She took him by the right shirt sleeve and said, "Get up." He got up and Elsie moved his chair across the aisle and then guided him over to sit down. He is blind.

Miss Jones, the aide, finished tucking the sheet around Mr. Stilter and went over to Mr. Sprocket's bed. She tugged him on the arm and said, "Sit over here—I want to make the bed." He looked at her and didn't say anything but got up and sat in the chair holding his head in his hands.

Gertrude Beck came into the room and went over to one of the beds and turned the patient on her side without saying anything except to another aide, Miss Jones. She pulled up the gown exposing the patient's buttocks and gave her an injection. I glanced back at the patient as Beck left the room and saw that the patient was still on her side, buttocks exposed, blood oozing from the injection site. Jones saw this about the same time I did and came over and pulled the sheet up and patted the blood with it without saying anything.

The patients, of course, know that they are not addressed by name not only because that's the way of the hospital but because often their names are not known—there are so many of them and they are moved around so much:

Miss Ruuzman, the head nurse, leaned over Mr. Cronach's bed to look at his name card at the head of his bed and then walked rapidly back up the ward and out. Mr. Cronach said indignantly, "If she looks at that bed-card much more she may remember my name." "Mr. Cronach, I presume," I said inanely.

Nameless, handled like things, deprived in the vast silences of the hospital of the opportunity to give and receive human re-

sponse; without property, and reduced almost below the capacity
to experience disgust by the hospital's enormous delay in cleaning up bedpans, commodes, and soiled bedclothes, the patient is
like a wanderer in one of Piranesi's prisons.

THE PROBLEM OF FALSE HOPE

As I passed through one of the wards I saw Mr. Yarmouth.
He waved and motioned for me to come over. The first thing
he asked was, "Do you live near my brother near King
Street?" It seems that Mr. Yarmouth wanted me to find out
if his brother was going to bring Mr. Yarmouth's other shoe.
He pointed to his feet and I could see that he had a shoe
on his right foot but none on his left. Mr. Yarmouth continued to tell me that he hoped his brother wouldn't let him
down; his brother was supposed to bring his other shoe. I
told him I lived on Maple and he said, "No, that isn't near
my brother." He said if he only had his other shoe he could
get up and around. He said that if his brother didn't get the
shoe for him Reverend Burr would. The Reverend had
promised that he would see about it. Mr. Yarmouth said,
"Let's see, today's Friday isn't it?" and I said, "Yes." He said,
"Well, there is still Saturday and Sunday maybe. I won't
give up hope, I never give up hope." I said, "No, don't ever
give up."

The record does not tell whether or not Mr. Yarmouth ever got
his other shoe; but his dependence on relatives and children—
who often do not come—for even a shoe, his anguish of hope, his
sense of being trapped, are repeated themes.

The history of Mr. Yarmouth's eyeglasses is more complete
than the brief tale of his missing shoe.

First day. Mr. Yarmouth waved at me and then motioned
for me to come over to where he sat in a chair at the foot
of his bed. I said, "Hi, how are you today?" He said "Fine,"
and then asked if I would make a phone call for him. I
said I'd be glad to if I could. He then asked if I had a dime
and I replied that I did not. It turned out that he wanted
reading glasses that his brother had. He said that he had
lost his and needed them badly. I told him that I would ask

Miss Everson and left him to do so. I found her and told her that Mr. Yarmouth had asked me to call his brother about his glasses and she walked to the desk and wrote this down in a little green book. She was very friendly and said that sometimes the men didn't even have relatives and that then the hospital tried to take care of these things. I replied that I would tell him that I'd talked with her about it and she said, "No" and wrote something in the book. I thanked her and went back to the ward. Mr. Yarmouth asked me if I had any money and I said no, and I told him I talked with Miss Everson, and he said, "Who's that?" I explained that she was the charge nurse and was going to take care of his glasses. He seemed satisfied.

Who is Miss Everson anyway, and what is Mr. Yarmouth to her? "Sometimes," says Miss Everson, "the men [those identity-less hundreds] don't even have relatives." As for this particular man, lacking particular eyeglasses, Miss Everson does not know whether or not he has a brother. Like a figure in a dream, writing in a phantom book where all that is written washes away, the charge nurse notes Mr. Yarmouth's request. But the act of writing is an act of magic and an act of pseudo-communication: by writing him down she has done away with Mr. Yarmouth, and the fact that Miss Everson is a make-believe listener writing a make-believe message makes the transmission of the observer's message and the writing in the book a pseudo-communication.

But to Mr. Yarmouth the communication was real:

Third day. Mr. Yarmouth, who was sitting in a chair at the foot of his bed, beckoned me to come over, "Did you get my brother about my glasses?" I was absolutely amazed. I told him that I hadn't been able to make the call but that Miss Everson had written the request down. "Who's Miss Everson?" he asked. "When does the mail come?" I said I didn't know but that I would go and ask Miss Everson about the mail and the glasses. He kept urging me to find out even though I assured him I would as soon as I could find Miss Everson. (Later) Mr. Yarmouth beckoned to me wildly. "You forgot me," he said,

"I knew you would." "No I didn't really forget you, Mr. Yarmouth, I just haven't found Miss Everson yet, but she's here somewhere." "Well, you be sure and tell me." I promised I would.

Mr. Yarmouth is sick—sick with false hope, a grave illness in the hospital. Symptoms of this disease are noisiness, demandingness, and the delusion that something one wants desperately is going to happen. The inner function of the delusion is to prevent the patient from thinking he is dead. Patients afflicted with false hope may become difficult to manage: for example, Mr. Yarmouth had the observer running back and forth stupidly between him and Miss Everson.

When I found Miss Everson I told her that I had been amazed that Mr. Yarmouth had remembered me, and that he had asked me about his glasses. Miss Everson was very nice and seemed surprised too. She said, "Just tell him *you're* working on it."
Then I went back to Mr. Yarmouth and told him "they're working on it—they're trying to get your glasses." He seemed satisfied and I left, waving at him as I went.

Miss Everson, who seems to understand the signs and symptoms well, handles the naive observer with sweet and consummate tact: "Just tell him *you're* working on it", she says. What else could she do? If the hospital were to call or write the patients' relatives for "every little thing" it would have to hire a special staff just to handle the phone calls and the correspondence.
The symptom that clinches the diagnosis of false hope is the anger of the staff at the patient.

Fifth day. I noticed that Mr. Yarmouth had been moved to the left corner of the ward in Mr. Worth's place. He saw me, waved and asked me, "Have they come yet?" I called back, "Not yet."

Sixth day. Mr. Yarmouth was still at his window. I went over to him and asked what he was doing in his new spot and he told me that they had moved him around, he didn't know why, and that he had nothing to do but look at the wall. I replied, "Don't do that, look out the window." "I'm trying to," he answered. He was very subdued today.

Mr. Yarmouth had been moved for being argumentative and noisy: frustration over the glasses was more than he could bear.

Eighth day. Mr. Yarmouth sat in exactly the same position he has been in since he was moved into this section. He was sitting by the window facing the wall by his bed. He is so subdued it is striking. . . . When he saw me Mr. Yarmouth beckoned to me to come over. He used to do this with a kind of devilishness but now he is almost lethargic, and when he asked me about his glasses and I told him I hadn't been able to find out about them he just accepted this, although in the past he has insisted that I let him know when I'll tell him. As I left he said, with a pathetic attempt to bolster his self-esteem, "Be sure to send the bill to me."

Mr. Yarmouth is "improving." He is giving up hope, yet his self-esteem still prods him into futile gestures of adequacy, as he clings to the idea and the memory of reading and of eyes that served him once:

Tenth day. Mr. Yarmouth with his back to the window. He asked me again about his glasses and I again told him that the order was written down. He knows he won't get them and so do I, so all of this is just a farce. I finally couldn't stand it any more and patting him on the shoulder told him I'd see him later.

Twelfth day. Mr. Yarmouth got out a Christian Science booklet to show me how he can read the larger headings but not the smaller print. "You know," he said, "I'm getting nervous, all I can do is sit here and read, and I have to have glasses." His request is only reasonable and I feel like a heel about it—how ineffectual can you be? Now he asks me about calling his nephew instead of his brother. We talked about Mr. Yarmouth's having been an oculist: "All the doctors used to call me and tell what they wanted and then I'd see that it was done and out on time. They depended on me."

Thus ends the saga of Mr. Yarmouth's glasses. Not once in his false hope did he make contact directly with one of the staff; his only channel of communication—or shall we say, pseudo-communication—was the observer. To him the hospital was a remote impersonal "They," inexorable and inscrutable like the prosecution in Kafka's *The Trial*. With not enough money for even a phone call, with nobody coming to see him, Mr. Yarmouth is marooned, and being marooned he is "nervous." When in his anxiety he argues with those around him, he is moved around and away from the patients he knows by the same "They" that promise to get his glasses but never do. He is punished for remaining human.

THE FEELING OF BEING DISCARDED

As one comes to know these patients one develops a feeling of unreality about their relatives: do they exist or don't they? Take the case of Mrs. Kohn.

She was sitting in her wheelchair beside her bed, embroidering. She showed me the pillow cases and showed me how to make French knots. At first she talked slowly, but when she got on the subject of her nieces she talked more rapidly. She took hold of my hand and held it. She said, "I have a niece living in town. Every year she goes to Wisconsin on vacation and sends me a card saying, 'I'll be seeing you soon,' and she never does come to see me."

The feeling of being discarded makes them cling to whoever shows a human interest. Holding on for dear life to their remnants of life and humanness is an idiosyncracy of human obsolescence:

I had only been in there for a few minutes when Mrs. Ramsey in her bed began calling out, "I'm cold, I'm cold. Cover me up." I walked over to her bed and she grabbed my hand and said, "Cover me, cover me up." I told her that her hands were cold and I pulled the covers up on them.

We have studied the process of becoming obsolete through the history of one man, Mr. Yarmouth; let us now observe a woman. Mrs. Prilmer was moved around, just like Mr. Yarmouth, because she was "noisy." Let us follow her for a few days:

First day. As I entered the ward Mrs. Prilmer who was sitting on the edge of her bed motioned for me to come over, calling, "Here, here." I went over to her and she took my hand and held on to my arm trying to pull herself up, saying, "Take me to the office, call me a cab, I want to go home. Help me, I can't walk." I said, "I can't do that," but she said, "Yes you can." A patient walked up and said, "Are you her daughter?" and I said, "No." Then the patient said, "She has a daughter and three sons," and Mrs. Prilmer affirmed, "Yes, my daughter lives in Boston; my son comes to visit me every day." So I suggested that she talk to her son about going home, but she replied, "He isn't coming today." I asked, "But I thought you said he came to see you every day?" and Mrs. Prilmer answered, "But he isn't coming today." So I walked over to the aide Miss Jones who was making a bed on the other side of the ward and told her what had happened. She laughed and said, "She used to be so quiet. Tell her her son will be here this afternoon." But I mentioned what I had told her and what answer I had received. "Maybe it would be better if you told her." So Miss Jones went over. Meanwhile I started talking with Mrs. Kohn and she said, "I've been waiting for physiotherapy to come after me. Sometimes I sit here and wait all day and they don't come. I think I'd be just as well off sitting at home." I nodded and Mrs. Kohn pointed to Mrs. Prilmer, saying, "She goes on like that all the time, even during the night. She stops anybody who'll talk to her; I think she's a little feeble-minded." Just then the aide walked away and Mrs. Prilmer called after her and said she wanted to go home. Jones answered, "I'll tell you what, I'll call the superintendent of the hospital; I'll send him over to see you, O.K.?" When Mrs. Prilmer said, "Yes," Jones and several of the patients laughed.

The record reads further: Finally I left just as an attendant was entering with a heavy cloth strap. Alice (another nurse-observer) asked if Mrs. Prilmer was going to be restrained with that. I said I thought so, but I didn't return to find out.

There prevails among us a nightmare *Dream of the Trap,* which is the opposite of the *Midsummer Night's Dream.* In the *Dream of the Trap* we are imprisoned by a malevolent "They"; we struggle to escape; we yearn for friends who never come. In our midnight terror we sometimes whimper, sometimes scream without sound. This dream is fear of desertion, of failure, of loss of self to coercive "forces." The hospital is the dream come true. The benign observer, of course, was an intruder in the dream, and had she not spoken to Miss Jones about Mrs. Prilmer the old lady would have been ignored. Mrs. Prilmer, starring in her last role, performed it as if she had practiced it many times in dreams: she seized the observer, clung to her, and tried to escape, through her, back to the outer world that had buried her here.

The other patients, usually too ignorant or too much in need themselves, attack one another, so that instead of helping they make things worse. So Mrs. Kohn, who has clung to the observer herself, assails Mrs. Prilmer and, talking out loud as if she was not there to hear her, says, "I think she's a little feeble-minded." Mrs. Burns from her wheelchair tried to help Mrs. Prilmer, but it did little good: Mrs. Prilmer even antagonized Rosemary, a "good" aide:

Eighth day. From Mrs. Prilmer I could hear, "My son, my son." Mrs. Lorenz answered something and Mrs. Burns said, "You're mean." From her wheelchair she threw Mrs. Prilmer a rag saying, "Here, blow your nose."

The aide Rosemary was around doing chores and Mrs. Burns said, "We need some more Rosemarys." I agreed. Rosemary helped Mrs. Kohn off the bedpan and passed out clean but badly wrinkled towels. As Mrs. Burns took one she observed, "It seems to me they could run these things through the mangle; it would be easier on these people's skins, but they don't care about them." As Rosemary took care of Mrs. Prilmer she called the old lady "squeaky," remarking that Mrs. Prilmer "squeaks" all the time. "Are you gonna be quiet now?" Mrs. Prilmer nodded assent, but made a face and motioned with her hand for Rosemary to go away. Rosemary said, "Don't you like me?" and when Mrs. Prilmer answered, "No," Rosemary said, "O.K., if you don't like me I don't like you either." Rosemary left and went into the next ward and Mrs. Prilmer, looking agitated, sat tapping with her hand on the arm of her chair.

After all, what is there in life for an ignorant, poorly paid helper in a human junkyard? A minority discover that what can save *their* lives is to be good to the patients within the limits of miserly budgets and pressure toward routine. But when an ungrateful patient turns and says, "I don't like you," it is too much. A week later Mrs. Prilmer had been moved in with the "noisy" patients.

I noticed all the patients in this room have been changed since I was last in here. They moved all the "louder" patients into this room. Mrs. Prilmer sat over in the corner to the left. As soon as I entered the room she called "Nurse, nurse, nurse." I must say that I was slightly overwhelmed when I entered, but when I recovered I went over to Mrs. Prilmer and she seized my arm and pulled me down toward her, for she was sitting on a commode near her bed. Her stockings had fallen down to her ankles. She talked fast and furiously, "How is your mama? How is your papa?" She told me that her head hurt and that she wasn't feeling very good. As I talked to her she held my arm with one hand and stroked it with the other. She kept talking on and on: it seemed as though she would say anything just to keep me there.

Of course, one has to be sensible about these things: what are you going to do with noisy and distracted patients with phantom relatives? Where are you going to get the money to pay for enough help, let alone enough help skilled psychologically to deal with these people who have been cast aside like old fenders? An administrator threw up his hands:

> I've got to remember that some of the help can't do anything but give bed baths: they were hired right off the streets and they just don't know. Of course, I've got some that can't learn either. Some can hardly read or write.

So you put the noisy ones all together to get them out of the way of the quiet ones, to isolate them so they won't disturb the help, but especially as an implied threat to anyone with noisy inclinations: if he doesn't keep quiet that's where he'll end up.

DEHUMANIZATION AND DEATH

If in every human contact something is communicated, something learned, and something felt, it follows that where nothing is communicated, learned, or felt there is nothing human either. The vast hospital silences, particularly on the men's side, tell us that humanness is ebbing there. The very quietness, however, informs the inmates—not so much because they think it, but rather because they feel it—that they are not human beings. As long as they remain physically alive, nevertheless, they seem never to lose the ability to feel: the primordial capacity for adaptive radiation which is lost only when the cells die remains, expressed, however feebly, in attitude and behavior:

> Mr. Unger sat in his wheelchair by the foot of his bed. He was dressed and wore a black corduroy cap. He was holding a urinal in his lap like a spitoon, and the neck of it was bloody. I said, "Good morning, Mr. Unger, how are you?" He looked up at me (he sits with his head down), smiled, and reached out to shake my hand. I get a warm feeling from Mr. Unger and am fond of him. Next to him sat Mr. Butler, dressed, in a chair: he was just staring. A bedpan with dried feces sat uncovered in front of Mr. Butler's bedside table on the floor.

So they feel they are not human, and from this comes anguish that expresses itself in clinging. But silence is not the only form of dehumanizing communication to which these people are exposed. Empty walls, rows of beds close together, the dreariness of their fellow inmates, the bedpans, the odors, the routinization, all tell them they have become junk. Capping it all is the hostility of the patients to one another and the arbitrary movement from place to place like empty boxes in a storeroom. At the end is a degraded death.

I stopped at the desk to look at Mr. Naron's chart and noted what orders were written. The aide Myrtle saw me and told me, "He's going to die today. The priest[1] was up here this morning already." One of the orders I noted read, "Side rails to be applied," but on going back to the unit I saw that there were no side rails on Mr. Naron's bed. He was turning from side to side and was quite restless. The aides Elizabeth and Frost were standing by his bed. Elizabeth was fingering the soiled adhesive tape that was keeping the nasal oxygen tube in place, and she asked Frost, "Can you change this?" and Frost responded very hostilely, "No, they won't let me do it; I'm not supposed to be bright enough." Then she nodded in the direction of Mr. Naron and remarked, "He's keeping me from doing my work; I'm behind now." Elizabeth shrugged her shoulders and walked on.

Frost looked at Mr. Naron and then went over to another bed and began making it. Mr. Naron was not screened off from the rest of the patients although there was a screen against the wall, not in use. The patients who were sitting in chairs would occasionally look in Mr. Naron's direction, and as I passed by them I heard these comments: "Ain't he dead yet? The priest already been here. I wonder how much longer he's going to be." Most of the patients who were in chairs were just staring down at the floor. There was no conversation among them except for an occasional whispered, "Is he dead?"

---

[1] During the study no clergyman was seen on the wards.

Thus passed Mr. Naron: a nuisance to the end, interfering with people's work; surrounded, perhaps, in his last moments, by his own phantom community of brothers, sisters, and children. He died as he had lived: he was just a "he" and a "him" without a name; people talked about him as if he were not there. To the end people did not do what they were supposed to do, and to the end he was tended by help who barely knew their jobs. No one held his hand, there were no tears, only a corroding irritation that he was taking so long to die—while the social conscience stood piously by, trying its respectable best to keep Mr. Naron alive with an oxygen tube fastened to his nose with a piece of dirty adhesive. Society is satisfied that it has "done its best" when it pours oxygen into a dying man. That he has first been degraded to the level of social junk is none of its affair.

ROSEMONT: HELL'S VESTIBULE

Steaming from the pit, a vapour rose
  over the banks, crusting them with slime
  that sickened my eyes and hammered at my nose.

Once there, I peered down; and I saw long lines
  of people in a river of excrement
  that seemed the overflow of the world's latrines.

I saw among the felons of that pit
  one wraith who might or might not have been tonsured—
  one could not tell, he was so smeared with shit.

. . do you see that one
  scratching herself with dungy nails. . . . ?[1]

I have described a ward in Muni San (Municipal Sanitarium). It is bad, but not the worst place I have seen for obsolete paupers. In Muni San there is a sense of responsibility: somewhere among its vast reaches there are doctors who, though

[1] From *The Inferno*. Canto XVIII.

never encountered by our researchers, must exist, for patients have seen them, and doctors prescribe for them. Muni San furnishes medicines and dresses injuries; it provides diets for diabetics, and if they become gangrenous they receive surgery. Linens are dingy at Muni San, but they are changed and washed regularly, and the sheets of incontinent patients are removed as soon as the overworked staff can get to it, sometimes even in the dead of night. There is plenty of food, and water is always handy for the thirsty. The help is often busily about, and patients who make requests receive a response. Bedpans and urinals are provided, and the beds are not smeared with excrement. Patients are never beaten by the staff and staff must not let a patient fall. But each of these conditions could be reversed: there might be just one doctor for hundreds of patients just to meet "regulations"—and he might breeze through the establishment in an hour one day a week. There might be no diets; linens might be smeared with feces and washed only when the Health Department threatened; baths might be a rarity and given with dirty water. Patients might be half starved and made to beg for a drink. Urinals might be mere tin cans, and immobilized patients might have to beg to be taken to the toilet or else be considered incontinent. "Troublesome" patients might be beaten. None of this occurs at Muni San. Rather what the patients suffer most from there, perhaps, is the sense of being dumped and lost; the emptiness of the life, the vacant routine, the awareness of being considered a nuisance and of being inferior to the most insensitive employee.

But in Rosemont all the indecencies and filth that do not occur in Muni San are piled on top of an empty life. Rosemont[1] is the Vestibule of Hell.

[1] The ward described here has about a score of patients. The building holds around a hundred. For these there is a registered nurse and somewhat less than a score of other employees including licensed practical nurses (LPN's) and attendants. All of Rosemont contains about twice the number contained in the building we studied, and there is one physician, who comes once or twice a week and "sees everybody real fast," as the researcher put it, in about an hour. No researcher saw him, except one day when one happened to be in the main office. It should be added that nothing in Rosemont is very clear because of the great difficulty in getting anything straight from the Office.

OVERVIEW[1]

Rosemont is a private institution run for profit by Mrs. Dis. She is genial, cooperative, and always one legal step ahead of the Health Department. This report starts with an overview of a typical ward.

As I entered the ward a few of the men turned their heads in my direction. Others paid no attention or were asleep. Most of them were dressed in street clothes. A few were in pajamas and robes. The clothing looked old and poorly fitting and some of it was torn at the elbows. The ward smelled strongly of urine even though the windows were open. The beds were so close together that often there was room only for a chair between them. All walls were lined with beds and there were some in the center of the room. The mattresses were thin, the beds sagged in the middle, the sheets were dingy and some of them were smeared with dried feces. The beds with no assigned occupants were covered by a thin grayish cover; others had a faded blue, red, green, or brown blanket folded at the foot or spread over the bed. The upper half of the windows had dark curtains. On the walls were a picture of George Washington, one of Jesus, another of the Madonna and Child, and a religious calendar. A couple of men had clocks at the head of their beds. The dark floor was dotted with wet spots, and I noticed several men spitting on it. Most of them were staring into space and they did not talk to one another.

I could not but notice the contrast between the attractive flooring and the drabness of the rest. The floor is tiled in colored squares and at one place there is a crest set in tile bearing the letter R. The floor is clean and waxed but two walls are dingy and have soil spots. A third has unpainted areas where remodeling has been done. The fourth wall is a

---

[2] My discussion of Rosemont is based on 35 observation periods on each of two wards. Observations were made 'round the clock for one hour each day between the hours of 9 A.M. and 7 P.M.; and thereafter for half an hour.

flimsy partition between the two sides of the division. A picture of George Washington hangs askew on the wall above the negro patients, and there are two other pictures.

There was an odor of urine. My general impression of the patients was one of apathy and depression. Most of them were sitting slumped over, heads bowed, hands folded. The few who were moving did so slowly and without animation. . . . While I was standing near the center of the ward Mr. Nathan, a large man in a dirty green shirt walked slowly over to me. . . . He talked about how hungry he was, saying that this was true of all the patients. He had never had a large appetite, he said, but even he was hungry on the food they got here. While he was talking several patients walked over and looked at a clock on the south wall. Mr. Nathan explained, "You see, it's getting near lunch time and they're all hungry. That's what everyone does from eleven o'clock until lunch time—they look at the clock."

There was some activity at the east end of the division, so I walked over. Mr. Quilby and Mr. Segram, two dirty, thin, gray-haired little men were in the same bed. One was talking loudly and the other was paying no attention. The bed had no linens, and the mattress, which was slit from end to end, had several wet spots. A second bed was empty and it too had no linens. The empty bed had a large wet spot in the center. In the third bed Mr. Quert, a patient who seemed more oriented, was sitting on the side of his bed apparently keeping the two patients from getting into his bed. He explained that someone had to watch or they would hurt themselves. Mr. Quert seemed to be keeping the two men in the bed by putting a bedside table in front of them whenever they tried to get out. I noticed that Mr. Quert had a puddle of urine under his bed too. . . . The two men were the most depressing sight I have ever seen. They were only partially dressed and neither of them had shoes on. They bumped into each other as they constantly moved back and forth in the bed. One of them was kicking or scratching the other. One tried constantly to get out of

the bed, first on one side and then on the other, but was
always prevented by the table. As he turned from side to
side he would bump into the other man in the bed and
would lift his legs high to avoid bumping him. Horrified,
I stood watching for some time. I tried to speak to the men
but they seemed not to hear. Mr. Ansmot (a patient)
shouted at one to get into his own bed, but got no results. . . . From the way he moved, one of the men must
have been blind, for he always felt around with his feet or
hands before he moved in any direction.

When I had seen enough of this I walked out. As I went
through the north division I saw a white and a colored aide
sitting in chairs, and a white aide was calling loudly and
sternly to a patient who had had an incontinent stool and
had feces smeared all over himself and his bed, "Sam, you
get that sheet up over you."

I watched the patient in the second bed in the center for
a few moments. He had feces all over himself and the bed.
I failed to find out what his name was. He did not reply
when I spoke to him. I left the division feeling completely
depressed and contaminated.

I noticed that Mr. Link and Mr. Scope were both incontinent and that the odor was especially bad on this side
of the division. As I walked down this aisle I looked down
and noticed I was standing in a puddle of urine about an
inch deep. I jumped over it and looking back saw that the
urine had collected in the center aisle and ran almost all
the way from the east to the west end of the division. It
started from the beds of four patients, Link, Scope, Yankton and Merchant. I walked down the aisle carefully avoiding the stream of urine.

THE IRONY OF GOD AND SALVATION

Hell's Vestibule is a Place of Many Ironies. Let us start with
the Irony of God and Salvation.

The religious theme is expressed strongly in an interview with Mrs. Dis' Second in Command.[1]

> Second in Command put on the pained expression of a martyr and said, "I guess the good Lord intended for me to do this kind of work. I just love these old people—you never know what's going to happen when you get old, and, if the Lord intended for me to do this work, I certainly will be as good to them as I can. . . ." (The researcher says) "I thought it might be hard to get help out here, it's so far out. . . . Maybe Mrs. Dis pays better than other places?" "Well, I don't know exactly, but she does pay well. I never ask what the pay is. I guess the good Lord wouldn't want us to do it for the money." . . . "What would you say would be the qualities of a good person to do this kind of work?" "Kindness," she whined, "and practice of the Golden Rule, just like the good Lord intended. We all must be kind to these old people; Mrs. Dis just wouldn't tolerate anything else." "Sometimes these older patients get upset; what do you do then?" "Oh," said Second in Command, "they're just like children. I feed them good. Why, they can have almost anything they want to eat; there's always things in the refrigerator. Mrs. Dis always keeps it well-stocked. I talk with them and just be kind to them and they just calm right down. . . . Oh, I just love the patients; I just love to be around them—just anything at all. (Second in Command was never seen on the wards.) The only thing that bothers me is when they die and you have to take that scum out of their mouth," and she drew up her face in disgust. "I always tell the aides it has to be done for the poor dears; we never know when we'll be like that, and it's a part of the Lord's work." She asked if I'd like a soda or 7-Up. I thought I'd better take something out of the machine. They might bring me coffee, and I didn't want to drink anything out of that filthy kitchen.

[1] The interview with Mrs. Dis is not given because every question simply touched off a long digression, which, though giving insight into her personality, did not bear on the subject. Aside from this Mrs. Dis' interview contained protestations of affection for the patients and slightly veiled invitations to the interviewer to enter some questionable deals.

The Bible also is present in Rosemont. A very nice looking copy is owned by Ed Alvin, a cruel old man, who earns his keep by helping out with the work. Ed always keeps the Bible on his bed.

> Mr. Benton said to Ed, "Junior, you better take care of that," and handed Ed a nice looking Bible. An aide was feeding Mr. Quilby, and said to him, "Oh, shut up, will you? Wait a minute, I'm not ready to give it to you yet, you silly thing." Then the aide handed Mr. Quilby two pieces of white bread, but since she didn't look as she put them toward his hand they fell on the floor. She fussed about this and told him to watch what he was doing as she picked up the bread and gave it to him. He began to eat it. Mr. Quilby is blind.

It can be seen that advertising is not the only place where values are burlesqued. The following is from observations of blind Mr. Benjamin:

> Mr. Harlow came up to Mr. Benjamin and spoke to him and sat down on his bed. I could not understand all that Mr. Benjamin was saying but it had something to do with his paying money and not having anyone to care for him. As he was talking Mr. Harlow left without saying anything and Mr. Benjamin continued to talk. Mr. Harlow came back to Mr. Benjamin and Mr. Benjamin again spoke about no one's caring for him and about someone who was supposed to take care of him but did not. Mr. Harlow said something to him softly and Mr. Benjamin said, "I've been baptized," and started to cry. He said, "They shouldn't treat me this way. I hope to goodness you aren't treated this way. I'll pray for you." Mr. Harlow said, "I ain't got nothing in the world, John," and Mr. Benjamin said that he didn't have anything either and no money to buy anything either. He talked about his things having been stolen last night and how terrible it was that people should steal from a blind man. He continued in this vein for a long time and Mr. Harlow answered very sympathetically.

Mr. Benjamin entertains two illusions: the illusion of the power of the sacred in this world, and illusory expectations.

Since all his life Mr. Benjamin was taught how to be wooly-minded and uncritical—beginning with a school system that never taught him to think—now a blind old man, he still believes that baptism and blindness can deliver him from the evils of this world when he does not have the money.

THE BENEDICTION OF THE BATH

Since bathing is a secular, not a sacred, ritual in our culture, the bathing of Mr. Benjamin does not quite belong here. On the other hand, since it is associated so much with purification, relaxation, and surcease even in our culture, it seems a veritable lay benediction. Besides, in Rosemont, where we saw only two bathings in thirty-three days—both of Mr. Benjamin—bathing gives us a chance to witness, for the first time, one of the dominant traits of a hell—the union of opposites. In this case it is the conjunction of filth and cleanliness.

An aide came to Mr. Benjamin and said, "Come with me Mr. Benjamin" but Mr. Benjamin said, "I don't want to go anywhere." When she said, "You come with me," he said, "I ain't got no breeches on; I don't want to go around naked." She said, "That's all right." As he started to get up she helped him and was going to guide him out, but he said, "I can't get through; there's something in the way," but she said, "There's nothing, come on." As he started to move she began to help him walk out. A patient came in and said, "The water's getting pretty dirty," but the aide said, "I've only got two more."

HUNGER

Since social security checks are notoriously small; since the men in Rosemont, not being residents of The City, are not eligible for admission to Muni San; and since they either have no families or have families that will not take them in, there is nobody to receive them but Mrs. Dis. Meanwhile Mrs. Dis has to make a decent living. In what follows, therefore, one should guard against judging her too harshly. After all, what would happen to obsolete people if not for the Mrs. Dises?

Mr. Hill tells the researcher of a very serious accident. He was hit by a car driven by a maniac who then turned and drove over him. At County Hospital he had many operations and a complete surgical reconstitution of his legs. He has dried feces under his fingernails and there is a bedpan almost completely full of urine setting on his bedside table. He had been told he had to get up and start using his legs. He said also that the doctors had told him that he must eat a good diet, with lots of protein for tissue repair and he expressed concern about the diet he was receiving here. He said he was constantly hungry and that everybody here is constantly hungry. He said that for breakfast they had a small bowl half full of oatmeal without cream, sugar or butter, two slices of toast and coffee. Lunch wasn't bad, but not all that it should be. Supper was a small bowl of very thin soup and two slices of toast. I could not but wonder how beneficial this major surgical repair is if the patient is not given adequate diet and care. He said that here nobody cares about the patients.

Before discussing Mr. Hill I shall give one more example of the union of excrement and food.

As I entered the kitchen several women, apparently patients, were scraping and stacking dishes, and the smell of urine greeted me. This is indeed a shock to the nervous system—to see food, hear the clatter of dishes, and to smell urine.

Hell has its logic, just like any other culture, and a fundamental postulate of it is that *Hell is the meeting place of opposites*, for while The World is relatively ordered so that opposites are kept apart, Hell is chaos, so they come together. For this reason Hell contains many incongruities that seem ironical from our point of view. The first incongruity we noticed was the religious and patriotic pictures on the walls; now we see people eating with excreta on them and all around them.

The decline of the disgust function, so that a person can bring himself to eat amid filth, is an ultimate stage in dehumanization. So closely linked is the *disgust function* to humanness that there is no culture known to anthropology where people do not have it. My friends the Pilagá Indians believe they were expelled from heaven because Asien, their high-god, could not stand the smell of their feces.

Another irony is the discrepancy between the good medical attention Mr. Hill received at Muni Clinic and the bad feeding he gets at Rosemont, so that the latter destroys the value of the former.

I now present a selection of observations on hunger.

Mr. Edwards was lying down, and asked what time it was, and I told him it was about ten after twelve. He said, "That's good. I'm hungry and it should be time to eat soon." I said, "Yes, it should be. What time do you have breakfast?" He said, "I don't know. We had that a long time ago." I asked, "What did you have this morning?" and he said, "Oh, we had toast and oats. I saved some of my bread and I ate that just a little while ago. You have to have something to tide you over until the next meal." As I started to leave he put out his hand to me to shake my hand. I shook his. He said, "I've been here a long time—it's almost 12 years now. I had to come because I was paralyzed from my waist down. I could move my arms OK but not my legs." He continued with this and also talked about his hernia operation and other ills, even telling me about his being burned on the leg when he was a child. I listened a while longer and then went on to the next bed.

Mr. Nathan walked up to me, eating a slice of toast. He smiled smugly and explained, "They gave me two breakfasts by mistake this morning, so I ate all the cereal and saved the toast. This should tide me over until lunch; I wish this would happen every morning."

Mr. Triste was eating. Occasionally he would lick his plate, bending his head to the plate and drawing the food to his mouth.

Mr. Nathan saw Mr. Edwards licking his plate, and said to me, "See him lick his plate? They get so damn hungry here. I was too. I usually buy something from the bread man when he comes, but I must have been asleep today."

Mr. Inkle was at the kitchen door asking for bread, but they would not give him any, and said, "Go on; get back to your bed." Some of the patients who were sitting in the solarium kept telling him to leave, to go back to his bed, and he finally did. Mike, who works for his keep, said several times, "I don't want no bread."

He went to the women's side room to get their trays. When he came out with them he stopped by Mr. Jacks' bed and offered him some bread that one of the patients had left and Mr. Jacks took it eagerly and put it in his bedside table. Then Mike stopped by Mr. Roberts' bed and offered him the coffee a patient had not drunk. Mr. Roberts thanked him, took it, and quickly drank it so that Mike could take the cup out with the rest of the dishes.

Mike stopped by Mr. Jacks bedside and held out a partially eaten tray of food. He smiled and asked Mr. Jacks if he wanted the bread from the tray. Mr. Jacks said something, took the bread and placed it on the shelf of his bedside table.

Mr. Edwards had been asking for food again. Lilly, an aide, said, "Ed, get up and make Edwards leave Tom's tray alone."

For supper the patients had mush, coffee or milk, chocolate pudding, bread, and a graham cracker. The men ate rapidly, hungrily, and silently, and scraped their bowls.

Mr. Benjamin, who is blind, was talking as I approached. He said good morning to me when I spoke and went on talking. I did not get the impression that he was talking to me. He said, "We don't have anything to eat. Oh, we have lots of food around here, but we don't get anything to eat."

The Canine Metamorphosis. Dogs eat hungrily and silently, beg for food, eat leavings, and lick their bowls. Inasmuch as books on dog raising recommend that they not be fed to capacity, the canine transformation of the inmates of Rosemont is almost complete in this respect. Perhaps this is an exaggeration, for not all the inmates lick their plates, beg for food, or get a chance at leavings. Leavings go only to the favorites of Ed and Mike, two patient-workers, who get their keep in exchange for the reluctant and often punitive services they render the inmates. Thus one could say that canine traits are only sprinkled among the population. Other canine traits are bone-burying, which emerges in Rosemont as setting something aside to tide one over, and being told to get back out of the kitchen, etc., when one begs for food.

All pathological environments must metamorphose the creatures in it. Franz Kafka, transformed by his humiliating father, saw himself as cockroach, various animals, and "hunger artist." Pathogenic families change their children into bugs, horses, dogs, garbage pails, phantoms, and so on. Many psychiatric institutions transform patients into simple "animals" or, at a more benign level, into retarded children. Pathogenic institutions simply cannot handle a human being, for humanness is a threat. For a cruel institution to function within its cruelties, it has to redefine its inmates—hence the pathogenic, lethal metamorphosis. In a pathogenic society, negroes become animals; Jews become monsters and murderers; Chinese become evil, yellow, little men, and so on. This redefinition of a human being into a persecutable category I have called *pathogenic metamorphosis*. Of course, the transformation cannot be perfect unless the subject acquiesces, but obsolete paupers with no place to go have no choice. Let us look at further examples.

> With that silly grin on his face, Mr. Reach was watching as I talked to Mr. Heard. He motioned for me to come over, so I walked over and said hello. Still grinning, he said, "I'm hungry. Get me something to eat. Take me home with you." I told Mr. Reach that he had just finished lunch and that he shouldn't be hungry and that I couldn't take him home with me because I didn't know where he lived. He immediately supplied the address for me, and told me that he owned his own home. I walked over to say hello to Mr. Edwards.

I walked over to Mr. Ansmot and asked, "Is it good?" He was eating very rapidly, but said, "It's all right." The soup looked mostly like liquid, with very little vegetable or meat in it. Most of the men ate very rapidly and when finished just sat and stared.

If I define a person in a particular way, it follows that I must define his entire perceptual apparatus in accordance with that definition. If I define him as "child," I talk to him as to a child, i.e., misrepresent reality to him because children cannot comprehend much. If I define him as "dog," it must follow that I talk to him as if he did not understand a great deal aside from, let us say, "go away," "come here," "lie down," "stand up," "bone," "food," and a few other simple signals—unless, of course, he is a highly trained dog. *Every institution thus establishes a culture in terms of definitions of its inmates as special kinds of entities,* and in terms of its conceptions of the inmate's capacities for seeing, hearing, and understanding. Everyone entering the institution must act accordingly: the staff must behave towards the inmates according to the definitions, and the inmates must defer to the staff's formulation. This process is at work between the researcher and Mr. Reach: the researcher assumes that Mr. Reach is some mixture of child and dog, so she tells him that he cannot be hungry because he has just had a meal, and instead of telling him simply that she cannot take him home because that is forbidden, she lies. Thus she *challenges Mr. Reach's capacity to perceive correctly* his own hunger and his ability to understand. We therefore say that the researcher *has taken on the culture* of the institution—she acts and thinks like one of the personnel in terms of their definitions of the patients. A lethal component of pathogenic institutions is that *they challenge the soundness of the perceptual apparatus of the inmates,* thus forcing them to lose confidence in their own judgment and to become as they are defined.

Continuing, we find a different researcher functioning in much the same way, for perceiving that the lunch is miserable she yet asks Mr. Ansmot, "Is it good?" How does one account for this paradox except in terms of the theory, and in terms of the total detachment of inmate from staff engendered by the metamorphosis? The worlds of staff and inmate have become totally separate, so that the former does not enter into the world of the latter. It is obvious that if the staff at Rosemont *did* enter the world of the patient, the staff would quit.

Now we can state a *law of pathogenic metamorphosis: pathogenic institutions metamorphose the inmates into specific types and treat the perceptual apparatus of the inmates as if it belonged to the metamorphosis*—dog, cockroach, child, et cetera.

Some Ironies of Hunger. Hungry men may have obsessive phantasies of succulent fruits.

> I stopped to talk to a little man on the east end of the north row of beds. I think his name was Yankton. He smiled at me brightly and immediately told me, "I always work hard but I have a good appetite." I asked him about his work and he told me he was a produce man. He said, "You know, I sold, oh, apples, oranges, melons, and bananas. Oh, those bananas, um-m-m." He shook his head and smiled as he talked about bananas. Then he said, "I work hard but I love my mother." His eyes became moist as he spoke of his mother, and he told me how dearly he loved her. He said, "Whenever there would be a little argument . . . you know how it goes, I'd give my dad the devil. I always stuck up for my mother."

Mr. Yankton tries to escape the reality of chronic hunger by transmuting it into "good appetite." Then good appetite reminds him of the arch-feeder, his mother. Thus, in an effort to avoid the reality of hunger he reminisces, only to collide with the most poignant symbol of food.

Mr. Benton, on the other hand, escaped from hunger by thinking that it was not lack of food but rather poor cooking and the specialized character of the food that bothered him.

> Mr. Benton asked, "Do you eat here?" and I said, no. He said, "You're lucky you don't," but immediately added, "Oh, I don't mean to be sarcastic, it's just that they have diet food here and it's not as good as ordinary food would be." I said, "Home cooked food always seems better," and he said, "Yes it does."

Mr. Benton and Mr. Yankton both have *delusions of extrication*. Mr. Benton evades the full impact of chronic hunger by telling himself that he is merely taking the consequences of "diet foods" and bad cooking, and Mr. Yankton escapes it by converting hunger into a robust "appetite."

The final example of hunger's irony deals with Mr. Fenn, an inmate who, like Ed, receives his bed and board for helping with the incapacitated inmates. Like Ed and many other patients, he is callous and harsh to the weak and disoriented; but like them, he is hungry.

> Mr. Fenn was looking very tired, and when I said hello to him he said, "I certainly wish I could eat early. Since I have to do so much heavy work I get hungrier than if I just laid around all day. That's really hard work, getting some of those fellows up for their baths. That one weighs 230 pounds —you know, that colored fellow we were talking to." (Time is now between 12 and 1 P.M.) I asked him more about the kind of work he did and he said that he helped with everything that needed to be done if heavy lifting was involved. He said, "I don't get enough to eat for that kind of work."

Here the irony resides in Mr. Fenn's failure to understand that the profit drive in Rosemont leaves little room for consideration of even his strength, and that the staff does not care very much whether the work assigned to him is performed. If the inmates he is supposed to take to the toilet are incontinent because he is too tired and irritable to get them out of bed to the lavatory, and back again, the regular staff simply lets them lie in their urine and feces until they get around to wiping off the bed and the inmate. Then he learns to sleep on a rubber sheet or a plastic covered mattress.

Whoever Does Not Work Shall Not Eat. The next example contains a précis of almost everything that has been discussed in this section on hunger.

> Mr. Ansmot asked the aide, "Why didn't we have meat for dinner?" and the aide said, "We work, you don't," and Mr. Ansmot said, "Don't meat help make you strong?" and the aide replied, "You ask the cook." And Mr. Ansmot said,

"You live here, you ought to know." Mr. Quert walked to the cart full of dirty dishes and took a spoon out of a dirty cup to eat the rest of his lunch with. Ed handed Mr. Stone a partially drunk cup of coffee from another inmate's tray, and he drank it.

Meat appeared in Rosemont only twice during our study, though we observed eleven midday and evening meals; yet even minimal expectation was enough to keep alive in Mr. Ansmot the hope of getting it. Apparently, however, the staff did not get too much meat either.

Mr. Ansmot had not eaten his meat and Lilly said, "You going to eat that meat?" And when he said no, she said, "Ed, get that meat from him." Ed handed her Mr. Ansmot's tray and she said, "I'm not going to give it to him, I'm going to eat it myself," and she pointed to herself.

A hell where keepers envy victims is ironical. Perhaps this envy of people who eat but do not work makes the keepers good ones: since their food is unsatisfying too and they have to work, they may dislike the inmates enough to treat them like dogs. Since the aides' work is drudgery, all *they* may be able to see is that the inmates live a lazy life. In such a context Mr. Ansmot's question, "Don't meat help make you strong?" could only have seemed ridiculous to the aide—if she thought about it at all—especially in view of the fact that not strength but acquiescence and profit is what Rosemont wants. Mr. Ansmot's failure to understand this shows that he is afflicted with false hope.

Before going on let us review what we have found out so far. We have seen that Rosemont, besides being dirty and run down, is staffed by callous personnel and underfeeds the inmates. Rosemont is characterized by what I have called *pathogenic ironies,* paradoxes, or incongruities, which can be either material objects (like pictures of saviors) or attitudes (like the belief that one should be taken care of) which are out of place there. It was seen that such paradoxes occur because the institution is indifferent to values and because some of the inmates have *false hopes* and *delusions of extrication.* Because it is a pathogenic environment Rosemont transforms its inmates and then *defines their perceptual capacities in terms of the transformation,* thus dehumanizing them and undermining their ability to make correct judgments. Culturally imposed *definitions of persons* and culture-bound *delineations of perception* are universal human tendencies, but deviant, pathogenic environments impose pathogenic definitions of persons and perception. The difference between an Australian tribal definition of members as kangaroos, wallabies, witchetty grubs, and so on, and the definitions imposed by Rosemont and similar institutions, is that in an Australian tribe everybody is defined as an animal in accordance with his totemic status, whereas in Rosemont *the imposed definition grinds status and dignity to powder.*

THE FUNCTIONS OF REMINISCENCE

Among people in a home for the aged one finds much reminiscing, for through reminiscing the old and the obsolete become aware that they exist. They seem to be saying, "I reminisce, therefore I exist." In the discussion of the Ross family it was said:

> Since memories are a family's folk-lore, reminiscences about the happier moments of life affirm and stabilize the family, for the recollection of pleasure actualizes past solidarities and mutes whatever threatens the present. When a family is miserable, happy reminiscing becomes an idyllic quasi-life, narcotizing pain and lending the appearance of validity to real life. (To Roquentin the past) "was another way of existing" and "each event, when it had played its part, put itself meekly into a box and became an honorary event."

Even in Hell's Vestibule memory can serve similar functions; and sociable reminiscing creates transient social solidarities also. Meanwhile, one cannot escape the pervading ironies. We have observed some reminiscing in Mr. Yankton's conversation with the researcher about his former occupation as fruit vendor, and viewed this as ironical because Mr. Yankton was remembering succulent fruits where he was chronically hungry. The following is another example of a reminiscence of consumption:

> Hilda (an aide) was saying to Mr. Ansmot (Mr. Reeves was also included in the conversation), "Scotch, you've got

to develop a taste for that. The scotch and gin family are nasty." Mr. Ansmot said, "Stag was my favorite beer." Ethel (an aide) replied, "I used to drink Stag. I like that Old Forrester hundred proof whiskey. Don't give me none of that eighty or ninety-two. I always wake up with a headache with those others; but with that I come to work, work all day, and nobody ever knows the difference." Mr. Reeves broke into the conversation, saying, "That's the dark beer. I like that."

Here Mr. Ansmot reminisces about alcoholic beverages, although in Rosemont it is difficult to get even a drink of water. At the same time he gains a transient solidarity with Hilda, imbibing from her a kind of phantom selfhood; by talking to an active person he somehow gains the impression that he is like her. For a moment a kind of fleeting contagion passes from her to him; it is this *contagion of life* toward which the socially dead yearn with clinging minds and hands.

The next example shows more clearly the development of transient sociability.

Mr. Edwards and Mr. Ruben were still talking. Mr. Gregory was sitting on his bed looking in his bedside stand. Mr. Benton came in from the porch and said to Mr. Karst, "Well how'd you like to be back on the road there, junior?" Mr. Karst replied, "It'd be all right." Mr. Benton said, "You worked for Boyle, didn't you?" Mr. Karst nodded and said, "And I worked for Acme twice but I quit both times." Mr. Benton said, "I helped when he sold out to Boyle—that wasn't here, that was in New York. I worked in Los Angeles and New York both." Then Mr. Karst said, "I was in La Jolla, California." Mr. Benton replied, "That's one of the most beautiful spots in the United States. How far did you say it was from San Diego to La Jolla?" Mr. Karst replied, "Sixteen to eighteen miles." Mr. Benton said, "You're right," and Mr. Karst said, very indignantly "Certainly I'm right, I lived there." Mr. Benton was quiet for a little while and then said, "I used to work for Marshall Fields in Chicago." Mr. Karst did not respond.

Men who are obsolete cannot talk about the present for they have nothing to do; they can discuss past roles only, and since they end by boring each other they drift apart. Past lives devoted to doing what they had to do rather than what they wanted to do; to jobs requiring neither study, thought, nor speculation, do not prepare them for old age where there is nothing to do. So there is the all-pervading irony: this time it is talk of roles by men who have no role left but that of *acquiescent inmate,* and talk of the pleasure of travel by men who will travel no more. The cream of the irony is the pathetic little quarrel between Mr. Benton and Mr. Karst over the distance between San Diego and La Jolla. Yet for a little while these men are drawn together and are able, perhaps, to forget the miserable present.

Not all the reminiscing heard at Rosemont had this directly *narcotizing quality,* for some of it was sorrowful. Yet the recollection of suffering in the past might conceivably be less painful than looking the present in the eye. Mr. Link's memories seem to be an example of this.

Mr. Link was sitting in a chair beside his bed, and he expectorated from time to time into an old tin can on the floor. He talked about his daughter, saying something about her being very happy. I did not understand most of what Mr. Link said, nor did he answer questions or repeat statements when I asked him to. He asked me, "Are you happy? Are you married? Do you have children?" He talked about some business and financial problems of the past but again I understood only a little of what he said. I caught phrases like "big shot," "election," and "I had lots of money." Apparently he was telling me about some man who took his money away from him, but I didn't understand all of it. He alternated between a happy and a sad expression, and at one time I was smiling because I thought he was talking about something happy. He said what had happened to him was a terrible shame—that he could be rich and happy now had this not occurred. He repeated something about "happy" and then lowered his head as if he was about to cry; but he pulled himself together and began to talk about his daughter again.

On the verge of tears, alternating between thinking of his daughter and his money, Mr. Link sits incontinent of urine in Hell's Vestibule. In his case the union of the past and present is so close that beyond the thoughts of his daughter, memory can give him no comfort. Why is he compelled to remember, then? Surely the *recollection of past misfortune must serve some biological function,* some adaptive, preservative goal. Perhaps, sunk deep in an unhappy past, Mr. Link still blots out the unthinkable present. On the other hand, it may be that regardless of circumstances the corrective (cybernetic) function of memory drives on, constantly presenting us with our past mistakes so that we will not make them again. Memory too is a function of hope, for tormenting memories mean only that memory "hopes" things will be better next time. The adaptive functions of the brain do not die even in Hell's Vestibule because basic, indissoluble properties of the *cell* are hope and memory.

A NOTE ON ACQUIESCENCE

The dictionary definitions for *acquiesce* include the meanings "to assent tacitly, comply quietly without protesting," and since the outstanding characteristic of the inmates is acquiescence, it is necessary to say a few words in general about it. First, a few examples:

Mrs. Luna said to Mr. Ansmot in a very irritated way, "I told you you had to get in bed!" And with that Mr. Ansmot very quickly got into bed. Mr. Gregory asked Daisy something, and she said, "You don't need that. Go and sit down. Which is your bed?" When he pointed to his bed she said, in a very irritated voice, "Well, it ain't made yet. You go and sit down right back where you came from." He sat down on his own bed. Daisy said to Mr. Gregory, "Get off your bed. Go out there somewhere and sit down." She was even more irritated than before.

With Mr. Holz in it, Ed dragged Mr. Holz' chair over to Mr. Holz' bed, jerked him out of the chair, dumped him into the bed, and said, very harshly, "Sit, sit, sit." An aide said, "Quit aggravating him, Ed; he ain't ate." Ed was lying on his bed making funny noises like "meow, meow." Mr. Holz was calling, "Granma, granma, ask her if she's coming." Then Ed went, "Arf, arf," imitating a dog. I had the feeling he was making fun of Mr. Holz. An aide came in with a tray, put it on Mr. Holz' bed, and said, "You know you're a nuisance." She sat down in a chair, and as she started to feed him, she said harshly, "Keep the hand down. Here, take that bread. Here, open your mouth. Here, here."

Mr. Heard was awakened by Miss Luna's pulling the pillow from under his head without saying anything to him. She left the ward with it. Mr. Heard immediately went back to sleep.

Human beings everywhere are required to acquiesce in their material conditions of life and in the way they are socially defined (as free men, as servants of the state, as slaves, as members of the kangaroo totem, and so on), and the social definition of a person always imposes an attitude toward him by those who define his position in society. But acquiescence in material conditions and in one's social position always require one to take up an attitude toward one's Self, for it is obvious that if I am defined as slave my attitude toward my Self will be very different than if I am defined as a free man. The problem of acquiescence is more critical for modern than for primitive man, because the social structure in which the latter lives usually has been relatively stable for centuries, and all who live in it have traditional roles which they learn to desire very early and with which there is little tampering thereafter. In contemporary society, however, though men are taught they are free, they are constantly being compelled to accept material conditions and social positions they reject with their hearts and souls yet find that circumstances compel them to acquiesce. Thus it comes about that acquiescence runs a gamut from quiet social conformity to terror-stricken appeasement. Actually, in our culture, the problem of acquiescence is the problem of masochism, for the masochistic approach to life is merely an assent to life. The problem then arises, why are the men in Rosemont acquiescent? In the first place they are members of a relatively docile population. It is many generations since Americans fought anything but external enemies, and they have entered the armed forces mostly on pain of imprisonment. Controversy, the flare of political passions, righteous anger about or rebellion against anything is not much part of the American scene. But equally important are the following:

Powerlessness.   All the men in Rosemont have to their names is their preposterous social security checks. As Mrs. Dis put it, they have been dumped in Rosemont by their relatives and forgotten. So they have neither money enough nor friends to extricate them. This breeds hopelessness, and hopelessness is the parent of acquiescence. The feeling of powerlessness compels them to accept the treatment they receive.

The Social Definition.   The social definition of the inmates is that of near-paupers who are a mixture of dog, child, and lunatic; and the social definition makes it possible for the help to treat them like creatures without personality. On the other hand the powerlessness of the inmates makes it necessary for them to accept the definition and the treatment that goes along with it.

Psychic Mechanisms.   Delusions of extrication, reminiscence, and resignation—an aspect of hopelessness—make it possible for the inmates to accept. With their delusions of extrication they can imagine themselves in different circumstances; and reminiscence can preoccupy them while carrying them back to a former life. Finally, hopelessness itself assuages some pain, because hope presents images of better possibilities and so stirs discontent.

Terror.   Behind the arbitrariness, the anger, and the contempt of the help (and also of the inmates) loom the ultimate threats of restraint or expulsion for those who object too much, for since a "hospital" has enormous powers, it can "restrain" the troublesome inmate by tieing him to his bed or by expelling him.

There is only one important ingredient missing from Rosemont, and that is *reward,* or the hope of it, for in Rosemont, contrary to most other acquiescent situations outside of prisons, there are no rewards for acquiescence. The adolescent who conforms (acquiesces) to group behavior can have good times with his friends; the advertising man on Madison Avenue receives raises and promotions in exchange for his organizational acquiescences; and the child who gives the school teacher the answer she wants gets a smile, a pat on the head, and a good grade.

DISTORTED PEOPLE

An intact human being is sound in mind and body. This includes sight, sanity, hearing, and continence. But a distorted one is insane, or blind, or deaf, or incontinent, and so on. Some people are distorted in several ways. The more distorted a person, the greater the tendency of others to withdraw from him. Some distortions like incontinence, for example, are more repulsive than others. Of course, not everyone withdraws from distorted people; and it is probable that the more degraded an intact person is, the greater his tendency to withdraw from those who are distorted. It is hard to imagine that a person who has had love and good fortune would be as quick to withdraw from a distorted person as one whose life was a series of deprivations and humiliations. Thus the tendency of sound people to withdraw from distorted ones is related to the experience of the former with deprivation and degradation in their own lives. But withdrawal must somehow be related also to one's fear of the distorted person; if people are afraid of a distorted person, they will be more likely to turn away than if he is safe. Finally we may surmise that if a distorted person—let us say, a hunchback—has something to give, like human warmth or gifts, people will be less inclined to reject him. All of this can be summarized by what seems to be a kind of law of distortion and withdrawal: *the tendency of sound people to withdraw from distorted ones is determined by the extent and nature of the distortion, by the degree of degradation of the sound individuals and their fear of the distorted person,* and *by the distorted person's own resources,* e.g. human warmth, property, etc. The ability of the distorted person to "get around" plays an important part in the withdrawal of others also. For example, a blind incontinent patient can be terrifying in a crowded place like Rosemont because those around him are always afraid that, groping his way to their bed, instead of to his own, he might dirty it.

I have chosen what is, perhaps, a harsh word to refer to all those who suffer among us because they differ in extreme ways from the more fortunate who are well-formed and have all their faculties. But the word "distorted" seems to me to convey better than any other the inner meaning to us of such misfortunes. For what most people in our culture experience in contact with distorted people is not compassion or annoyance at some anticipated burden, but the cold sweat of revulsion.

Mr. Quilby, the little blind man with the bad toe, whom one of the researchers saw rolling around in bed with another man on the first day of her research, is a good illustration of the operation of the *law of distortion and withdrawal,* for not only is he blind, but he is psychotic, incontinent, and highly mobile. On the other hand, he has no resources at all. It is interesting that Mr. Benjamin, who is also blind and mobile, but has a little personal cache of aspirin, hot water bottles, and so forth that he is willing to make available, and who is not incontinent or psychotic, is not treated as badly as Mr. Quilby. But let us follow the natural history of Mr. Quilby for a month; this will tell us much about the law and provide further knowledge of Rosemont.

> Mr. Quilby hallucinating and talking loudly. Chased from Mr. Ansmot's bed: "You get off my bed—get away from here." Mr. Quilby walks smack with his head into a wall but simply reverses. Yvonne was sweeping the floor on this side and she said to Mr. Quilby, "You get in your bed now or sit down in your chair, or you'll hurt your toe again." On Yvonne's instruction the researcher took him by the arm and directed him to his chair and he sat down with no resistance.

Human beings, like most other warm-blooded animals, appropriate and defend territory. In Rosemont we have the culturally determined expression of this territoriality emerging as *defense of the bed.* Yvonne is hard to explain—she was a decent human being with a real feeling for the inmates.

> The aide feeding Mr. Quilby replied, "I'm going to give him a whole loaf of bread some day," and Daisy said, "You think he'll eat it?" and the aide replied, "Sure he will." Daisy said, "Yeh, I guess he will." Then the aide who was feeding Mr. Quilby said, "I'm not talking to you. Keep your mouth shut." Then she immediately said, "Open your mouth." Mr. Quilby said something about being fed too fast and the aide said, "Don't tell me I'm feeding you too fast." Ed said, "He's for the birds."

Here the sarcasm and contempt of the aides is echoed by Ed, who works for his keep. The pig metamorphosis ("I'm going to give him a whole loaf of bread some day") is an institutional irony: men who are underfed are likened to pigs because they are hungry. We can see that Mr. Quilby is a nuisance, yet he has to be fed because if he feeds himself he will make too big a mess.

The aide was finished feeding Mr. Quilby. His tray was empty and she said to the other aide, as she got up to leave, "Watch him holler for water." The aide replied, "No, you've had enough for now" and left. The other aide continued to sit on Mr. Triste's bed. Mr. Ansmot said, "He's been hollering for water for a long time." Mr. Ansmot and the aide were talking very softly and I couldn't hear what they were saying. . . . Mr. Quilby said, "Guess there ain't no water in that jug." Then he began calling, "Alice, Alice, Big Alice will be down next week." He repeated this several times. When Daisy came back into the ward she looked as if she was eating either an orange section or a piece of orange candy. She went to Mr. Quilby's bed and gave him a piece of it, saying to him, "Don't bite my hand now."

The bit of orange is pseudo-expiation—a gesture to the conscience that guarantees that, since the feeble conscience has been satisfied by a sop, the behavior will be repeated.

Mr. Quilby got up and started walking toward Mr. Ansmot, who yelled, "Get away!" but Mr. Quilby kept going toward him. Ed, who was lying on his bed at that end of the hall, got up, slapped Mr. Quilby, dragged him back to his bed, and laid him down. During this Mr. Quilby was saying, "I've got to wash myself; let me go, I've got to wash myself." Ed said, "Shut up!" several times; and then "Stay in bed; them guys don't want to be bothered with you." When Ed lay down, Mr. Quilby got right up, and Ed said, "All right girls, he's all yours now." Daisy came in from the other side and put Mr. Quilby back in bed, saying, "Get on that bed." When he started pulling the sheets off and then taking his pants off, Daisy called to Ed and said, "Look what he's doing, Ed. Help me." But Ed ignored her and Daisy said in a louder voice, "Come on, Ed, and help me. Don't you see what he wants?" Ed got up and took Mr. Quilby to the lavatory and Daisy straightened his bed while he was gone. Ed turned Mr. Quilby loose at the door of the lavatory and he wandered rudderless. Ed returned and handled Mr. Quilby roughly. He got him to his bed and set him down in it quite roughly, saying, "You stay there; I'm sick of you," and lay down in his own bed. Daisy was sitting there, and when Ed kept saying over and over again how sick he was of looking at Mr. Quilby she said, "Maybe some people are sick of you too."

Ed had a Bible lying on the top corner of his bed. Mr. Charles seemed concerned that it might fall and started moving it over toward the center of the bed. Ed said, in a very nice tone of voice, "That's okay, I want it there."

Over and over again blind, psychotic inmates try to excrete but get into trouble either because they cannot find their urinals or because no one will take them to the toilet. "Incontinence" is related to inability to excrete decently because the patient cannot get to the lavatory or cannot find his urinal. Mr. Benjamin who is blind but not psychotic puts it concisely:

Mr. Benjamin began feeling around where he was sitting, and as he did so he reached out further and further until he was no longer sitting on his bed. Mr. Ansmot, who was at the opposite end of the ward, yelled, "Get on your bed." Mr. Benjamin moved over to the next bed, which is Mr. Nathan's, and Mr. Ansmot called out in a very loud voice, "Get on your own bed before they tie you in!" Mr. Benjamin paid no attention but kept moving around. Ed came in carrying a long, narrow cabinet. He had to pass through the aisle in which Mr. Benjamin was, and said, "Get out of my way, Benjamin. Come on, move." Mr. Benjamin did, and Ed went on. Then Mr. Benjamin started to walk around again and groped around as if he were trying to find something. I thought he was trying to find the can he uses as a urinal. He said, "I can't see." Mr. Nathan came in and stood close to me, and said, "He doesn't know what he's doing. He's out of

his place," and walked on past Mr. Benjamin to the lavatory.
. . . Mr. Benjamin finally sat on Mr. Ruffe's bed, and Mr.
Ruffe looked kind of upset by this and got up out of his
chair, pulling the blanket at the foot of the bed away so that
Mr. Benjamin could not touch it. . . . Mr. Benjamin, sitting
on Mr. Ruffe's bed, kept reaching out and asking at intervals
for "my pee-bottle." As last he said, "If you don't give me
my pee-bottle I'm going to go on the floor." . . . Mr. Fenn
came in and said to Mr. Benjamin, "What's wrong?" and
took Mr. Benjamin to the lavatory.

During this time three members of the staff were in and out of
the ward and several patients were looking on.

Mr. Quilby, because he is blind and disoriented, and because
no one wants to help him, is pushed to incontinence and then
penalized. This can only disorient him further, increase his anxiety,
and make him even more likely to be incontinent. The *provocation–punishment* cycle is present in feeding too: Mr. Quilby has
to be fed, but since he is unable to see and is disoriented, he does
not eat as the aide wants him to, so she curses him, which makes
him inept, which brings further scolding, and so on.

Mr. Quilby was bouncing on Mr. Segram's bed and Mr.
Segram was sitting on the end of it. Mr. Segram was hitting
at Mr. Quilby. Ed came in pushing a mop bucket of steaming water. He went to Mr. Quilby's bedside, grabbed him by
the arms and bounced him down on his own bed. Turning
to Mr. Segram, he said harshly, "And you get on this chair."
Yvonne came into the ward carrying a tray which she took
to Mr. Quilby's bedside. She said to him, "Come over this
way Mr. Quilby, I've got your supper. That's it, come over;
that's good." She said this softly, not roughly as many of the
aides and attendants do. Yvonne smiled and laughed frequently and appeared to be talking with Mr. Quilby as she
fed him.

Ed is at least as cruel as any of the regular help; to him the
inmates are merely a burden, and since they remind him of his
own degradation he vents his spleen on them. The researcher's
observation is particularly striking because it throws Ed's harshness into relief against Yvonne's kindness.

What follows now is a long extract from the nineteenth study day. Mixed in with observations of Mr. Quilby is much of the life of the ward.

Mr. Quilby had just urinated into a urinal and then poured the urine on the floor under his bed. Mr. Fenn (an inmate working for his keep) came in from the northeast entrance pushing Mr. Ansmot in a wheel chair. He helped Mr. Ansmot into bed, talking to him. Mr. Ansmot asked, "Get my spout (urinal) before someone else gets it." Mr. Fenn replied, "Right away?" and then went out to the north ward. Mr. Ansmot said, "Yes, right away." A bell clanged three times. Mr. Quilby was saying, "I want this door opened so I can get in." He was crawling around on his bed as if he was looking for something. Mr. Ansmot turned to Mr. Triste and said, "How are you feeling today?" I couldn't hear Mr. Triste's response. Mr. Quilby said, "Oh shit." Mr. Fenn brought the urinal to Mr. Ansmot. He saw Mr. Quilby crawling and stumbling about his bed, shrugged his shoulders and left the ward. Mr. Fenn went to Mr. Quilby, and said, quite harshly, "Wait a minute." Mr. Quilby was pushing and pulling chairs about that were at his bedside. There were three in the direct vicinity of his bed. Mr. Fenn said, "Put it down; now sit it down." Then he said, "Oh, the hell with you," and left the ward. Mr. Quilby then turned one chair over, another one and another one upside down, stacking them one on top of the other until there was a maze of chairs. He was mumbling all the time, and the only thing I could understand was, "Where is that good rocking chair?" Mr. Ansmot and Mr. Triste were watching. Mr. Quert said to Mr. Stone, "He's crazy." Mr. Quert replied, "Yeh." Mr. Ansmot said to Mr. Quilby, "That's a chair you're turning over."

At the same time at the other end of the ward Mr. Benjamin (also blind) was talking aloud. No one was paying much attention to him. He was saying, "Now you'd better bring my shoes now. I told you last time you'd better bring my shoes." The floor was wet under Mr. Quert's bed and chair too. Mr. Edwards was also yelling at this time, "Bring my supper. Damn you, bring it, you slow pokes. I'll dy-

namite you, you bitch." Mr. Benjamin was continuing to call
out that someone had stolen his shoes. Mr. Ansmot said to
Mr. Quilby as Mr. Quilby approached Mr. Ansmot's bed,
"Leave my bed alone. Get away from here." Then Mr.
Stone went into the north ward. Mr. Benjamin was still
talking about his shoes, "Bring those shoes back and put
them where you got them from." Mr. Edwards was damning
the staff about supper. Mr. Quilby was saying something
about, "I can't get over" and Mr. Ansmot was slapping at
Mr. Quilby with a towel, telling him to get away, "Get out
of my bed, get!" Mr. Quilby was sitting on Mr. Ansmot's
bed, and Mr. Ansmot said, again, "Get back. Don't wet
on my bed." Meanwhile the TV was blaring though no one
was watching it. Mr. Benjamin continued to talk for quite
some time. Suddenly Mr. Ansmot yelled for Ed. Mr. Nathan
came into the ward and looked at the clock above Mr.
Roberts' bed. Mr. Triste stood up by his bed and watched
Mr. Quilby. Mr. Ansmot was still trying to get Mr. Quilby
to go away from his bedside, saying, "Get away from there.
Leave that bed alone." Then Mr. Quilby went to the chairs
he had stacked and scattered about on the floor. He sat on
the floor and crawled about, over towards Mr. Harlow's and
Mr. Benton's beds. Mr. Edwards left the ward yelling,
"Dynamite." Mr. Ansmot yelled for Ed again and Mr.
Quilby said, "Now I can't pee at all." Mr Harlow
yelled at Mr. Quilby, "Get out of here," four times, and
then said, "Turn around," but Mr. Quilby said, "I can't," and
Mr. Harlow slapped him. Then Mr. Harlow and Mr. Quilby
seemed to be struggling with Mr. Harlow's chair. . . . Mr.
Benton slapped Mr. Quilby's face, and Mr. Quilby said,
"Quit slapping me on the face," and sat down on Mr. Benton's bed. Mr. Benton pushed him rather gently with his
foot, saying, "Get over to your own bed. . . ." Mr. Quilby
and Mr. Harlow are now struggling with each other and Mr.
Harlow is trying to push Mr. Quilby toward the latter's
bed. When Mr. Quilby got on Mr. Reeves' bed Mr. Benton
got up, went to Mr. Quilby and slapped his buttocks, pulled
him over to his rightful bed, hit him hard again on the
buttocks, and bounced him onto his bed. Then he straightened the overturned chairs and said to Mr. Quilby, "Damn

you," and went to his own bed, saying, "He'd drive a man crazy." Mr. Quilby continued to mumble to himself. . . . Many of the patients did not seem to be aware of the scuffling going on. . . . Mr. Quilby was up again, groping about his bed. He moved it to and fro, as he talked to himself. He bounced his mattress, crawled across his bed, stepped into urine and then toward Mr. Segram's bed. As he moved Mr. Segram's chair he patted his foot in the urine on the floor. "Door" was the theme of his mumbling. When he pulled Mr. Segram's bed about two feet toward his own Mr. Segram said, "Oh, get the hell out of here." . . . Mr. Benton said to Mr. Charles, "He hasn't got any mind to cope with. No other method works except to be rough with him."

A consequence of the operation of the processes of distortion and withdrawal is to drive a badly distorted person to ever more extreme expressions of distortion, as extreme withdrawal increases his inability to cope with the environment. This increases his distortion, and society responds by withdrawing further. Mr. Quilby walks in urine and pats his foot in it, making himself more disgusting and accentuating tendencies to withdraw. When a person is distorted an ideology develops about how to deal with him. Mr. Benton says, for example, that since Mr. Quilby "hasn't got any mind to cope with, no other method works on him except to be rough with him." This is part of the ideology of hostile withdrawal.

During the researcher's hour of observation no regular staff appeared, so that the "handling" of Mr. Quilby was left entirely to the inmates, including Mr. Fenn and Ed. Though this "handling" was more of a crushing, the law of distortion helps us to understand the process: this highly mobile, disoriented, and incontinent old man threatens the only integrity left to the degraded inmates—their *bed-territories*. Whoever's bed he alights on and dirties is blasted. Hence a massive though transient solidarity is mobilized to defeat him. It is the excremental patriotism of the degraded and the lost.

Daisy (an aide) brought in another tray and went to feed Mr. Quilby. She tugged at his shirt and said very harshly, "Sit up, sit up." Mr. Quilby sat on the side of the bed and

Daisy poked food into his mouth. Supper was soup, coffee or milk, two slices of bread, two medium cookies, and a dish of apricot-colored pudding or something of similar consistency.

Daisy had given Mr. Quilby seven pieces of bread and he was eating the last two now. As Mr. Quilby went toward Mr. Jacks he picked up his cane and hit and poked Mr. Quilby, saying, "Get out of here." Mr. Twine, who had been trying to overtake Mr. Quilby, at last caught up with him and taking his arm, led him to bed, and he left. Mr. Quilby was up walking around again and climbed up on Ed's bed. Ed came into the ward and jerked him off his bed and Mr. Quilby screamed, "Oh, oh!" Mr. Edwards laughed as he watched. Mr. Quilby began to yell, "Hey, Mary (his sister)." Mr. Edwards muttered to himself, "Him and Mary." Mr. Quilby was saying, "I want to see my sister, Mary." He yelled particularly loudly, "Mary!" and Mr. Ruben said, "Oh, shut up." Mr. Segram talked to Mr. Quilby and I could hear Mr. Quilby say, "Somebody's going to get hung in here tonight. They're going to hang me and then get a needle and thread and sew me up." Someone else yelled, "Oh, shut up." Mr. Twine went to Mr. Quilby and Mr. Quilby yelled, "Go away, go away!" Ed went to Mr. Roberts' bedside, picked up his bedside table, put it on his head, wiggled his hips and sang. Mr. Roberts looked disgusted. Mr. Quilby was still yelling and Mr. Twine was holding him down in bed.

Mr. Quilby continued to talk and soon began to cry loudly. As Mr. Fenn passed him he bent down to Mr. Quilby's ear and yelled, "Ow!" and left the ward. On his way back into the ward he went over to Mr. Quilby and said in his ear, "Arr, arr, ow!"

It will have been observed that the law of distortion and withdrawal does not state what becomes of the distorted person, but simply that others withdraw from him. I have pointed out, however, that the withdrawal of others increases his anxiety and disorientation and thus further increases withdrawal. Mr. Quilby's anxiety has reached such a pitch that he expects to be hanged and sewn into a shroud. The unimpeded working out of the law would thus lead ultimately to a pervading sense of doom and finally, perhaps, to suicide. Before this, however, the distorted person will engage in ever-widening swings of disorientation until he becomes totally intolerable and is beaten, tied up, or killed. We have already seen Mr. Quilby beaten.

> Mr. Quilby is restrained, flat in his bed, with leather straps on his wrists and ankles. Ropes are attached to the straps and tied to the legs of the bed. A sheet is over his head and he appears to be asleep. He appears to be tied tightly.

> Everything was quiet except for Mr. Quilby. He seemed to be moaning softly. He was restrained and lying on a bare mattress and was partially covered by a sheet.

> Everything on the division is quiet: there is no activity and no noise. Suddenly Mr. Quilby sat upright in bed and said, "Well, who passed away this time?" After a few minutes of silence he said, "It looks like we're all here again this morning—well, thank God for that."

Thus the law suggests increasing rejection of the distorted person by the environment leading to more and more punitive measures and the development in him of a *pervading sense of doom*. Obviously all of this can occur only in the presence of degraded fellow inmates and in an absence of controls. We have seen just this in Rosemont, a private home for obsolete paupers.

SOMETHING ABOUT THE HELP

Before bringing this section to a close I will present some more of the rather scant materials on the staff. From the observations and from the interview with the Second in Command, the reader will already have formed some opinion of their general indifference and callousness. The data I present now are intended to give insight into the poor self-conception of the staff, for it is important to restate the idea that unless a person feels degraded himself he will not be able to degrade others. It does not follow, of course, that all degraded people will try to degrade others; I suggest rather that a person with strong self-respect has no need to degrade his fellows.

Our first piece of data derives from an interview with Josephine Pike, an aide.

> A huge woman in a dark print cotton dress entered the room. "Do you wanna see me?" she asked. "Yes, I do." I introduced myself, and since she didn't say anything but, "Howdy," I asked her name. "Pike," she said. Her dress was torn in a couple of places and her body odor was terrific; however, it was the hottest night of the year. Her tongue seemed too large for her mouth, and she was difficult to understand. Occasionally she drooled, and I wondered if she'd had a stroke. I didn't smell any liquor. She sort of sprawled down into a chair and draped the upper part of her body across the table, laying her head on one arm so as to face me. "Man," she said, "it's hot," and turned to brush a cockroach away. The cockroach kept inching up and she would nonchalantly throw out her arm to make him move. A couple of times she tried to swat him. This went on during most of the interview. . . . I first asked her the question about the qualities of a good aide, and she listed kindness, conscientiousness, and understanding the patient. . . . When I asked her, "What do you do when a patient gets upset," she brightened and sat up and said, "Well, I talk with 'em. I'm a Christian woman and I'm kind. I go and fix 'em a glass of milk or a jelly sandwich, because those men are hungry. You know, men: just love 'em and feed 'em and they're happy."

Perhaps not the dirt and the rags but the nonchalant familiarity with roaches is the symbol of degradation here. The reader's attention should be called to the fact that both Josephine and the Second in Command responded to the question, "What do you do when a patient gets upset?" by saying that they feed them, thus certifying to the fact that hunger is a chronic problem.

In the next example the researcher gets into a conversation with Lilly, an aide.

> Lilly was feeding Mr. Quilby, and I heard her say to him sternly, "Shut up. Eat this. I said eat it." She told me that

Mr. Quilby could feed himself but that she didn't like to see him do it—"The poor thing can't see and he makes such a mess." She put the cup to his mouth and he drank a big swallow of milk. Lilly said, "Oh, he likes his bread and milk. You'd live on it, practically, wouldn't you?" She said she would like to do more for all the patients but that it was impossible for her to do it all alone. She said there are 88 patients and that most of them would rather have her take care of them than anyone else, but that she isn't able to do it all.

Lilly said, "I'm a nurse, you know—or I could be if I would just go ahead and finish." She sounded proud and a little defensive. I said something noncommital and she went on, "I could finish without half trying, and I'm sure I will some day; I think I should. I wouldn't have to do anything. Mrs. Dis said she could get it for me, and I'm sure she could. I could just get it from working under her. Then I could be a licensed practical nurse." The aide who always wears the black velvet hat came up to Lilly and me. Lilly said to me, "This is my helper." I said, "Well, that's nice." Lilly said, "Well, I have to have some help around here; I can't do it all myself."

The aide in the black cap then proceeded to give Lilly, her "superior," orders, including telling her to wipe up the puddles of milk on Mr. Quilby's bed, and Lilly obeyed.

It would be a misunderstanding of Josephine, Lilly, and Second in Command to interpret their misrepresentations as defense of the institution only. They may be far more interested in defending themselves—not against outer, but rather against inner criticism. When they talk as they do to the researchers they seem to be addressing their own consciences, saying, "I am really a human being; and you, my conscience, and I, are really one; you are not buried and alienated at all."

SUMMARY AND CONCLUSIONS

Every institution establishes a "national character" of inmates and staff in accordance with the remorseless requirements of the institution and in relation to the characteristics brought to it by inmates and staff. Given the commitment of Rosemont to profit, the laughable social security checks of the inmates, and the cost of food, comfort, and a high standard of living, certain consequences have to follow. In order for Mrs. Dis to be comfortable and make a good profit, according to her lights, she has no choice but to extract as much as she can from the pensions of the inmates and the salaries of her help and to limit the standard of living of both. That of the inmates is cut to a level just above starvation but below that of a good prison. In order to do this a fundamental transformation has to be brought in the mode of life and the self-conception of the inmates and in the staff's way of perceiving them. In short, Mrs. Dis makes it necessary for her institution, as personified in her staff, to conceptualize the inmates as child-animals, and to treat them accordingly. This in turn is made possible because in our culture personality exists to the extent of ability to pay, and in terms of performance of the culturally necessary tasks of production, reproduction, and consumption.

But the transformations are possible in Rosemont only because of the acquiescence of the inmates; and this is obtained not only because the inmates are old and powerless, having been abandoned by their relatives and a miserly Government, but because, with one or two exceptions, they recognize that being obsolete they have no rights; because they understand that having nothing they are not going to get anything. Meanwhile their degradation is intensified by the fact that while economically poor they are intellectually poor too; for the schooling they received, and the culture in which they have lived, provide no resources for making life in a filthy hole more bearable. They can neither read nor carry on conversations of interest to one another; nor, having lost faith, do they have the culture of worship. Rather they spend their time staring into space, defending their beds against the gropings of the blind, the incontinent, and the disoriented, or watching the behavior of their blind and psychotic fellows, while they wait obsessively for the next meager meal.

Thus the "national character" of all the inmates becomes reduced to several simple components under the tyranny of the institution. These components are apathy, obsessive preoccupation with food and excreta, the adoption of the role of child-animal, and defense of the bed. To this may be added general acquiescence in everything the institution does, decline of the disgust function, and preoccupation with reminiscence.

THE TOWER NURSING HOME

Having seen Muni San and Rosemont, we ought to visit a place where good will is expressed in an atmosphere of relative tranquility. Tower charges less than some private hospitals but enough to limit patients to the upper middle class and above. Tower patients read more and seem better educated than those at Muni San and Rosemont, and some have had careers in business or the professions. Though there is a ward with over a dozen beds, most of the patients share rooms with one or two others, and some have private rooms with their own furniture, family pictures, and other amenities. A number of patients have their own TV sets or radios, even though there is a TV set in the lounge on each floor.

There are about 100 patients in Tower—four times as many women as men. They are under the care of between 50 and 60 regular employees assisted by a few male orderlies, and some of the patients have private nurses. The staff enjoys the work, most of them have been there for years, and they are gentle and solicitous.

Tower is clean and almost entirely odorless, linens are ironed and white, and bed-baths are given every day. Patients' private doctors are available by phone; many of the patients are very sick indeed, many must be fed with a syringe or by tube, and some are incontinent, confused, or psychotic.

Tower is proud of its gleaming kitchen, its carefully calibrated diets, and its food and linens stacked high in storage bins.

Every day is visitors' day at Tower, at the appropriate hours, and the place sometimes buzzes with the noise. Whole family groups—young grandchildren and all—are not infrequent; and even when a patient is so disoriented or so far gone that he cannot respond, his visitors will sometimes come and merely sit.

THE AGED UPPER-MIDDLE-CLASS AMERICAN WOMAN

Introduction. This section is devoted largely to the exploration of the mind of the aged upper-middle-class American woman, not only because women outnumber the men by four to one at Tower, but also because many of the men are in such bad condition physically and mentally that contact with them is problematic. Meanwhile, since women sixty-five and over outnumber men of that age in our society, especially above seventy-five years of age[1] it is important to learn as much as possible about them. In a 1958 publication the Bureau of the Census[2] reported that in 1960 women of eighty-five and over would outnumber men by 46 per cent, but that by 1980 they would have a numerical superiority of 75 per cent. But survival is not the only issue, for since men surviving at very advanced ages tend to be in worse physical and mental condition than women of comparable age, the understanding of the mind of the aged woman is doubly important.

In discussing the mind of the aged woman I have concentrated on the cultural content of what she says and on the attitudes of those taking care of her. Perhaps this section ought to be called "On the persistence of the cultural configuration in the aged, upper-middle-class American woman." The cultural content of a mind will be seen to have some diagnostic implications, for it is largely (though not entirely) the capacity to keep the cultural configuration in order in one's mind that makes the difference between the mentally well and unwell.[3] Involved also

[1] Inasmuch as there were only about 9 per cent more women than men sixty-five years of age and over (45.31 to 54.69%) in the population in 1960, the striking ratio in Tower is not accounted for by the survival statistics. As one ascends the age scale the differences between the number of surviving males and females changes rapidly. For example, whereas between the ages of seventy and seventy-four females outnumber males by about 15 per cent, in the age group of eighty-five and over females outnumber males by 36 per cent. (Figures are from the 1960 census and the calculations were made by Professor David Carpenter of Washington University.)

[2] Bureau of the Census, *Current Population Reports.* Population estimate series p. 25, No. 187, Washington, 1958.

[3] The reader is referred to the extract from "Recent research in prevention of mental disorders at later age levels" by V. A. Kral, M.D. in Appendix B for an expert orientation to this problem. Dr. Kral's paper

in the problem of the mind of the aged is the culture's tolerance for hallucination. A person who manages all aspects of the cultural configuration well may yet have "little" hallucinations, such as suddenly imagining he sees birds where there are none; so long as hallucinations do not interfere with social functioning or endanger life, a benign and enlightened society finds no difficulty in accepting them.

I am concerned to show also that even in the relatively kindly atmosphere of Tower, old people, with their reduced capacity to deal with stress, may be poorly handled at times by personnel who, while committed to an ideology of benign patience, nevertheless do not understand the aged, cannot truly empathize with them, and so may gloss everything over with the attitude that the aged are confused babies. On the other hand, the inability of the patients to empathize with one another is of particular significance in Tower because of the solicitous orientation of the institution itself. In this atmosphere of kindliness and care the patients too often seem to dissipate their last energies in blind and spiteful conflict with one another.

In attempting to understand these people, one remembers that they are not merely aged, but that they are aged people *in an institution,* cut off from family and friends except during visiting hours, and that they are being cared for by people who are paid to do it. True, many times it is better to be attended by those animated by pecuniary benevolence than by a family animated by no benevolence at all. Still, the choice may be hard and may constitute a serious stress for people ill equipped, because of their age, to deal with it. The difficulties inherent in being aged in our culture are enhanced, even under conditions of pecuniary benevolence, by an institution's need for orderliness, routine, and profit, all of which exert a coercive power. It is safe to say that some people would not be in Tower at all if given free choice—which, of course, they do not have because feebleness, illness, money, and the inability or unwillingness of family to take care of them have made Tower the only solution. For many not even the solicitousness of Tower can erase the "weariness, the fever, and the fret" consequent on being old in our society.

appeared in *Recent Research Looking Toward Preventive Intervention,* Ralph H. Ojemann (ed.), State University of Iowa, 1961.

The Setting

The patient in room 25 appeared to be straining to see who was in the hall and seemed to be anxious that I stop and see her. She was in bed, and the covers were neat. I introduced myself and told her that I was a graduate nurse from University. . . . Her room was neat and clean, and the walls were bright yellow. The dresser appeared to be one that ought to belong to the patient, and on it were photographs, toiletries, and a heart-shaped box of candy. The patient's hair was curled and combed and had a ribbon in it. She wore powder, rouge and lipstick. . . . A practical nurse introduced me, telling me that the patient was Mrs. Gort (age 78). Then the nurse motioned me out in the hall, where she told me that Mrs. Gort was quite vain and liked people to tell her how pretty she was. Back in Mrs. Gort's room she told her, "Yes, you are very pretty. Oh, yes, you are very pretty," and left. Mrs. Gort smiled broadly while the practical nurse was saying this.

The patient in 13 was not there. The room had pink walls and there was a lavender bedspread. The lavender and the pink were very intense. . . . The patient in room 28 was in a wheel chair. I introduced myself and she seemed to grimace or to smile at me, but she did not reply. Her room was blue, with a peach spread on the bed and many pictures of the patient's family around the room. There were also some plants.

I knocked and entered room 211. To me this is the most pleasing room on Division 1. It is bright, cheerful, and more like a room one would expect to find in someone's home. The other rooms on this division, even though furnished with maybe more of the patient's personal possessions, seemed more crowded and hospital-like.

In the hall were a record player, a television set, a bookcase with current novels, plants, and pictures. It is a pleasant area and seems to be the closest thing to a lounge or sitting room for the patients on the first floor.

The main hall is much wider than the two wings and much more attractive. Walls are a pleasing yellow, the ceilings white, and the overhead pipes and clumsy radiators at both ends of the hall match the color of the structures behind them. The floor is tiled with a gray and black pattern bordered with black. For its entire length, the hall is lined on both sides with chairs, and there are divans near the east and west ends, where most of the patients gather. The most comfortable chairs are grouped around a small table, and in the east end there is a television set. An antique umbrella stand is against one wall, and in an alcove that looks as if it had been made for that purpose, is a religious statue on a marble pedestal. The thumb has been broken off and glued back in place. Birds and flowers scenes embroidered on Japanese silk framed in bamboo decorate the walls. New upholstery on a few chairs and on the divans make the other chairs look rather shabby, although everything about the hall is clean and in good repair.

I am sitting facing an immense, beautiful stained glass window, which reads "Since ye have done it unto the least of them, ye have done it also unto Me." With the sun shining through, I am impressed with what a warm, peaceful, and cheerful area this is. The only activity during this time has been the sound of the two aides handling trays in the west wing.

Mrs. Leacock is asleep in her room, and a steam inhalator is bubbling on a table by her bed. Her room is especially ornate, with approximately six 9×12 family photographs plus cologne bottles, cocktail glasses, radio, etc. Patient Rhea (age 65) in 182 is dressed in a dark dress and is propped up in bed with three divan cushions and is watching television.

The nurses' work areas on this east wing are the most unattractive part of the third floor. Into what obviously used to be a bathroom, are crowded a medicine cabinet, a tiny, unattractive desk, and a bathtub . . . thus allowing only one person to be there at a time. In the hall is an old fashioned, ugly chest, which seems to serve only as a table on which to put things. On the refrigerator next to the chest a sign says, "No one is to open this icebox except the nurses on the floor." On a tiny bulletin board are fire regulations for first, second, and third floors, telling nurses how to evacuate patients. A notice written in pencil on a scrap of paper tells which patients need help in preparing to eat and which patients' trays come up at 7 A.M. Patients who can't feed themselves must wait until the day shift comes on and others eat at 6 A.M.

In the corner of the bulletin board is a worn, flower-bedecked, card with a poem called "The Nurses' Prayer," which is about a devoted, ever-smiling nurse, who wants to wear her cap and pin in Heaven. Beyond this area is a utility room. . . . Although not actually dirty, this is a very cluttered, unattractive area, drastically in need of paint. As I walked down to the west wing I was keenly aware of how drab both wings are in comparison with the main hall. The hallways in the west wing are narrow, undecorated, with discolored yellow paint, and several cracks in the plaster.

Patient Sorge (age 68) was sleeping soundly and I watched her for several minutes to be sure she was breathing. She is dressed in a very lacy nylon gown which is, to say the least, impractical, considering her condition. Mr. Botrom (age 99) was asleep in his room. Mrs. Leicht (age 82) was sitting propped up at the head of her bed. Her room is very small and dreary, with darkened and chipped paint and cracked plaster. I wonder whether a patient more aware of her surroundings would be placed in this room. I said hello to her and she replied by asking me how the weather is outside. She pointed to the dirty torn window blind, which was drawn across the window, and said, "I never know. They do it, but what can I do about it; what can I say?" I told Mrs. Leicht that it was raining, and I went over to the window blind to show her. Much to my surprise the sun was shining. As I raised the blind Mrs. Leicht saw the sun and said, "I think you're mixed up; it doesn't look like rain today." I explained to Mrs. Leicht that it had been cloudy, and I felt a little foolish when I realized I was trying to convince her that I wasn't confused. I changed the subject by asking Mrs. Leicht if she was going to get up soon, and she said, "Whenever they decide to lift me, I suppose. I don't know. What can I do about it?"

I stopped in the utility room or bathroom on the west wing. It has an empty room with a bathtub in it, as well as a partitioned-off area which contains two bathtubs with a walk in between them. Like the room at the east hall, this room is cluttered and unattractive. It contains sinks for shampooing as well as some items of equipment such as bedpans and urinals.

The linens on the beds appear to be clean, white, and wrinkle-free. All the beds are covered with bedspreads, and there seems to be a different color or design in each room.

Some Sketches of Patients

Mrs. Manger (age 80) and Mrs. Mintner (age 80). I walked into Mrs. Manger's room. It is long and narrow, with two beds, two bedside tables, a dresser, a toilet, and a big chair. She was sitting in the big chair with the TV table in front of her. On her right was another table with her radio on it. Near her was a straight chair with a Bible and newspaper on it. As I entered I said, "Hello, may I come in and talk with you?" She said, "Oh, yes. Come in. It's so nice to see you." She began to take the papers off the chair and put them on the table. She said, "Sit down here." I put the Bible on the table and sat down. She extended her hand and I took it and she held my hand for several minutes. She asked, "How is the weather out?" and when I said, "It's cloudy, but not cold," she said, "It must be the weather that's making my voice this way. I don't like it when I talk like this." I said, "You sound hoarse, do you have a cold?" And she said, "No, I'm sure it's not that. The weather must be doing it."

The old and sick cling to the young and able, holding onto them physically and mentally, involving them in conversation.

The more alert the minds of the aged the more they are able to cling, through progressively enmeshing the young in conversation. Weather is important to the aged, as well as to prisoners, lunatics, and others confined against their will. It is not merely a subject for value-free chit-chat, but is a veritable *actualizer of existence*; if one can be moved by the weather one is not yet dead.

> Mrs. Manger said, suddenly, "Do you often go to Reynolds' —you know, the store downtown?" I said, "Once in awhile, but I haven't been downtown since Christmas." She said, "I have a charge account there, and I would like to have them send me some hairpins. I only have five hairpins to my name, and you know you can't do much with only five. I can't go shopping myself, my heart is too bad. The doctor said I might drop dead any time."

Where most of life's business is well taken care of by the institution, one's mind may drift to personal trifles, if one is not in pain, because such preoccupation narcotizes dissolution-anxiety.

An apparent ease with death, side by side with the anxiety to prolong life, is related to a culture which, emphasizing survival, does not prepare the mind for extinction. Since, also, sensuousness and appearance are prominent in the culture, decline and death are pushed out of view as well as out of awareness. It is logical that obsolescence-anxiety and fear of death should be countered with the persisting symbols of sensuousness and appearance. Hence the desire for hairpins, filmy nightgowns, and nice clothes in women at death's door. Hence, also, the following:

> Mrs. Seaman (78 years old) is a well-nourished, hearty-looking older woman with gray hair. She has a great deal of bright red rouge on her cheeks, long fingernails painted a bright red, lipstick, and a great deal of jewelry. She has a metal brace on her left leg, and I noticed crutches leaning against the wall behind her wheel chair. She said, "So you're learning how to run a nursing home, are you? Well, there is a lot of room for improvement." Mr. Starr (age 74) immediately interrupted and said, "Good food is probably the most important thing in keeping people happy," and Mrs.

Seaman said, "I think the most important thing is to have a good place so people can have baths and showers as they need them." She seemed very indignant.

When one considers that the usual picture of the aged primitive woman is that, half naked and unkempt she does not conceal from view her spent body, one wonders when our culture decided not to let old, socially dead women abandon the fancy scenery of femaleness.

I said, "Yes, it does seem nice here," and I asked, "Do you have a roommate?" Mrs. Manger said, "Yes, but I don't like her. I've been thinking of asking for a room to myself. No one can get along with her. She always brags. She says she has a visitor every day, and that would be 365 visitors a year. No one could have that many visitors. I don't talk to her unless I have to. Nobody likes to talk to her." She made several more similar comments about her roommate, Mrs. Mintner (age 80).

The ability to hate probably endures as long as the power to love. If at death's door the capacity to love still exists, probably the same is true of hate, and this must mean that *how* and *what* to hate are lessons early and well learned.

Mrs. Mintner seems an angry woman. She usually turned her head away or closed her eyes when the researcher entered the room, and Mrs. Manger detested her. To say that one has visitors every day is galling to phantom people who count their visitors like beads on a rosary. Thus Mrs. Mintner has retained *the power to hurt*, just as Mrs. Manger has retained the capacity to hate. Mrs. Mintner must therefore be very alert, for if she were not she would not know so well how to hurt. If it is true that the value to a culture of an idea or feeling can be measured by how long it lives in a dying body, it follows that since the capacities to love, to hate, and to hurt seem to last as long as alertness itself, the culture must set great store by them. Between the patients in Tower there is no love but much hostility. Love is a visitor in Tower, between the hours of two and four on Tuesday, Thursday, Saturday, and Sunday, and six and seven in the evening on Monday, Wednesday, and Friday. It is something the patients reserve for family and friends, meanwhile venting their spleen on one another.

I have said that visitors are counted like beads on a rosary, and so they *must* be by people slipping away from life. But, "I have many visitors while you have few" is also an invidious comparison that raises Mrs. Mintner's status while lowering Mrs. Manger's: it *thrusts the achievement drive into the face of Death himself.* Thus this drive, so well learned by all of us, persists, along with love, hate, and the capacity to hurt, to the end of life, because the culture values it highly.

"Basically hostile" people like Mrs. Mintner may become lambs when treated humanely. Somewhat later that day the researcher had a chance to talk to her alone.

> Mrs. Mintner was sitting in the hall, and since I was curious about her after Mrs. Manger's comments, I sat down beside her and said, "I see you've finished reading your paper," and she smiled and said, "Yes. I enjoy reading the paper. Are you from University?" I said, "Yes, I am," and she said, "I thought you might be. What are you studying?" "Nursing—I'm a registered nurse, and I'm getting further education." Mrs. Mintner nodded, and said, "Education is good," and she asked if I had been where the tornado hit in town, and we discussed that for several minutes.

But it was impossible for the researcher to repeat this experience.

A couple of days later at 7:30 in the morning the researcher noted:

> (The researcher is talking to Mrs. Manger and Mrs. Mintner says) "Stop talking so loud," and Mrs. Manger said, "She can't tell me to stop talking. We both pay for this room and I pay as much as she does." She went on to talk about how difficult Mrs. Mintner was to get along with, and asked, "How old is she?" I said I didn't know, and Mrs. Manger said, "Well, I don't think she's so old that she should be that cranky—but nobody can get along with her. You just don't know how bad she is."

Cooped up in the same room, unable to escape from one another because of the rigid framework of the institution—because each room costs a certain amount and the rooms are filled—these two are doomed to pour their hatred on each other, until death silences one of them. But it is not only the institution that binds them to their hate; culture does it too. In our culture, sleep and quiet have somehow become related, although it is rare in primitive culture that one treads softly or lowers one's voice because the "rights of sleep" demand it. Mrs. Manger, however, lays claim to the right to talk in a loud voice because it comes with the room. Along with her part of the room, she has bought the privilege of keeping her roommate awake; she owns the privilege of violating her roommate's right to have quiet when she is trying to sleep. This too is private property. Mrs. Manger asserts her right belligerently, not only because it has been bought, but because, like any other tough American, "nobody is going to tell her what to do." Though her heart may stop beating at any moment, she uses what weapons the culture gives her against a person she detests, in last efforts to maintain autonomy. Finally, in order to strengthen her Self further and to enhance her status in the eyes of the researcher, she accuses Mrs. Mintner of one of the worst crimes, that "nobody can get along with her."

It will be helpful to digress a moment to illustrate a different possibility.

Mrs. Weil was a somewhat confused woman of eighty, with a serious disturbance of the central nervous system which, though not preventing her from walking, made it difficult for her to walk without lurching sideways. She talked without stopping, and was so difficult to understand that one of the aides thought she talked only "jew-talk." Her fellows tended to shun her, and the help to treat her offhandedly. Not so Mrs. Leicht.

I walked over to Mrs. Weil and Mrs. Leicht (age 82), who had been conversing for sometime, and I said to Mrs. Leicht, "I believe you can understand her, can't you?" and Mrs. Leicht answered, with a shrug of her shoulders, "Well, what can I do honey?" I questioned her hard about this, and in between her characteristic "What can I do?" and "That's the way things are," I managed to piece together the thought that Mrs. Leicht could not understand Mrs. Weil, but was pretending that she could. "It makes her feel good," said Mrs. Leicht, "and she likes it, so what can I do about it?"

Mrs. Leicht persisted in saying no and laughing when I suggested that she could understand Mrs. Weil.

It is not being thrown together in a room with another person or merely being confined to an institution that makes people unendurable to one another, but rather the lack of compassionate understanding. Instead of turning away from Mrs. Weil, Mrs. Leicht was humane, expressing in this way her feeling that one subjects one's self to fate and that whatever makes miserable people "feel good" is what must be done.

We return now to Mrs. Manger:

"I used to like to go to plays," said Mrs. Manger, "but now I can't, because I'm sick." She asked about various theatres, such as the Lyric and the Woodland, which I had not heard of, and spoke of some actors and actresses, whom I had heard of but not seen.

In our culture aged people may begin to lose touch with younger ones when the places they once knew and frequented disappear, but in primitive culture, where the spacial configuration endures, young and old can still communicate within the same frame of space. What is true of space is true also of people, for although in primitive society many people personally known to the aged may never have been seen by the young, they still are vividly present to them because of close kinship ties and meaningful stories. This too makes communication between the generations easy and so does not shut the aged out. Thus in our culture its quality of evanescence has long made it difficult for young and old to talk to one another.

But we must take into consideration also the value of what is remembered. In primitive culture there is a certain parsimoniousness about memory—what is remembered by the aged seems to be what *sustains the culture*. On the other hand, much that might enter communication between the old and the young in our culture becomes obsolete and is of little or no consequence to the culture. Of what value is it to the researcher to know about the vanished Lyric and Woodland theatres? And what good does it do her to know about actors and actresses of the past? Thus, if primitive culture is an unchanging mountain, ours is an avalanche falling into a Sea of Nonexistence. Who can remember it? If, in primitive society, one's personal community is a rope fastened in a mythic past and continuing into a future without end, ours is a bit of string that falls from our hands when we die.

There was a slight pause and Mrs. Manger asked, "What do you do?" I said, "I go to University," and she said, "That's nice. You look healthy; I bet you never even get a cold," and I said, "Once in awhile I do," and she said, "I have a bad heart. The doctor says I musn't exert myself. He's surprised I'm still alive. He said I might go anytime. He says I have to take a lot of rest." I asked, "Do you have your meals here in your room?" and she said, "Oh, yes, it would be too much to go to the dining room. They have wonderful food here. Just wonderful."

When people are worried about dying they often try to mask it under a cheerful and talkative exterior, but one can feel the anxiety beneath because they bring death into the conversation over and over again and take the most circuitous pathways in order to return to it obsessively. Thus, Mrs. Manger's need of hairpins leads her to speak of the danger to her heart if she goes downtown; when she talks about TV programs (not mentioned here) she gets on to her fear of going to the theatre, and the researcher's healthy look merely reminds Mrs. Manger of her own bad heart. When a person like her (probably old American, upper middle class) talks easily about death, she is hiding her fear of it.

Mrs. Manger said, "I'm so glad you came back. I'm still in bed. They're so late getting us up today. What time is it?" I said, "It's about a quarter to nine," and she said, "Is that all it is? I thought it was afternoon already." I said, "They aren't so late after all." "No, they aren't, but sometimes time seems to drag so. Pull up a chair and sit down. . . . I like to get up and move around," she said, "I wish they would hurry and give me my bath. Then I could sit up in that chair and later take a walk down the hall." I asked, "Do you sit out in the hall?" and she answered, "I used to when I had friends out there, but they've all gone, so I'd rather stay in here."

A clear and alert mind is sensitive to the contingency of events and feels time fly or drag. If one still knows that one thing has to be done in order that another can occur; if one still perceives that activity has a *causal structure,* like first taking a bath and then getting up and then walking down the hall, one's brain is still alert. The capacity to wish things to happen, to expect them to happen in a certain real sequence, and to imagine their happening, are all characteristics of an intact mind. As Mrs. Manger lies in bed, feeble with illness and old age, she is still capable of the *psycho-cultural experience of time.* The fact that even her body still resonates to the time configurations she incorporated long ago, that she still has a good sense of the logical structure of activity, and that she can still wish, expect, and imagine all of it, prove that she is tied to, not disengaged from, life.

The following expands the problem of time as it affected many patients.

5-7 P.M. The practical nurse was feeding the patients who had nasal tubes. Mrs. Geist (age 77) was awake and I stopped and spoke to her. She said, "It's such a long time to lie in bed. They put us in bed before supper (around 3 P.M.) and I won't be able to get up until after 9 o'clock (tomorrow morning). Sometimes it's 10 before I can get up. I get so tired lying here." Mrs. Cuzlitz and Mrs. Firm were sound asleep.

The time spent in bed against their will was the commonest complaint of the patients who were able to be up and about. The statement "I get so tired lying here" must be taken literally to mean physically tired. *Institutional enfeeblement,* brought about by making the patients stay in bed for 18-19 hours can only accentuate the natural debilitating processes of old age. When three quarters of the day are spent in bed it reduces also the patient's social contacts and other forms of experience that might help to keep him alert.

The fact that inmates of all institutions must, without question, subordinate eating, sleeping, and mobility to an inflexible working day, with no chance for collective bargaining with the management or the help, illustrates the fact that an adult who *falls* sick in our culture *falls* into a lower status. Whoever falls sick in our society becomes its symbolic prisoner. This is due in part to the fact that in institutions attendance on the sick is not a mercy but a job. If one attained grace through tending the sick they would not be symbolic prisoners.

Mrs. Launfaughl (age 86). I walked into Mrs. Launfaughl's room. She was in bed. When I spoke she said, "Come in and sit down. Do you have time?" I said, "Yes, I have plenty of time. Am I interrupting a nap?" and Mrs. Launfaughl said, "No, I don't feel good today, so I'm lying down. It's nothing special, I'm just getting old. I'm over 80, you know. I never tell anyone just exactly how old I am; I just say, over 80. When I came here they put my age down at 89, but I'm not even that old now, and that was eight years ago. Are you at University?" I said I was. Mrs. Launfaughl said, "I don't really need anyone to take care of me. I can take my own bath. There are some really sick people here."

She then went on to tell me about having studied Spanish; about having spent a summer in Mexico with a native family, and having planned to spend some time in Spain, though it never worked out. She said she had read Eleanor Roosevelt's column in the paper and that she did not like her though she did like Franklin Roosevelt. She said the country was going to the dogs, and then laughed and said, "Don't tell the people at University I said that." She also discussed trying to reach the Moon, Winston Churchill, and the persecution of the Irish Catholics by the English. She went on steadily, with little participation by me beyond an occasional nod.

While I was listening to her two practical nurses came in and silently changed the two other patients in the room.

In attempting to estimate the state of anybody's intelligence, one must know *the number of frames of reference* a person is able to deal with simultaneously and clearly. In Mrs. Launfaughl's conversation with the researcher the following appeared: (1) etiquette, (2) the socialization of time, (3) the cultural configuration of care, (4) status-relevance of activity and conversation, (5) the extension of space, (6) political structure, (7) the cultural configuration of fear.

(1) *Etiquette.* When Mrs. Launfaughl says, "Come in and sit down. Do you have time?" she shows her sensitivity to the etiquette of creating a guest.

(2) *The socialization of time.* Perception of the socialization of time means that one is aware of the existence of competing obligations; that the culture always has a lien on a person's time, and that one cannot usually give all of it to one individual, especially to a stranger, unless one is paid for it. The perception of the socialization of time implies also that one never reveals one's age without thinking about whether it might harm one. One should retain this age-paranoia if one is to be considered truly intact, even though the fear may no longer be relevant because one has become obsolete. When one is obsolete it makes no difference how obsolete one is!

(3) *The cultural configuration of care.* A pervading American attitude toward care is that one should not accept it until one has passed beyond the point where he has ceased to be able to "take care of himself." Even after one no longer can take care of himself physically he must make the effort; and ideally, only after he fails can his conscience and the attitude of people around him permit his being helped. So Mrs. Launfaughl protests that there are others, weaker than she, who *really* need help. The *right* to give up and to accept help and its antithesis, the *obligation* to continue and to refuse help, are ancient and abiding moral alternatives in our culture. As tests of moral worth they have been as much at home in the kitchen as on the battle-field. While spartan attitudes toward care might be related to the "Protestant ethic," it seems irrelevant in a society where *ethics* are obsolescent. But the attitude is relevant to a productive system where one does not withdraw his capital—including himself—from production unless he is forced to.

(4) *Status-relevance of activity and conversation.* In conversation one must always talk about matters that will maintain or enhance one's status, and it is mildly status-enhancing to talk about Spain, Spanish, and Mexico, rather than about food or one's sickness. Only when an illness literally engulfs one may one, perhaps, lose his sensitivity to status-relevant topics of conversation.

(5) *The extension of space.* An alert, educated person has an expansive perception of space, reaching out across oceans and borders to the Moon and into outer space, so although an institutionalized old lady may not know where she is in The City, she may know definitely where she is in the universe. Changing *cultural* orientations thus make necessary a different measure of *individual* orientations.

(6) *Political structure.* Perhaps "political personalities" is a better term than "political structure," for most people know next to nothing about the structure of political *institutions* though they may be able to talk brightly about political *personalities.*

(7) *The cultural configuration of fear.* Mrs. Launfaughl has a healthy fear of being "turned in" because she dares to say that the country is "going to the dogs." Thus having located another bit of socially patterned paranoia in Mrs. Launfaughl, we can finally pronounce her "mentally sound." It is important to remember, in judging the mental status of the aged, that they should not only have their frames of reference sharp but have their fears set well in the culturally regulated channels also.

Mrs. Launfaughl said, "you know, it's pretty expensive here, and I could use a little more money. I'm lucky though, I have some good stocks," and she mentioned various companies and the dividends they paid on their stocks. One of the patients in the room moaned a little and Mrs. Launfaughl said, "Those two poor souls are worse off than I am, but I'll probably slip away before either of them. When it's your time you have to go. I'm thankful I still have a clear mind. It's not as good as it used to be. I forget things once in a while, but I can still think clearly." She told me about various tests she had taken in high school and how she had figured out how many miles from The City to the equator. Her teachers had not expected her to do well, she said, because her penmanship was so poor, but she had ranked second in her class.

The ancient rule, that when miserable one should reflect on those who are worse off, has never been well observed because in order to think of those more miserable than we it is necessary to have some social solidarity with them. Here, however, in an exquisitely sensitive weighing of death against pain, Mrs. Launfaughl pities the other women because they are suffering, even though she feels on the brink of death. Like most of us, she wants to think of death as a slipping away, a quiet dissolution without pain. Few have asked primitive man how he wished to die, but it is not clear that all have desired to go without pain. The Indian warriors of our woodlands—the Choctaw, the Chickasaw, the Iroquois, and the Creeks—expected to die in torture, if not in battle, screaming insults at their enemies. Pain can become a goal in such cultures, whereas in others, like our own, pain-avoidance and pleasure-seeking can be so much part of education that they seem natural conditions of existence.

Man in our culture wants to retain his "mind" until he dies, for to lose it is to be despised, as if one were poor. Primitive culture can at times be more tolerant of derangement because primitive culture is simpler and because it values hallucinations, whereas we fear and despise them because we cannot use them. It is very simple: Indians needed hallucinations for their religions; we require stone, mortar, glass, steel, and a parking lot.

> I walked past Mrs. Launfaughl's room and she called out, "Here's the one I owe money. I sent down for some so I could give you the dime I owe you." I said, "You don't owe me any money." She looked at me and said, "Didn't I borrow a dime from you?" I said, "You don't owe me any money." She said, "Didn't I borrow a dime from you? No, I guess you're not the one. I'm writing postcards to send to the 'Treasure Chest' (a TV program in which a number of the old people are interested) and then I'm going to work the puzzle." I said, "I hope you win something." She smiled and said, "I haven't yet, but I always keep trying."

Remembering debts, sensitivity to luck and competition, and the capacity to "keep trying" help to distinguish intact people from others, and even though Mrs. Launfaughl is on the verge of "slipping away" these components of the cultural configuration still resonate in her. *The test of the existence of a cultural configuration is its persistence in the threatened or dying organism.*

In view of the dreadful state of television it is interesting to see that here it helps to keep people mentally alive. TV does more than while away their time; it activates the cultural configuration, maintaining the old people because it breathes life into the culture-in-the-cell. Meanwhile the old people can experience some solidarity with others who participate in the same programs.

Mrs. Kirsch (age 81) had joined the group watching television and Mrs. Ortway (age 86) had returned to it. Mrs. Seeley, a practical nurse, was sitting in a two-bed woman's room working a cash crossword puzzle, while both patients were in bed.

As Mrs. Launfaughl lies in bed thinking of many little things, her mind constantly reverts to death:

Mrs. Launfaughl said, "When I was little I used to go to mission meetings. They used to talk about all kinds of things at these meetings, but they started out first talking about Hell and the next time they talked about Purgatory and then they talked about Heaven. I guess this was to make people afraid of going to Hell first and then they showed them in the end that they could go to Heaven. I had funny ideas then. I was afraid of dying suddenly in a state of sin. I used to really worry about that, and I'd wonder when I was walking down the street whether I'd get to the next corner without dying." She sort of laughed and said, "Isn't that funny?" I said, "Meetings like that often make a big impression on children," and she said, "Yes, they do. You know, my mother died when I was a child. I was only about three or four and my aunt raised us. There were six of us and I was the youngest. My aunt took over after my mother died and she was good to us. She's the one I used to go to those meetings with." She asked, "Have you heard the term *globus hystericus*?"[1] I said, "Yes I have," and she said, "I guess I used to have that. I wouldn't eat anything but soup because I was afraid I'd choke. That was silly wasn't it? But I can always remember my twin brother when he choked to death. He ran from my aunt to my mother and back again but they couldn't do anything for

[1] A choking sensation due to emotional factors.

him. I guess I was afraid I'd choke too. I wouldn't eat
with the other people when I was going to school—I'd go
by myself and buy a bowl of soup and try to eat that.
Then one day I decided, this is silly—I can't go on this way.
If I choke I choke, and from then on I hadn't any trouble.
I take three pills this big at one time (and she showed me
the size with her finger). Sometimes you have to make
yourself get over those things."

At the edge of death, as thoughts of sin, Purgatory, and Hell
press in upon her, Mrs. Launfaughl's mind goes back to her
greatest "sin"—that she survived her twin brother who choked
to death in childhood.

> *Mrs. Heine* (*age 86*). In the large ward I stopped to
> talk to Sarah, whose last name I do not know. She was still
> in the wheelchair, tied to the post, but the chair was facing
> in a different direction. She took my hand as I walked up,
> and said, "Your hand is cold." I said, "You'll have to warm it
> for me," and she took my hand in both of hers and patted
> and rubbed it. She then put her hand on the arm of the
> chair and said something else I could not understand.
> She picked the hem of her dress up and folded and un-
> folded it several times. I said, "That's a nice dress you have
> on," and she said, "I like it. It's not common; nobody else
> has one like it."

A primordial asset of warm-blooded animals is the capacity to
give and receive physical warmth, and to want to give and to
receive it. But in man the exchange of warmth is everywhere
culturally elaborated. In our culture, the warming of cold hands
resonates with love. Although Sarah's condition is so precarious
that she has to be bound into her chair so she will not fall out
of it, she yet understands the significance of the admonition to
warm the researcher's hand, and the researcher understands
Sarah's "Your hand is cold" as an invitation to communion. So,
though much of what Sarah says, as we shall see, seems to have
the unintelligible irrelevance of confused old age, she still
comprehends the cultural invitation to communion. So also her
desire for status remains strong—she does not want to be

"common." She is as alive to the status implications of dress as any high school girl. The status drive is a strong component of the cultural configuration and the nearness of death does not destroy it.

I am not sure that I have made myself clear. Here are people so old that they have to be tied in their chairs, who expect to die at any moment, and yet the culture is as alive in them—one almost feels more alive—as their breathing. It is almost as if the culture had been imprinted on them. Culture is *like* an instinct —the littlest details, the most subtle motivations imprinted by it remain palpitating and vigorous even when the people, the bearers of the culture, are at death's door and *perception itself is faltering*.

> I stopped by Sarah Heine, and she said, "How's your sister?" I was rather startled, but said, "Just fine." A practical nurse came up at this time and said, "Sarah's our doll," and Sarah replied, "A very troublesome doll," but the nurse said, "No, you're no trouble." Sarah said to me, "We need a little trouble in the world, otherwise people wouldn't be satisfied."

Since Mrs. Heine's perception is faltering she is confused about people. Since the researcher never talked about her sister to Mrs. Heine, the researcher's sister is a bizarre element in the conversation. Mrs. Heine's hold on the cultural configuration is stronger than her hold on the components of the material world. Consider also her hold on the cultural clichés. She justifies her own troublesomeness with a cliché, saying that the trouble she causes other people makes it possible for them to enjoy their satisfactions more. This enables her to legitimize her own existence: nuisance though she is, she thinks, it is nuisances like her that give piquancy to available pleasures. So, she argues, though she is obsolete in some ways, she still serves a psychosocial function.

Culture, one might say, is a system of conflicts held together by a network of clichés. Hence the tendency of the aged to be cliché-prone, for clichés are fundamental links between actions. The capacity of the aged to verbalize clichés is an index of mental intactness—just as it is in the young.

As I walked up to Sarah she said, "How's your husband?" and I said, "I'm not married," but Sarah said, "You aren't? I thought you were." At this time a practical nurse who had been taking care of one of the patients next to Sarah, came over and said, "Sarah's our girl, aren't you?" Sarah looked at her face and said, "Am I?" The practical nurse said, "Sure you are. You're my girl."

Loss of the capacity to participate in an amiable misrepresentation of one's self is the natural complement of loss of the capacity to identify others, for obviously if all people are becoming vague figures, then one's own identity must become unclear also. If, almost at random, people have sisters, husbands, and so on that do not exist, then, if a well-meaning nurse says, "You're my girl," one may not see this as an amiable misrepresentation, for it might be true.

Mrs. Letts (age 80) and Mrs. White (age 82). I spoke to Mrs. Letts and she answered me, and Mrs. White immediately said, "You're so nice to come and visit the sick, and you look so healthy too. I hope you have health until the time you die." I asked Mrs. Letts how she was this morning and she said she didn't feel so good and that she had not felt well yesterday either. Mrs. White said to me in a low voice, "I don't think she's going to get out of here; she's not going to make it." Every time I tried to talk to Mrs. Letts, Mrs. White seemed to interrupt. She continued with, "I hope I get out of here soon. I'm feeling better. Every day I feel better and I want to get well enough so I can leave. My heart is a lot better than it used to be."

I commented on her flowers, for she had just gotten a large and beautiful azalea plant. She said, "I don't even know the people who sent it—they're a club my son and daughter-in-law belong to, they don't know me—I just got them because of my son and daughter-in-law. Everybody who does nice things for me does it because of other people, not because of me. A lot of people send me cards and do things for me, but they're friends of my husband or my son—not my friends." I didn't quite know how to answer this.

Although it is true that the feeling that she is not valued for herself may be a personal peculiarity of Mrs. White, it occurs often enough in everybody to suggest that it has ramifying cultural roots. Let us begin exploration of them with the fact that people put the high-rising standard of living in place of their veritable Selves, and do not cultivate a Self but rather a living standard. We then go on to the realization that our culture provides us with no way of evaluating our Selves with certainty —that we must always do it by means of externals, for example, possessions or school grades. We also lose friends, who seem to drop us for no apparent reason or who simply move away, so that there is no stable personal community in which our true worth can be reflected. Hence the difficulty in believing ourselves loveable—quite apart from what our parents may have done to us. These underlying conditions are aggravated in old age, for then many who loved us have died, and many of those around us are much younger and therefore find us boring or weird. We are roleless and obsolete. Put it all together and you have enough to produce Mrs. White's belief that "Everybody who does nice things for me does it because of other people, not because of me."

Mrs. White strikes us as rather "pushy"—whenever the researcher tries to talk to Mrs. Letts, Mrs. White barges in. Perhaps we can understand her now. Perhaps she was always a "pushy sort," but *now* her pushiness implies, "Nobody really cares about me," and also, perhaps, a sense of the impending end.

> During my entire conversation with Mrs. Letts, Mrs. White was lying with her eyes closed and moaning, and she gave no sign of being aware that I was there. Mrs. Letts said, "I'm not feeling so good today," and I asked, "What happened—didn't you rest well last night?" She said, "Oh, I think I had too much company yesterday," and I said, "I noticed that you had some visitors yesterday afternoon." Mrs. White continued to moan, and I said, "Your roommate doesn't seem to feel so good today." Mrs. Letts said, "Oh, she suffers a lot. She's had a terrible morning. . . ." (Later) Mrs. White opened her eyes and smiled. I said, "I

was in here earlier but I didn't have a chance to talk to you." She said, "I had a terrible morning. I've had pain that goes to here and all the way through to my back." She gestured toward her right side and how it went through from this point to her back. She went on, "I needed three nurses to make me comfortable this morning and even then they couldn't make me feel good. I couldn't eat any lunch today either. I just feel terrible." I said, "It's nice you have such a quiet roommate who doesn't bother you," and she said, "Yes. She's very nice and when she suffers she suffers just as much as I do." I told her I would let her rest and would see her again tomorrow. As I left she asked, "Would you turn the TV off?" This is Mrs. Letts' TV and I didn't want to turn it off without consulting her. Mrs. Letts didn't seem to understand what was wanted, or otherwise this was just her way of keeping the TV on. But she didn't agree to its being turned off, and I left the room. As I left Mrs. Letts and Mrs. White were still discussing whether or not the TV should be on.

The struggle for survival of the Self continues unabated between these two who are in almost constant pain, and one woman cannot yield to the other. Since the will to live prolongs life, it is natural that when a Self is keeping a person alive it will be vigorous. But since it is a Self molded by our culture, vigor implies that even at death's door the Self will not yield to another person. Hence the battle of wills between these women, in pain, at death's door, but holding onto life. A good painting of the gateway to Hell would show the shades from our culture fighting for first place. Meanwhile the conflict between Mrs. Letts and Mrs. White takes on a nightmarishly burlesque quality because Mrs. Letts is so confused that at times she does not know whether the TV is on or off, or whether she is watching it or not. Culture outlasts perception.

I walked into Mrs. Letts' room. Her TV was not on, and I said, "Do you like the early morning TV programs? I notice your TV set isn't on yet," but she said, "It's on; I've been watching it all morning." I didn't know what to say in answer to that, and after a slight pause, she said, "We had an explosion here last night." I said, "You did?" She said, "Yes. You know, we're near the power plant, and I saw it and heard it. Do you see that house over there?" and she pointed through the window to a house next door. I nodded. She said, "Those windows were blackened by the explosion." Several of the windows of the house have screens on them and look rather black. She said, "I didn't get hurt, but it was a terrible shock. I had the doctor out last week, and he told me the only reason I am here is shock. I want to get well so I can go home."

Here almost nothing is right: the TV set was not on though Mrs. Letts thought it was; Tower is not near a power plant; and there was no explosion. The windows of the house across the street, however, do appear black. Thus color is the only persisting accuracy, while events and their causes are all wrong. By insisting that the TV is on when it is not, and that she has been watching it when she has not, Mrs. Letts insists also that her mind is intact when it is not. A mind that is failing, or has failed, may at the same time refuse to acknowledge the fact; or, to put it another way, it has lost the power to perceive that it is failing or has failed, for the reason that a characteristic of mental failure is often the inability to perceive it.

THE FALTERING OF THE SYSTEM

In Tower the staff tries to be nice to its decrepit charges, and an atmosphere of indulgent patience permeates our interviews with the staff: everybody agrees that the patients are children or babies. But this *homogenization by metamorphosis* and *reduction*—by reducing all the patients to babies—permits the development of the kind of superordinate callousness often seen in insensitive parents and elementary school teachers. In Tower it not infrequently has consequences that are terrifying for the patients.

Panic in the Dream

As I was sitting in the hall I heard a male voice call desperately, "Oh nurse, oh nurse," then, "Call the nurse right away." I couldn't decide where the voice was coming from or who it could be. The voice called, "Oh nurse" several more times, and there seemed to be no one around to hear it. By this time I decided that the voice was coming from Room 113, so I decided I would go down and see what was going on. By the time I got to Room 113, patient Forrest (age 90) was standing in the door calling, "Oh nurse" for patient Barnes (age 86), who was sitting in a chair, also calling, "Oh nurse." As I came up to the door, patient Forrest said, "Are you a nurse? We need one in here." As I walked into the room, patient Barnes was pulling at the restraints which held him in the chair. Patient Barnes said in an agitated voice, "Look here—I can't even get loose. You've got to take these things off of me. Will you tell the nurse to come here and take them off of me? I'm not guilty of anything, and there's no reason to tie me up like this. If anything happened to my daughter I couldn't even help her. You've got to get them off." I suggested to Mr. Forrest that they were just there to remind him to stay in the chair. I told Mr. Barnes that of course he wasn't guilty of anything. Mr. Barnes went on, "But I promised Mrs. Furcht I wouldn't move without her permission, so there's no reason for these. I can't have them on here, look here, I can't even move. Now you go get the nurse to take them off." I told Mr. Barnes that I could not take them off, but that I would tell the nurse what he said, and I left the room.

As I was looking for aide Cash, aide Love was standing at the elevator and said, "I'm going to dinner now." I said, "Do you want me to tell Mrs. Cash when I see her?" and aide Love laughed and said, no that she would tell her. I told aide Love that I was looking for Mrs. Cash anyway, and that I would be glad to tell her. We found aide Cash in the medicine room, pouring a laxative and aide Love told her she was going to supper, and then I told aide Cash about Mr. Barnes. Aide Cash said in a friendly manner, "Oh I know, I know."

Apparently patient Forrest called one of the orderlies into Room 113, because I heard patient Barnes saying,

"Get me out of here, I'm not a thief." One of the boys answered, "We've already told her, Mr. Barnes." The boys walked back down the hall and got onto the elevator. Then I heard patient Barnes saying, "Mr. Forrest, will you tell her right away I want to see her." Mr. Forrest answered politely, "Certainly I will, Mr. Barnes." Mr. Barnes added, "Tell her right away I want to see her, that I want to see her right away." Mr. Forrest replied, "I certainly will tell her Mr. Barnes, as soon as I see her." Patient Barnes said sharply, "How soon will you see her?" Mr. Barnes was talking loudly and continuously now, about how he was innocent and wanted to be untied. I heard him say, "Tell the aide I want to see her right away—I've got to see her right away." Aide Cash was in the medicine room during some of this, and I'm sure she heard patient Barnes talking. She did not come out into the main hall, however. I heard singing coming from the east wing, and I guessed this was aide Cash singing as she worked in Room 125. I saw aide Cash in the hall, and told her I was going for a break, and she said, "Fine." As I was waiting for the elevator, patient Barnes was still calling out loudly, and patient Forrest was talking to him in a very stern voice. I think I heard patient Forrest say something about, "Behave yourself, noise won't get you any place, and the nurse is busy."

In institutions of good will like Tower, one of the most important reasons for using restraints is the fear that if a patient is permitted free he may wander around and come to harm—that he may fall or go out into the street and catch cold or be hit by a car—for then the institution would be subject to a damage suit. On the other hand, if Mr. Barnes could afford a private nurse who would be with him all the time, the danger would be much less. If Mr. Forrest, Mr. Barnes' roommate, who is relatively intact and has his own nurse, were solicitous and compassionate and willing to dedicate himself to Mr. Barnes, the danger to Mr. Barnes would also be less. And, of course, if there were a flying squadron of help—possibly two at the most—to take care of emergencies, Mr. Barnes would have been relieved at once. But a flying squadron would cut Tower's income or raise the cost of care. Finally, if the very idea of tieing an old man (a practice unknown in the world outside of the "developed nations") were repulsive, some way would surely have been found to deal with Mr. Barnes aside from the simple-minded, direct, and mechanical procedure of binding him. Thus many currents have flowed together to produce Mr. Barnes' psychotic agitation.

The reaction to Mr. Barnes' panic underscores the bland acceptance of the hospital system by the personnel: the laughter of aide Love and her going off to dinner; Mrs. Cash's singing and her unruffled continuation of the preparation of laxatives—which have no urgency; and, finally the researcher's own indifference, as she takes her coffee break right in the middle of the episode.

Mr. Barnes imagines he is tied up because he is accused of a crime. This is the emergence from his unconscious of the *Dream of the Trap*. Since he is disoriented, he is a mobile distorted person; and because in hurting himself he may injure the institution too, Tower is frightened and so ties him up. Then, however, under stress, Mr. Barnes' *general* disorientation expands into an immense terror, which generalizes to panic expressed as fear of imprisonment and as alarm about his daughter. As he becomes panic-stricken, his roommate, Mr. Forrest reacts in the predictable direction of hostile withdrawal, while the help turn away also.

One sometimes suspects that the sudden emergence of the entrapment syndrome is simply an open expression of the unexpressed feeling that the aged person had all along that he is imprisoned.

Milly (a researcher) walked over to Mrs. Wood (age 84) to say hello and Mrs. Wood said, "They have me locked up here—I haven't done anything wrong and I shouldn't be locked up." Milly said this wasn't a bad place to be locked up, and I said to Mrs. Wood that I thought she liked it here. . . . Aide Scott was waiting for the elevator and stepped into it when it came. Mrs. Wood watched this process carefully, and then said, "Is that an elevator?" I replied that it was, and Mrs. Wood said in amazement,

"She just got right onto it, didn't she?" I imagine Mrs. Wood was putting two and two together and planning her trip to the store.

While it is true that being subject to arbitrary power may give almost anyone a feeling of imprisonment, this becomes reality in a confused patient like Mrs. Wood who, in spite of long periods of clarity, is always under the impression that she has to go out and run her (nonexistent) grocery store. Her interest in the elevator seems more like part of a plan for a prison break than for a trip to the store.

Shut Out in the Hall

Mrs. Weil (age 80). As I sat down in the main hall, patient Weil headed toward me. She looked tired, her hair stood on end, her shoes were untied, her stockings were sagging, her dress was half-way unzipped, her slip showed at both ends, and she was talking a mile a minute. Mrs. Weil was walking with her feet set wide apart, and taking such small steps that she was going more from side to side than she was forward. She looked for all the world like she had been on a three-day spree as she staggered toward us. Aide James and aide Jefferson had gathered in the hall by me at this time, and were watching Mrs. Weil come down the hall. Aide Jefferson said, "My God, Mrs. Weil, you look like you've had it." Mrs. Weil stuck her tongue out and made a face in response to this remark.

Aide Jefferson went into Room 218, and Mrs. Weil followed her, talking rapidly and saying, among other things, "Oh you go on." Aide Jefferson had not spoken kindly to Mrs. Weil, and she was shaking her head in dismay as she talked. As Mrs. Weil followed her into the room, aide Jefferson turned to her and said very politely, "I'm going to have to close the door now—you wait out here and I will be with you in just a few moments, as soon as I can, so you sit down right here."

Mrs. Weil sat down in the chair that had been indicated for her, and started talking to me. Then she saw aide James, who apparently is a favorite of hers and she walked into the

west wing to talk to her. I could hear aide James saying to
Mrs. Weil, "Mama Weil, you poor old thing, you look like
you've been talking all night. Have you? I'll bet you have."
Mrs. Weil came back and was talking to me. I could not
understand most of what she said. But from her gestures
and a few scattered words, I discovered that Mrs. Weil
was trying to bribe me into helping her get through the
door. She told me that she had a baby to take care of at
home and then she listed, by counting on her fingers, many
good things to eat that she would give me if I went with
her.

Mrs. Furcht the Head Nurse had gone through the hall
during this time, apparently giving linen to the various
private duty aides. The young colored boy was going
through the halls with a cart collecting dirty linen at this
time and he was very careful to avoid running into Mrs.
Weil as he passed. Mrs. Weil said hello to him and he
waved to her. Mrs. Weil was still asking me to help her get
out the door, and I told her that I would get in trouble if
I did that. She shook her head no, and said that she had
done it many times before and she had never gotten into
trouble. Mrs. Weil asked me if I lived here, and I said no.
She replied, "It's no wonder you don't want to leave then."
I asked Mrs. Weil if she would like for me to walk her
down to her room so she could rest, and she said yes. As we
walked down the hall I noticed that Mrs. Weil appears to
have periods of dizziness, for she reels or staggers occasionally as she walks. When we got to her room, there was
a place mat on a table with a picture of George Washington on it. I asked Mrs. Weil if she knew who that was and
she said, "No." I pointed to the picture again and said that
it was George Washington, and I asked Mrs. Weil if she
knew who George Washington was. Mrs. Weil said, "Why
sure, of course I do—he was a neighbor of mine for years."
I laughed and reminded Mrs. Weil that George Washington was the one with the cherry tree, and then she laughed
at herself and said, sure she knew who it was, but she
continued to talk about a neighbor of hers. I told Mrs.
Weil good-bye.

Everything that happened to Mrs. Weil occurred as a consequence of her mistaking Room 218 for her own. Her confusion brought from the staff and the researcher some cultural clichés and stimulated irrepressible feelings of amusement and depreciation, which only aggravated Mrs. Weil's confusion: it is of no consequence to Mrs. Weil's condition that she gives the staff various "as-if" cliché impressions, when what she needs is specific help. Their similes do her no good.

It is possible to discern some compassion here, but what one misses are physical contact and an effort to *do* something for Mrs. Weil. At any rate, none of the responses satisfied her: she stuck out her tongue at one of the aides, and remarked to the researcher that she understands why the researcher doesn't want to leave Tower—because the researcher doesn't live there (i.e. where Mrs. Weil feels mistreated). Mrs. Weil was not "abused"; she was merely mishandled.

Another example of mishandling is the following:

I sat down again by nurse Livvy, and Mrs. Weil, who was finally becoming so discouraged by the rather unfriendly behavior of the visitors, came over to me. She seemed more agitated than usual and she was talking very rapidly. I can usually understand a word here and there, but today I could not make out anything she was saying. I told her that I didn't understand, and nurse Livvy said, "That's right Mrs. Weil, you're right." I had the feeling that nurse Livvy was showing me the best way to handle Mrs. Weil, so I said, "That's right Mrs. Weil," too. . . . Mrs. Weil kept talking to me, and since I have generally found that Mrs. Weil has something in mind when she talks, if I can only guess what it is, I started my procedure of pinning her down. I asked her if she wanted me to do something and she said yes. I asked her if she wanted me to go some place and she said, "Well of course, of course, let's get away from here, and go down there," pointing to the west end of the hall. I told Mrs. Weil I would be glad to go to the other end of the hall with her and stood up. Patient Weil careened, head first, and sideways, several steps away from me. I grabbed her arm and steadied her, and she straightened herself up. I asked patient Weil what happened that she did this, and she replied something about "dizzy." I asked patient Weil if she always felt dizzy when this happened and she said that she did. I asked patient Weil if her head ached and she said that it did not. We walked to the end of the hall, and had a considerable discussion about which chairs we would sit in. Patient Weil wanted us to sit side by side, but in red chairs, and the two red chairs weren't side by side. Patient Weil wanted to move the two red chairs together, but I finally convinced her to let me sit in a gray chair.

Mrs. Weil pulled a handful of torn-up tissue out of her pocket at this time, and started to throw it on the floor. I told her to give it to me and I would throw it in the wastebasket. With this she walked over to the window and tried to open it; with the intention of throwing the tissue out, I suppose. I told her she would be a litter bug if she did that, and she laughed at me and gave the tissue to me, and I threw it into the wastebasket. As I came back in the main hall Mrs. Weil was starting into Room 218. I asked her if she would like to go back to her own room, because it was almost dinner time, and she said that she would, so we started down the hall. Two girls were wheeling a cart of linen down the hall as we walked by, and Mrs. Weil examined it closely and started to reach out for one of the towels. The two girls laughed at her, but went on down the hall with the cart before she could get a towel. I took Mrs. Weil into her room and left her.

To say to a confused patient with impaired and, perhaps, conceptually disordered speech, "That's right, you're right," is not yet so bad. It is not the correct thing to do, but it could be worse; for if one says, "That's right Mrs. Weil" one at least acknowledges her existence! To ignore her or laugh is much worse, but still not as bad as saying, "Shut up." The researcher, however, does the right thing. First, she understands that Mrs. Weil generally "has something in mind," and she gets at it by asking Mrs. Weil simple, direct questions. Second, she indicates to Mrs. Weil that she will do something for her. Third, she shows specific concern for a specific condition (Mrs. Weil's careening), not just a vague, "What's the matter?" Fourth, the researcher sat with Mrs. Weil. Fifth, the remark that Mrs. Weil would be a "litter bug" if she threw the tissue out the window draws Mrs. Weil into a clear-cut, rational, cultural context, within Mrs. Weil's comprehension. Sixth, the offer to take Mrs. Weil to her room performs the function of orientation. Thus if we put together *specific solicitude, simplicity, directness,* the *effort to truly understand,* the presentation of a *clear-cut cultural context, orientation,* and *proximity,* we have six very good rules for therapy for *any* mental disorder. And what are these but *primordial rules of human discourse* anywhere?

SUMMARY

If one were to attempt to derive but one law from this section it would be that *culture outlasts body and mind,* for even as the body remains barely alive and the mind declines into a senile rigidity, beset by hallucinations, the cultural configuration remains as part of mind. Long after she can no longer move, the American upper-middle-class woman is concerned with appearance and status, and her capacity to hate and to hurt follow channels determined by the culture. Bedridden though she may be, listening for her heart to stop beating, she still retains the lesson she learned when she was strong: that it is easier to be hostile than compassionate. So, cooped up in narrow quarters with others, she is unable to sacrifice an illusory autonomy to the wishes of those with whom she shares her room.

Since the frames of reference of the cultural configuration are the *content* of mind—if not, indeed, mind *itself*—the extent to which these frames are retained by aged people becomes an index of the intactness of their minds. Sensitivity to space–time, to moods of weather, to the importance of appearance and status, alertness to competition and luck, and the capacity to participate in amiable misrepresentations, are all measures of the mental state of an aging person of either sex. So also are insistence on one's rights and the capacity to enmesh another person in a meaningful conversation. This involves an understanding of the cultural theories of causality and probability.

As one reads these conversations between the researchers and the patients in Tower, one is impressed with the uniqueness of our culture's orientation toward aging and death: its denial of death; its expectation that at death's very door women will dress up; its acceptance of the fact that the aged may be bound even while all the ingenuity of science is used to keep them alive. Meanwhile the vast effort to maintain life is technical and impersonal; and at the patient's death, those who exerted the greatest efforts to keep him *alive*—the technical staff—are least moved, for his personal death is his family's affair.

One is also impressed with the gulf between the aged and the young, even when the aged are mentally alert; and this is because our culture is an avalanche of obsolescence hurling itself into the Sea of Nonexistence. And so it is with the personal community: our friends and those we love are a bit of string that falls from our hands when we die, and youth will never use it to tie up anything.

An effort to formulate a "national character" for Tower yields the following: the staff, though animated by *solicitude* and *kindliness* seems to maintain an attitude of *indulgent superiority* to the patients whom they consider *disoriented children,* in need of care, but whose confusion is to be brushed off, while their *bodily needs* are assiduously looked after. Tower is oriented toward body and not toward mind. The mind of the patients gets in the way of the real business of the institution, which is medical care, feeding, and asepsis. Anything rational that the patient wants is given him as quickly as possible in the brisk discharge of duty, and harsh words are rare. At the same time the staff seems to have *minimal understanding of the mental characteristics of an aged person.*

As for the patients, they live out their last days in long stretches of *anxiety* and *silent reminiscing,* punctuated by outbursts of *petulance* at one another, by TV viewing, and by visits from their relatives. There is no inner peace, and *social life is minimal.* Meanwhile the patients *reach out* to the researcher and would engage her endlessly in conversation if she would stay. There is a *yearning after communion but no real ability to achieve it.* In this we are all very much like them.

L'ENVOI

❧ ❧

There was a listening fear in her regard,
As if calamity had but begun;
As if the vanward clouds of evil days
Had spent their malice, and the sullen rear
Was with its stored thunder labouring up.

JOHN KEATS: Hyperion

❧

TWO CULTURES

In Western Culture today one must make a distinction between the culture of life and the culture of death. In the minds of most people science has become synonymous with destructive weapons, i.e., with death—to such a degree, indeed, that college students' associations to the word *nuclear* is often "destruction."[1] The culture of death, which every day draws more and more of

---

[1] *Nuclear* obviously is a neutral word meaning *central.* When Freshmen in a large social science survey course at Washington University were asked to write down their "immediate association to the word *nuclear*," first associations with destruction were about 45 per cent. The counting of second associations would bring the number of associations to well above 50%.

the élite, does not include mathematicians, physicists, and chemists only. Biologists and physicians do research in biological warfare; sociologists and anthropologists engage in systems analysis (the study of the integration of weapons, radar systems, people, and machines) and the study of the make-up of bombing and missile crews; economists work on global strategies for economic warfare, the economics of weaponry and contract allocation, logistics, and so on. It is impossible to calculate just how much American scientific talent has been put out to pasture on the rank grasses of death: university research and consultantship, nonprofit "defense" corporations, industrial research "parks," and so on. Probably 50 per cent would be a low estimate. Together with the engineers and technicians they constitute the well-fed, comfortably housed culture of death. Thus we have an élite of death that we support in relative luxury. We must bear in mind that this is not the hasty mobilization of brains against a short-lived threat, but rather the long-sustained (perhaps for fifty years) training of tens of thousands of the most acute brains in the country in thinking about a world charnelhouse.

Where is the culture of life? The culture of life resides in all those people who, inarticulate, frightened, and confused, are wondering "where it will all end." Thus the forces of death are confident and organized while the forces of life—the people who long for peace—are, for the most part, scattered, inarticulate, and wooly-minded, overwhelmed by their own impotence. Death struts about the house while Life cowers in the corner.

ABOUT CRITICISM AND HOPE

All books of social criticism of the United States by Americans should end on a note of happy possibility these days, even though Hollywood, in the spirit of the times, is going in for tragedy. It is also argued that whoever criticizes without making suggestions for improvement ought to keep quiet. This seems to me like saying that a person who cannot make a roast should say nothing about one that is served burnt. I suspect it belongs also in the same category as the miserable argument that anybody who cannot solve the Russian problem should not object to nuclear testing. Such complaints are merely ways of silencing the opposition. At any rate, I do not quite belong among the social critics who have nothing to put in place of the irritating carbuncle, as Morris Cohen used to say. I have offered ideas where I consider myself qualified by long experience: I have made some suggestions about the emotional problems of children, about the schools, and about institutions for the aged. Even without experience I have even dared to suggest the resumption of trade with the Soviet Union as a way to peace. But in a democracy everyone is by birthright and opinion-poll-right an authority on foreign policy.

Meanwhile, I do end on a note of optimism! The ascent of man from the lower animals and the brutality of "civilized" history show that Nature has destined man to move from one misery to another; but the record proves also that man has sometimes been *forced* by misery into enlightenment although he has never accepted it without a bitter fight. This, perhaps, is Nature's plan for *Homo sapiens,* until some time hence, if he has not destroyed himself, he will realize, through misery, that destiny of perfection she holds mysteriously in store for him.

Man's most desperate problem is to know his fears and not be so ruled by them that they destroy his creative resources, making it impossible for him to anticipate the ramifying consequences of his actions. Socrates said, "Know thyself"; and this must naturally include, "Know thy fear."

Appendix A

An Analysis of Contacts Between Georgie Ross and His Mother

Table 1. *Analysis of Contacts by Duration and Intensity*

DURATION	INTENSITY			
	warm	mixed	distant	totals
long	2	5	1	8
moderate	4	1	5	10
short	4	6	3	13
totals	10	12	9	31

Table 2. *Analysis of Contacts by Occasions and Intensity*

OCCASION	INTENSITY			
	warm	mixed	distant	totals
social climax	7	6	8	21
random	3	6	1	10
totals	10	12	9	31

Table 3. *Analysis of Occasions of Social Climax by Intensity and Duration*

DURATION	INTENSITY			
	warm	mixed	distant	totals
long	—	—	—	—
moderate	4	1	4	9
short	3	5	4	12
totals	7	6	8	21

Table 4. *Analysis of Random Occasions by Intensity and Duration*

DURATION	INTENSITY			
	warm	mixed	distant	totals
long	2	5	—	7
moderate	—	—	1	1
short	1	1	—	2
totals	3	6	1	10

Appendix B[1]

Extracts from Dr. V. A. Kral's Paper "Recent Research in Prevention of Mental Disorders at Later Age Levels"

Three or four decades ago, and in some places even today, practically all mental disorders of the later years were considered as manifestations of structural changes of the brain of either the parenchymatous (senile) or the vascular (arteriosclerotic) type. Today, however, such a simple view is not tenable. The steadily increasing number of elderly patients seen by psychiatrists, and also the greater interest which psychiatry takes in the older age group, have taught us that the mental disorders of the senescent part of our population comprise a variety of nosological entities.

M. Roth studied a population of individuals sixty years of age and over hospitalized in a mental institution in Britain. He found that out of 450 patients, 266 (that is 59.3 per cent) were suffering from functional psychoses. Of these, 220 (49.1 per cent) suffered from affective disorders, and 46 (10.2 per cent) from late paraphrenia. Acute and subacute confusional states were found in 36 (8.5 per cent) cases. Only the remaining 146 patients (32.2 per cent) were actually suffering from psychoses due to organic brain disease: 36 (that is, 8 per cent) had arteriosclerotic psychoses and 110 (24.2 per cent) were suffering from senile psychoses.

Roth's study suggests that affective psychoses, late paraphrenia, and acute confusion are distinct from the two main causes of progressive dementia in old age; namely, senile and arteriosclerotic psychoses. In addition, the study also provided some validity as to the distinction between these two dementing psychoses,

[1] Excerpts from "Recent research in prevention of mental disorders at later age levels" by V. A. Kral, M.D. in *Recent Research Looking Toward Preventive Intervention*, Ralph H. Ojemann (ed.). Proceedings of the Third Institute on Preventive Psychiatry. State University of Iowa, April 1961. Reprinted by permission.

although the clinical differentiation may be difficult in a given case.

Admittedly, Roth's study is at variance with the statistics representing the admission rates of aged patients to mental hospitals of large areas or entire states. These usually show the admission rates for arteriosclerotic and senile psychoses far above the figures for other types of mental disorders. However, the fact that Roth's findings are not a mass statistic but are, rather, based on careful and unbiased analyses of individual case records by an experienced clinician using strict criteria makes his study a valuable contribution. Using the same criteria, we recently reviewed the material of the geriatric service of the Verdun Protestant Hospital in Montreal. Out of 360 patients of both sexes, nearly 50 per cent were found to be suffering from functional psychoses, although on admission a diagnosis of psychosis with senile brain disease had been made in a number of them.

We turn now to those patients whose mental disorders are not severe enough to warrant hospitalization and who are seen in psychiatric geriatric clinics and in private practice.

A study of this type recently undertaken by our group showed the following: Out of 210 cases seen by the psychiatrists in a geriatric out-patient clinic, 19 (that is, 9 per cent) were found without psychiatric disorder on clinical psychiatric examination; 91 (43 per cent) were suffering from neurotic conditions; 41 (19.5 per cent) were found to have senile psychoses; 12 (5.7 per cent), arteriosclerotic psychoses; and 41 (19.5 per cent), functional psychoses. Among the latter, endogenous depressions of the manic-depressive and the involutional type prevailed. These were found in 34 of the 41 cases, whereas late paraphrenia was present in the remaining seven cases. It is interesting to note that as regards the functional psychoses, our material shows the same percentage distribution as that described by Roth. The main difference between the two studies consists in the fact that in Roth's material, which comprises the cases of a closed mental hospital, affective psychosis was the most frequent diagnosis; whereas in our clinical material the main bulk of the cases consisted of "neuroses of later maturity." The difference with regard to the organic disorders was surprisingly small.

Neither study, however, gives an indication as to the proportion of the mentally well-preserved persons in the senescent population. An approximate indication seems to emerge from the study of the population of an old people's home. This study showed that out of 162 residents, 67 (41.3 per cent) were found without mental disorders; 24 (14.8 per cent) had a history or signs of functional psychosis, but no signs of organic brain disease; and 71 (43.9 per cent) were suffering from psychiatric disorders due to organic brain disease of either the senile or the arteriosclerotic type. This percentage might appear relatively high when compared with the two previous studies. This seems to be due to the fact that in this particular home residents who become sick after admission are kept, if possible, until their deaths. The advent of modern psychiatric treatment methods, particularly tranquilizers, anti-depressants, group and occupational therapy, and specialized nursing care, makes it possible to keep practically all of the mentally sick in the home as residents. The interesting finding that neurotic conditions were practically absent in this material is probably due to the fact that the residents live in a sheltered environment, that the feeling of isolation is apparently minimal, and that the factor of loss of prestige and stature hardly applies.

I have dealt with these studies at some length because they form the clinical background for the prophylactic endeavors with which we are concerned here. In summarizing them, we arrive at the following conclusions:

1. In the senescent segment of our population there occur at least six kinds of mental disorders of numerical importance which differ as to symptomatology, course, and outcome.

2. The psychotic conditions due to structural brain disease of the senile and arteriosclerotic type are numerically less important than previously assumed.

3. Functional disorders of the affective type, particularly endogenous depressions, form a considerable part of the mental disorders of older patients in and outside mental hospitals.

4. Among the non-hospitalized old people, neurotic conditions form the most frequently encountered type of mental disorders.

In view of what was said above we have now to consider what is known about the etiology of the mental disorders mentioned and what measures are presently available to eliminate or modify the most important etiological factors. Unfortunately our knowledge in respect to the etiology of these mental disorders is still limited.

Of the six nosological entities there is only one where we are fairly certain about the main causative factor; that is the group of the neurotic reactions in later life which comprises the main bulk of the cases which psychiatrists see outside a mental hospital. The problems of these patients are primarily those of adjustment to the biological, psychological, and social facts of aging. They have to adjust to new and mostly unfavorable situations at a time of life when the capacity for adaptation weakens. The most important factors involved are loss of prestige among family and friends, loss of a lifelong occupation (be it a job or housekeeping), decreased earning capacity, and, frequently, a drastically decreased income. This leads to increasing dependence on others, at a time when the spouse or lifelong friends are being lost. In addition, there is in men the realization of loss of strength, endurance, and sexual potency, and in women, the loss of attractiveness.

Clinically, a small number of these cases shows a picture of neurotic reactions as they occur in younger age groups—phobic reactions, anxiety reactions or obsessive-compulsive neuroses, and chronic personality disorders. Most cases of this group, however, present the clinical picture of a flat depression with feelings of weakness, tiredness, irritability, and sometimes even hostility toward one or more members of the family. Most of them complain of sleeplessness and loss of appetite; some show obsessive eating, particularly at night. Nearly all patients of this group have many somatic complaints, only some of which have any substantiation in fact. Hypochrondriacal fears regarding the heart, lungs, the gastrointestinal tract, and occasionally also, of impending mental disease are frequent.

The main dynamic factor in these neurotic conditions is anxiety —the aging person's anxiety of getting old, of losing his role in society, and of becoming isolated and rejected. There is also the anxiety of the younger members of society about their own future aging, which leads to a tendency on their part to separate themselves from the aging person, to close their eyes to his problems, and to disregard the positive sides of aging—greater experience, better judgment, less emotional reactivity, and better control of some of the drives which motivate and govern the younger years in life. This largely unconscious anxiety of the younger members of society is rationalized behind the attitude best expressed in the Latin saying: *Senectus ipsa morbus* ("Old age is in itself a disease").

The stressor effect in these cases is unspecific. The stress acts on the patient at a time in life when his stress tolerance is apparently diminished. A condition which is harmless and easily tolerable for the healthy adult and the middle-aged person may become a danger to the mental health of the old person or may possibly even lead to death as shown in the figures of Roth's study. The immediate conclusion to be drawn from such observations is that acute stress of any kind should be avoided in old persons; in other words, that the recommendations of physical hygiene and medicine should strictly be observed by members of this age group. Responsibility for the necessary supervision and the frequently needed help rests, of course, with the younger members of society.

INDEX

absurdity, 286, 287-8, 291, 294, 297, 299, 308, 320

acquiescence, 122, 123, 246, 286, 291, 347, 354, 364, 366-8, 374, 382, 421, 424, 425-7, 440; pathological, 366-8, 417

adaptive radiation, 42, 43-4, 404

adolescence: Coca-Cola bacchanals, 219, 263-7; conscience, 281; conservatism, 212; culture, 205, 238, 259, 281; delinquents, 245; etiquette, 244-5; girls' morality, 211; pecuniary view of, 272-3; proto-, 218-20, 267-8; sex, 210-12, 219, 230, 247, 267, 272, 276-7

advertising, 20-2, 41, 114; campaigns, 52; children and, 68-76; creativity, 92; and culture, 94; deceptive, 50, 73-6, 92, 97; as "dishonorable," 97; double talk, 92, 94; expenditures for, 92, 97; fear in, 89, 91, 93-4; language, 92-3; morality, 52-4; pecuniary philosophy, 45-99; public image, 91; and scientists, 32-7, 41-2; slogans, 46, 52; Standard Oil, 262-72, 273; as a subculture, 94-5

aged, the, 443; and autonomy, 451; as children, 443; clinging, 400-403, 447, 460; and communication, 452; and hallucinations, 443; intelligence of, 455-7; lack of empathy among, 443, 452; lack of understanding of, 443; and stress, 443; and weather, 448

aircraft industry, 41

alienation, 95, 259, 291, 294, 320, 340, 379, 439

America, 5, 17

American home, 384

Americans, 5-8, 14, 15, 28, 29, 30, 39, 43

anesthetic (see narcotize)

anger, 138-9, 145-6

anthropology, 19

anxiety, 128; and absurdity, 66; and advertising, 66, 73, 89; and competition, 76; dissolution, 448; and the Pentagon, 120; and pride, 104; and survival, 96; and teen-age relations, 154, 155, 160, 181, 211

armaments, 8, 31, 41-2; as balance wheel, 110-12; and civilians, 105-6; and Congress, 112-13; contracts, 120; dependence of economy on, 102, 109-13; and economic euphoria, 102, 122; expenditures for, 101, 111-112; and military personnel, 105-6; profits in, 103-4; race, 84, 100-8

armed forces, 7, 14

Ashanti, 18

asymmetry, 17, 18

athletes, 192-3

athletics, 173; Rome High, 184-93; scholarships, 185, 187; and Selfhood, 190-2

automation, 17, 24, 103, 220n

Automation and Technological Change, 24

automobile industry, 41

babies, 26, 81; "good," 325-6; isolation of, 326, 348n, 387n; as private enterprise, 331-2

banks, 40, 104

baseball, 299-301

About the Author

JULES HENRY studied under Franz Boas and Ruth Benedict at Columbia University, where he received his doctorate in anthropology. His subsequent career of teaching and research has taken him on field trips to the Kaingang Indians of Santa Cararina, Brazil, to the Pilagá Indians of Argentina, and among the Indians of Mexico. Closer to home, he has taught at the University of Chicago, Columbia University, and Washington University in St. Louis, where he is Professor of Anthropology and Sociology. A five-year study of old-age homes and a two-year study of the families of psychotic children provided much valuable data for this book. His knowledge of contemporary education stems from many years of direct observation and research in elementary and secondary schools. He has also been co-director of the Youth Project—a research undertaking of the U.S. Children's Bureau—and a consultant to the National Institute of Mental Health and the World Health Organization.

A NOTE ON THE TYPE

The text of this book is set in Caledonia, a Linotype face designed by W. A. Dwiggins, the man responsible for so much that is good in contemporary book design and typography. Caledonia belongs to the family of printing types called "modern face" by printers—a term used to mark the change in style of type-letters that occurred about 1800. Caledonia borders on the general design of Scotch Modern but is more freely drawn than that letter.